Praise for Joel Kotkin and
The Next Hundred Million: America in 2050

"Given the viral finger-pointing and hand-wringing over what's seen as America's decline these days, Mr. Kotkin's book provides a timely and welcome . . . antidote." —*New York Times*

"Kotkin . . . offers a well-researched—and very sunny—forecast for the American economy. . . . His confidence is well-supported and is a reassuring balm amid the political and economic turmoil of the moment."
—*Publishers Weekly*

"A fascinating glimpse into a crystal ball, rich in implications that are alternately disturbing and exhilarating." —*Kirkus Reviews*

"Kotkin provides a well-argued, well-researched and refreshingly calm perspective." —*Globe and Mail*

"For Mr. Kotkin, population growth translates into economic vitality— the capacity to create wealth, raise the standard of living and meet the burdens of future commitments. Thus a country with a youthful demographic, in relative terms, enjoys a big advantage over its global counterparts." —*Wall Street Journal*

"Lamenting its own decline has long been an American weakness. . . . Those given to such declinism may derive a little comfort from Joel Kotkin's latest book." —*Economist*

"Kotkin has a striking ability to envision how global forces will shape daily family life, and his conclusions can be thought-provoking as well as counterintuitive." —WBUR-FM, Boston's NPR news station

Praise for *The New Class Conflict*

"Were progressives serious about what used to preoccupy America's left—entrenched elites, crony capitalism and other impediments to upward mobility—they would study 'The New Class Conflict,' by Joel Kotkin." —*Washington Post*

"In having the courage to junk the old nostrums, [Kotkin] has taken an important step forward." —*Financial Times*

"Joel Kotkin's important new book, *The New Class Conflict*, suggests that America's real class problems are deeper, and more damaging, than election rhetoric." —*USA Today*

"Kotkin is to be commended for seeing past the daily bric-à-brac of American politics to perceive the newly emerging class divisions."
—*Washington Free Beacon*

"[This book] paints a dire picture of the undeclared war on the middle class." —*New York Post*

"This original and provocative book should stimulate fresh thinking— and produce vigorous dissent." —*Foreign Affairs*

"A provocative and useful contribution to the literature on class."
—*Reason*

"Kotkin's willingness to look beyond conventional labels and challenge trendy theories has made him stand out." —*spiked*

Praise for *The City: A Global History*

"This fast read succeeds most with Kotkin as storyteller, flying through time and around the world to weave so many disparate histories into one urban tapestry."
—*Planetizen's Fifth Annual Top 10 Books List, 2006 Edition*

"No one knows more about cities than Joel Kotkin, and has more to teach us about them. In *The City*, Kotkin takes us on a brisk and invigorating tour of cities from the Babylon of ancient times to the burgeoning exurbs of today. It is impossible not to learn a lot from this book."
—*U.S. News & World Report*

"[*The City*] offers fascinating insight into the ideologies that have created different city designs, and into the natural human desire to gather together to live and for commerce." —*Orange County Register*

"The book is taut, elegant, informative and lots of fun to read. When I got to the end, I wished it had been longer." —*Governing*

The Human City
Urbanism for the Rest of Us

■ ■ ■■

Joel Kotkin

AN AGATE IMPRINT

CHICAGO

Printed in the United States.

Library of Congress Cataloging-in-Publication Data

Names: Kotkin, Joel, author.
Title: The human city : urbanism for the rest of us / Joel Kotkin.
Description: Chicago : Agate B2, [2016]
Identifiers: LCCN 2015050503 | ISBN 9781572841727 (hardback)
Subjects: LCSH: Urbanization. | Sociology, Urban. | City planning. |
   Community development, Urban. | Urban policy. | BISAC: SOCIAL SCIENCE /
   Sociology / Urban. | SOCIAL SCIENCE / Human Geography. | POLITICAL SCIENCE /
   Public Policy / City Planning & Urban Development. | ARCHITECTURE / Urban &
   Land Use Planning.
Classification: LCC HT361 .K686 2016 | DDC 307.76--dc23
LC record available at http://lccn.loc.gov/2015050503

10 9 8 7 6 5 4 3 2 1   16 17 18 19 20

B2 is an imprint of Agate Publishing. Agate books are available in bulk at discount prices.

agatepublishing.com

To Grammy and Mémé—who came from the hard places of Brooklyn and Paris—and found the human city

CONTENTS

INTRODUCTION

■ ■ ■

Books have many origins, and that is also the case with this one. I started thinking about a new approach to urbanism after being exposed to a series of views—largely in favor of cramming people into ever-denser spaces—that now dominates most thinking about cities. I had also been exposed repeatedly to analyses, including some of my own, that rated cities largely from the perspective of their economic productivity.

Economic growth, of course, is critical to urban health and the lives of urban citizens. But how growth impacts daily life, I came to realize, is also important. If we build cities, as we increasingly do, in ways that accentuate divisions among the classes and decrease the quality of life for families—even to the point of discouraging people from having children—what have we accomplished? Even if skylines rise and architects create hitherto impossible-to-imagine structures, a city still primarily needs to be, as Descartes noted, "an inventory of the possible"[1] for the vast majority of its citizens.

These thoughts came together for me when I was working in Singapore. Here was arguably the best-planned dense urban area in the world, a model of modernist design and post-industrial prosperity. Yet in doing scores of interviews and reviewing survey data, it became obvious to me that high-density living, coupled with enormous career pressures, was also producing high levels of anxiety and breaking down what had been an exceptionally strong familial culture.

I articulated these thoughts in a speech called "What Is a City For?" that I gave to the Singapore University of Technology and Design in the spring of 2013. It was published later that year by the Lee Kuan Yew Centre for Innovative Cities.[2] In that address, I began to search out answers to that question. My thinking was further shaped by a suggestion from one of my colleagues, geographer Ali Modarres, to look at Aristotle, first and foremost, for some basic principles.

In the ensuing two years, the book began to take shape, although I knew much of it ran very much contrary to the prevailing wisdom about cities. Yet as I went through the historical literature and observed cities around the world, it became clear that there was an enormous gap between what planners, politicians, and much of the business community were advocating for—ever more density—and the everyday desires of most people, particularly working- and middle-class families. It seemed only proper that someone speak to these aspirations as well.

In no way do I consider this book, in its essentials, anti-urban. Instead, the task here is to *redefine* the city in a way that fits with modern realities and the needs of families. In this respect, the urban experience is simply not only confined to the inner city or old neighborhoods but also to the "sprawl" that now surrounds them in virtually every vibrant urban area in the world. As Gregg Easterbrook, contributing editor of the *Atlantic* and the *Washington Monthly*, asks, "Sprawl is caused by affluence and population growth, and which of these, exactly, do we propose to inhibit?"[3]

Many voices influenced this book. These include the writings of Fernand Braudel, Lewis Mumford, Frank Lloyd Wright, Peter Hall, H. G. Wells, Herbert Gans, and, although I differed from her on many ideas, Jane Jacobs. These figures from the past informed my reporting on the present; their focus on how people actually live, and what they desire, gave me necessary inspiration.

No field of study—technical or in the humanities—thrives when only one side or perspective is allowed free reign and granted a dispensation from criticism. The question of the future of cities is too important to be hemmed in by dogma and should, instead, invite vigorous debate and discussion. My hope is that this book sparks at least a modicum of that debate by challenging the conventional thinking on the future of cities and the urban form. This book was written with that hope.

JOEL KOTKIN
Orange, California, Fall 2015

CHAPTER 1

What Is a City For?

■ ■■■

WHAT IS A CITY FOR? In this urban age, it's a question of crucial importance but one that is not often asked. Long ago, Aristotle reminded us that the city is a place where people come to live, and they remain there in order to live better: "A city comes into being for the sake of life but exists for the sake of living well."[1]

But what does "living well" mean? Is it about accumulating as much wealth as possible? Is it about consuming amenities and collecting the most unique experiences? Is the city a way to reduce the impact of human beings on the environment? Is it about positioning the polis—the city—to serve primarily as an engine in the world economy? Is it about establishing the dominion of the powerful and well connected, those persons who can achieve a high quality of life near the urban core? These are the principles that often guide the thinking of most urbanists today.

I start at a different place. If we are to "live well" in the city, it should, first and foremost, address the needs of future generations, as sustainability advocates rightfully state. This starts with focusing on those areas where families—the new generations—are likely to be raised, rather than primarily focusing on the individual and places where relatively few youngsters grow into adolescence and maturity. We must not forget that without parents, children, and the neighborhoods that sustain them, it would be impossible to imagine how we, as a society, could "live well" or even survive as a species. This is the essence of what I call "the human city."

5

This book is not primarily an argument for any particular urban form. Urban areas now account for 55 percent of the world's population, up from 30 percent in 1950.[2] These areas range from small towns to suburbs to megacities (cities with populations of over 10 million residents). Most have some unique qualities to offer their residents and provide solutions, economic or otherwise, for them.[3] Ideally, urban areas should provide the widest range of living options—from exurbs and suburbs to a thriving urban core—that provide for different people at different stages of life. Living well should not be about where one *should* live but about how one *wants* to live and for whom.

Cities, in my definition, are more than what today's planners and urban theorists insist they must be—dense and crowded places. To some advocates, these are the only places that matter because they express "superior" urban virtues pertaining to environmental or cultural values. A few years ago, for example, Seattle's the *Stranger* outright scorned the periphery—where "people are fatter and slower and dumber"—and claimed cities own "a superior way of life" full of "sanity, liberalism and compassion"—although this compassion hardly seems to apply to those benighted non-urbanites.[4]

Rather than dismiss the expanding city, we need to include it as part of the contiguous region of settlement, what British authorities call the "built-up urban area."[5] As we'll see, this dispersion is the common reality, more or less, for almost all large cities in the world. Cities are much more than places with arresting architecture or the most attractive places for culture or tourism. Instead, a city's heart exists where its people choose to settle. "After all is said and done, he—the *citizen*—is really the city," Frank Lloyd Wright suggested. "The city is going wherever he goes."[6]

THE CULT OF DENSITY

Wright's observation places emphasis in the right place—on those who live in the city. People love their places not for general reasons but for specific reasons that relate to their own needs and aspirations. In our contemporary setting, the desires of many citizens often conflict with those of urban planners and consultants. This centers largely on the dominant urbanist notion—what may be best called "retro-urbanism"—that cities, in order to be successful, must be made ever denser, much as they were in the late 19th and early 20th centuries. Some, including many New Urbanists, favor doing so on a somewhat human scale, with Paris-style levels of density. Others, influential perhaps more in the developing world, embrace a vision of urban density expressed boldly in high-rise apartment blocks and soaring office towers, which has defined the urban vision ever since high-rise steel frame construction began in late 1880s America.[7]

Perhaps the most powerful case for the high-rise city was first articulated by the brilliant architect Charles-Édouard Jeanneret-Gris, also known as Le Corbusier. He envisioned packed buildings surrounded by vast tracts of open land.[8] A bold thinker, Le Corbusier was inspired by 1920s and 1930s Manhattan, the city that most approximated his ideal. But Gotham's many poorer districts and its ramshackle appearance offended him. To him, New York City was not dense enough, its skyscrapers "too small." His goal was to conjure the city as "a miracle of machine civilization" with "glass skyscrapers" that "rise like crystals" and serve as "a magnificent instrument for the concentration of population."[9] These cities, he believed, represented the urban future, an idea widely shared, at least broadly, by many urban thinkers today.

Le Corbusier's work, much of which was written in the late 1920s, epitomized a kind of technological optimism, one that was centered on the application of geometry, mathematics, and mechanics to city building. "A town," he wrote, "is a tool." In his vision, cities required "order," and that order was necessary if the city was not to "thwart" its ambitions. His theory was "a struggle against chance, against disorder, against a policy of drift."

Le Corbusier detested the disorder of the traditional city, its mishmash of building types, its competing densities, and its street-level spontaneity. His was a city of order imposed from above, as had been the case in the earliest times; this order allowed Hellenistic cities to develop in a manner not seen in the cities of early Greece, which also tended to be somewhat haphazard in design.[10] Le Corbusier, perhaps not too surprisingly, showed an unseemly admiration for dictators, be they Napoleon III, who rebuilt Paris, or Adolf Hitler, a failed artist who relished massive urban building projects. Like many of today's planners, Le Corbusier saw in dense developments the salvation of society. The Corbusian vision of a "city of skyscrapers" would allow society to make sufficient economic progress to enhance further the grandeur of the city. [11]

Today's density advocates are rarely as audacious as Le Corbusier, but they also claim numerous benefits from their sense of a highly centralized urban "order"; some organizations, such as the Urban Land Institute (ULI), have been fighting decentralization and suburbanization since the late 1930s.[12] There is a widespread notion that higher density will increase productivity, calm the climate, and lower living costs, albeit at the price of homeownership.[13] In the following pages, I outline the retro-urbanist argument for each of these purported benefits.

THE ECONOMIC EQUATION

Some retro-urbanists, such as Richard Florida, point to studies such as those from the Santa Fe Institute that show the great productivity of large cities, claiming that "bigger, denser cities literally speed up the metabolism of daily life." The notion that innovation needs to take place in dense urban settings is now widely accepted. Yet in reality, as the study's authors note, their findings were about the population of an area, not the density, and had little to do with the urban form.[14]

After all, many of the nation's most innovative firms are located not in downtown cores but in sprawling regions, whether that's in Silicon Valley, the north Dallas suburbs, or the "energy corridor" west of central Houston. Dense San Francisco proper has seen a significant boom in high-tech-related business services in recent years, yet neighboring San Mateo County still holds more than five times as many jobs in software publishing as San Francisco.[15] And despite the recent expansion of tech-related business in San Francisco, the majority of the Bay Area's total employment remains 10 miles from the city center—and is more dispersed than even the national average.[16]

Likewise, most STEM (science, technology, engineering, and mathematics) employment, a large driver of economic growth, remains firmly in suburbanized areas with lower density development and little in the way of mass transit usage.[17] Lower density regions as diverse as Durham, Madison, Denver, Detroit, Baltimore, Colorado Springs, and Albany are among the places with the highest shares of STEM jobs, and in many cases, they are creating new STEM jobs faster than the high-tech stalwarts. Charleston, Provo, Fayetteville, Raleigh, and Des Moines are among the fastest-growing STEM regions since 2001, each with STEM employment up at least 29 percent.[18]

Much has been written about how large, dense cities are the best places to grow jobs and, increasingly, to find opportunities.[19] Yet in reality, the central core has become progressively less important economically, in terms of employment.[20] Today, only 9 percent of employment is located in the central business districts, with an additional 10 percent in the balance of the urban cores.[21]

America's metropolitan areas were largely monocentric—that is, dominated by the single strong core of downtown—during the immediate post-World War II period, but since have largely become polycentric. Job dispersion is now a reality in virtually every metropolitan area, with twice as many jobs located 10 miles from city centers as in those centers. Between 1998 and 2006, 95 out of 98 metro areas saw a decrease in the share of jobs located within three miles of downtown, according to a Brookings Institution report.[22] The outermost parts of these metro areas saw employment increase by 17 percent, compared to a gain of less than 1 percent in the urban core. Overall, the report found, only 21 percent of employees in the top 98 metros in America lived within three miles of the center of their city. More than 80 percent of employment growth from 2007 to 2013 was in the newer suburbs and exurban areas.[23]

CITIES, SUBURBS, AND ENVIRONMENT

In addition to economic arguments, claims of environmental superiority also drive the push for densification. Some environmentalists also celebrate the demographic impact of densification, seeing in denser cities a natural contraceptive against population growth, which is seen as a major contributor to environmental destruction. Stewart Brand, founder of the green handbook *Whole Earth Catalog*, embraces denser urbanization, particularly in developing countries, as a way of "stopping the population explosion cold."[24]

Concerns over climate change have been added to justify greater density. "What is causing global warming is the lifestyle of the American middle class," insists New Urbanist architect Andrés Duany, a major developer of dense housing himself and arguably the movement's most important voice.[25] To advocates such as Duany, a return to old urban forms encourages transit riding over cars, which is one way to reduce carbon emissions.

But besides being environmentally imperative, the shift to denser development is also seen as somehow morally justified. Retro-urbanists—those who long for a return to the traditional pre-1950 city—represent a kind of moral imperative. Typically, this is cast as a choice between 4,000-square-foot McMansions and unbridled consumption on one side and more sustainable high-density urban living on the other. Columbia University's Earth Institute executive director Steven Cohen speaks of a future "with smaller personal spaces, more frequent use of public spaces, bikes, parks, high-tech media, and constant attention to one's environmental footprint."[26] Prince Charles's vision of "eco-cities"—although more medieval than modern in its form—also embraces a similar viewpoint, urging British people to live in smaller spaces and grow their food in community gardens. One doubts, however, that either Charles or many of his acolytes are living in the same modest fashion.[27] Retro-urbanist David Owen, for example, suggests in his book *Green Metropolis* that people need to live in densities associated with his former Manhattan home, although he himself moved to bucolic Connecticut.[28]

Sadly, much of the research advocating density as a solution to climate change is deeply flawed since it usually excludes greenhouse gas (GHG) emissions from common-area elevators, lighting, space heating, and air conditioning—often because that data is not available. Research by environmental group EnergyAustralia, which took this and overall consumer energy spending into account, found that both townhouses and detached housing produced less GHG emissions per capita than high-density housing when common-area GHG emissions were included.[29] Further, one recent study from the National Academy of Sciences found that New York City—despite its mass transit system and high density—was the most environmentally wasteful of the world's roughly 30 megacities, well ahead of more dispersed, car-dominated Los Angeles.[30]

In one of the most comprehensive national reviews of GHG emissions, the Australian Conservation Foundation found per capita emissions to *decline* from the urban core, through suburban rings, to the suburbs.[31] Another study, this one in Halifax, Nova Scotia, found the carbon footprints of core residents and suburbanites to be approximately the same.[32]

THE HIGH COST OF CITY LIVING

Finally, there is the often-repeated notion among retro-urbanists that higher density will solve the problem of affordability, now a major concern in cities around the world. Yet in many ways, pro-density policies *worsen* affordability. Groups such as the Sierra Club argue that every level of government (local, state, and federal) should enact policies making people live closer together so that they rely less on cars. In order to do this, these groups advocate establishing urban growth boundaries, which ban new development beyond the urban fringe.[33] This makes it impossible to build affordable starter homes, which rely in part on lower-priced land on the urban fringe. These groups have embraced the smart growth movement's tendency to enforce their vision by promoting "more scientific planning" for how land will be used, buttressed of course by strict regulations.[34]

At the core of this problem are simple economics. The issue facing big coastal cities, notes one progressive blogger, is their lack of "semi-density, mid-rise construction."[35] Yet by most measurements, it turns out that higher-density housing is far more expensive to build. Gerard Mildner, the academic director at the Center for Real Estate at Portland State University, notes that the cost of developing a garden apartment is roughly one-third that of developing a high-rise.[36]

Even higher construction costs are reported in the San Francisco Bay Area, where townhome developments can cost up to double that of detached houses per square foot (excluding land costs), and units in high-rise condominium buildings can cost up to 7.5 times as much.[37] In reality, "affordable" high-density housing is often extraordinarily expensive to build, which translates into higher rents and mortgages. This then requires high levels of subsidization by the public to even approach affordability. Ultimately, even the most ambitious public housing projects cannot meet the demand for affordable housing. In New York, the city with arguably the strongest high-density subsidized housing program, the odds of getting a subsidized apartment run something like 50 to 1 against.[38]

CITIZENS AND THE SEARCH FOR HUMAN SCALE

Today, many developers and consultants associate density with the largely unsupported notion that ever more people want to move "back to the city."[39] Real estate magnate Sam Zell confidently predicts that cities will become denser, with people eager to engage in "reurbanization" by moving into 300-square-foot "micro-units" where they can enjoy a bit of "privacy" for themselves amid the excitement of the city around them. Such units and smaller have already been developed in cities as diverse as New York, Vancouver, Providence, Seattle, and Tokyo.[40]

Around the world, planners, politicians, and pundits often wax poetic about these massive new building projects and soaring residences made up of hundreds of tiny stacked units, but there's just one problem with this brave new condensed world: most people, including many inner-city residents, aren't crazy about it. People care deeply about where they live, and they often aren't thrilled with the kind of urban vision held by many city leaders. Instead, urbanites prefer that their cities retain a more livable, human scale—an important aspect of the human city. This reflects not only a concern for greater comfort and less congestion but also, as we will see later, a desire to maintain the unique character of our geographies, whatever the size.

This can be seen in the increased resistance to densification and gigantism—that is, the worship of scale for its own sake—throughout the world. Protesters in Istanbul, opposing major building projects near the heart of the city, favored a drive for "healthy urbanization and [a] livable city" and opposed President Recep Tayyip Erdoğan's desire to push his grandiose vision of the city as "the financial center of the world." Rallying against construction around Taksim Square, protesters decried what has been described as "authoritarian building"[41]—the demolition of older, more human-scaled neighborhoods in favor of denser high-rise construction, massive malls, and other iconic projects.[42]

Similar protests over urban development priorities have occurred in São Paulo and other cities across Brazil,[43] where the government is accused of putting mega-projects ahead of basic services such as public transport, education, and health care, particularly in the run-up to the 2014 FIFA World Cup and the 2016 Summer Olympics.[44]

Comparable conflicts have also arisen in high-income countries. Even in New York City, the red-hot center of American ultra-density, eight of Manhattan's 10 community boards[45] opposed former Mayor Bloomberg's attempts to further densify already congested Midtown.[46] The Midtown project prompted Yale architect Robert Stern, a devoted advocate for dense cities and no opponent of density, to warn that too much high-rise development creates a dehumanized aesthetic that chases away creative businesses and tourists, while preserving older districts attracts them.[47] Retro-urbanist Richard Florida, usually a reliable supporter of density, also expresses concern that high-rise density does not appeal much to the "creative class," who prefer more human-scaled neighborhoods.[48]

Similarly, in Los Angeles, neighborhood councils, notably in Hollywood, have rallied against attempts to build denser buildings, which generate more congestion and erode both the area's livability and its distinct urban identity.[49] In London, too, attempts to build what the *Independent* describes as "the tall, the ostentatious, the showy and 'iconic'" have been widely criticized for undermining the human-scaled character of London. Densification may be revealed religion to British planners, but this faith is not so well accepted by citizens. British novelist Will Self notes the "Wizard of Oz–hollowness" of these structures and says that while they seek to inspire, they also "belittle us" with their mass and scale and stand against the city's historic grain.[50]

Like their more urban counterparts, suburbanites do not want the character of their places radically transformed by "visionary" architects and planners. They often are particularly galled that "smart growth" policies are actually "a stalking horse for developers who want to attract government subsidies," as well as sanctioned seizures of small-property owners stuck in the way of a particular definition of "progress."[51]

THE AGE OF DISPERSION

These objections, from both core city residents and suburbanites, reflect a growing disconnect between the residents and the visions of most pundits, urban real estate interests, and much of the planning community. Planners may crave more density, but the secular trend in the marketplace is toward ever more dispersion. As I will discuss further in later chapters, almost all of the world's 34 megacities have declined in urban density from their peaks, even as they have continued to add population.[52] This has nothing to do with cities becoming smaller. Instead, it illustrates that cities nearly always become less dense as they become larger. This, notes New York University professor Shlomo Angel in his landmark book *Planet of Cities*, is true in both developing and developed countries. Cities in the developing world are indeed getting more populous, but they are spreading out even faster.[53]

To understand why, we must examine the basic realities of how cities develop. As the interior parts of cities become denser, or dominated by commercial structures, land on the fringe often provides a cheaper alternative. As I mentioned earlier, one- or two-story structures constructed on the periphery are usually much less expensive to build, and they can sometimes even accommodate small gardens and some domestic animals. Refusal to acknowledge these realities simply makes it harder to make dispersion work smoothly. "Urban expansion," Angel warns, "must be prepared for in advance or not at all."[54]

These trends are particularly pronounced in high-income countries like the United States where the massive, postwar shift to suburbia is now well over a half century old. In 1950, only half of the residents of today's major metropolitan areas lived in suburbs,[55] but since that time, 90 percent of metropolitan growth has been on the periphery.[56]

Today, nearly 75 percent of metropolitan area residents live in suburban areas. Overall, 44 million Americans live in the core cities of 51 major metropolitan areas, while nearly 122 million Americans live in the suburbs. Additionally, more than half of the core city populations live in districts that are functionally suburban or exurban with low density and high automobile use.[57]

There is no doubt that there remains a strong, and arguably expanding, number of people who seek a more urban lifestyle. Greater densities certainly appeal to a specific, though relatively small, segment of the population. But overall growth, as we will see, has been concentrated in peripheral areas, with some exceptions, for many decades.

HERE COMES THE CHILDLESS CITY

In the high-income world, the issue of a rapidly aging—and in some places declining—population has reached critical proportions. In some parts of the world, notably western Europe, eastern Asia, and even parts of North America, low birth rates are threatening the fiscal health of governments, the future of the workforce, and the consumer base.[58] In many cases, as is already evident in Europe, the choice is increasingly to either accept large numbers of immigrants or face gradual demographic decline.

Here, the question of what families need and prefer should be central. In her heyday in the 1960s, Jane Jacobs asserted that "suburbs must be a difficult place to raise children."[59] Jacobs's ideal city, dense but human-scaled, indeed was once a congenial place for families. But a quick look at demographic changes in places like Greenwich Village shows how far we have traveled from Jacobs's ideal city. The area today—which my own grandmother knew as a child—now largely consists of students, wealthy people, and pensioners. Although their numbers have grown somewhat, there are relatively few children, compared to both the nation and the rest of New York City.[60] Overall, Manhattan has one of the lowest percentages of children in the country; the majority of its households are made up of singles. In the Village, despite the presence of many young people, the portion of people aged 5 to 17 is 6 percent, far below the norm for New York City and less than half of the 13.1 percent found across the United States' 52 largest metropolitan areas.[61]

This suggests a very different role for cities as they relate to families. Urban theorist Terry Nichols Clark of the University of Chicago notes that, today, childlessness drives the "new American metropolis," which revolves around a dramatically "thinner family" and appeals to those who prefer a less conventional, childless lifestyle.[62] This is a universal phenomenon. For all their impressive achievements, and sometimes inspiring architecture, high-density cores such as those in Manhattan, Seattle, San Francisco, Boston, and Washington, DC, have the lowest percentages of children. At the same time, the ultra-dense cities of eastern Asia—Hong Kong, Singapore, and Seoul—exhibit the lowest fertility rates on the planet, sometimes less than half the number required to simply replace the current population.[63] Due largely to crowding and high housing prices, 45 percent of couples in Hong Kong say they have given up having children.[64]

Some of Asia's urban residents, if they can, are now looking to leave these cities—among the most widely praised by urbanists—for more affordable and lower-density locales. This is evident in the rising emigration from cities such as Hong Kong and Singapore, where roughly one in 10 citizens[65] now chooses to settle abroad and nearly half would consider a move, mostly to lower-density countries like Australia, Canada, and the United States.[66] Some Chinese mothers, in order to give birth to future American citizens, actually indulge in "birth tourism" so they can have their children in places such as Los Angeles and Orange Counties, where the vast majority of Asians live in family-centric suburban communities.[67]

The reluctance of people to have children in dense cities suggests that super-urbanity often serves as a kind of way station in which people spend only a portion—often an exciting and career-enhancing one—of their early lives. But when they grow older, and particularly when they decide to start families, their tendency to leave remains, as we can see in the patterns of migration. According to the US census, in 2011, children aged 5 to 14 constituted about 7 percent of the population in core districts across the United States, roughly half the portion seen in suburbs and exurbs.

This reflects a trend that has existed for decades and one that we'll discuss in more detail later. In the last decennial census, the US urban-core population aged 5 to 14 dropped by 600,000, almost three times the net gain of residents aged 20 to 29. Core cities continue to attract the young but generally lose residents as they age and start families. By 2011, people in their 20s constituted roughly one-quarter of residents in the urban cores but only 14 percent or less of those who lived in suburbs, where the bulk of people go as they enter the age of family formation.[68]

RECASTING THE URBAN DEBATE: CORE CITIES AND LIFE'S STAGES

In this way, if not for any other reason, the suburbs are essential to the health of an urban organism. Without places for people to move farther out in the periphery, these core cities, with their low birth rates and high levels of income inequality, are hardly sustainable in the long run. Many of them, as we will discuss later, can only survive by importing people, whether it be those from their own hinterlands (including young people nurtured in suburbs), immigrants from abroad, or in some places, people from the overpopulated countryside.

The renaissance that has taken place in the heart of some urban cores, clearly a welcome development, is more long-standing than many may assume. As early as 1959, Harvard's Raymond Vernon identified two parallel developments: the relative decline of dense urban areas and an upswing in select core neighborhoods. He noted, however, that these changes would be, compared to the metropolis, somewhat "minuscule."[69]

Sadly, few planners and powerful urban land interests acknowledge these demographics when pushing policies that discourage suburban development in favor of density. Their notion of improving cities is less about luring people there with amenities that appeal to families and more about shoving development into dense transit nodes, increasing the "sustainability" and profitability of their developments.

But this approach tends to make it impossible for all but the highly affluent to buy houses, financially stressing families who tend to favor such housing. Reacting to draconian regulations that mandate densification, one Bay Area blogger charged[70] that "suburb hating is anti-child" because it seeks to undermine single-family neighborhoods.[71]

The issue of the urban future is simply too important to allow the grip of ideology to weaken the natural, organic development of cities and their peripheries. Young people may improve their lives and careers by heading to the urban core, but most are unlikely to stay for the duration, or if they do, it may well be without having children or getting married. In the human city, we have to welcome a broad array of options that can address the varying needs of urbanites, not only today but also through their life cycles as their aspirations change.[72] To flourish, cities need to be flexible and responsive to changing human needs—from birth to the end of life.

CHAPTER 2

The Importance of Everyday Life

■ ■ ■ ■

THROUGHOUT HISTORY, urban areas have taken on many functions, which have often changed over time. Today, this trend continues as technology, globalization, and information technology both undermine and transform the nature of urban life. Developing a new urban paradigm requires, first and foremost, integrating the traditional roles of cities—religious, political, economic—with the new realities and possibilities of the age. Most importantly, we need to see how we can preserve the best, and most critical, aspects of urbanism. Cities should not be made to serve some ideological or aesthetic principle, but they should make life better for the vast majority of citizens.

In building a new approach to urbanism, I propose starting at the ground level. "Everyday life," observed the French historian Fernand Braudel, "consists of the little things one hardly notices in time and space."[1] Braudel's work focused on people who lived largely mundane lives, worried about feeding and housing their families, and concerned with their place in local society. Towns may differ in their form, noted Braudel, but ultimately, they all "speak the same basic language" that has persisted throughout history.[2]

Contemporary urban students can adopt Braudel's approach to the modern day by focusing on how people live every day and understanding the pragmatic choices they make that determine where and how they live. By focusing on these mundane aspects of life, particularly those of families and middle-class households, we can move beyond the dominant contemporary narrative about cities, which concentrates mostly on the young "creative" population and the global wealthy.

This is not a break with the urban tradition but a validation of older and more venerable ideals of what city life should be about. Cities, in a word, are about people, and to survive as sustainable entities they need to focus on helping residents achieve the material and spiritual rewards that have come with urban life throughout history.

Cities have thrived most when they have attracted newcomers hoping to find better conditions for themselves and their families and when they have improved conditions for already settled residents. Critical here are not only schools, roads, and basic forms of transport, which depend on the government, but also a host of other benefits—special events, sports leagues, church festivals—that can be experienced at the neighborhood, community, and family levels.

This urban *terroir*—the soil upon which cities and communities thrive—has far less to do with actions taken from above than is commonly assumed by students of urban life. Instead, it is part of what New York folklorist Barbara Kirshenblatt-Gimblett calls, "everyday urbanism," which "take[s] shape outside planning, design, zoning, regulation, and covenants, if not in spite of them."[3]

This divergence in perspective, notes Los Angeles architect John Kaliski, stems in part from the desire of planners and architects to construct "the conceptually pure notion of what a city is or should be." The search for a planned utopia, he says, also ignores the "situational rhythm" that fits each specific place and responds to the demand of consumers in the marketplace. No surprise then that grand ideas, epitomized by soaring towers, often prove less successful than those more pragmatic, market-oriented efforts of, say, Victor Gruen to recreate the plaza and urban streetscape within the framework of modern-day suburbia.

So rather than just focusing on grand narratives about how to transform the metropolis and its denizens, we need to pay more attention to what people actually do, what they prefer, and those things to which they can reasonably aspire. The history of successful cities reveals that, although their functions change, cities have to achieve two things: a better way of life for their residents and a degree of transcendence critical to their identities.

In addressing the wider issues faced by urban residents, we need to also draw on older urban traditions that have emerged over the last three millennia. Jane Jacobs's idealistic notions of cities, however outdated, contain meaningful insights—about the importance of diverse, child-friendly, dense city neighborhoods, for example.[4] By exploring the deeper veins of urbanity—spiritual, political, economic—we can begin to hone our efforts to improve and develop our cities so that they are more pleasant, and particularly more accommodating, for people as they go through the various stages of life.

THE CITY OF GOD

Early cities rested largely on urban studies scholar Robert Park's notion of cities as "a state of mind [and] a body of customs and traditions."[5] The earliest urban residents built their cities with the idea that they were part of something larger than themselves, connected not only to their own traditions but to divinity itself. Great ancient cities were almost always spiritual centers, and as the great urban historian Lewis Mumford noted, religion provided a critical unifying principle for the city and its civic identity:

> Behind the wall of the city life rested on a common foundation, set as deep as the universe itself: the city was nothing less than the home of a powerful god. The architectural and sculptural symbols that made this fact visible lifted the city far above the village or country town. . . . To be a resident of the city was to have a place in man's true home, the great cosmos itself.[6]

In the decidedly non-urban world of early times, the city's spiritual power helped define a place and animate its residents with a sense of common identity. This attachment still remains notable in cities such as Jerusalem and Mecca.[7] Jerusalem, shortly after its conquest by the Hebrews, began as a powerful and strategic fortress but evolved, with the building of David's temple, into the "holy city," a status it has maintained for three major religions to this day. "Jerusalem," notes one historian, "had no natural industries but holiness."[8] Even today, as political scientist Avner de-Shalit suggests, "Many Jerusalemites are proud of living in a city where spirituality is more important than materialism and wealth."[9]

Many other cities, perhaps less cherished for holiness, have served as repositories for essential cultural ideas and ethnic memories—a role that still exists today. The special appeal of cities such as Kyoto, Beijing, Rome, Paris, and Mexico City stems in part from their being built on foundations of earlier civilizations, even those like the Aztecs' ancient Tenochtitlan, whose religious structures were systematically destroyed and replaced by those of their Catholic conquerors.[10]

In this sense, great cities—even as they expanded via armed conquest and the control of an ever-expanding hinterland—cultivated the notion of their distinct connection to eternity. In many cases, from Babylon to China, kingship was "lowered from heaven," thus connecting early theologically-based urbanism to the notion of power. In Babylon, for example, all property was theologically under the sovereignty of god, for whom the human ruler served as "steward."[11]

Today, urban thinkers barely reflect on such considerations, particularly those concerning religion or the role of the sacred, which has been historically critical to creating the moral order that sustains cities. Indeed, some have argued that higher degrees of secularism are essential to the creation of a more advanced and progressive society.[12]

But one does not have to view traditional religious underpinnings as the only way to nurture "sacred space." Today, notes urban analyst Aaron Renn, this sense of identity often extends to secular places like Times Square in New York or the Indiana War Memorial in Indianapolis; it could be the Eiffel Tower in Paris, Trafalgar Square in London, or the mountains visible from the great cities of the American West: Los Angeles, Denver, Phoenix, San Francisco, Seattle, and Portland.[13] Cities in continental Europe have been defined by their countless squares, such as Place de la République in Paris, Piazza del Duomo in Milan, and the Grote Markt in Brussels, as well as the manicured parks in Australian and Chinese city centers, such as Sydney's Hyde Park and Beijing's Beihai Park.

THE IMPERIAL CITY

If the divine, or its modern equivalents, drove city life to aspire to higher ideals, the notion of power—notably that of the supreme and absolute monarch—was critical in the development of the first giant cities. The imperial city not only expressed the egotism of rulers and the ambition of builders but also reflected the ideal that the city was more connected to a sense of transcendence than other, less exalted places. Peter the Great, for example, believed that in Saint Petersburg, he was building something divine on earth. "Truly," he commented, "we live here in heaven."[14]

Saint Petersburg epitomized another critical role of cities: to function as windows, or gateways, to a wider world. The late British philosopher Stephen Toulmin suggested that, in the merger of "the polis" with "cosmos," the city takes the lead in ordering nature and society alike.[15] This sense of possibility, of creating better and newer ways of life, has long been an important function of cities.

In the imperial city, God was hardly banished; instead, the focus turned more toward mastery of the human condition. Imperial Athens, for example, sought to export not so much religion but rather a more generalized culture that reflected the Greek way of life, such as its political forms, art, and fashion. The Greek city-states also exported such prosaic practices as the use of olive oil to both trading partners and conquered territories. Here we first see a distinct urban culture on the march, defiant about its superiority over the countryside. As Socrates is said to have remarked: "The country places and trees won't teach me anything, and the people in the city do."[16]

Athens's successor, Rome, was built on the idea of the state—the *res publica*, which Romans perceived as being inherently superior and deserving of global preeminence. There was clearly a spiritual element here. Ancient Roman historian Titus Livius Patavinus, known today as Livy, spoke of how the Gods "inhabit[ed]" the city—but the primary exports of Rome were its power, systems of urbanization, and legal system.

With Rome, we also see the emergence, for the first time, of a city with a population of 1 million or more, bringing with it the great challenges still faced by large cities today.[17] Most Romans were descended from slaves and many, like their contemporaries in today's megacities, lived in crowded, unsanitary, and dangerous conditions—and often paid exorbitant rents. As the empire expanded, many of the old plebeian class were driven into poverty as they were replaced with slave labor. As we'll discuss later, this misery amid all the splendor and elegance associated with the imperial elite has remained a common reality in great cities throughout much of urban history.[18]

This "princely city" dominated by political power, as German sociologist Max Weber noted, produced what Weber identified as "the consumer city," a place driven by the wealth of individuals connected to the political or clerical regime. These areas were dominated by privileged rentiers, and the large servile class, free or not, was employed to tend to their needs.[19]

This earliest consumer city—tied to the presence of the court and courtiers—was a precursor of the luxury urban cores of today. As Rome declined, this role was assumed by the new capital, Byzantium (later Constantinople), which emerged as the world's largest city, reaching its peak population in 500 AD. The city's power was based largely on its serving as center of what remained of the empire as well as the headquarters of the Orthodox Church. As a result, it created a large consuming class of priests, bureaucrats, and soldiers who enjoyed its many pleasures.[20]

Over the next two millennia, similar patterns could be seen in Beijing, Damascus, Tokyo, Paris, Vienna, and Cairo, all of which grew largely as the result of imperial expansion and centralized government, with its attendant need for bureaucrats, scribes, and religious leaders. For example, Vienna, a city not noted for its commercial prowess, grew fivefold between 1600 and 1800, outpacing the other cities of central Europe. Such centralization of power often led to ambitious building projects, not only in Vienna but also in Imperial Paris and later in the capital of a rising Prussian and then German empire, Berlin.[21]

In some cases, such as in Washington, DC, political power, rather than the patronage of the rich, transformed a once sleepy metropolis. As late as 1990, the British geographer Emrys Jones considered it "doubtful" that Washington could ever be considered among the world's leading cities.[22] Yet, as the US federal government grew in size and complexity, so, too, did the area. Washington is now very much a global metropolis and has enjoyed one of the strongest economies in North America and a growing immigrant population.[23]

Some of today's large Asian cities—Beijing, Seoul, and Tokyo—also derive their importance, in part, from serving as centers of political power. In the case of Beijing, this focus on centralization remained intact after the Communist takeover in 1949, with party cadres playing the leading role and turning the capital into the country's dominant city over the old commercial capital of Shanghai.[24] In all of these capitals, the central governments exercised inordinate influence over both the economy and society.

THE PRODUCER CITY

Most major cities today depend largely on their prowess as economic units. This development, as Karl Marx suggested, reflected the replacement of the wealthy land-owning aristocracy with the merchant and money-lending classes, the earliest capitalists. In contrast to the aforementioned consumer city dominated by princes, Weber described these as "producer cities." Venice was an early example. This Italian city-state pioneered the use of industrial districts built largely to meet export demand. Venice was primarily a mercantile city, dependent on the export of goods and services to the rest of the world for its livelihood.[25]

Arguably, the most evolved of the early producer cities emerged in the Netherlands, a place that limited both imperial and ecclesiastical power. The Netherlands crafted a great urban legacy that, in its initial phases, involved rising living standards and remarkable social mobility. These trends led the Dutch to be widely denounced as avaricious people who valued physical possessions more than spiritual or cultural values.

Yet this urban culture, as English historian Simon Schama noted, offered a high quality of life to its middle and working classes and even served its poorest class reasonably well.[26] These Dutch cities—home to over 40 percent of Netherlanders—not only remained wealthier than those of other European countries but also managed to improve such things as hygiene and provide a better environment for children and families. They also accommodated many outsiders, a pattern still seen today, particularly in key global cities. Many outsiders, such as Jews and Huguenots, flocked to Dutch cities, in large part for both economic opportunities and greater religious freedom. The religious and ethnic heterogeneity of the Dutch cities also encouraged independent thinking and the mixing of cultures; in the second half of the 17th century, over one-third of Amsterdam's new citizens came from outside the Netherlands. This openness was critical to developing innovative approaches to the arts and philosophy, such as the groundbreaking writings of Baruch Spinoza.[27]

The producer city provided the template for a city that served its commercial interests *and* nurtured a middle class, rather than being built around the needs of kings, aristocrats, prelates, and bureaucrats. These cities were both expansive and outward-looking, in part because artillery made walled cities infeasible. This encouraged these cities to spread into the countryside, as their security increasingly came to rely on the mobilization of armed citizens or mercenaries. In contrast to the walled-in city of the imperial era, the producer city's walls were moved back, and new populations were absorbed into suburbs, much like in the modern city.[28]

THE RISE OF THE INDUSTRIAL CITY

The modern city emerged from the producer city but in ways fundamentally transformed by the Industrial Revolution. Futurist and author Alvin Toffler points out that this "second wave," or industrial, society accelerated urban density and concentration, in part due to the need to keep the workforces of new factories and associated businesses in close proximity. It did so by "stripping the countryside of people and relocating them in giant urban centers."[29] This was most notable in Britain in the centuries leading up to the Industrial Revolution. Britain's urban population grew 600 percent between the dawn of the 17th century and that of the 19th century, six times the country's overall rate of increase.[30]

The capitalist-driven industrial city exacted a huge toll, at least initially, on its residents. Artisans who had been living in smaller villages and towns moved into cities that served as homes for giant factories. Many came to the city not for love of adventure or opportunity but due to dramatic changes in the pattern of land ownership in the countryside, particularly in Britain after the Enclosure Act of 1801, which took property that had been considered common and placed it under private ownership. As we see today in the megacities of the developing world, this decline in local fortunes sparked an urban migration as farmers lost access to fields and pastures.[31]

Once in the city, migrants often found conditions harsher than when they lived in smaller towns or villages; their life spans were shortened by crowded conditions, incessant labor, and lack of leisure.[32] Yet at the same time, a rising affluent class enjoyed unprecedented wealth and access to country estates that allowed them to skip the worst aspects of urban living, particularly in the summer. "The townsman," noted one observer of Manchester and London in the 1860s, "does everything in his power not to be a townsman and tries to fit a country house and a bit of the country into a corner of the town."[33]

Conditions were so hard for the working classes—and the wealth of the upper classes so great—that roughly 15 percent of London's population worked in domestic service while an estimated 35 percent lived in poverty.[34] For those who did not have the chance to live in the relative comfort of "downstairs," life became, as one doctor observed, "infernal," made much worse by "vile housing conditions."[35] Death rates soared well above those seen in the British countryside by as much as 40 percent.[36] The German observer Friedrich Engels notes in his searing 1845 book, *The Condition of the Working Class in England,* that cities like Manchester and London were marked by "the most distressing scenes of misery and poverty to be found anywhere." Crowding and density, he noted, had an impact on the character of British city dwellers:

> *The more that Londoners are packed into a tiny space, the more repulsive and disgraceful becomes the brutal indiffer-ence with which they ignore their neighbours and selfishly concentrate upon their private affairs.*[37]

Later, these conditions also spread to North America, despite the continent's ample landmass. As early as the 1820s, slums where whole families were confined to a room or two were spreading in cities such as Cincinnati. In the 1850s, a local reporter found families in that city clus-tered in a "small, dirty, dilapidated" tenement room, containing "con-fused rags for beds and a meager supply of old and broken furniture."

Overcrowding was generally worse in the older Northeast cities, particularly in New York City, and the achievement of homeownership extremely rare.[38] Densities on New York's Lower East Side reached as high as 100,000 an acre in the late 19th century, which was equal to those in inner London, Paris, and even Bombay, according to historian Robert Fogelson. Meanwhile, Chicago, the industrial hub of the era, was described by one Swedish visitor as "one of the most miserable and ugly cities I have seen in America."[39] Yet people, largely immigrants, contin-ued to go to Chicago, making it the fastest-growing large city of its time.

It was not until later in the 19th century—and even more so in the 20th century—that many of the depravities of the early industrial city diminished. Living standards improved, as did life expectancy and the quality of housing. These advancements came in part as a result of reform movements that pushed for improvements in hygiene and san-itation, as well as for the development of parks.[40] But perhaps the most important answer to the ills of the industrial city came about—in a manner many thought, and continue to believe, unsuitable—through urban expansion into the countryside.

ONE OPTION: THE RISE OF SUBURBIA

Some early progressive reformers, such as H. G. Wells, advocated the dispersion of the population into the periphery as a means to improve the lot of urban residents. As early as the mid-19th century, London was already spreading out, losing density in its core as middle- and working-class people sought out a less cramped, more pleasant existence. In many cases, the new locales also gave them easy access to employment, which was growing more rapidly in the suburbs.[41] Between 1911 and 1981, the population of inner London declined by 45 percent.[42] Similarly, by the 21st century, the inner arrondissements of Paris lost well over half of their population in 1860.[43]

This movement also included attempts to create what the British visionary planner Sir Ebenezer Howard labeled the "garden city."[44] Horrified by the disorder, disease, and crime of the early 20th-century industrial metropolis, he advocated the creation of "garden cities" on the suburban periphery. These self-contained towns, with populations of roughly 30,000, would have their own employment base, neighborhoods of pleasant cottages, and rural surroundings.

Determined to turn his theories into reality, Howard was the driving force behind two of England's first planned towns, Letchworth in 1903 and Welwyn in 1912.[45] These garden cities were meant to be planned, self-sufficient communities surrounded by "greenbelts," which included proportional areas of residence, industry, and agriculture. Howard's approach, focused on the needs of normal citizens, was in sharp contrast to not only the denser grandiosity brilliantly expressed by Napoleon III's Paris but also to Hitler's proposed brutalist Germania, the socialist cities of Eastern Europe, and the ambitions of some of today's retro-urbanists. In contrast, Howard saw instead "the great value of little things if done in the right manner and in the right spirit."[46] By the late 19th century, Howard's "garden city" model of development soon influenced planners around the world—in America, Germany, Australia, Japan, and elsewhere.[47] In the United States, innovative urban thinkers—such as Frederick Law Olmsted—suggested the idea of building at a modest density in a multipolar environment built around basic human needs.[48]

The new suburban ethos fit well in America. If anything, as Alexis de Tocqueville and others noted, Americans had a peculiar penchant for settling in small towns and villages. Like many contemporary critics of America's cities and suburbs, some, particularly those from Europe, denounced the sameness that characterized the country's seemingly endless progression of smaller towns. The auto-centered nature of to-day's metropolis reflects the essentially pragmatic and functional ori-entation common to American settlements.[49]

By the 1920s, noted *National Geographic*, the United States were "spreading out."[50] Once a nation of farms and cities, America was being transformed into a primarily suburban country. No longer con-fined to old towns or "streetcar suburbs" near the urban core, subur-banites increasingly lived in ever more spread-out new developments such as Levittown, which arose out on the Long Island flatlands in the late 1940s and early 1950s.[51] The suburbs, noted historian Jon C. Tea-ford, provided more than an endless procession of lawns and carports as well as "a mixture of escapism and reality."[52]

Although much of this building was uninspired, there were at-tempts to develop a better kind of community. One of the earliest and most innovative examples emerged in 1929 with the development of Radburn, New Jersey. Visualized as "a town for the motor age," the community offered a wide range of residential units, with interior parklands and access to walkways. Car and pedestrian traffic was to be strictly separated, with houses grouped around cul-de-sacs with a small access road. To Lewis Mumford, Radburn represented "the first departure in city planning since Venice."[53]

Radburn focused on creating a secure and healthful environment for the residents. There were extensive recreation opportunities for the com-munity, and the town emphasized providing an ideal environment for raising children. Initially planned to house 25,000 people, the Radburn development sadly was derailed by the Great Depression, which drove the builder into bankruptcy. Today, the city houses some 3,100 residents.[54]

The architects of the New Deal also embraced suburban develop-ment. Early efforts to develop garden cities in America received a huge boost during the New Deal, which led to the construction of the first great master-planned communities—Greenbelt, Maryland; Greenhills, Ohio, near Cincinnati; and Greendale, Wisconsin, outside Milwaukee. These communities were designed with offices, industrial facilities, parks, and playgrounds. Provisions were also made for a diversity of housing units and income groups.

Eventually, these federal efforts were stymied by strong opposition from builders and conservatives who denounced them as "communist farms." Plans to build some 3,000 such towns were never realized. Yet after the war, the principles behind such places were observed in the breach as massive demand, fueled by new federal loan programs, led to the building of massive conventional production suburbs that incorporated a few of these principles.[55]

Even without the planned towns, the movement of people into the suburbs—which took place with both government assistance and the enthusiastic participation of the populace—was great enough to shrink the industrial city. Inner-city areas, which had constituted half of metropolitan populations by 1950, have dropped to barely 25 percent today. The prospect of single-family houses within the metropolitan region, once reserved for the more affluent, was suddenly within reach of most working-class families.[56]

THE TRANSACTIONAL CITY—AND THOSE LEFT BEHIND

By the 1950s and 1960s, the growing popularity of suburbs—for both businesses and residents—generated a harsh reaction from urbanist intellectuals such as Jane Jacobs, who saw the suburbs taking the middle class away from what they perceived as a socially and culturally richer experience in the city. It also led some developers and city officials to find ways to resuscitate their city cores, an effort that continues to this day. Some of the early attempts to reinvent the city center worked, notably in more attractive "legacy" cities—such as New York, Chicago, Boston, and San Francisco—which possessed a strong trading tradition, great universities, unique architecture, and attractive physical settings. This approach was not as effective, generally, in cities whose origins lay in the manufacturing era or whose demographics and economic structures were not ideally suited for the transition to an information-based economy.

Those places that managed to emerge triumphantly out of the wreckage of the industrial era were no longer defined by smoke-belching industrial plants. The symbol of the new successful city was the high-rise office or residential tower, the arts district, and other high-end amenities.

The visionary urbanist Jean Gottmann envisioned the emergence of what he called "the transactional city" over three decades ago. Like cities such as Amsterdam and Venice in the early modern period, which managed the trade and financial needs of vastly larger territories, these cities would benefit from the need for the production of information and the coordination of both services and finance in a globalized economy. Gottmann predicted that the suburbs would also grow, but he placed emphasis on the strong expansion of city cores, which he said would benefit most from serving as "crossroads for economic transactions."[57]

In the emerging urban hierarchy, the best-positioned cities—New York, San Francisco, Boston—were able to rebound smartly, often through redevelopment and the cultivation of knowledge-based industries. This often also had the effect of displacing whole communities, primarily working-class whites and African Americans, while replacing them with higher-income, more educated residents. But the revitalization efforts of the 1970s and 1980s that succeeded in places like Boston's Quincy Market, notes historian John C. Teaford, were notably less successful in far less historically blessed places, such as Buffalo, Cleveland, and Toledo.[58] While some cities were able to transform themselves into successful information-era hubs, many other cities—and their residents—were left behind.

By the dawn of the 21st century, 70 percent of children in New Orleans, nearly 60 percent in Cleveland, and 41 percent in Baltimore lived in poverty. Cities such as Chicago, Cleveland, and Detroit continued to lose population. Detroit, a century earlier renowned for its "broad and cleanly streets," presented arguably the worst-case scenario, losing most of its residents as both industry and the middle class decamped for the periphery and other parts of the country. "This," author Scott Martelle wrote about Detroit, "is what the abject collapse of an industrial society looks like."[59]

ANOTHER OPTION: THE SOCIALIST CITY

Some planners sought to remedy the predicament of the industrial city without suburbanization. Their response to the failures of industrialism drew from a socialist ideology, which some thought would aid them in creating cities along more equitable lines. Like some of to-day's retro-urbanists, socialist city-builders evolved their own planning "religion," albeit in a more oppressive form, to address the problems associated with growing cities.

The socialist vision of the city found early expression in the writings of German sociologist Ferdinand Tönnies. Heavily influenced by Marx, Tönnies envisioned a future in which the entire world would become "one large city" run not by the populace in general but "by thinkers, scholars, and writers" who would construct and control this planetary metropolis.[60]

Once established, the Soviet Union provided the primary model for this new urban ideal. Under Joseph Stalin's rule from 1929 to 1953, numerous "socialist cities" were built by importing the peasantry from the countryside, sometimes through coercion and forced migration. This was intended both to further enlarge the working class and to accelerate the transformation of the Soviet Union into an industrial superpower. Built from scratch, the new factory towns "were intended to prove, definitively, that when unhindered by pre-existing economic relationships, central planning could produce more rapid economic growth than capitalism."[61]

At the same time, large existing cities also were transformed to fit the model of "socialist cities." As they sought to rebuild the former Saint Petersburg, Petrograd (soon to be renamed Leningrad), and Moscow, the Bolsheviks quickly occupied many of the old mansions and fashionable apartments of the aristocracy and the bourgeoisie, whom they had overthrown.[62] But the rest of the population was instructed to live as the party required. As novelist Aleksey Tolstoy suggested, this was a society where "everything was cancelled" including, he noted "the right to live as one wished."[63]

The new Communist rulers sought to build their urban areas by obliterating the civic past—not too unlike, as we'll see, the redevelopers in the West during the 1960s and 1970s. Stalin, for example, demolished the Cathedral of Christ the Saviour, which had been completed in 1882 after 40 years of construction. In its place, the Soviet regime constructed the new Palace of the Soviets. Thousands of other historic buildings also went down under Bolshevik edicts. "In reconstructing Moscow," proclaimed Nikita Khrushchev in 1937, "we should not be afraid to remove a tree, a little church, or some cathedral or other." When his own architects asked him to spare some historical monuments, the future Soviet leader responded that his crew would continue "sharpening [their] axes."[64]

But the goal was not merely to transform the physical city. Socialist planners also saw cities as the ideal place to create a new kind of urban person, what some critics labeled *Homo sovieticus*, or "Soviet Man." As one historian wrote, the socialist city was to be a place "free of historical burdens, where a new human being was to come into existence, the city and the factory were to be a laboratory of a future society, culture, and way of life."[65]

Socialist planners sought to achieve this new urban paradigm by constructing cities along lines they believed would promote their notion of community. Nurseries and preschools were built within walking distance of residential areas. Theaters and sports halls were also placed nearby. Instead of individual kitchens, communal eating areas were developed. Private space was minimized while planners constructed wide boulevards crucial for marches and impressive public structures. Sadly, the construction was often shoddy—despite Soviet propaganda depicting ideal construction sites with happy workers and well-managed cities with happy families. "In the new socialist cities," writes historian Anne Applebaum, "the gap between the utopian propaganda and the sometimes catastrophic reality of daily life was so wide that the communist parties scrambled constantly to explain it away."[66]

What did a "socialist" city look like? It certainly did not resemble contemporary suburbs in the West. The new model—much like that of today's retro-urbanists—favored multistory apartment blocks over leafy suburbs.[67] Alexei Gutnov, one of the authors of the book *The Ideal Communist City*, acknowledged that suburban development provided "ideal conditions for rest and privacy . . . offered by the individual house situated in the midst of nature . . ."[68] But this approach, he decided, did not fit the communist ideal of a more egalitarian, socially reconstructed society. Gutnov feared that[69] the highly private nature of such housing might lead the citizen to "separate himself from others, rest, sleep, and live his family life," which would make it harder for the state to steer him toward the proper "cultural options."[70]

As part of its commitment to equality, the socialist city sought to provide equal mobility for all residents, with each neighborhood being at equal walking distance from the center of the community and from the rural area surrounding it. Like the radiant city of Le Corbusier, these dense developments would be surrounded by open land on at least two sides, creating a green belt. Not surprisingly, socialist planners also strongly preferred public transportation over privately owned vehicles, high-density apartment housing over detached private homes, and maximizing common areas over private backyards.[71]

These notions, notes Applebaum, were quickly adopted by the Soviet satellites in Eastern Europe, who sought out "the destruction of the property-owning classes," which included small homeowners.[72] Influenced by modernist ideas, identical pre-fab tower blocks in park-like settings were mass produced all over the Soviet Union and its satellite states. Called *Plattenbau* in German and *paneláky* in Czech and Slovak,[73] these panel buildings were constructed of pre-fabricated, pre-pressed concrete and often poorly constructed. One-third of all Czechs still live in a *panelák*.[74]

One particularly sad example of socialist planning—and its authoritarian Nazi counterpoint—could be seen in and around Berlin. In the prewar era, Berlin's raucous lifestyle and socialist leanings offended both conservatives and Nazis. The Nazi Party leader for Berlin (and later, Hitler's Propaganda Minister), Joseph Goebbels, initially denounced the city as "a sink of inequity." But as the capital became synonymous with the Third Reich, Goebbels began to describe it as "magnificent," "electric," and a city that exhaled "the breath of history." Hitler himself, to the consternation of his *völkisch*, rural-oriented supporters, centralized power in the capital and determined to make Berlin the most magnificent city in Europe.[75] Before being halted by their defeat in World War II, the Nazis planned to turn Berlin into a monumental city of Germania, which would have been one of the most extensive urban building projects in history.

The Communist inheritors of the then-ruined eastern half of Berlin may have shared Hitler's passion for authoritarian ideology, but unlike the Nazis, they never possessed enough resources to rebuild the city.[76] Following the Bolshevik model, party leaders seized what was left for their own good, absconding with country estates and the few remaining comfortable city apartments. But they also followed Soviet ideas in how they constructed the urban environment for their supposed masters, the proletarians. East German architects and planners made the obligatory pilgrimages to Moscow, Kiev, Leningrad, and Stalingrad to find out what a socialist city looked like. They soon learned that their Soviet colleagues, among other things, preferred large apartment blocks to tree-lined, lower-density suburbs.[77]

The results were depressingly bleak. The city, with its dense apartment blocks and blocky office buildings, reflected much of the modernist tradition but in a particularly uninspired and dehumanized manner.[78] As anyone who visited there at the time could recall, socialist Berlin loomed as a very gray city with little charm; once the East German state disappeared, many residents of Berlin and other urban centers left for the more frankly capitalist cities in the West.[79]

THE EMERGENCE OF THE NEW CONSUMER CITY

Even as many of the old industrial cities continued to fail—not only in America but also in eastern Asia and Europe—Gottmann's "transactional city" burgeoned in pockets around the world. By the 1980s, these revitalized cities were beginning to newly invigorate the urban role as centers of consumption and wealth.

In this new calculus, a city's value had less to do with its physical geography—for example, access to rivers or power sources—than with its ability to attract high-service industries and a workforce that could operate them. Unlike the more industrially based cities throughout the world, which were left with little after the factories closed, these cities enjoyed a smoother transition into the information era. The new consumer city also represented, fundamentally, a city of choice—that is, a place where certain consumers came not so much for opportunity but rather to partake in the pleasures of high-end urban life.

Factories in Detroit and Manchester lay idle and useless for decades, but the centers of the transaction economy often succeeded by repurposing the residue of the old industrial era. In some places, old warehouses and factories were brilliantly transformed into areas for higher-level services as well as restaurants, bars, and retail shops. This was particularly true along rivers and lakefronts.[80] Similarly, churches, which had served as the fulcrum for Renaissance urbanism, were shut down, and even more will be in the future. It's been predicted that in the next 20 years, some two-thirds of the 1,600 churches now operating in Germany will close—but they may find new life as boutiques, entertainment venues, or luxury condos.[81]

This trend started as early as the 1960s. English author and journalist A. N. Wilson, for example, wrote about the shift in London from its dock and manufacturing economy to one dominated increasingly by media and finance, as well as the shift toward more luxury consumption, clubs, and shops. This new urban economy, Wilson noted, allowed London, with its concentration of business, financial services, and media, to remain remarkably vibrant, while the old industrial cities of the Midlands, like their counterparts elsewhere, essentially lost their fundamental purpose and faced a secular decline from which they have not recovered.[82]

With its rich array of cultural amenities, the new consumer city exercises an almost magnetic attraction for the very wealthy, students, and people at the early stages of their careers. Its core economy revolves around the arts and high-end managerial and financial positions. Modern, post-industrial London, observed English novelist Ford Madox Ford, is irresistible to some as it "attracts men from a distance with a glamour like that of a great and green gaming table."[83]

This trend evolved, if anything, even more profoundly in America's premier city, New York. In 1950, notes historian Fernand Braudel, New York was "the dominant industrial city in the world," populated largely by small, specialized firms that often employed 30 people or fewer. Collectively, they employed a million people and were key to the rise of many immigrant families, including my own. Today, the city has fewer than 200,000 people working in industry; the loss of these firms, Braudel notes, left "a gap in the heart of New York which will never be filled."[84]

Yet if the industrial heart was emptied, New York was not without recourse. The old industry base was supplanted by the "information economy," which as early as 1982 already accounted for the majority of Manhattan's jobs. So while plants were slowly going dark throughout the city, new office towers were rising over Gotham. In many ways, this transformation built on New York's early history of being, first and foremost, a trading and port city. The difference was that the primary raw material was no longer in trading commodities but rather in harnessing skills in the production of information.

This successful evolution led some, including Terry Nichols Clark, to suggest that urban success depends not so much on new office construction, or even corporate expansion, but on the locational decisions of individuals who rely largely on the city's cultural and lifestyle attributes. Clearly, locational preferences play an important role in sustaining these cities. The same spectacular scenery of such cities as Seattle or San Francisco that appeals to visitors also lures well-heeled populations who can live every day amid the splendor that most experience only as tourists.[85]

As we'll explore in later chapters, the new consumer city depends upon attracting those who seek out the thrills of urban life—a trend that Clark defines as "the city as entertainment machine." In this approach to urbanity, a city thrives by creating an ideal locale for hipsters and older, sophisticated urban dwellers, becoming a kind of adult Disneyland with plenty of chic restaurants, shops, and festivals. In Clark's estimation, amenities and a "cool" factor make up the essence of the modern city, where perception is as important as reality, if not more so. He suggests:

> . . . for persons pondering where to live and work, restaurants are more than food on the plate. The presence of distinct restaurants redefines the context, even for people who do not eat in them. They are part of the local market basket of amenities that vary from place to place.[86]

THE NEW GEOGRAPHY OF INEQUALITY

In this new consumer city, the role that priests and aristocrats played in imperial cities has been assumed by the global wealthy, financial engineers, media moguls, and other top business executives and service providers. One thing the new consumer city does share with its historic counterpart is a limited role for an expanding middle class.

Some of this stems from the structure of the successful transactional city. In recent decades, these cities have grown two ends of their economies: an affluent, well-educated, tech-savvy base and an ever-expanding poor service class. Mass middle-class employment is fading. Unlike in the 1960s and 1970s, these cities have not produced anything like the office towers built to house middle managers, clerical staff, and others who are neither rich nor poor. In fact, by 2014, office space was being built at barely one-tenth the level in American cities as that of the 1980s. Instead, the new consumer city expresses itself largely through the construction of residential structures, aimed largely at the high-skilled workforce as well as a nomadic population made up of wealthy, highly gifted, or top specialists.[87] The growth of these cities, note historians John Logan and Harvey Molotch, was less a result of local economic expansion as it was of the cities' ability to use their capital to acquire firms from elsewhere, which helped secure their place in "the hierarchy of urban dominance."[88]

This frankly elitist vision of the city is widely embraced by many urban developers and politicians. Former New York Mayor Michael Bloomberg suggests that today, a successful city must be primarily "a luxury product," a place that focuses on the very wealthy, whose surplus can underwrite the rest of the population. "If we can find a bunch of billionaires around the world to move here, that would be a godsend," Bloomberg, himself a multibillionaire, says. "Because that's where the revenue comes to take care of everybody else."[89]

This reliance on the rich, notes a Citigroup study, creates an urban employment structure based on "plutonomy," an economy and society driven largely by the wealthy class's investment and spending.[90] In this way, the playground of these "luxury cores" around the world, as will be discussed later, serve less as places of aspiration than as geographies of inequality. New York, for example, is by some measurements the most unequal of American major cities, with a level of inequality that approximates South Africa *before* apartheid. New York's wealthiest 1 percent earn a third of the entire municipality's personal income[91]— almost twice the proportion for the rest of the country.[92]

Other luxury cores exhibit somewhat similar patterns. A recent Brookings Institution report found that virtually all the most unequal metropolitan areas—with the exception of Atlanta and Miami—are luxury-oriented cities, including San Francisco, Boston, New York, Chicago, Los Angeles, and Washington, DC.[93] As urban studies author Stephen J. K. Walters notes, these cities tend to develop highly bifurcated economies, divided between an elite sector and a large service class. "This," he notes, "is the opposite of [Jane] Jacobs's vision of cities . . . as places they are 'constantly transforming many poor people into middle-class people.'"[94] These trends are particularly notable in places such as Kendall Square in Cambridge, just across the Charles River from Boston. Long a working-class redoubt, the expansion of technology and biomedical firms has transformed the area into an increasingly bifurcated society divided between the affluent and highly educated and a large poor population. The median price of a one-bedroom apartment in Cambridge is $2,200 a month, according to the online real estate company Zillow—more than many [local] residents make in a month. As the *Boston Globe* reports:

> As global pharmaceutical companies build new labs, Internet giants Google and Twitter expand, and startups snap up office space at ever-higher rents, families living in the shadow of the innovation economy are flocking to the local food pantry at three times the rate of a decade ago. The waiting list for public housing is double what it was five years ago. The beds in the Salvation Army homeless shelter on Massachusetts Avenue are always full . . . .[95]

These patterns contradict the notion of the middle-class, family-oriented city that Jane Jacobs so evocatively raised. On the ground, as Witold Rybczynski notes, the rise of successful urban cores increasingly has very little to do with Jacobs's romantic notions about bottom-up organic urbanism:

> *The most successful urban neighborhoods have attracted not the blue-collar families that she celebrated, but the rich and the young. The urban vitality that she espoused—and correctly saw as a barometer of healthy city life—has found new expressions in planned commercial and residential developments whose scale rivals that of the urban renewal of which she was so critical. These developments are the work of real estate entrepreneurs, who were absent from the city described . . . but loom large today, having long ago replaced planners and our chief urban strategists.[96]*

As Rybczynski notes, the current rise of "urban vitality" derives not from the idiosyncratic, diverse, and, if you will, democratic form that Jacobs celebrated but from something more an expression of self-conscious corporate marketing. This is very much the experience of modern Paris, London, Brussels, Hong Kong, and Singapore, where high housing prices are driving many longtime residents and even some affluent families out of the core city and, in some cases, out the country.

In the process, we see a city that is increasingly divided by class and provides limited options for upward mobility. In the past decade, for example, there has been considerable gentrification around Chicago's lakefront. But during this period, Chicago's middle class has declined precipitously. At the same time, despite all the talk about "the great inversion" with the poor replaced by the rich, it turns out that it is mostly the middle and working classes who have exited.

Urban analyst Pete Saunders suggests that Chicago is really two different cities now, with different geographies and sizes. Prosperous and greatly hyped "super-global Chicago" has income and education levels well above those of the suburban areas, but the majority of city residents live in "rust belt Chicago," with education and income levels well below suburban levels. "Chicago," Saunders says, "may be better understood in thirds—one-third San Francisco, two-thirds Detroit."[97]

It's ironic that many of the cities that have done best in the post-industrial era have also been those that have become ever less diverse; they have evolved in ways that contradict Jacobs's idealized urbanity, in which dense neighborhoods seemed to be the most permanent as opposed to the most transient.[98] Successful transactional centers increasingly have less room for either the poor or the middle-class families who have traditionally inhabited them. San Francisco's black population, for example, is a fraction of what it was in 1970.[99] In Portland, the nation's whitest major city, African Americans are being driven out of the urban core by gentrification, partly supported by city funding.[100] Similar phenomena can be seen in Seattle[101] and Boston,[102] where long-existing black communities are gradually disappearing.[103]

Whatever their successes, the transactional cities have not found a way to address the problem of inequality, the role of families, or the preservation of the urban middle class. Most shocking of all, the shift to an information-based economy has not succeeded in eliminating poverty. Indeed, during the first 10 years of the new millennium, neighborhoods with entrenched urban poverty actually grew, increasing in numbers from 1,100 to 3,100 and in population from 2 to 4 million. "This growing concentration of poverty," note urban researchers Joe Cortright and Dillon Mahmoudi, "is the biggest problem confronting American cities."[104]

TOWARD A NEW URBAN PARADIGM

The transactional city model, it is clear, does not provide a workable urban future for the vast majority of society. For one thing, due to their high prices, these cities are profoundly challenged in providing what most residents of the metropolis actually want: homeownership, rapid access to employment throughout the metropolitan area, good schools, and human-scaled neighborhoods.

Instead, the transactional city represents a profound sociological departure from the more democratic form of urbanism that emerged first in the 17th century and again in the 20th century. Their appeal is not for middle-income families or ambitious newcomers from out-side but rather for those attracted to—and able to afford—what Terry Nichols Clark refers to as the urban "basket of amenities."[105] As we've seen, these primarily include the educated young, the childless afflu-ent, and, most particularly, the very wealthy.

The current urban discussion all too often ignores the issue of how to offer opportunity to the vast majority of the population. In a world where most people live in cities and towns, all efforts should be made to make these places accessible and livable for the vast majority of citi-zens. The dense, luxury city model may work well for certain people at particular points in their lives, but the greatest challenge remains, as it was in the past, accommodating the aspirations of the majority, who have long gone to the city for opportunity, cultural inspiration, and a sense of identity.

GENUINE SUSTAINABILITY

No doubt the luxury core model will continue to flourish in places, particularly for the well-heeled and those located in a limited number of historic cities that boast historical structures, unique amenities, and usually excellent mass transit. But this paradigm is not applica-ble, in any case, to a whole city—even a New York or London—where most people live outside the glamorous districts. If we want an ur-banism that works for most, cities need to develop a very different focus, emphasizing such things as economic growth and opportu-nity—a geography that increases the opportunities for a broad array of citizens.

Properly defined, sustainability must extend beyond the environ-ment, around which the term "sustainability" is usually hung, to a broader concept that includes the health of the entire society. In the past, the city—and later the suburb—provided "a profoundly demo-cratic phenomenon," which upgraded the living conditions of the middle and working classes.[106] In contrast, the evolution of the new consumer city works against the improvement of middle- and work-ing-class residents. Planning policies to restrict peripheral growth, so favored in the luxury cities, also serve to raise rents and home prices, as is most evident in highly regulated places like California, Australia, and the United Kingdom.[107]

In this sense, then, we need to look at social sustainability—that is, the preservation and expansion of the middle class—as a critical value for the future of society and its overall health. Building out into the periphery has provided this option more than any other model. "Sprawl," notes author Kenneth Kolson, "serves their [the middle class's] interest far more than the growth girdles and other market restraints of 'smart growth.'"[108]

Our definition of "sustainable" needs to go beyond a program that promotes the lower standards of living and higher levels of poverty that occur when we force human beings into ever smaller, and usually more expensive, places. The attempt to reduce the space and privacy enjoyed by households is not "progressive" but fundamentally regressive. In this sense, notes British author Austin Williams, sustainability has evolved into "an insidiously dangerous concept, masquerading as progress." By limiting housing options and focusing on the most affluent quarters, sustainability advocates sometimes suggest policies that make things more expensive for the middle and working classes. They also make the formation of families increasingly difficult. In this most basic biological sense, Williams says, "the ideology of sustainability is unsustainable."[109]

Instead of focusing only on environmental and design concerns, we need to place far more emphasis on the *human* factor as we construct and develop our cities. Residents may, and generally do, desire cleaner air and water, but they may not think this also means they have to accept crowded conditions that they may find depressing, too expensive, and inimical to family formation.[110]

Perhaps most maddening is that many of those who most actively push densification do not have to live with the consequences. Increasingly, those calling for more densification are people who, as one Los Angeles newspaper found, enjoy the very lifestyle—in gated communities and large houses located far from transit routes—they wish to eradicate for others.[111]

The ultimate absurdity of this new approach to urbanity was on display at the World Economic Forum's 2015 Davos meeting, epitomized in the focus on climate change by people who used some 1,700 private jets to attend the Swiss event.[112] The people blowing fuel on private jets somehow feel empowered to ask everyone else to live more modestly. One has to wonder about Davos-goers like billionaire real estate investor Jeff Greene, who says that to fight climate change, America needs to "live a smaller existence." This coming from a man who has owned as many as five houses, including an un-small $195 million Beverly Hills estate that was, at the time, possibly the country's priciest residence.[113]

SEARCHING FOR THE HUMAN CITY

In many ways, we are faced with a crisis that parallels that of the industrial city, with ever-widening inequality, widespread poverty, and social alienation.

Frank Lloyd Wright came up with what may be seen as the most ambitious vision in response to the current emphasis on ever-increasing density. Wright detested the way high-rise buildings cast shadows on the urban landscape, and in his proposals for Broadacre City, made in 1958, he posited a model in which many urban functions were dispersed into the countryside. In sharp contradiction to Le Corbusier, Wright saw the densification of cities as a "destructive fixation." Universal electrification and modern transportation, he argued, had made densification unnecessary and made possible a greater dispersion of cities. He equated decentralization with democratic principles and with the provision of a better life for those strangled by "urban constriction." Wright, perhaps somewhat impractically, thereby proposed "an acre to each individual man, woman and child."[114]

Wright's ideas, or those of Ebenezer Howard, for that matter, were never fully adopted, but these principles—developed in reaction to the industrial city—remain highly applicable in the information age as well. The desire for space, light, and access to green spaces has not changed; these are universal and intrinsically human desires. This is true for the low-density cities of the West but also, if anything, more imperative in the dense cities of Asia, where most people do not have access to their own backyards.[115]

Great cities that want to attract and retain families must maintain that spiritual nourishment that comes from contact with nature. Olmsted's vision of Central Park, for example, was to provide working-class families "a specimen of God's handiwork."[116] Today, many of the most ambitious programs for park-building are taking place in suburbs, such as Orange County's Great Park,[117] which is slated to be twice the size of Central Park, or in sprawling family-friendly cities, such as Raleigh's nearly completed $30 million Neuse River Trail,[118] which cuts through 28 miles of heavily forested areas. There's Houston's rapidly developing bayou park system and Dallas's plans for a vast new 6,000-acre reserve along the Trinity River that easily overshadows New York's 840-acre Central Park. These ambitious new parks often start close to the urban core but also provide open space for the widely dispersed settlements attached to them.[119]

This suggests a radically different approach to the urban future, one that can be not only "greener" but also, most importantly, better for people and their families. In the end, it is not the magnificence of a city that matters, or its degree of hipness, but how well people live, both in terms of their standard of living and their ability to rise economically. It is a question of accomplishing those things that have made cities work in the past: an expansive economy, thriving families, and a powerful sense of place.

In reality, for most residents of cities, life is not about engaging the urban "entertainment machine" or enjoying the most spectacular views from a high-rise tower. To them, the goal is to achieve residence in a small home in a modest neighborhood, whether in a suburb or in the city, where children can be raised and also where, of increasing importance, seniors can grow old amid familiar places and faces. As the Southern California writer D. J. Waldie writes of his home in working-class Lakewood:

> I believe that people and places form each other . . . the touch
> of one returning the touch of the other. What we seek, I think,
> is tenderness in this encounter, but that goes both ways, too.
> I believe that places acquire their sacredness through this

*giving and taking. And with that ever-returning touch, we
acquire something sacred from the place where we live. What
we acquire, of course, is a home.*[120]

Such a notion of "home" remains generally undervalued in our
current discussion of the urban form. People clustering in ever more
crowded cities, living atop one another, may fulfill the ambitions of corporate leaders, urbanist visionaries, and planners. But in the end, such
ambitions may not fulfill, for most people, what a less congested place
or a house cooled by even a touch of green and trees might provide. As
the world urbanizes, this is not merely an American or high-income
country issue but one of increased global significance.

CHAPTER 3

The Problem with Megacities

WHEN ASHOK DATAR was growing up in Mumbai, he heard the cries of hyenas and the calls of myriad tropical birds. At that time, jackals still visited the city occasionally, much as coyotes can be found in cities in North America today. The last hyenas in Mumbai were shot dead in the 1990s, supplanted by the ceaseless, dense development of the great Indian city.[1] Sitting in his cramped apartment in a predominantly Muslim section of the central city, Datar notes that tropical birds are also nearly extinct there now, leaving a fauna of commonplace rats, squirrels, and pigeons. The city, he says, has become largely denatured from its surroundings.

But it's not just nature that has struggled in Datar's hometown. Chairman of the Mumbai Environmental Social Network and a long-time adviser to the Ambani family interests, Datar sees a city where the human species faces ever-increasing pressure. In the hurried, crowded, polluted, and jumbled streets are all the worst attributes of the 19th-century European industrial city—massive slums, huge gaps between rich and poor, and a way of life that seems detrimental to basic human needs.

The masses moving into Mumbai and other cities are coming from a countryside rife with poverty to a place of limited opportunity. Datar wonders whether this model of ever-growing numbers of people transferring from the countryside to megacities will prove the best way to meet the needs of a population as vast and as predominantly poor as that of India.

To be sure, India—with a still-growing population and increasing education levels—clearly is growing and developing its economy, and it is likely to become one of the great powers of this century. But the question remains whether ever-expanding megacity development is necessary at a time when employment, in the West and elsewhere, is dispersing. "We are copying the Western experience in our own stupid and silly way," Datar says. "For every tech geek, we have two to three servants. This is not the future we would have envisioned."

Indeed, given the problems associated with dense development, many countries might consider other options. Datar suggests that developing countries need to better promote the growth of smaller, more manageable cities and try bringing more economic opportunity to the villages. They also need to address the underlying cause of Mumbai's unbearable crowdedness: rural village economies that are emptying their surplus populations into the cities rather than sustaining themselves. These areas have lagged behind in India's boom, and as long as they do, they will continue to send ever more people to the cities, including Mumbai.[2] "To save the city," Datar suggests, "we will have to save the village too."

THE RISE OF THE MODERN MEGACITY

The rapid growth of population in megacities, particularly in the developing world, is coming at a time when virtually all global population growth is taking place in the poorest parts of the planet. Indeed, according to UN population estimates, 99 percent of all population growth between 2010 and 2100 is expected to take place in developing countries, predominantly in Africa but also in Asia. Together, these two regions, which are now rapidly urbanizing, will account for some 96 percent of the world's population growth.[3] According to UN projections, India's urban population will increase by nearly 250 million in 20 years—an even greater increase than what is projected for rapidly urbanizing China.[4]

Driven by these demographic forces, the growth of megacities like Mumbai—urban regions with over 10 million residents[5]—poses new and often enormous challenges for the urban future. Even as they demonstrate the enormous appeal of city life, these new megacities also represent an enormous break in urban history in two critical ways: their unprecedented size and their relative lack of the kind of economic base that drove urban development in Europe, America, and more recently, eastern Asia. No city in the 19th or 20th century was nearly as large, or grew in countries as poor, as those we see today.

Today's megacities, first of all, reflect a profound shift in urban scale. In 1800, only Beijing had a population exceeding 1 million. In 1900, greater London was the world's largest urban center with 6.5 million people.[6] Today, there are more than 50 cities with larger populations, including the largest, Tokyo, whose population exceeds 35 million.[7]

Until 1975, Tokyo was one of only three megacities—New York and Mexico City being the others. Over the next 40 years, megacities cropped up around the planet. There were 34 such cities in 2014, which now account for roughly 13 percent of the world's urban population and 7 percent of the world's total population. Overall, the population of the world's 100 largest cities has grown to 10 times what their combined size was in 1900.[8] As in Mumbai, most of this growth has been driven by the migration of rural people to the city. This reflects Marx's notion that modernity is essentially "the urbanization of the countryside." What differs today is the unprecedented scale of this migration.[9]

The other big divergence lies in the economic underpinnings of urban growth. In the past, urban growth generally occurred most rapidly in the most prosperous and fastest-growing regions. Cities like Tokyo and Osaka, originally castle towns, expanded rapidly by developing their industrial and trading economies. This closely followed what had already occurred throughout the West in places like New York and London, which became large due to their varied and expanding economies.[10] More recently, Seoul and China's megacities have also grown within the context of rapid industrialization and a powerful export economy.

In contrast, the wealthiest urban centers increasingly no longer dominate the ranks of the world's largest cities. Today, these advanced high- and mid-income cities account for merely 10 of the world's 34 megacities, including Tokyo (1), Seoul-Incheon (5), New York (9), Osaka-Kobe-Kyoto (14), Moscow (15), Los Angeles (18), Istanbul (23), Paris (29), London (32), and Nagoya (33).

For the most part, outside of Istanbul—which may soon be Europe's largest city—few of these cities are growing rapidly.[11] But listing Istanbul among the advanced cities has some limitations. For all its growth and relative prosperity, it is still something of a developing-world city. Roughly half of the city's dwelling units were constructed illegally, suggesting it may have more in common with poorer megacities than might be commonly assumed.[12]

Overall, though, the megacities in the United States and the high-income countries in Europe, where population tracking is more reliable, show slower growth. Between 2002 and 2012, London and Moscow were the only megacities with a purchasing power adjusted GDP of over US$40,000 that registered population growth over 10 percent. In contrast, the population of Paris grew 8 percent, Los Angeles grew 6 percent, and New York barely grew 3 percent over the past decade.[13]

Japan, one of the world's most urbanized major countries, has logged even slower growth. Tokyo, the great outlier in that country's stagnant population profile, expanded 7 percent, Nagoya grew 6 percent, and Osaka-Kobe-Kyoto grew a weak 2 percent. The rapid population depletion in the rest of the country along with a lack of foreign immigrants will limit future migration to Tokyo. This suggest Japan's great cities will grow even slower in the years ahead, especially as the country runs short on young people in general.[14]

The contrast with megacities in the developing world is breathtaking. Over the past 30 to 40 years, the most rapid population increases have taken place in areas that remain relatively undeveloped and poor, primarily in Africa, southern Asia, and Latin America.[15] In the first years of the 21st century, urban growth was three times faster in low-income countries than in their higher-income counterparts.[16]

Among the poor megacities, Karachi, Pakistan, has led the growth charge, with reports of a more than 80 percent expansion in its population from 2000 to 2010.[17] Other rapidly growing megacities are scattered throughout the developing world. In Nigeria, Lagos saw its population swell by over 48 percent over the past decade; the Thai capital of Bangkok and Dhaka, Bangladesh, both grew some 45 percent. The world's second-largest megacity, Jakarta, expanded 34 percent and now exceeds 30 million.

Rapid urbanization has also spread to Latin America, although, unlike Africa and India, these countries urbanized quite early. By 1930, Buenos Aires, Mexico City, and Rio de Janeiro all had a million people. The United Nations Population Division estimates that over 80 percent of the Latin American population now resides in urban areas and that 87 percent will live in cities by 2050. Argentina will reach the highest urbanization rate by 2050, at 95 percent. To put these numbers into perspective, more than 19 of every 20 Argentines will live in cities. The urbanization rates of other Latin American countries will not fall far behind: Chile, Brazil, Venezuela, and Uruguay will also surpass 90 percent, and Mexico, Panama, Colombia, Ecuador, Peru, and Suriname will exhibit urbanization rates above 80 percent.[18]

These numbers suggest that the future of megacities will be in the developing world. This will be most marked in those countries that still have large rural hinterlands that can export surplus populations to the urban centers, something increasingly unavailable in high-income countries where the countryside has already been largely depopulated. These poor places—most with median incomes between Dhaka at US$3,100 per capita and Bangkok at US$23,000 per capita—will continue to grow, although their growth rates may also slow due to smaller family size and competition from other generally smaller cities.

China, not surprisingly, is home to six megacities, the most of any country, reflecting the country's extraordinarily rapid urbanization. The second-fastest-growing megacity over the past decade, Shenzhen, was a small fishing village before it became a focus of former Chinese leader Deng Xiaoping's first wave of modernization policies. In 1979, the village had roughly 30,000 people;[19] now, it is a thriving metropolis of 12 million whose population grew 56 percent in the past decade. Its rise has been so recent and quick that the Asia Society has labeled it "a city without a history."[20]

India matches Japan with three megacities, all growing much faster than any city in the high-income world. The population of Delhi, the world's third-largest city, expanded 40 percent over the past decade; Mumbai, almost 20 percent; and Kolkata (Calcutta) roughly 10 percent, a relatively low rate for a city in a developing country. And there are likely to be more megacities of this kind in the future.[21] By 2025, the ranks of megacities in poor countries seem certain to expand. United Nations growth projections to 2025[22] suggest nine more megacities could emerge by 2030, including Chennai, Bangalore, Hyderabad, Ahmedabad (all in India), Ho Chi Minh City (Vietnam), Bogotá (Colombia), Johannesburg-East Rand (South Africa), Luanda (Angola), and Hangzhou (China).[23]

SIZE IS NOT ENOUGH

Conventional wisdom suggests that these dense urban areas are the key to creating prosperity and a better life for the population of developing countries. A 2009 World Bank report, for example, insists that large urban concentrations—the denser, the better—represent the key to improved prosperity. "To spread out economic growth," it argues, "is to discourage it." And it is certainly true that as countries modernize, they also urbanize, often quite rapidly. In the developing world, urban growth has been accelerated by international investment and aid.[24]

Over time, some of these cities—like those that emerged during the European Industrial Revolution—may well emerge as great engines of economic opportunity. This may be most likely in places like China that have developed powerful industrial and technological sectors and enjoy an expanding domestic market. But most megacities, as presently constituted, have little chance of gaining international economic prominence. For one thing, they generally lack the characteristics—such as ethnic diversity, legal structures, technology, or manufacturing prowess—necessary to create the kind of economy that underpins successful global cities. These megacities are often very important to their countries, in large part due to political centralization, but none has come close to collecting the critical assets—in terms of infrastructure,

education, health care, and even basic sanitation—necessary for becoming a competitive global city.[25]

In reality, megacities are plagued by inefficiencies and inherent
problems that may keep most people from achieving prosperity and
securing a powerful international role. For example, global management consulting firm A. T. Kearney supplemented its 2014 Global
Cities Index with an Emerging Cities Outlook. This ranking gauged
the potential for cities outside the high-income world to "improve
their global standing" over the next 10 to 20 years. Jakarta, Manila,
and Delhi ranked in the top four positions (along with Addis Ababa
in Ethiopia), and Karachi ranked last on the list.[26] Over time, some of
these cities may move up in the rankings, but analysts such as those
at McKinsey & Company don't project any will rank among the top 10
global cities by 2025.[27]

Rapid growth, as author Suketu Mehta suggests, may not make
these megacities more competitive but rather less so. More congested,
more crime-ridden places like Mexico City have become, if anything,
less competitive, less economically important, and more dependent on
transfers from the rest of the country. By the end of the 1970s, Mexico
City's share of the national GDP had slipped from 45 percent to 37
percent. Long a net contributor to the national budget, it had become
a drain.[28] "Supergrowth," author Jonathan Kandell notes, "has robbed
Mexico [City] of economic logic."[29]

Similar conditions exist in many of Africa's largest cities, which
are growing as fast as any in the world.[30] In the past decade, their economic growth has barely kept up with their population. This may get
worse given the slowdown in the once much-heralded BRICS countries—Brazil, Russia, India, China, and South Africa. Most of these
countries have seen their growth rates slacken, often by as much as 50
percent, from a decade earlier.[31]

Rather than future New Yorks or Tokyos, most megacities represent not a triumph of urbanism but a testament to its worst short-
comings. Writing about Mexico City, author David Lida suggests a
pattern of city building that does not follow the traditional European
or American playbook:

*The orderly European model for cities, and even the bustling
but carefully planned United States archetypes that followed
it, have already given way to another version, in which much
of the world's population lives—enormous improvised hy-
permetropoli which, with virtually no planning whatsoever,
have expanded to accommodate monstrously multiplying
populations.*[32]

These realities suggest that perhaps the enthusiasm about the
emerging megacities expressed in some accounts may be misplaced.[33]
Sometimes, it appears, observers conflate the street-level vibrancy of
these cities with economic progress. "Bombay is a fast-paced, even
hectic city," Mehta says, "but it is not, in the end, a competitive one."[34]

A SHORT HISTORY OF "MEGAPOLITAN ELEPHANTIASIS"

From the earliest periods, large-scale urbanization and swelling populations challenged the ability of rulers to maintain basic health and
order. None of these cities remotely approached the size of today's megacities, but they only had access to less advanced levels of technology for
coping with urban growth. This was not so much a product of the Greek
experience since Greece's cities were relatively small; the greatest Greek
city-state at its peak, the Athens of Aristotle's time, numbered no more
than 275,000. It was Athens's inheritor, Rome, that stepped into un-
known territory by becoming the ancient equivalent of a megacity.[35]

With its magnificent public structures, forums, marketplaces, and
temples, Rome displayed many of the most exciting characteristics of
the modern megacity. As the first city to surpass 1 million by the second century AD, it also demonstrated many of the problems that have
afflicted giant urban settlements. The city grew for many reasons, primarily because it served as capital of a vast empire that controlled most
of the ancient Western world. But its density was also made possible by
improvements in construction methods and materials that allowed for
the building of ever-taller structures.[36]

Much of what we now learn about Rome stems from accounts
from its aristocratic families, who could live in the city with gardens

and ample space. But, as in the emerging megacities of today, for the vast majority, life in Rome meant existing in often shoddily built tenements, or *insulae*; estimates are there was only one private house for every 26 blocks of apartments. These *insulae* often were prone to fire or collapse in earthquakes, dirty, profoundly unhealthy—and ferociously expensive. The streets of these dense areas were also dangerous, particularly as night, in the words of historian Jérôme Carcopino, "fell over the city like the shadow of a great danger, diffused, sinister and menacing."[37]

These unhealthful conditions made life in the city more lethal than in the countryside. Rome's sewer system may have been well ahead of its time, but the higher floors in buildings lacked plumbing hookups, which made this system less than effective in stemming disease.[38] Not surprisingly, some poorer Romans moved to the outskirts of the city for both lower rents and a chance to breathe clear air; many of their patrician and wealthy counterparts headed farther out, into the more scenic countryside, often staying there not just on weekends but more or less permanently.[39]

Lewis Mumford would later describe Rome as suffering from "megapolitan elephantiasis," a kind of collective dysfunction that left it with "pathological cells" that multiplied out of control. Eventually Rome, perhaps presaging the current megacity, became too large, bloated, and congested to sustain its role as the center of the empire. The emperors eventually moved their capital, first to Milan and later to Ravenna in the west and Byzantium on the Bosphorus in the east. Later named Constantinople, this great city grew to house well over 300,000 people in the fifth century and soon suffered many of Rome's ailments. The largest city in the Mediterranean at the time, the Byzantine capital was afflicted by constant riots and high crime; filthy conditions helped spread disease. Indeed, in the middle of the sixth century, upward of half the population died from the plague.[40]

In China, some cities, such as Beijing, grew, but their expansion was limited by walls, which also served as a means to regulate movement into the city. By the late 18th century, further migration into Beijing was banned. Not surprisingly, as in the case of most larger cities, many with means also chose to leave the dense core for the comfort of lower-density areas nearby.[41]

In the Muslim world, noted the Arab historian Ibn Khaldūn, the largest cities were particularly susceptible to the plagues that swept through the Middle East, North Africa, and eastern Asia. Cairo, which in the 14th century had a population of 400,000, or eight times that of contemporary London,[42] lost much of its population when rulers and high officials escaped to avoid repeated epidemics. So great were these plagues, Khaldūn noted, that buildings and even palaces were abandoned, and "the entire inhabited world changed."[43]

THE CRISIS OF THE EARLY INDUSTRIAL CITIES

Arguably, the industrial cities of the West provide the most compelling precursor of what is occurring in megacities today. One writer described London's East End slums of the 19th century as "an Empire of hunger," a prime breeding ground for disease and every kind of social dysfunction.[44] London, then the world's largest city, suffered mortality rates higher than those in the countryside until the 1920s. Friedrich Engels describes London's St. Giles in terms that would have also applied to the Roman *insulae*:

> *The houses are packed from cellar to attic and they are as dirty inside as outside. No human being would willingly inhabit such dens. Yet even worse conditions are to be found in the houses that lay off the main road down narrow alleys that lead to the courts. The extent to which these filthy passages are falling into decay beggars all description.*[45]

These conditions were present in late 19th-century America as well. Many cities suffered rates of infant mortality many times greater than those found in less dense and rural areas.[46] Removal, especially in the summer, helped the more affluent, but for the average urban resident, this was not an option before the rise of mass suburbia. There existed, notes Fernand Braudel, "a separate demography for the rich," as opposed to those who could not easily escape the city.[47]

These conditions were, if anything, worse on the continent. Raw sewage ran down the streets of Berlin as late as the 1870s; only 8 percent of housing had water closets. Not surprisingly, as Berliners dumped their sewage into the river, there were recurrent outbreaks of cholera, typhus, and other devastating diseases.[48] As cities such as Berlin and Paris grew to well over 3 million people by the dawn of the 20th century, most people struggled with exceptionally high rents and slum conditions.[49]

Overall, through much of the 19th century, living conditions in large European cities remained very unhealthy. In Vienna, then capital of the vast Habsburg Empire, only 7 percent of households had their own bathrooms and toilets, and barely 1 percent lived in single-family houses. In conditions more than twice as crowded as Paris, tuberculosis and other diseases were frightfully common.[50] In Saint Petersburg, at the dawn of the Russian Revolution, living conditions were even worse than Berlin's; nearly half of all deaths in the city were traceable to infectious diseases.[51]

HOW THE URBAN CRISIS WAS AVERTED

Rather than accept mass poverty and celebrate dysfunction, late 19th-century European cities confronted their challenges in ways that made life better for many of their citizens. One key goal of prefect Georges-Eugène Haussmann's renovation of Paris, commissioned by Napoleon III in the mid-1800s, was to improve its dreadful sanitary systems and provide a network of parks for its citizens. The quantity of fresh water per citizen more than doubled during the time of the great city's reconstruction, leading to health improvements that would be emulated elsewhere.[52] As one historian notes, Haussmann's work, which involved razing many older working-class areas, "reduced the worst terrors and debasements" that were so common in the modern large city.[53]

These improvements were financially possible, in large part, because cities like Paris, London, and Berlin were also productive economic centers with the resources to address their worst problems. By 1900, as urban economist Edwin Mills has shown, urbanization brought in its wake improved incomes and more employment opportunities, and it created conditions that made business investments more lucrative.[54] In Europe, Japan, and North America, cities eventually improved their living conditions, often through the movement of population to the periphery or, particularly in North America, a shift to emerging metropolitan regions, particularly in the south and west.[55]

THE LEGACY OF COLONIALISM

This success, born of both struggle and prosperity, may prove difficult to repeat in the current era. Economic structure here is key. Paris, London, and Berlin, not to mention New York and Chicago, had prosperous economies atop the world economic system; extra income could be generated to make widespread improvements.

Unfortunately, most megacities today do not enjoy this kind of surplus. To some extent, this reflects vestiges of their colonial past. Some of the most important emerging megacities—Mumbai (Bombay), Jakarta (Batavia), Kolkata (Calcutta), and Kinshasa (Leopoldville)—all started out as colonial outposts. This created a very different relationship between the ruler and the city. Whereas a European city builder was constructing a future for his people's culture, country, and family, the developers of colonial centers were not as concerned with improving long-term conditions for local residents. And where improvements were made, the highest quality sanitation, parks, and transport links generally enveloped those zones inhabited by Europeans and, to some extent, their indigenous allies and functionaries.

The Europeans often shielded themselves through segregation, legal or informal. In some parts of eastern and southern Africa, the indigenous population was even forbidden to live permanently in those sections preferred by Europeans. The colonial rulers of Mexico City, itself placed on the site of a great Aztec metropolis, made a conscious attempt to separate Spaniards—who were considered racially superior—from the indigenous population.[56]

This legacy from the colonial period helped create cities that, as they achieved independence, lacked many of the necessary structures to be successful on their own. British officials did not want to see their network of colonial cities compete with Manchester or London;

Japanese colonialists in Korea certainly did not envision Seoul as a rival for Tokyo, whose rulers saw it as the capital of "a new British empire," a London or New York on the Pacific.[57] This even occurred, notes historian André Raymond, in those cities such as Cairo that were nominally independent and had a long glorious history behind them but found themselves subordinated within the European-dominated world economy. When it came to most business sectors, Europeans presided over what was essentially "a colonized nation."[58]

This legacy of colonial domination applied to India, even in cities such as Bombay and Calcutta that had significant industry. Indians were not expected to provide heavy industry; they were expected to fulfill only those niches that the imperial rulers thought advantageous, notably producing textiles using local cotton. As a result, in part, India was poorly suited for rapid industrial growth. Even today, the manufacturing share of Indian GDP is half that of China.[59]

In contrast, the absence of colonial rule may have contributed to Tokyo's rapid ascendancy. There, the wealthy had a great interest in developing world-class transportation, port and industrial facilities, and an extensive basic education system. Tokyo's resurgence after World War II would not have been so rapid but for its decades-long accumulation of industrial prowess and high education levels that contemporary megacities enjoyed at their time of independence.[60]

THE CITY OF DISAPPOINTMENT

This difference in industrial structure and development may well determine the future of megacities; those that lack productive capacity may have trouble ever achieving basic affluence under current conditions. "The old cities developed out of industrialization," says Deborah Balk, an urbanization specialist with the CUNY Institute for Demographic Research in New York City. "But you don't see that happening now." Instead, these cities are getting huge but without becoming wealthy. "These are poor cities, and that divide is really important," Balk says. "There was poverty in London, New York, and Paris, and Tokyo 100 years ago—and there still is poverty in some of those cities—but they never had slums in the way you see in today's contemporary poor cities."

Indeed many megacities—including one of the fastest-growing, Dhaka—are essentially conurbations, that is, spread-out areas of contiguous urbanization, dominated by very low-income people; roughly 70 percent of Dhaka households earn under US$170 a month, and many of them earn far less. They may be cities filled with aspiring people, but few get to fulfill their dreams. "The megacity of the poor" is how urban geographer Nazrul Islam describes Dhaka, his hometown.[61]

These conditions represent a break—hopefully not a permanent one—from the role that cities have served as engines of opportunity. This role was once true of many of the current megacities, particularly those that grew rapidly in the 1960s and 1970s. And even today, as these cities become more dystopic, the lure of the megacity for those stuck in rural poverty remains magnetic. As one factory supervisor, who in the 1990s migrated to Mumbai from a village 200 kilometers away, told me:

> *I migrated because there was no option in my village—there was no water, no school, no work. This is a tough place, but at least I have aspirations of owning a vehicle, a home, maybe a small business. My aspiration may be to go somewhere else, but for now, this is where my hopes are, however hard they may be to achieve.*[62]

Yet, as this migrant already suspects, Mumbai may not end up improving his life. This represents a major reversal in how people experience cities. In the past, they came with greater expectations of improvement. Now, many confront what geographer Ali Modarres has labeled "cities of disappointment," where they experience not progress but a pervasive lack of social mobility. People come to these cities, Modarres suggests, but do not find the opportunities that earlier generations might have.

This could affect China in the decades ahead, as an estimated 170 million rural migrants, most of them only modestly skilled, find themselves permanently stuck on the fringes of China's great cities, in most cases separated from their families. They often lack the skills to succeed in an increasingly sophisticated population and are also highly vulnerable to declines in the country's industrial and construction sectors. This kind of floating population has now formed a permanent underclass in many of the country's massive cities.[63] Ultimately, they could prove to be a very volatile population, caught between staying in a place where they are not welcome, with little chance of ever successfully integrating, and achieving the wherewithal to live in decent conditions.[64]

We can already see this in Mexico City, the first city in a developing country to achieve megacity status. As has also occurred in the high-income world, the shift to services has hollowed out opportunities that were once offered to La Capital's upwardly mobile working class. According to studies done in the 1970s, rapid industrialization provided similarly high rates of upward mobility to both city natives and rural immigrants.[65]

In recent years, as industry has moved away from the city, such gains have slowed, with fewer moving up from the poorest class. Only four out of 100 persons whose parents belonged to the 20 percent poorest sector of the population have been able to join the wealthiest 20 percent. Close to 50 percent of those who were born in the poorest sector have not been able to ascend socioeconomically, and close to 60 percent of those who were born in the richest sector have not descended.[66] Overall, Mexico City's middle class now constitutes only about 15 percent of its population, suggesting that the great urban process of upward mobility has stalled.[67]

"The middle class in Mexico is going down," says Adolfo Arrendondo, who runs a small school for aspiring residents located in largely lower-middle-class Iztacalco, one of Mexico City's 16 diverse *delegaciones*, or boroughs. They are, he suggests, trumped by "both the superrich and the criminal poor. We are squeezed in the middle of the sandwich . . . . The poor justify themselves because of their condition; the rich have impunity because of their position, arrogance, and predatory behavior, while the middle class suffers from both."[68]

This sense of disappointment is common in other developing-world megacities. In cities such as Cairo, Jakarta, Manila, Lagos,

Mumbai, and Kolkata, the vast majority continue to live in "informal" housing that is often unhygienic, dangerous, and subject to all kinds of disasters, natural or man-made. In India's three largest cities, over 16 million people live in slums.[69]

Moreover, many of these unmanageable megacities—most notably Karachi[70]—offer ideal conditions for gang-led rule and unceasing ethnic conflict,[71] which further threaten their economic development.[72] National security experts Peter Liotta and James Miskel detail how megacity residents are highly subject to security challenges, including "anarchy, governmental collapse, ethnic rivalry, cultural grievances, religious-ideological extremism, environmental degradation, natural resource depletion, competition for economic resources, drug trafficking, alliances between narco-traffickers and terrorists, the proliferation of 'inhuman weapons' and the spread of infectious diseases."[73]

To these problems, there also remains a growing class divide, as a small section of the population benefits from globalization, but most do not. In Mumbai, scholar Jan Nijman suggests, most gains in recent years have accrued to the upper echelons of the middle class while "the ranks of the lower middle-income classes have shrunk, and the ranks of the poor have expanded rapidly." Much of the growth in a perceived middle class, Nijman argues, is based not on income but on consumption driven by credit.[74]

Essentially, we see both the growth of slums and the celebration of luxury housing in the central parts of Mumbai, which suggests a more general prosperity to some in the West. Yet beyond this impressive façade of modern, Corbusian splendor, new employment in the city takes place in the "informal sector," that is, jobs that frequently lack any real social benefits. These jobs—drivers, stall-owners, repairmen, household workers—are generally poorly paid and account for much of the employment growth in both Mumbai and Mexico City.[75]

Ultimately, notes Modarres, the prospect for the developing world's megacities rests on restoring some sense of economic mobility and returning to a more human scale of development. Rates of economic growth and job creation, he suggests, are often well below the level needed to keep the local population sufficiently employed.

These cities become "centers of consumption"—much of it in the form of foreign aid—but remain less competitive economic entities, a startling shift from the patterns of urban commerce that have driven successful cities from the market revolution of the 17th century to the recent rise of China.[76]

HEALTH AND QUALITY OF LIFE

The life spans of urban residents—even in the West—have been shorter than those in the countryside for most of history. This is still true in many megacities today. One telling indication of the difficulties newcomers to Mumbai face is the relatively low level of life expectancy in the city—roughly 57 years—which is nearly seven years below India's national average.[77] Gaps in life expectancy can be found in other developing-world megacities as well, including Tehran, Cairo, and Buenos Aires.[78]

Urbanization is often portrayed as a means to achieving greater wealth and a higher standard of living, but this is not the case for most residents of many emerging megacities. The vast majority are forced to live in unhealthful and even abominable conditions. Such problems are often ignored or minimized by those who inhabit what commentator Rajiv Desai has described as "the VIP zone of cities," where there is "reliable electric power, adequate water supply and any sanitation at all." Outside the zone, Desai notes, even much of the middle class has to "endure inhuman conditions" of congested, cratered roads, unreliable energy, and undrinkable water.[79]

Clearly many of the emerging megacities are ill prepared to handle rapid growth. Dhaka grows largely in its slums, which are mostly filled with former rural residents. These rural populations likely move to the megacity not for the bright lights but to escape hopeless poverty and even the threat of starvation. Similarly in India, much of the population—rural and urban—remains desperately poor, with nearly 380 million living on less than US$1 dollar a day and half the children suffering from malnourishment.[80]

More serious still, slum dwellers face a host of health challenges that recall the degradations of Dickensian London. As Dr. Marc Riedl, a specialist in respiratory disease at UCLA, puts it, "megacity life is an unprecedented insult to the immune system."[81] In Africa, according to one researcher, the environmental and economic conditions are essentially diminishing the returns of urbanization, grinding conditions down to resemble—in terms of economic, social, and physical well-being—those of the very countryside that so many have escaped.[82]

High density is associated with higher rates of coronary disease, as well as psychiatric disturbances, notes a 2006 article evaluating the ecological consequences of the land use changes in Asia.[83] In cities such as Manila, roughly one in three residents lives in shantytowns, which carry high degrees of infectious diseases—including pneumonia, measles, and cholera—rarely seen in higher-income countries.[84]

Excessive concentration, according to a 2013 Chinese study, engenders more obesity, particularly among the young, who get less exercise and spend more time desk-bound. Not surprisingly, stroke and heart disease have become leading causes of death in Chinese cities.[85]

As in earlier times, dense places also demonstrate a greater susceptibility to epidemic diseases.[86] The SARS epidemic in Hong Kong, for example, was made far worse by the extreme crowding in that affluent but heavily congested city.[87] These dangers are, if anything, greater in developing megacities, many of which are located on polluted marshlands and brownfields.[88]

But perhaps the most physically evident result from intensified urbanization can be seen outside any window: pervasive air pollution. Half of the 20 most polluted cities, in terms of particulates, are in India, according to a World Health Organization report.[89] Among megacities, Beijing usually ranks among the most polluted, but Delhi now suffers the worst air conditions of any major city in the world.[90]

Packing people into cities does not improve the environment; in fact, air pollution[91] increases with density. There is consistent evidence that proximity to busy roads, high-traffic density, and increased exposure to pollution are linked to a variety of respiratory ailments that range from severe conditions to minor irritations.[92]

Several studies relate low birth weight to air pollution. A South Korean report,[93] for example, found that carbon monoxide, nitrogen dioxide, sulfur dioxide, and total suspended particle concentrations in the first trimester of pregnancy are significant risk factors for low birth weight.[94] Air pollution particulates[95] are associated with killing more people than traffic accidents. Pollutants such as those emitted by vehicles are significantly associated with an increase in the risk of heart attacks[96] and early death.[97]

Even in authoritarian China, such concerns about quality of life have sparked grassroots protests, many of them targeted at new industrial plants located near cities such as Shanghai, Dalian, and Hangzhou. High degrees of pollution have led at least some affluent urban Chinese to move back toward the countryside or to cleaner, less congested regions in Australia, New Zealand, and North America.[98]

THE INFRASTRUCTURE CHALLENGE

To address these issues, emerging megacities are racing to manage their population growth by building sufficient infrastructure to maintain, and ideally improve, the lives of their citizens. Throughout the history of cities, infrastructure has generally underpinned growth; this was true in France, where roads helped make Paris a powerful economic force; in the United Kingdom, and later in Meiji-era Japan, where extensive canals and railroads connected major cities; and in North America, where a network of freeways built in the second half of the 20th century connected vast expanses of the continent.[99]

Under any circumstances, these burgeoning cities in the developing world will require enormous investments in order to both make themselves more competitive and to improve their residents' quality of life. A 2014 McKinsey & Company study suggests that developing countries will require US$10 trillion more in capital investments to keep running, despite the slower overall growth in their populations.[100]

Even now, many of these cities are losing the race to keep up with their population. In the past, European, American, and Japanese cities grew their infrastructure to keep up with their growth and expansion. But in most megacities today, traffic congestion, for example, is worsening. Traffic, as anyone who has spent time in these cities easily notices, poses particular threats to riders and pedestrians alike. According to researchers Tim and Alana Campbell,[101] developing countries now experience a "neglected epidemic" of road-related injuries, which account for 85 percent of the world's traffic fatalities.[102]

Lack of adequate urban infrastructure is particularly acute in India, where spending on roads and other key infrastructure, by some estimates, is only one-fifth of what the government itself says it needs.[103] In Mumbai, the average commuter spends 47 minutes each way getting to work, while in Delhi, the trip takes 43 minutes. This is longer than in smaller rivals such as Chennai or Hyderabad. Not surprisingly, 50 percent of formal sector workers in Mumbai expressed the desire to move elsewhere, in part to escape brutal train or car commutes; only a third of workers in other cities, usually smaller and less dense, expressed this sentiment.[104]

Mumbai's problems are further worsened by an over-concentration of employment in the island city core. With so many pouring into the narrow streets, road congestion is almost unbearable for much of the day, and finding a parking place can be a major challenge. "The wars of the 21st century," jokes Suketu Mehta, "will be fought over parking places."[105]

Other megacities also suffer significant congestion issues. Commutes take roughly 35 minutes one way in New York and 29 minutes in Los Angeles;[106] in São Paulo, they take 75 minutes, and in Mexico City, almost 100. Whether on congested roads or over-packed trains or buses, denizens of new megacities often face grave challenges accessing places of employment or amenities in other parts of their cities.[107]

But, arguably, the most critical long-term infrastructure issue relates to basic sanitation and water. In some megacities, between one-third and one-half of solid waste is neither collected nor treated.[108] In Dhaka, for example, the sewer system covers barely 25 percent of the city, something that would seem strange to a denizen of imperial Rome, let alone modern London or New York.[109] Nearly two-thirds of sewage in the megacity, with a population of 16 million people, is untreated.[110] Mexico City, which enjoyed an advanced water delivery system[111] under the Aztecs, now loses upward of 40 percent of its water due to leakage or illegal connections, notes researcher Cecilia

Tortajada. The water quality is so poor that the area has one of the highest per capita consumption rates of bottled water, twice the rate seen in the United States.[112]

Incessant rain also causes drainage problems in megacities such as Mumbai and Kolkata. Many of these cities are low-lying and prone to flooding. The threat of higher sea levels predicted by many climate scientists suggests even greater threats to these cities, as well as other coast-hugging megacities such as Jakarta, Manila, and Lagos. [113] Some experts project annual flood losses worldwide to grow to US$52 billion over the coming decade,[114] up from US$6 billion in 2005.[115]

Even in China, where the government has invested heavily in water systems, half of the content of China's largest lakes and reservoirs is unsuitable for human consumption. China's more than 4,700 underground water-quality testing stations show that nearly three-fifths of all water supplies are "relatively bad" or worse. At this stage of development, most industrial countries throughout history have more or less solved this issue, but residents of China's relatively rich megacities still endure some of the same water-related challenges experienced in poorer Asian or African cities. There are even indications that toxicity levels in the water supply in some cities, such as Nanjing, could impact reproductive health.[116]

Housing may prove to be the greatest of all infrastructure problems. In Cairo, over 80 percent of the population lives in slums, as do roughly one in five in São Paulo.[117] Similar problems can be seen in Mumbai, where crowded living conditions are the norm. Two-thirds of the city's population live on a mere 5 percent of the land. Some parts of the city have densities of 1 million people per square mile, among the highest such concentration on the planet. Dharavi, the city's largest slum, has a density 13 times that of Manhattan, and its living conditions are characterized by poor sanitation and rickety housing. The average housing unit is 190 square feet, shared by a family of six. In Dhaka, densities can be even higher, reaching 2.5 million people per square mile.[118]

Tragically, even with solid economic growth and a growing middle-class population, Mumbai's slums have grown ever larger. In 1971, slum dwellers accounted for one in six Mumbaikars; now they constitute an absolute majority. Inflated real estate prices drive even modestly affluent people into slums. A modest one-bedroom apartment in the Mumbai suburbs, notes R. N. Sharma of the Mumbai-based Tata Institute of Social Sciences, averages around 10,000 rupees a month, double the average worker's monthly income.[119]

Researcher Vatsala Pant estimates a monthly total "middle-class" household income in Mumbai at 40,000 to 50,000 rupees; equivalent to less than US$1,000. Yet monthly salaries for teachers, police officers, and other mid-level jobs are often half that amount. Not surprisingly, given the city's high housing prices, even these kinds of workers often find themselves living in slum neighborhoods, which are also known as *jhopad-patti* or *jhuggi-jhopadi*. "It's the dream of an immigrant for a place in Mumbai . . . and ends up with a slum," Pant notes.[120]

"IN PRAISE OF SLUMS"

What is perhaps most remarkable is that, in the face of all these well-documented problems, some Western observers actually feel these developing cities are not dense enough, even though they are from two to five times as dense as those in the United States and the European Union. Some demand that Chinese authorities curb suburban "sprawl." It is hard to see how making these places denser will make them any more healthful, or even more economically beneficial, for the vast majority of their residents.[121]

Still, some experts praise the rise of megacities and see them as naturally occurring phenomena tied to "globalization and technological change."[122] Other Western pundits assert that "the inexorable logic of the mega-city" can address virtually every problem, from climate change to technology. These issues, they say, can be solved most efficiently by building ever more massive urban systems.[123] It is often stated by architects and developers that high-density development is the future, particularly in fast-growing parts of Asia. Minoru Mori, whose development firm has built high-rise structures throughout Asia, suggests a developing Asian model of "vertical cities" that will encompass an ever-greater part of the continent's huge population.[124] Not surprisingly, these ideas are widely championed by firms such as Siemens, which develops transit systems and manages large construction projects in countries like China and is thus in the best position to benefit from such vertical cities.[125]

A 2012 article in *Foreign Policy* was bizarrely titled "In Praise of Slums." This is based in part on the idea that life in the villages is worse than living in the slums, although, the author admits, people in the slums often suffer more exposure to pollution, disease, and violence. He argues, however, that the slums, however horrible, remain "a force for good" because they provide more opportunities than the villages.[126] In light of current urban growth trends, writers like him have lots to celebrate; slums, according to the United Nations, will accommodate 75 to 90 percent of future urban growth around the world.[127] But given the high degree of poverty, low education levels, and dysfunction in these slums and in most developing megacities, this writer and other Western pundits might reconsider their celebration of such places. A 2014 *National Geographic* article, for example, feted the intrepid entrepreneurial spirit of Kinshasa's slum dwellers but underplayed the miserable conditions in which the majority of Kinshasa's 11 million residents are forced to live. That city, which Belgian researchers described as an example of "aborted urban development," suffers from high crime, poor drinking water, and pervasive informal housing.[128]

Others argue that today's slum dwellers are better off than those in the past because they ride motorcycles and have cell phones. Yet access to the wonders of transportation and information technology is unlikely able to compensate for physical conditions that are demonstrably even worse than those endured by poor Depression-era New Yorkers, who at least could drink water out of a tap and expect consistent electricity—privileges not taken for granted by their modern-day counterparts in Manila or Mumbai.[129]

In the long run, the rise of megacities in the developing world—rather than affirming "the triumph of the city"—may be laying the foundation for an emerging crisis of urbanity. People crowd into giant cities that lack the economic and political infrastructure to materially improve their lives. Rather than an exemplar for the urban future, the megacity could become a dangerous cul-de-sac that offers neither greater promise nor a better life for its residents.

Remarkably, as stated earlier, some in the West seem to feel that these residents should not be encouraged to become more affluent, to try to achieve higher income standards. This is based in part on concerns about a potential strain on resources and perhaps the encroachment of cities on rural land. The growth of slums, suggests environmental pundit Stewart Brand, is a positive development for the planet. It takes people out of remote villages, where subsistence farming threatens forests and topsoil, and puts them into slums, where they consume little in the way of energy and leave the rural landscape alone. Rather than a problem for future humanity, Brand and others see slums as part of "the solution" to the world's environmental and social dilemmas.[130]

IS THERE A BETTER ALTERNATIVE?

Given the evidence, it's not surprising that some experts in the developing world increasingly challenge the logic of promoting megacities. To be sure, it is clear that urbanization will continue, but we too rarely ask, in what form? Future urbanization does not need to be a choice between rural hopelessness and urban despair. The rise of a mass of poor slumdwellers—estimated to be as high as 1 billion—threatens the social stability of not only the countries they inhabit but also the world, as they tend to generate high levels of both random violence and more organized forms of thuggery, including terrorism.[131] Simply put, these cities are out of control; they resemble, as one Mexico City writer suggests, "something Philip K. Dick dreamed up after swallowing a fistful of amphetamines."[132]

Clearly, there is a need for alternative approaches to urbanization. An impressive 2014 study by the McKinsey Global Institute, called "Mapping the Economic Power of Cities,"[133] found that "contrary to common perception, megacities have not been driving global growth for the past 15 years." Many, the report concludes, have not grown faster than their host economies.[134]

This suggests that it may be more feasible to emphasize urban growth not in just a few giant cities but in an expansive array of smaller conurbations. In the coming decade, McKinsey predicts that growth will shift to 577 "fast-growing middleweights," many of them in China and India, while, in contrast, megacities will underperform economically and demographically. The rapid rise of agricultural productivity—the "green revolution"—may depress the demand for labor in more rural villages, but efforts could be made there to expand opportunity in smaller, often provincial towns and cities.[135]

There are signs, indeed, that this trend of decentralization may be taking root. This can be seen in patterns in Mexico, where growth has moved decisively to smaller cities. The liberalization of Mexico's economy in 1985, notes the World Bank, shifted the basis of growth from a producer's distance to La Capital to its relationship to the US border.[136] At the same time, the organic growth of Mexico City itself has shifted ever more to the periphery, where the relative cost of housing, for example, is much cheaper. This second dispersive pattern is occurring virtually everywhere.[137]

With the shift of economic growth, there has been a significant change in Mexico City's own demographic trajectory. It was once predicted, for example, that Mexico City would become the world's largest city, with some 30 million people by the beginning of the 21st century. Yet, its growth has slowed to a modest rate, and its current population is 20 million. Lower Mexican birth rates and the development of other urban alternatives have made La Capital far less of a growth hub than once imagined.

Similar trends of slowing megacity growth can be seen elsewhere in Latin America. In the first decade of the new millennium, population growth was 15 percent in São Paulo, 12 percent in Mexico City, and 10 percent in Rio de Janeiro. These represent huge declines from their peak growth rates between 1965 and 1975 when São Paulo grew 75 percent, Mexico City 60 percent, and Rio de Janeiro 40 percent.[138] Similarly, in Brazil, India, and Turkey, megacity population growth was less than that of cities with populations of 1 million to 10 million between 2000 and 2010.[139] In China, megacity growth also appears to be slowing down, as annual growth rates have declined in both Shanghai and Beijing.[140] Overall, migration from the countryside has slowed to 2 percent annually, down from much higher rates, as rural wages rise along with urban costs.[141]

This trend, notes Singapore-based scholar Kris Hartley, also reflects a growing shift of industrial and even service businesses to more rural locales, particularly in Asia. As megacities become more crowded, congested, and difficult to manage, Hartley suggests, companies are finding it more convenient, less costly, and—critically—better for the families of their employees to locate farther from giant cities.[142]

This pattern is particularly notable in India, where migration to large cities already has begun to slow down, as more potential migrants weigh the costs and opportunities of making such a move as opposed to staying closer to home.[143] In many cases, the most rapid growth has taken place in mid-sized cities—not yet megacities—such as Hyderabad, Pune, Chennai, and Bangalore, as well as in smaller cities like Coimbatore, home to 2.5 million, that have seen much of the industrial and tech growth in the country. For example, India's national government has established an objective of adding 25 million more jobs to the Indian auto industry by 2016.[144] It appears most will go to states such as Gujarat (home to Prime Minister Narendra Modi), West Bengal, and Tamil Nadu or to ascendant, somewhat smaller cities such as Chennai and Ahmedabad but not to Mumbai.[145] This type of economic diffusion could help sustain these smaller cities.[146]

CAN URBANIZATION BE HUMANIZED?

As we look into the urban future, it seems logical to place a far greater emphasis on both peripheral areas and smaller cities. These areas already account for the vast majority of the global urban population—worldwide megacities account for only 13 percent of urban residents[147]—and they may be more capable, R. N. Sharma suggests, to cope with growth. In megacities like Mumbai, he says, political leaders have pledged to reduce slum conditions but, as we have seen, with little effect. High prices in these congested, crowded cities make upward mobility, even with growth, difficult and housing prohibitive.

"All megacities," Sharma writes, "are therefore a 'costly affair' beyond sustainable resources and beyond the priority needs of the majority of Indians."[148]

This is made worse, he suggests, by obsessive attempts in cities like Mumbai to convert into "a world-class city." Yet in their quest for greater size, luxury housing, and high-end retail, these advocates—what Sharma calls "the builder mafia in connivance with the greedy politicians and bureaucrats"—do little to address the basic needs of most Mumbaikars.[149] People who live in a mega-slum like Dharavi are productive—the area is a beehive of activity, serving as home to 15,000 "hutment" factories that produce pots, toys, and recycled materials[150]—but this hard work has not produced better living conditions, in large part due to the high cost of housing and the stress of an ultra-dense urban environment.

What India needs is not bigger cities, notes analyst Kanti Bajpai, but better cities that can better reward entrepreneurship and hard work. Improvements could include not only the expansion of the urban periphery around megacities but also the construction of a host of "completely new cities"—as occurred in the United States and the United Kingdom following their periods of rapid urbanization. These would offer more opportunities for the middle and working classes to live "in well-planned, clean, and gracious spaces." Bajpai argues that part of the solution to the megacity problem also lies in the revitalization of the countryside. Villages in India are still home to the vast majority, and they also serve as the primary source of new urban migrants. One solution may be to find ways to rehabilitate and improve these areas.[151] In response to a national program to provide greater unskilled employment in rural areas,[152] the 2011 census of India indicated that an unprecedented number of villages had transitioned from rural to urban (predominantly non-agricultural employment).[153]

This move is likely to impact firms now located in megacities. "We are inevitably getting more competition from elsewhere," notes R. Suresh Kumar, human resource manager at Mumbai-based Associated Capsules. "2,000 rupees a month means nothing in Mumbai, but in Uttar Pradesh, it really is meaningful."

In the years ahead, companies like Associated Capsules are likely to relocate most of their operations to these cheaper areas.[154] This phenomenon has been called "rurbanization," and it was an important provision of the campaign of Prime Minister Narendra Modi, who implemented such programs as Chief Minister of the state of Gujarat. Modi speaks of human settlements with the "heart of a village" and developing "the facilities of the city."[155]

THE LIMITS OF DENSITY

As we consider the urban future, it may be time to rethink how this process should best take place. Even in China, which has done more than most emerging countries to address the challenge of urbanization through massive investment in highways, trains, subways, and airports, improvements are often overwhelmed by the crush of newcomers. In most cases, as Emrys Jones noted a quarter century ago, "theorizing is overtaken by new waves of migrants."

One does not have to be a Gandhian idealist to suggest that dispersion, not concentration, provides a better model for future urban growth in developing countries, offering more space, privacy, and connection to nature. In Africa, note social scientists Robert and Rose Obudho, policymakers should "first seriously consider the improvement of the welfare of the people in the rural informal sector, as well as smaller cities." A focus on large city development, they suggest, will exacerbate problems, while shifting toward smaller-scale areas could encourage more "self-reliance, spatial equity, [and] local participation."[156]

Ultimately, a shift toward dispersion—both within regions and between them—has been made more feasible in the developing world, as in the west, by new technology. Smaller cities and even villages are no longer as economically isolated and are brought closer to the outside world through the use of cell phones and the Internet. Economic growth in these places could help stem the tide of megacity migration by closing the gaps in living standards of rural people relative to their urban counterparts, as has occurred in western countries.[157]

This redirection of growth also reflects a growing appreciation of what some identify as "diseconomies of concentration," with elevated levels of pollution and congestion, that ultimately drive people and business to less dense locales.[158] The benefits of dispersion could be enormous, particularly for the vast majority of people. It would allow people more living space and, if employment also was dispersed, a quicker and less rigorous commute, with related benefits gained both in terms of time and energy conservation.[159]

China, where some 250 million people are expected to move from the countryside to urban areas over the next decade, represents perhaps the greatest test for this approach. Today, notes Tao Ran, an expert on land issues at Beijing's Renmin University, many smaller towns are swallowed up by industrial development schemes, weakening the countryside for the benefit of the urban core, particularly for industrial purposes. Smaller units, which may thrive on their own, get gobbled up by ever-larger ones. "Of course urbanization is good for China," Tao says, "but not this kind of urbanization."[160]

In some megacities, it may be too late to reverse these trends. But a shift toward dispersion could still help many other cities, such as Hanoi, that are on the cusp of rapid growth but are not yet megacities. Dang Giang, founder of the nonprofit Action for the City, explains that rapid growth is already degrading the quality of Hanoi's urban life, affecting everything from food safety to water quality to traffic congestion. Houses that once accommodated one family, she notes, now often have two or three.

The prospect of expanding Hanoi's nearly 4 million people, almost four times its population in the 1980s, to 10 million or more may thrill urban land speculators and ambitious government planners, but it may not prove so thrilling for city residents. Like her counterpart Ashok Datar in Mumbai, Dang favors conditions that shift growth to both smaller cities and the Vietnamese countryside. "The city is already becoming unlivable," Dang insists. "More people, more highrises will not make it better. Maybe it's time to give up the stupid dream of the megacity."[161]

Such voices are all too rarely heard in the discussion about cities in the developing world. But we need to confront the urban future with radical new thinking. Rather than foster an urban form that demands heroic survival, perhaps we should focus on ways to create cities that offer a more prosperous, healthful, and even pleasant life for their citizens.

CHAPTER 4

Inside the "Glamour Zone"

∎ ▪ ▪ ∎

A NATIVE OF SINGAPORE, Calvin Soh is as comfortable chatting in his father's southern Chinese dialect as he is in English. The 47-year-old former head of Publicis Asia, now head of a new software start-up,[1] and his family live in an attractive apartment near the city's oceanfront. He enjoys all the amenities—from good food to safe streets to excellent schools—that come with living in a place of almost surreal efficiency and centrally directed purpose.

Yet beneath the impressive façade, Soh wonders about what Singapore has given up in its headlong path to success. Once among the most unique urban environments in the world, the area has become increasingly generic—the same shops, the same clothes, the same trendy restaurants, the same overpriced housing that we find in many of the most successful global cities.

"We are becoming not a place or a people but a Hotel Singapore," he said over dinner in an outdoor eatery in Geylang, the city's lively red-light district, which is incongruously filled with mosques and Buddhist temples. "We are still trying to figure out what it is to be a Singaporean."

Directed for a half century by well-educated and thoughtful civil servants, the tiny island republic is arguably the best run, most successful, dense urban place on the planet—a sharp contrast to its megacity counterparts in other developing nations. Whereas many megacities fail to meet the standards of economic success and social stability, Singapore excels in almost all statistical measurements. According to the US

Bureau of Labor Statistics, the city-state has a per capita GDP estimated at US$55,000, above that of the United States and well ahead of those of Japan, Germany, France, and its old colonial master, Great Britain.[2]

Yet with greater wealth have come new problems. Once known as highly egalitarian and verging on puritanical, Singapore is also becoming an abode of the rich and, of all things, a gambling mecca. There are now 188,000 millionaire households among its residents, including a growing group of migrants from the rest of Asia, Europe, Oceania, and even America, who are attracted to the low-tax, clean, safe, and orderly city.[3]

This influx of foreigners and, even more so, their money, has created an importation of cultural riches from around the world, which has eroded local culture and, by many accounts, made life harder for ordinary Singaporeans. Even as GDP growth continues to chug along at somewhat close to 5 percent per annum, real wages for ordinary Singaporeans have stagnated.[4] From 1998 to 2008, the income of the bottom 20 percent of households dropped an average of 2.7 percent, while the salaries of the richest 20 percent rose by more than half.[5] The residents of this highly successful city-state are now among the most pessimistic of peoples, alongside the understandably dour residents of Greece, Spain, Cyprus, Slovenia, and Haiti.[6]

For many Singaporeans, discontent is leading them to consider a move elsewhere. Already, some 300,000, or almost one in every 10 citizens, now live abroad. As many as half of Singaporeans would migrate if given a choice, according to a recent survey.[7] Many Singaporeans, Soh notes, watch their city change in ways they do not want but feel they have little means to stop from happening. "We have become a country where people are efficient, obedient followers," he says. "Yet we don't know who we are and what we want to be. We are in danger of becoming more of a global rest stop than a real place."

THE EMERGENCE OF THE GLOBAL CITY

Singapore's evolution from trading post to global city[8] reflects the emergence in Asia of what author Saskia Sassen has described as the urban "glamour zone." These areas are now found in most eastern

Asian cities, as well as in leading European and North American cities. At a time when ever more megacities are evolving into large places that are simply swelling with migrants from their impoverished hinterlands, these glamour zones, and global cities that surround them, play a disproportionate role in the world economy.

The term "world city" has been in use since at least 1915, the time of pioneering urban planner Patrick Geddes. In 1966, Peter Hall published his seminal work, *The World Cities*. Hall's world cities were all predominant cities in large nation-states.[9] Later on, the concept of "global cities," based largely on concentrations of business service firms, emerged as the primary terminology used to describe such international centers.

The preeminence of these "world" or "global" cities rests largely on unique assets such as the world's great universities, research labs, hospitals, financial institutions, corporate headquarters, and trendsetting cultural industries. These cities also disproportionately attract the rich and serve as centers of luxury shopping, dining, and entertainment—hence Sassen's term "the glamour zone." This has been their role since the 18th-century emergence of London as the first true world city. As the painter Thomas Gainsborough, whose portraits portray the elegant scions of the city's upper classes, remarked: "We are all Adam's children, but silk makes the difference."[10]

Global cities today benefit, in part, from the declining power of nation-states in a globalized economy. In an era of megacities, far smaller places like Singapore, Hong Kong, the Randstad, Dubai, and the San Francisco Bay Area have shown that girth is not the key to global influence. In this respect, global cities follow a path pioneered by ancient outposts along the Mediterranean—Tyre, Carthage, Athens, and a host of other Greek cities—in the years before the consolidation of the Roman Empire. During another era of dispersed power, Venice, Antwerp, and Amsterdam emerged, all smallish cities with vast influence. Similarly, in Asia, global influence often stemmed not from the often-larger imperial capitals—such as Kaifeng and later Beijing in China[11]—but from smaller cities such as Cambay (India), Melaka (Malaysia), and Zaitun (now Quanzhou in China).[12]

RETHINKING THE URBAN HIERARCHY

In examining the world's most influential cities, scholars and analysts usually look to the largest urban agglomerations—large contiguous developed areas—particularly in the high-income world. Many of these cities—London, Paris, Tokyo, Berlin, Moscow—grew in part by becoming centers of vast empires. The great exception was non-government anomaly New York, which gained influence much more quickly than Washington, a relatively minor city until recently.[13]

But in the modern era, we increasingly need to look beyond the great, sprawling cities of Europe and North America,[14] as well as Tokyo,[15] and pay greater attention to much smaller cities such as Singapore, Dubai, Houston, or the San Francisco Bay Area,[16] all of which are well below megacity size.[17] These cities generally do not sport the largest raw number of service and financial firms, factors that have dominated research on global cities.[18] Instead, their power comes from occupying critical roles in the intersection of international trade or from having powerful influence in those industries that are increasingly important in the world economy. Because of the unique industrial heritage of these cities, they tend to possess "deep knowledge" unique to these key business sectors—notably entertainment, technology, media, energy, and the arts.[19]

Rather than count employees of large accounting firms whose work can be spread around the world, these cities are home to people with unique, highly specialized skills—actors, directors, app writers, oil geologists, specialized financial consultants—who are often sole proprietors or employed by smaller firms. These workers tend to cluster in areas that specialize in their fields and provide the best marketplace for their services.[20]

Global cities, Emrys Jones noted a quarter century ago, have been shifting their focus from quantity to quality.[21] In the future[22]—in a world with widespread, instantaneous communications and quick travel—global influence among regions will depend upon these regions' specialization in particular critical industries. As we saw with the megacity, it is not size that matters but competence and efficiency. This allows Singapore, Hong Kong, Los Angeles, Houston, Dallas-Fort

Worth, and the San Francisco Bay Area to be far more influential in the world economy than their much larger counterparts. Together they form the basis, notes urban geographer Paul Knox, for the development of an "archipelago of technologically high developed city regions," gradually replacing nation-states as wielders of economic power and influence.[23]

These cities do many things that fit into our framework of human cities. Notably, they tend to have decent infrastructure, a high degree of cleanliness, and excellent cultural and recreational facilities. They generally lack the extreme congestion, high crime, and sanitation challenges common to poorer megacities of the developing world.

In large part, it is these characteristics that attract foreign capital and talent to these particular cities. One indication can be seen in the location of foreign subsidiaries; efficient, globally focused Singapore now has more than twice as many regional headquarters than far-larger Tokyo, not to mention Asia's less affluent megacities.[24] Global hubs often are helped by their populace's facility with English—the world's primary language of finance, culture, and most critically, technology. English dominates in most of the key global cities from New York and London to Singapore and Dubai. This linguistic, digital, and cultural congruence concerns major rivals to these cities, including those in Russia and mainland China, as well it should.[25]

TRACKING "NECESSARY" CITIES

The top global cities, as we will see, often fail as places for the middle and working classes, but they do well economically despite this. In part, this reflects their role as "necessary" cities. As critical nodes in particular regions or industries, they become places that people need to interact with, whether they choose to settle there or not. Good examples can be seen in cities as diverse as Los Angeles (entertainment), Houston (energy), and Hong Kong (financial services).

Perhaps the most conspicuous modern example of a "necessary" region may be the San Francisco Bay Area, the headquarters for the largest concentration of cutting-edge tech firms in the world. This region plays a profound role in globalization, particularly since its innovations increasingly shape the environment in which companies in other sectors—from manufacturing to retail to media—operate. Indeed, according to one study, three Bay Area counties—San Francisco, San Mateo, and Santa Clara—rank as the top three in terms of America's concentration of tech jobs, as well as among the leaders in tech job growth.[26]

Although the Bay Area dominates this important field, other even smaller areas show surprising tech strength, including Seattle, Tel Aviv—an expression of Israel's status as a "start-up nation"—and Singapore, the preferred regional base for many top technology firms. It's important to note that none of these emerging regions is large enough to be a megacity at this stage. In fact, they would be considered midsized cities in heavily populated, urbanized places like Japan, not to mention mainland China, where there are 13 cities that are larger than the city of Singapore.[27]

PHYSICAL CONNECTIVITY

A successful global city needs to maintain the strongest possible physical connectivity with other cities around the world. The earliest models of global cities, such as Athens and Rome, were largely connected through sea travel, as well as the magnificent roads built during the Roman epoch.[28] During the Song dynasty in the 9th to 11th centuries AD, China's cities developed both a complex system of canals that crisscrossed large parts of the country and large ports for the nation's first great overseas expansion.[29] Britain's industrial revolution, which catapulted London into preeminence, was forged in part through the development of canals and then trains. Global cities, such as New York, Hong Kong, and San Francisco, were all port cities; investments in trade brought with them the resources of the world and opened up the business of servicing that trade.[30]

In today's global economy, a "connected" city still benefits from striding along the world's most critical maritime trade routes. Singapore's prosperity, for example, stems in part from its being the second-largest container port in the world.[31] Beyond the port, Singapore has developed arguably the best urban infrastructure in the world.

Driving in Singapore is a revelation after life in congested New York or Los Angeles, not to mention such megacities as Mexico City or Jakarta. Cars generally run along smoothly, with few blaring horns. The subway and buses, although crowded, are clean and generally well functioning.[32]

The most "connected" cities—Dubai, London, and Frankfurt— have all developed strong airport systems. Although being a hub for air travel does not necessarily create a global city, it is critical to many businesses that function on an international level. These "airplane cities," such as Dallas-Fort Worth and Los Angeles, have developed airport-based "business districts" focused heavily on international trade, according to North Carolina-based analyst John Kasarda.[33]

Even in today's high-tech economy, physical connectivity remains an important asset for successful global cities. Cities with airports that handle extensive international traffic, such as Dubai, Singapore, Beijing, and Abu Dhabi, have advantages over their less connected competitors. Indeed, Dubai's strategy to become a global city starts, in many ways, with its ports at Jebel Ali and Port Rashid, the largest in the Arab world, as well as its enormous airport, which helps the city be more central in global business than its regional rivals, many of which are much larger.[34]

HUMAN CONNECTIVITY

Since the earliest emergence of global cities, another kind of connectivity—a human one—has been arguably at least as important. In their period of ascendency, Athens, Rome, Constantinople, Baghdad, and later, Venice accommodated uniquely diverse populations compared to other cities of their time. The foreign quarters in Chinese entrepôts, such as Canton during the Song dynasty, hosted a large foreign contingent, mostly from Islamic countries. Chinese merchants in Southeast Asia mixed closely with local Malays, often intermarrying with them and creating a unique *Peranakan* culture. They also often spread religious ideas—Hindu, Buddhist, Islamic, and Christian—in the markets they served. A growing acceptance of outsiders and their beliefs helped boost trade, particularly under the Yuan, or Mongol, dynasty.[35]

Perhaps the best early example of the importance of human connectivity evolved in the Netherlands. By the 17th century, as discussed
earlier, roughly 45 percent of Amsterdam's population was from outside the country, largely Germans and outsider groups such as Jews
and Christian dissenters from primarily Catholic countries.[36] In a
world of sharp racial and religious prejudice, such cities, noted Fernand Braudel, offered outsiders a "haven of comparative security."
"The miracle of toleration was to be found," he observed, "wherever
the community of trade convened."[37]

This close relationship between trade and diversity also applied,
perhaps even more so, to the city that developed from the Dutch colony
of New Amsterdam. As the novelist James Fenimore Cooper noted in
1828, New York's remarkably diverse society bore "a strong impression
of its commercial character." Migration from abroad, as well as from
the rural hinterland, made sure that New York did not stagnate, bringing new economic forces and entrepreneurs into the city and keeping
Gotham in what he called "a state of effervescence."[38]

A city's appeal to newcomers has remained critical in modern
times. One notable example was the mass migration of skilled migrants and entrepreneurs from Hitler's Europe, which flooded London
as well as New York and Los Angeles. These people brought with them
their skills, connections, and creative input. This critical migration has
continued to the modern day, although the countries that people come
from are now more diverse and less European in origin. Some predict
the United Kingdom will receive 2 million foreigners every 10 years, a
large proportion of whom will settle in the London area. With the on-
going migration from Syria and other Islamic countries, other leading
European cities, notably those in Germany, will see their populations
rapidly diversify.[39]

The growth of the foreign-born population, like any individual
measurement, has to be seen in context. In some cities, notably those
in English-speaking countries, foreign workers and managers play
a critical role and are generally integrated into the urban economy,
although not without some conflict along the way. In contrast, in regions such as Dubai-Sharjah, where approximately 85 percent of the

population is foreign born, or Jeddah, Saudi Arabia, where roughly half of the population is from another country, the immigrant population is heavily low skilled and temporary. These regions offer little chance for even highly skilled newcomers to assume citizenship or even permanent residency.[40]

On the other hand, many cities in Asia have chosen to be far less open to immigration. In contrast to the high percentages of immigrants seen in Western global cities, as well as Singapore, cities such as Seoul, Shanghai, and Beijing are predominantly made up of nationals, although, as in the case of virtually all large developing world cities, many originated from the countryside or smaller cities.[41]

THE POWER OF INERTIA

Inertia, noted Braudel, "is one of the great artisans of history."[42] Global cities, particularly the leading ones, owe much to their early origins— and the culture, ideas, and infrastructure rooted in their evolution over time. Three of the leading global cities in Asia—Mumbai, Singapore, and Hong Kong—started as outposts of the British Empire. Shanghai emerged largely as a European-dominated business center with extraterritorial rights,[43] while Tokyo emerged largely as the center of the Tokugawa regime[44] and then as the capital of an empire, which, at its height in the early 1940s, extended from Manchuria to Indonesia.

Even today, with the clear rise of eastern Asia as the potentially dominant center of the world economy, the leading global cities remain those that emerged from the first melding of the worldwide economy. For example, London and New York still sit atop most lists of global cities. No other place is close to either of these great cities in most rankings.[45] They possess almost everything that leads to global influence—power in finance, great global connectivity, diversity, a powerful media—all of which remain unmatched anywhere else. These cities also retain the certain sense of excitement that so impressed Walt Whitman more than 150 years ago:

> *A million people—manners free superb—open voices—Hospitality—the most courageous and friendly young men. City*

of hurried and sparkling waters. City of spires and masts.
City nestled in bays. My city![46]

Today, great cities like New York depend less on "spires and masts" and more on office complexes and communications arrays, but their vitality remains in a form Whitman might have appreciated. However, their economic function is much different from what it was in the 19th and early 20th centuries. To a large extent, these cities have morphed from primarily production and trade centers into Jean Gottmann's "transactional" cities. They serve primarily as "centers of transactions, for the performance of meaningful rituals, for the processing of information." As we've seen, many who work in or travel to these cities may live on their periphery or even in entirely different parts of the world but, as Gottmann notes, must journey there for certain interactions and expertise that do not exist anywhere else.[47]

London's origin as the first true global city, with tentacles that reached virtually everywhere on the planet, grew from its status as the capital of the British Empire. This gave it power, not only in its historic island core but also in its English-speaking colonies and vast territories.[48] Today, that legacy, even in the face of Britain's retreat from political and military power, lives on in its role as not only a global financial capital but also a critical hub for the cultural, legal, and business practices that define global capitalism.[49]

A half century after the fall of the British Empire, London remains, along with New York, the world's dominant global financial center—the Global Financial Centres Index ranked it first in the world in 2014[50] and second in 2015.[51] Although New York is part of a far larger economy, London retains many advantages as a financial hub, including a regulatory environment considered superior to those imposed by governments elsewhere, including the United States and the eurozone. London also has the second-best global air connections of any city outside of Dubai, and its time zone is better suited than New York's for dealings in Asia.

Critically, London is also a major advertising center and a media hub—home to the BBC, the *Financial Times*, and the *Economist*, arguably three of the world's most influential and respected news organizations. Websites for London newspapers like the *Daily Mail* and the *Guardian* are among the most visited in the world. Additionally, as an important entertainment hub, London ranks second globally in total spending by international visitors.[52]

London's geographic centrality and long-standing protections for corporations continue to make it a popular location for the regional headquarters of many multinationals. Yet at the same time, it has also emerged as Europe's top technology start-up center, according to the Startup Genome project.[53] The city has upward of 3,000 tech start-ups[54] as well as Google's largest office outside of Silicon Valley.[55]

New York similarly benefits from a long historical legacy, albeit considerably shorter than that of its British rival. The city is home to most of the world's top investment banks and hedge funds and retains its primacy in stock market volume (value of trading), according to the World Federation of Exchanges. New York's volume (NYSE and NASDAQ) is nearly four times that of second-place Tokyo and more than 10 times that of London.[56]

Like London, New York's power is increasingly based on not just money but also its grip on information industries and culture. It serves as home to dominant market data providers such as Dow Jones and Bloomberg and is home to all four of America's largest news networks. It remains a global leader in media and advertising, as well as in the music industry, serving as home to Warner Music Group and Sony Music Entertainment, two of the "big three" labels.

But perhaps New York's most unassailable advantage lies in how it is the epitome of a high-density urban future, particularly in regards to the spending habits of the wealthy through its role as a fashion and design center; along with London, it is both a productive center and the quintessential "consumer city." With iconic landmarks galore, international visitors spend more money in New York each year than in any other city in the world.[57]

THE SINGAPORE MODEL: FROM THIRD WORLD TO FIRST

New York and London remain preeminent, but the urban glamour zone has expanded decisively to eastern Asia over the past few decades.

Asia now boasts five legitimate global cities: Tokyo, Hong Kong, Singapore, Beijing, and Shanghai.[58] None of these approaches New York or London in importance, but their emergence and potential preeminence will be felt in the decades to come. Unlike the great cities of the West, the Asian ascendency has been distinctly authoritarian, largely guided by the direction of civil servants, party functionaries, or in the case of Hong Kong before 1997, colonial officials. Their progress has been rapid and, in many ways, unexpected.

At the time of its independence in the mid-1960s, no one would have expected the emergence of Singapore into the top ranks. It was a rough-edged Asian metropolis with a GDP of roughly US$2,600 per capita, which put it ahead of China and most of its Southeast Asian neighbors but below such countries as the Philippines, Brazil, Yugoslavia, Bolivia, Argentina, Greece, Spain, and the United Kingdom.[59]

When the quasi-socialist People's Action Party (PAP) took power in 1965, Singapore was divided between feuding ethnic groups and reeling from the departure of the British, who had founded and run the city from its inception in 1819. Surrounding Muslim nations Malaysia and Indonesia regarded the predominantly Chinese city-state with suspicion, and many in the West questioned its survival. The (London) Times predicted the economy "might collapse" without the big British military presence.[60]

The PAP's leader, Lee Kuan Yew, believed that the city needed to diversify the economy as a way to provide jobs and a path to upward mobility. Lee was determined to escape the corruption afflicting most non-aligned countries as well as the crushing rigidities of Communism. A scion of an old Hakka Chinese trading family, Lee created a system that British historian C. M. Turnbull called "an authoritarian constitutional democracy."[61]

It was also a party dictatorship like the one we see today in China. In his 1980 biography of the Singapore Premier, author Alex Josey compared his leadership of the PAP to Mao Tse-tung's role in the Chinese Communist Party. But Lee played things very differently. He was as much a product of Great Britain—he was educated at Cambridge—as of Chinese culture. He came to Fabian socialism directly from the source; he was a pragmatic socialist and, as Josey put it, "a patient revolutionary."[62]

Although Singapore was originally a trade and manufacturing hub, Lee and his mandarins correctly planned for the evolution of an economy more dependent on technology and high-end services. Education was a critical component, and from the start it was seen as the primary way to build both the state and the economy. This policy resulted in a high proportion of technically trained professionals, leading the Center on International Education Benchmarking to name the country "among the most technically competent in the world."[63]

THE RISE OF CHINESE GLOBAL CITIES

Arguably, the most important export of Singapore was its system. When the Chinese leader Deng Xiaoping visited the country in 1978, he quickly saw an ideal formula for elevating his own then very poor country. Deng, Lee would later recall, was most captivated by Singapore's modern prosperity. "What he saw in Singapore in 1978," Lee writes, "had become the point of reference as the minimum the Chinese people should achieve." Singapore presented an appealing model to the feisty Communist autocrat: a top-down, mandarin-led system that also could appeal to global capitalists.[64]

Anyone visiting China today can see the results of Deng's insight: gleaming cities, a massive expansion of education, modern roads and transit systems, and most of all, the general prosperity that has lifted the mother country of most Singaporeans to almost unimagined heights. China's share of the world economy grew from 5 percent in 1994 to 14 percent in 2012, which in turn greatly enhanced the role of China's key urban areas. Already, three Chinese cities have risen to the ranks of global cities, and it is not unlikely that one of these will rank among the two or three most important cities on the planet later this century.[65]

Hong Kong has long been a major global hub, but the biggest shift has been in the rise of two of China's mainland cities, Shanghai and Beijing. A Roland Berger study that traced corporate investment noted that Shanghai is becoming an attractive alternative to Singapore and Hong Kong as a location to establish regional headquarters. In 2010 alone, 24 companies relocated their Asia-Pacific headquarters to Shanghai, including Disney, Kraft, and Novartis.[66]

In the future, Shanghai's most significant Chinese competition will come from Beijing. The venerable capital city has the advantage of being the country's all-powerful political center, as well as the site of its most elite educational institutions and its most innovative companies.[67] Like its rival Shanghai, Beijing is an increasingly popular location for companies to locate their Asia-Pacific headquarters. Companies doing so include Amazon, Volkswagen, Nokia, and Caterpillar. Given China's power, it seems that one, if not both, of these cities will catapult into the ranks of top global cities within the next 10 to 20 years.

GLOBAL CITIES AND THE MIDDLE CLASS

As we've seen, since the 17th century, great cities have nurtured not only the rich, the well-connected, and their servants but also the aspirational middle and lower classes

Amsterdam, Holland's primary city, was noteworthy not so much for its heroic statues and great boulevards, churches, and palaces but for its teeming alleys, bustling wharves, and clean, comfortable residences. Having won its independence at great cost, the Dutch middle class carried out its trade with minimum interference. Consumer cities, as Weber noted, not only consumed the luxury goods that dominated the aristocratic cities but also produced and traded basic goods and commodities. They also became places where merchants achieved political power and shaped the national culture.[68]

The same trend repeated itself elsewhere, most notably in Britain and the United States.[69] In early 19th-century New York, artisans and small shopkeepers comprised the "reservoir of people" who could join the land-owning class and afford spacious places to live.[70] The ability of these great cities to improve people's lives from North America to Europe to Asia—what historian Peter Hall called the "unique creativity of great cities"[71]—stands as one of the greatest social achievements of modern times.

From their origins, modern global cities are simply different from other, less influential conurbations; they are unique in every way, from how they operate to how they function in the international economic system. "New York," observed American journalist John Gunther in 1946, "is at once the climactic synthesis of America and yet the negation of America."[72]

The rewards of being a truly globalized city can be enormous. It creates a market for more diverse cultural amenities, better food, and a greater concentration of luxurious facilities, compared to other cities of similar or even much larger size. Yet intense globalization—easing the flow of capital and people to such places—also increasingly distorts and threatens the local middle class by raising property prices, undermining the indigenous economy, and compromising the prospects for upward mobility.

FORCES UNDERMINING THE MIDDLE CLASS IN GLOBAL CITIES

In the second half of the late 20th century, broad-based economic growth and suburbanization addressed many of the worst disparities that developed during the Industrial Revolution. But as discussed previously, today's urban economy—driven by rapid globalization, technology, and migration—has revived some aspects of the increasingly hierarchical urban culture that was associated with cities well before the Industrial Revolution.

This transition has been building for decades. Manuel Castells, writing as early as the 1980s, believed that an "informational city" would generate nodes of prosperity that communicated largely among themselves while shunning the rest of the metropolitan areas. The local metropolitan population, historically a key source of customers and workers for major businesses, would now, he predicted, have a "decreased relevance," while the benefits of "post-industrialism" would concentrate in selected parts of metropolitan regions but not in the entire city or country as a whole.[73]

In the past, urban growth generated blue-collar and middle-class opportunities across a broad spectrum. But increasingly, the primary sectors now driving key urban areas—high-technology, media, and financial services—are far less reliant on the mass mobilization of labor, both skilled and unskilled, than activities in manufacturing, trade, logistics, or even routine business services.[74] Former higher-wage blue- and white-collar employment has shifted to the suburbs or smaller cities.[75] Much of what else is produced, Hall observed, has become increasingly decentralized in back offices that are usually located in smaller cities and on the periphery, as well as in "homes and local work stations."

Increasingly, global cities flourish best in fields that require regular face-to-face contact, such as fashion design, high-end finance, and media.[76] This transformation can be seen in London, the archetypical international hub. The modern London renaissance, marked by the revival of many once working-class areas such as Shoreditch, Islington, and Putney, has also created a city increasingly bifurcated between a post-industrial elite and a growing underclass. As author James Heartfield observes:

> The vacated shells of industrial London were turned into expensive houses or art galleries. With rising home prices, it was working-class London that was being driven into the suburbs.[77]

For those at the top end, particularly those with holdings in real estate, this transformation has worked brilliantly. London may, by recent accounts, have more billionaires than any city on the planet. But the results have been less benign for other neighborhoods. Overall, the region (i.e., the Greater London Authority) also suffers the *highest* incidence of child poverty in the United Kingdom, even more than the beleaguered Northeast.[78] Poverty affects 30 percent of working-age adults, over one-third of pensioners in inner London, and roughly one in five in outer London. The inner London poverty rates are among the worst in Britain.[79]

These trends can be seen in other global centers. Even in traditionally egalitarian Toronto, recent projections for that region show a strong increase in the population of wealthy individuals and even more so in the poor population, while the middle class is expected to decline significantly. A recent study of Toronto, for example, found that between 1970 and 2001, the portion of middle-income neighborhoods in the core city dropped from two-thirds to one-third, while the portion of poor districts more than doubled to 40 percent. By 2020, according to the researchers, the portion of middle-income neighborhoods could fall to less than 10 percent, with the balance made up of both affluent and poor residents.[80]

Inequality is also increasing in Europe's cities. Many low-wage workers congregate in the closer-in suburbs, as has happened in Paris, the continent's leading global city.[81] The social protections of the European Union may have ameliorated, for the time being, the shift toward an increasingly bifurcated society, but greater inequality seems likely in the future. In this era of powerful oligarchs and growing inequality, global cities are increasingly less likely places for upward mobility than in the past.

Even Tokyo, once widely seen as among the most egalitarian societies on earth and where foreigners account for less than 2 percent of the population,[82] has become distinctly less equal. Starting in the mid-1980s, Japan overall became less socially mobile and more stratified as the city moved toward its current "post-industrial form." In the period of the *endaka*, or restructuring, that took place in the 1980s, Tokyo shifted from being a largely industrial capital to a financial one.

As has occurred in many other global cities, this economic transformation has helped reverse the enormous social mobility that accompanied Japan's postwar boom, notes social analyst Jan Woronoff. "The narrow gates," he suggests, may well be "getting narrower," as the benefits of Japan's high-tech and increasingly globalized economy become more concentrated.[83] There are now an estimated 15,000 people living on the streets of Tokyo, and the poverty rate has risen to its highest level in recent decades.[84]

These trends are, if anything, more pronounced in the United States, home to more major global cities than any country. Like Tokyo and London, New York, Chicago, and Los Angeles used to be renowned as places of opportunity for those with lower levels of

education, particularly immigrants. But the shift in economic structure has served to alter this reality.

In New York, whole industries, largely garment and specialty manufacturing, have faded, while Chicago lost its old heavy industry base
and Los Angeles lost its once vibrant aerospace and related industries.[85] These businesses employed many working- and middle-class
people; some provided entrepreneurial opportunities, particularly for
immigrants. The loss of these industries has accelerated the growth of
inequality, with many blue-collar workers in suddenly "hip" neighborhoods such as Williamsburg often finding themselves forced out of the
city by a difficult admixture of high rents and reduced opportunities.[86]

As I touched on in previous chapters, we are beginning to see—in
the most successful global cities in particular—an era reminiscent of
the Victorian period, when a huge proportion of workers labored in
the servile class. Social historian Pamela Cox explains that in 1901,
one in four people, mostly women, were domestic servants. This is the
world so popularly portrayed in TV shows such as *Downton Abbey* and
Upstairs, Downstairs, but is this the social form we wish to promote?[87]

Today, as opportunities for middle-class families disappear, more
people are earning a living serving the wealthy and their needs as nan-
nies, restaurant employees, dog walkers, and other service workers.
This can be seen, for example, in the city of New York, where over
one-third of workers labor in low-wage service jobs, a portion that has
increased steadily throughout the economic recovery, according to a
recent study by the Center for an Urban Future.[88]

Another key driver of the new global city is the abundance of inherited and rentier wealth. This trend has been amplified by the global
recovery from the Great Recession, which notably benefited those
with inherited wealth as the returns on capital have surpassed those
of labor.[89]

It is increasingly the wealthy that shape "the glamour zone" and
fuel the growing gap between the classes. According to an analysis
of census data by Mark Schill of Praxis Strategy Group, Manhattan was the leader among the nation's core cities in asset-based
wealth, while the Bronx, just across the Harlem River, ranked at the

absolute bottom. This inherited wealth is increasingly diffused among multiple cities as members of the expanding ranks of the ultra-rich purchase apartments in numerous locations, sometimes in condominiums within hotels.[90]

Manhattan, the densest and most influential urban environment in North America, exhibits the most profound level of inequality and bifurcated class structure in the United States.[91] Even in nouveau hipster and increasingly expensive Brooklyn, nearly a quarter of residents—mainly African American and Latino—are below the poverty line. While the wealthy gentry shop at artisanal cheese shops and frequent trendy restaurants, one in four Brooklynites receives food stamps. In fact, New York has experienced the biggest rise in its number of homeless in the nation, and its number of children sleeping in shelters has risen steadily, even as its elite economy has "boomed."[92]

THE FOREIGN INVASION

As would be expected, growing flows of capital and people across international borders have had a powerful impact on the evolution of global cities. London, for example, has been the prime destination for newcomers to Europe; economist Tony Travers at the London School of Economics estimated that during the last decade, London received more immigrants, many from the rest of the European Union, than did such American magnets as New York or Los Angeles. Although some of these newcomers were from the global elite, most have found work in London's lower-end service jobs in restaurants and retail, as well as in construction. More than 70 percent of the jobs created between 1997 and 2007 in the United Kingdom went to foreigners.[93]

These patterns can be seen across all global cities. In Dubai, the workforce is already primarily made up of foreigners—at both the low and high levels. Singapore leads the rising Asian cities with a foreign-born population estimated at 42.6 percent,[94] slightly ahead of Hong Kong, where 39.5 percent of the population came from elsewhere, most of them migrants from the Chinese mainland. In Europe, the London and Paris regions are now over 20 percent foreign-born. A number of key North American metropolitan areas—notably Miami,

Los Angeles, New York, Houston, Toronto, and Chicago—have foreign-born populations of between 15 and 50 percent. Meanwhile in Australia, Sydney's foreign-born population is also high, at 40.1 percent, while Melbourne's is 36.7 percent.

As we saw earlier in this chapter, the cities that attract immigrants traditionally benefit greatly from their skills and energy, especially in countries where immigrants can integrate into the larger society. "A Polish Jew changes into an English Hebrew," observed Ford Madox Ford in 1995, "and then into a Londoner without any legislative enactments, without knowing anything about it."[95] Until the end of the last century, the same pattern occurred in France, the Netherlands, Canada, and the United States, as newcomers gradually integrated into their new countries.

Yet there are reasons to believe that, in Europe at least, this model may no longer work. Despite their growing dependence on immigrants, Europeans are increasingly resentful of newcomers, particularly those from Africa and the Middle East, whose numbers have expanded dramatically since 2015.[96] Some two-thirds of Spaniards, Italians, and British citizens, according to an Ipsos poll, believe there are already "too many immigrants," while majorities in countries as diverse as Germany, Russia, and Turkey also hold negative views about newcomers in their midst.[97]

The French fear of immigration, stoked by the recent terrorist incidents there, has made the far-right National Front's Marine Le Pen into a legitimate national force,[98] while the emergence of the UK Independence Party stems partly from angst over immigration, particularly among working- and middle-class voters.[99] Countries such as Denmark, Sweden, Finland, and the Netherlands, once considered paragons of multicultural tolerance, have produced potent anti-immigration movements.[100]

Even tightly controlled and officially multicultural cities such as Singapore have started feeling resentment toward immigration. As both local skilled and inexpensive labor has become less available over the past few decades, the city has become more dependent on imported labor. As recently as 1980, over 90 percent of residents were citizens. Today, that percentage is 63 percent, and by 2030, if the government's plans to grow through increased immigration succeed, foreigners will outnumber the natives. Many Singaporeans, even sophisticated people like Calvin Soh, feel the foreign influx is turning them into strangers in their own city.[101]

In other global cities, like New York, Los Angeles, London, and Toronto, these effects could be mitigated by the movement of people—including newcomers—away from the congested core and into the suburbs or less expensive cities. But immigration-induced population growth (as in other dense cities, Singapore's birth rates are well below replacement level) is more intensely felt in severely space-constrained Singapore.

Singapore's growing foreign presence has engendered unease among the citizenry, whose lives are increasingly stressful and who feel crowded by the newcomers. Officials were much disturbed by a particular post on Facebook about Indians, whose curry-cooking ways disturbed the olfactory senses of some Chinese nationals. The ensuing controversy was captured in a play about this conundrum, *Cook a Pot of Curry* by local playwright Alfian Sa'at, that upset many government officials, who found the play somewhat antithetical to their engineered social harmony.[102]

In conversation, many Singaporeans also express concern about competition from skilled foreigners, including those from India, China, Europe, and North America.[103] In 2013, concern over the influx of talent, and its effect on Singaporean graduates, led the government to take measures to force employers to give priority to local job applicants.[104] Perhaps even more threatening, however, has been the agitation among the city's many south Indian and Sri Lankan immigrants, who occupy much of the lower tier of the employment pyramid. Keeping construction labor and household help relatively cheap has long been a government priority. In 2013, there was a riot—the first since 1969—in Singapore's Little India district, as police experienced disorder from some foreign workers, some of whom were inebriated. The growing concern about at least low-end economic migrants has led to moves to impose stronger controls on them.[105]

But ultimately, the conflict over immigration in Singapore relates to space. With 5.3 million people crammed onto an island of only 225 square miles, many feel the city-state is already too crowded. Residents are uneasy about suggestions by the city's planning and business elites to raise the city's current population to roughly 7 million by 2030, largely through immigration. They are also hesitant to embrace the proposals for coping with this growth, which would require building a vast underground city with shopping malls, public spaces, pedestrian walkways, and even cycling trails. Even otherwise adaptable and sociable Singaporeans may not want to spend their lives like Morlocks in H. G. Wells's *The Time Machine*.[106]

HOUSING INFLATION

In many global cities, the foreign influx has aligned closely with ever-higher housing prices. Much of this has been driven by rising investments from the global rich, notably from China, the Indian diaspora, and the Middle East. In Singapore and elsewhere, the arrival of these wealthy people is viewed as undermining the basis for a more egalitarian society and broader property ownership.[107]

This trend is likely to increase in most dense cities but particularly in global cities. A 2013 study by real estate investment firm CBRE found Asian financial institutions looking to place $150 billion in real estate assets, much of it in global-city leaders London and New York, as well as in Dubai and Sydney, long a magnet for Asian investment.[108] In New York, Chinese investors have even crossed the East River, looking to invest in Brooklyn's upscale expansion.[109]

Some of this is being driven by a trend among the rich to buy multiple residences. Given the buoyancy of the real estate market, a pied-à-terre in Manhattan, Singapore, Shanghai, London, or Miami can appear to be not only a good investment but also a convenient base for having a good time. In many cases, these wealthy foreigners are not full-time residents but people who come to the city for the occasional business or shopping trip. In some of New York's luxury buildings, less than one in 10 are full-time residents; for most, it's just one of their several residences scattered around the world.[110] Similarly,

London prices are being pushed up by an onslaught of primarily Asian buyers, who now, by one estimate, purchase two-thirds of the city's newly built houses and are primary players in the massive densification of the city.[111]

Overall, foreign investment, particularly in residential properties, has contributed to extraordinarily high housing prices, relative to income ratios, in such cities as New York, Hong Kong, the San Francisco Bay Area, coastal Los Angeles, and London. For example, although house prices in affordable markets, such as Texas, tend to average three times that of household incomes (price to income ratio), prices in the top 10 global cities tend to be much higher, often by a factor of three or more. In Hong Kong, house prices are 15 times higher than household incomes—the highest among high-income cities.[112]

These trends have had a devastating impact on the ability of many middle- and working-class families to buy or rent decent housing. "It's almost impossible for ordinary people to purchase a flat," Ng Sai-leung, director of the Chinese University of Hong Kong's Centre for Quality of Life, says of the current conditions in Hong Kong.[113] Although the Hong Kong case is extreme, this phenomenon of all but the wealthiest residents being pushed out of key parts of the property market has become standard.[114] For young people in areas such as London, the possibility of homeownership has begun to evaporate, not due to preference, as some have suggested, but as one agent put it, "by necessity."[115]

Recent trends in the San Francisco Bay Area reflect how a concentration of wealthy individuals can impact local residents and property prices in disturbing ways. As the core city of San Francisco has become particularly popular with younger employees at some of the world's largest information technology firms, such as Google, Facebook, and Apple, the city's housing market has evolved into the most expensive in the country.

This has led to an intense conflict between the new money and the more settled citizens, many of whom feel priced out by the tech-driven explosion. To make matters worse, some feel they have become second-class citizens in their own city. For example, firms like Google provide luxury bus service from the city to their corporate headquarters, located 30 miles or more away in the far more suburban surroundings of Silicon Valley. In contrast, ordinary San Franciscans are forced to rely on the city's historically underperforming public transportation system.

Opposition to the Google buses reflects deeper concerns about how the tech influx has driven up demand for housing and, consequently, the price of rent, making the city far more costly for those who have lived there for years.[116] In 2013, San Francisco voters also recoiled against plans to develop high-rises along its waterfront; many residents suggested that rather than add to the middle-class housing stock, the new construction would benefit mostly wealthy investors, including those from overseas.[117]

Similar concerns about being priced out contributed to New York's 2013 election of strong left-wing mayor Bill de Blasio. The longtime progressive activist's campaign focused on the concern of working- and middle-class Gothamites that they were becoming superfluous in a town many could no longer afford.[118]

INEQUALITY IN THE CHINESE GLAMOUR ZONE

Perhaps the most rapid growth of inequality has taken place in the once very egalitarian-minded global cities of China. These cities may be ruled under a red banner, but they seem, from a social perspective, more like pre-reform urban Britain than a model of communist fraternity. This is most evident in the most advanced cities, such as Shenzhen and Hong Kong, which have some of the most skewed income distributions in all of Asia. As repositories for foreign investors, and the mobile rich, these cities have become wealthy but in a decidedly far-from-egalitarian manner.[119]

Indeed, as China has urbanized and its major cities have expanded, it has become ever more unequal. Over the past 20 years, its income distribution pattern has shifted from one similar to that of Sweden, Japan, or Germany to one that is closer to that of Argentina or Mexico. By 2006, China's measurement of inequality was greater than the United States, Vietnam, the United Kingdom, and India. Not surprisingly, class anger has reached alarming proportions, with almost 96 percent of respondents to one recent survey agreeing that they "resent the rich."[120]

As China continues to urbanize in the coming decade and economic growth inevitably slackens, these class distinctions could deepen further. The glut of college graduates—concentrated in urban areas—will need to compete with an aging workforce for a still-limited number of positions. Ironically, the domination of the Communist Party appears to further concentrate wealth and power; most of the richest people in China are linked to the party.[121]

This all poses a threat of ever-greater social conflict in China's emerging "glamour zones," as young people—even the educated and well off—are forced to live in smaller spaces and face prices that make purchasing a residence prohibitive. This is leading many residents, as in other countries, to look for a better quality of life elsewhere. As many as two-thirds of China's wealthiest people either have emigrated or plan to. Whereas the rich in the British Industrial Revolution removed themselves to the countryside, many of those who did best from the great Chinese urban boom are looking to relocate to other countries entirely.[122]

THE ISSUE OF IDENTITY

Globalization has fostered an urban form that epitomizes, as two academic authors put it, the "widening, deepening, and speeding up of worldwide connectedness in all aspects of contemporary social life."[123] This reflects an old tradition of cosmopolitanism, which was present in the ancient world. But even then, globalization took place within the context of a broadly common culture, a strong family structure, and in many cases, a common faith.[124]

There is a tendency in global cities to de-emphasize the sacred or unique. This follows the notion of Le Corbusier to see cities as "machines for living."[125] Yet in the past, the irrational attachment to, for example, a particular neighborhood served as a counterbalance to the anonymity and cosmopolitan nature of a great city. As British essayist G. K. Chesterton observed:

> If there arose a man who loved Pimlico, then Pimlico would rise into ivory towers and golden pinnacles; Pimlico would attire herself as a woman does when she is loved. For decoration

is not given to hide horrible things: but to decorate things already adorable. A mother does not give her child a blue bow because she is so ugly without it. A lover does not give a girl a necklace to hide her neck. If men loved Pimlico as mothers love children, arbitrarily, because it is THEIRS, Pimlico in a year or two might be fairer than Florence. Some readers will say that this is a mere fantasy. I answer that this is the actual history of mankind. This, as a fact, is how cities did grow great. Go back to the darkest roots of civilization and you will find them knotted round some sacred stone or encircling some sacred well. People first paid honour to a spot and afterwards gained glory for it. Men did not love Rome because she was great. She was great because they had loved her.[126]

Rather than establishing strong local roots tied to a specific neighborhood, today's global city tends increasingly toward homogenization. There is a "flattening of cultures," as political scientists Daniel A. Bell and Avner de-Shalit recently suggested, that is a direct result of the dynamism of our "liberal" political economy, its ascendency accelerated by the ever-widening span of both technology and global capital. They posit that cities are the place where the resistance to this trend will occur, and cities could benefit by stressing their distinctiveness in the future.[127] This notion certainly has some compelling logic, but it could end up, as sometimes happens, as little more than a celebration of cultural oddities.

In some senses, city dwellers may be even more susceptible to this "flattening" because they are most likely to be more secular, less traditional, and more transient. In Singapore, where the city and the state are one, patriotic sentiments are particularly muted. Despite massive government efforts to promote civic engagement and patriotism, a recent survey found half of all Singaporeans are indifferent to maintaining their citizenship as long as their wealth could be maintained. Rather than being tied to tradition, religion, and family, Singapore is increasingly dominated by an ideology that former foreign minister S. Rajaratnam labeled "moneytheism."[128]

These non-specific, unmoored values find physical expression in the architecture that dominates many global cities. As you travel these places, you see the same structures, be it from Frank Gehry or some other "starchitect," in myriad cities. Increasingly, city skylines and waterfront developments appear remarkably similar—from London's Docklands to Tokyo's waterfront developments to Shanghai's Pudong.[129] By appealing to cosmopolitan tastes, these global centers are becoming what architect Rem Koolhaas labeled "the generic city." Reflecting the concerns of Calvin Soh, Koolhaas described Singapore in particular as "a city without qualities" and a "Potemkin metropolis."[130] Some, like retro-urbanist architect Roger K. Lewis, heap part of the blame on the efforts of practitioners like Koolhaas to undermine local distinctiveness:

> *Many of us love to visit character-laden cities such as St. Petersburg, Paris, Rome, Venice, Agra, and Bangkok or wander through picturesque towns and villages in Tunisia, Greece, Spain, Mexico, and Japan—or, for that matter, in the United States. Much of what appeals to us about these places is traditional architecture that is locally distinct. We admire historic buildings, neighborhoods, and communities shaped by site, climate, history, native culture, and locally available materials and construction technology. But are such unique places at risk of being engulfed by the rise of "global" cities that eventually could look more or less the same, full of buildings that could be anywhere? Is architecture becoming increasingly globalized, standardized, sanitized?*[131]

Lewis adds that the street-side experience also tends to be much of the same in all global cities, stores stocked with the same foods and the same fashions, with roughly universal forms of entertainment. As he puts it, "The experience of strolling through malls at Canary Wharf in London's Docklands, at Potsdamer Platz in Berlin, and at Manege Square in Moscow is fundamentally the same."[132]

These changes may be felt most profoundly in the emerging cities of Asia. Once distinct districts like Singapore's Orchard Road are not much different in their offerings from Fifth Avenue in New York or Regent Street in London. In fact, many of these same shops and restaurants have expanded into second-tier cities and suburbs. To find a unique local business in the central parts of Singapore is increasingly difficult, as so much of the local shopping is generic, dominated by global brands from Europe, North America, and Japan.

The monotonic quality now common in global "glamour zones" no doubt reflects their huge wealth. Rising real estate prices have pushed locally owned, distinctive businesses from areas where rents are simply too high for merchants. Areas like Chicago's Magnificent Mile, once expressive of the city's own retail culture, now has virtually no locally-based stores, much as is the case on Fifth Avenue. In the words of one local journalist, the physically arresting space of North Michigan Avenue has devolved into a "long mall." This trend even threatens businesses long identified with a place—say delis or Greek coffee shops in New York, bistros in Paris, or pubs in London—which are steadily being replaced by national and global brands.[133]

The globalization of finance—now expanding to Shanghai, Dubai, and Singapore—also plays an important role in the homogenization of global cities.[134] Global cities, says New York researcher Sharon Zukin, have enjoyed a remarkable expansion of credit for real estate in their cores, "bringing in the same development ideas—and the same conspicuous textual allusions and iconic corporate logos inevitably affixed to downtown architectural trophies—to cities across the globe."[135]

THE SOCIAL CRISIS

In its wake, the glamorization of global cities also has exacted social costs, particularly for working-class and poor residents. In the global city, Zukin writes, elite leaders see their audience less as their citizens and more as wealthy investors and powerful corporations. The result sought, she suspects, is to make the city "safer and less strange to outsiders' eyes: those of tourists, expatriates, media producers, and affluent consumers—the very people those developers want to attract to their respective cities."[136] These newcomers, they hope, will inhabit homogenized superblocks and high-rise towers that are barely indistinguishable from one global city to another.[137] Even an utterly unique place like New Orleans, notes Tulane University geographer Richard Campanella, has suffered a gradual loss of character. There, some of America's most storied neighborhoods feature restaurants specializing not in Cajun cuisine but in dishes like beet-filled ravioli—the kind of thing one expects to find in Portland, Williamsburg, Brooklyn, and other favorite hipster locales.[138]

This conflicts with the often self-conscious image of these urban centers as different and unique. City officials and business boosters often promote festivals, arts districts, cafes, and restaurants that, they believe, will express a kind of "coolness." Planners in Seoul, for example, have placed great emphasis on creating a "cultural district" in the Hongdae area in an attempt to transform the Korean city into a world-class one. Even smaller up-and-coming cities aim to compete by developing their own minicores in a similar manner; more than 150 cities worldwide hold an annual or semi-annual Fashion and Design Festival.[139]

This civic striving for "coolness," ironically, comes at a time when many creative professionals—such as artists and musicians—find the going increasingly rough in cities like New York, where housing prices have soared out of their reach. Musician Patti Smith laments that "New York has closed itself off to the young and the struggling. New York City has been taken away from you."[140]

In some ways, globalization is doing to great cities what so many critics repeatedly criticize suburbs for—essentially recreating the same environment everywhere. The form is not, of course, the single-family houses or garden apartments of the suburbs but the luxury high-rises that attract the young, the footloose, and the wealthy to the urban core.

Yet what is increasingly missing is the kind of affordable, flexible space—the reconverted house or warehouse, the reclaimed old Victorian—that often appeals to the creative types. "Hipness here," writes one Toronto author, "has a fear of heights." Huge towers tend to dominate and change the tenor of neighborhoods, and in some cases, they even block out the light that once brightened the city streets and cast shadows over local parks, a classic case of how products for the wealthy impinge on the shared space of a city.[141] After hearing about plans for yet more luxury high-rises, one Toronto resident seethed:

> *Three jazzy overpriced condo towers owned by global inves-*
> *tors? The city doesn't need that. The base, full of cultural*
> *facilities and art galleries, paid for by the condo sales? How*
> *about taking the developer money and putting [it] into areas*
> *that need amenity and spreading the social benefit around[?]*
> *And a Frank Gehry monument to make Toronto world*
> *class? Please.[142]*

Even city core-oriented people question the need for ever-denser housing developments. Some fear the "recovery" of the core, in the form it has taken, supplants local residents with a new demographic dominated by a global elite class and those who serve them. As green architect and commentator Lloyd Alter asks: "But what are we getting when we throw away height limits and barriers to development, stop worrying about shadows and views, and let the developers loose? Also, importantly, who are we getting?"[143]

SAVING THE DISTINCTIVENESS OF GLOBAL CITIES

Faced with these challenges, some residents of global cities struggle to preserve something of their local culture. Whether it's Calvin Soh in Singapore or an aging hipster in New York, residents worry, as one London writer put it, about their city losing its "soul" to globalized capital, migration, and tourism.[144]

This presents a unique issue, even for the most successful cities. "No amount of analysis and forward planning," says longtime government adviser Peter Ho, "will eliminate volatility and uncertainty in a complex world." The economics-driven managerial model, he concedes, so successful in the past, is not so effective in dealing with issues of identity and growing pressure on the middle class, particularly with the reduction in high-wage, blue-collar work.

To thrive in the future, Singapore, like other great global cities, will have to find its way without a pre-drawn map. As Asia modernizes and develops a modern infrastructure, Singaporeans cannot remain competitive merely by being more efficient or better educated. The city-state will have to rediscover the boldness of its founding generation, even while discarding many of its methods. "We will have to be pioneers again," notes Calvin Soh, "and recognize that we don't have the same strategic advantages that we used to have. We have to start planning for the next 10 years from that viewpoint. And that plan has to come from the grassroots, not from above."

This, indeed, is the challenge that faces global cities—how to serve their economic function, maintain their local character, and nurture new generations. This is in some ways a conflict between the irreplaceable and the interchangeable—the sacred and that which is produced by automation and globalized finance. A city can either nurture its uniqueness or become a hotel for a nomadic global population. Such nomads are no doubt necessary, particularly in a global hub, but it is one thing to accommodate this class and another for the transient elite to dominate the urban landscape. At the same time, these pressures have also inspired more dangerous reactions, notably nativism and a growing chasm between guest workers and residents.[145]

In the end, the fundamental challenge facing the global city ultimately lies in accommodating two identities, a global one and a local one. As the Roman writer Seneca wrote, citizens live with "two commonwealths—the one, a vast and truly common state, which embraces alike gods and men, in which we look neither to this corner of earth nor to that, but measure our city's bounds by the path of the sun; the other to which we have been assigned by birth."[146] The global city fully embraces the cosmopolitan economy, but it also needs grassroots businesses catered to families and neighborhoods—what Hong Kong scholar Lau Siu-Kai labeled "utilitarianistic familialism."[147]

The future direction of global cities will depend largely on how they serve these "two commonwealths," the expansive and the familiar. To work as a great global city, it is critical to serve not just global business but also the local economy and the needs of local residents. The world beckons and must be accommodated, but a city must be more than a fancy theme park or a collection of luxury office and residential towers. A great city, even a global one, requires a middle and a working class, not just the global rich and their servants. It needs families and ordinary residents who may rarely leave town, not just globe-trotting individuals. It needs to be true to itself and to the people who created these special places in the first place.

CHAPTER 5

Post-Familial Places

■ ▤ ▦ ▩

When my father was growing up in Flatbush in Brooklyn in the 1930s, it was very much a place for middle-class families. There my grandfather bought a house, raised three children, and commuted daily to a factory in Manhattan, a half hour or more away. People without children were a rarity; entertainment was familial, with cousins, aunts, and uncles coming for Thanksgiving, birthdays, and the Jewish holidays.

My mother, whose family was very poor, back then lived in Brownsville, a hardscrabble Brooklyn neighborhood, both then and now. Yet she and her four brothers and sisters (one brother, for whom the author was named, died of kidney failure in his early 20s) were still part of a large family, as was common at the time. Urban life, even in the poorest sections, thrived in ways that are increasingly rare in our cities today.

Families today face a difficult challenge. A generation reared largely in the comparative spaciousness of suburbia may yearn for city life but find its ability to buy or even rent a family residence along Flatbush's tree-lined streets all but prohibited. In a city where space is often at a premium, choosing to raise a family can pose difficult, even impossible choices.

"The cost of space is the biggest issue in Brooklyn," notes local resident Michael Milch, whose wife attends dental school at NYU. "The issue becomes, can you get some personal green space and a place for the kids to wander?" Of course, people living and settling in areas such as Ditmas Park or nearby Kensington, where many homes are large but often prohibitively expensive, willingly pay a premium for the pleasure of living in New York. But their vision of space is not diametrically different from that of suburban residents. They are seeking environments that are only moderately dense and perceived as friendly to families. Jason Walker, 45, a father of two, left Washington, DC—a core city with one of the highest percentages of childless households in the nation[1]—and moved to the Ditmas Park area in order to escape "a culture dominated by childless people leery of the existence of kids."

The Walkers—living in a two-bedroom apartment—have decided to put up their home for sale and look for another in the area or elsewhere. "It's pretty sad to look at how my kids have to live," Walker said. "What we need and want is a home."

Such opportunities exist in places like Kensington and even more so in neighborhoods of other American cities, where single-family homes are sometimes just a short walk, or certainly a short ride, from the urban core. These represent places where great cities—like New York—can once again welcome the middle class.

This may not be the urban future imagined by city planners, developers, and many urban pundits. Instead, their focus is often on high-rise projects, which usually target the highly affluent, or on ultra-small units for singles. New housing on a more human scale, notably single-family houses that tend to be farther out on the city's periphery, are generally less favored by the planning and development community, which is more concerned with engineering density for a population that, frankly, will have fewer couples and even fewer children.[2]

FAMILIES AND CITIES: A BRIEF HISTORY

The city of my parents, as well as that portrayed by Jane Jacobs, was human scaled, even when dense. It was anchored by strong institutions—churches, synagogues, ethnic associations, and voluntary organizations—that tied families to each other and to their community. Cities were many things to many people, but they also were familial in ways that are increasingly rare.

In the past, families struggled to survive in places that were disease-ridden and unsanitary. These conditions kept death rates high, particularly among the young.[3] Yet cities continued to accommodate families, who often braved difficult conditions and disruption of their own culture to settle there.

Familialism was critical to survival in these new environments. Families, or clans, provided much of the "intermediary institutions" that made a city, or a particular neighborhood, function. In some cases, extended family groups provided funding for businesses and sometimes also served to protect their urban "turf" from outsiders. The family in large part provided what the government of those times could not supply.

The societies of both ancient Greece and Rome relied heavily on blood ties along highly patriarchal lines.[4] In fact, pagan religion was closely tied to the home and hearth; family had a kind of semi-religious significance. But similar allegiances were also common in monotheistic religions such as Judaism,[5] Christianity, and Islam.[6] The same applied also to Buddhist[7] and Hindu scriptures[8] and traditional Chinese family-based faiths. Kinship defined both the Sinic and European cultures, which accounted for at least half of the global population around the birth of Christ.[9]

In Rome, as in today's cities, family structures weakened in the later centuries. This trend was accelerated to some extent by the efforts of early Christians, who worked to reduce the primacy of kinship in order to assert a more universal message that transcended blood lines or deeply felt civic loyalties. Even in the early modern period, many sought out a life as priests or as nuns, as the church, seen as the bearer of all knowledge, provided security and opportunities, particularly for learning, that were not so available elsewhere. As many as one in 10 women in 16th-century Florence were celibate.[10] These patterns shifted in the ensuing centuries, as religious and social views changed and the economy became more dynamic.

But as we saw earlier, the family resurged in the 17th century, particularly in advanced communities like those in the Netherlands, which developed what historian Simon Schama describes as "the Republic of children."[11] Critically, this focus on family did not mean a neo-traditionalist approach to women's place in society. Females in the Golden Age of the Dutch Republic were instructed in such fields as geometry and applied mathematics and enjoyed a freedom of action that shocked many French and English observers.[12]

Familialism also played a critical role in the earliest rise of capitalism. During the Italian Renaissance, the prime drivers were family businesses, where blood ties provided "the decisive bonds" for enterprise.[13] But there was also a significant change in society's attitude toward children. As Harvard's Steven Ozment notes, the emergence of a worldview centered around children, breaking with the relative indifference towards them that characterized Medieval culture, had its origins in this early capitalist era.[14] Protestantism, too, certainly played a role, as the elimination of monasteries and convents reduced outlets for celibacy for both men and women and thus increased the pool of potential parents. In the ensuing centuries, cities became primary incubators for a new family-centric culture, notably in the Netherlands. In the domestic reality of places like Holland, painted so poignantly by Rembrandt and the other Dutch masters, medievalist Philippe Ariès notes, "the child has taken a central place in the family."[15]

Chinese civilization, from its earliest times, was largely built around a large extended family, often with several generations under the same roof. The tradition of "regulating the family" was seen as critical to both "ordering the state" and pacifying the world. Three of Confucianism's five key relationships were familial, led by the all-important father-son tie.[16] Individual achievement and struggles were encapsulated within the context of the family; one never took credit, or shouldered blame, alone.[17]

As the Chinese began to spread to Southeast Asia and beyond, they carried elements of this family-centric culture with them. The traditional fealty to Emperor and later state faded amid the vibrant capitalist culture developed by the Chinese diaspora. As late as the 1980s, surveys in places like Hong Kong found that the number of people who put family ties first was five times more than the number who placed priority on their obligation to overall society.[18] Kinship ties, notes the sociologist Peter Berger, constituted "the absolutely central institution" of Chinese businesses in the Americas, Europe, Africa, and Australia.[19]

THE POST-MALTHUSIAN CITY

Until the 19th century, cities depended on the countryside to constantly replenish their populations. Urban death rates remained higher than those in the surrounding countryside,[20] where birth rates also tended to be higher.[21] Some historians describe an "urban graveyard thesis," which notes that plagues and higher infant mortality in cities were only offset by migration from the countryside. "What life added," notes Fernand Braudel, "death took away."[22]

Under such conditions, urban growth, to a large extent, reflected the ability of cities to lure people from the countryside with the promise of economic gain. Ancient Rome, Byzantium, and Renaissance Venice all expanded their populations by welcoming migrants drawn by opportunity. Fecund in their heyday, these cities became far less so as they declined. Similar patterns could be seen in the early modern period, when cities such as Milan and Amsterdam suffered sagging birth rates as their economic positions deteriorated.[23]

Only at the end of the 19th century did humanity—mostly in Europe and North America—manage to depart what some historians call the "era of Malthusian stagnation." This departure came in the form of rapid population growth, not only from the traditional source, the countryside, but also from a surplus of births over deaths. This resurgence was also predicated on advances in the world food supply, most notably through the development of mass agriculture in places such as the United States, Canada, Australia, and Argentina.[24]

The industrial era transformed urban demographics in a particularly dramatic fashion. In Britain alone, the population grew from 8 million in 1790 to almost 18 million in 1850, and a growing surplus of rural population headed for the cities, much as we see in the megacities of the developing world today. Some migrants came from rural backwaters as far away as Ireland, Scotland, and Wales. As those areas depopulated, London grew from under 1 million in 1801 to over 7 million in 1910; its rivals New York, Manchester, and Berlin expanded even faster.[25]

Initially the filth, overcrowding, and crime incubated in these cities reinforced their dependence on the countryside. But by the second half of the 19th century, efforts to improve sanitation in western Europe—demonstrated most dramatically by the redevelopment of Paris under Georges-Eugène Haussmann—significantly reduced urban mortality rates.[26] A spate of improvement also swept through American cities, including such rough-and-tumble industrial places as Chicago and Cleveland, where new parks, roads, public transport, and modern sanitary systems improved the health of the growing urban masses.[27]

Yet by the 1950s and 1960s, families, particularly from the expanding middle class in Europe, North America, Australia, and parts of eastern Asia, started heading toward the periphery for more and cheaper space, better schools, and safety. This left cities increasingly denuded of middle-class families and led to a new demographic configuration in cities that has become more conducive to singles or couples who don't have children. While cities have resurged in many places, increased their levels of safety, and retained important economic functions, the old familial city has still not returned.

THE EMERGENCE OF THE POST-FAMILIAL CITY

Modern urbanism has engendered something new in history: the post-familial city, one that is increasingly childless and more focused on the individual. As we'll see, a confluence of factors has contributed to this cultural shift, including trends toward ever-increasing density, the related phenomena of high costs, the weakness of urban education systems, and increasingly, the ability of people to perform functions remotely via the Internet.

As touched on in previous chapters, the link between density and childlessness is fairly clear-cut. It is most pronounced in the hearts of the most vibrant urban cores—from small North American global cities to European metropolises to Asia's biggest megacities. The notion that height is a symbol of modernity, efficiency, and even aesthetics is common among urbanists. Today's physically developing city has become increasingly Corbusian in its ambitions and its rationale.

In contrast to singles and childless couples, families generally avoid high-density housing; in the United States, the percentage of childless people is highest in denser districts.[28] Generally, the densest areas also house the highest percentage of women who have never had children. The highest percentage of women over 40 with no children—a remarkable 70 percent—can be found in expensive, and dense, Washington, DC. In Manhattan, half of households are single.[29]

Simply put, modern families in higher-income countries require space and are thus generally unwilling to live in crowded conditions.[30] In the United States, some 52 percent of non-family households live in single-unit dwellings (detached, semi-detached, and townhouse), as opposed to apartments or mobile homes, but 62 percent of single-head-of-household families and an astounding 83 percent of married-couple families, most of whom had children living with them at some point, live in this form of housing. Married couples constitute 12 percent of apartment occupants, compared to 38 percent in other households.[31]

Perhaps the ultimate primary example of the new child-free city is San Francisco,[32] where there are now 80,000 more dogs than children.[33] San Francisco has the highest percentage of households without children 18 or younger of any major US core city.[34] The 2010 census revealed a San Francisco getting older while its count of people aged 20 to 44 had dropped. Meanwhile nearly half of parents of young children in the city said they planned to leave in the next three years, according to one survey by the mayor's office.[35]

These patterns are evident in a host of key cities, particularly those in the high-income world. In Chicago, for example, the 2010 census found that the city's overall population fell by 7 percent, but its share of people aged 5 to 19 fell by 19 percent.[36] In the suburbs of Toronto, Montreal, and Vancouver, the ratio of children per woman of child-bearing age is roughly 80 percent higher than in the urban cores.[37]

THE EUROPEAN URBAN MODEL

These trends are, if anything, more marked in European cities such as London, Paris, and Berlin.[38] One way to measure this is through an examination of fertility rates, or the number of children born to the average woman of child-bearing age (15 to 44 years). Inner London, notes demographer Wendell Cox, has a fertility rate of 1.6, which is well below the replacement rate of 2.1. In the outer reaches of London, this rate hits 2.0, roughly a third higher.

Even countries with a strong welfare state that often provides subsidies for families are seeing these patterns take shape. A Max Planck Institute study of total fertility rates within four countries—Denmark, Finland, Norway, and Sweden—found a strong correlation between higher fertility rates (the number of children borne by women in their lifetime) and less dense suburban locations. These suburban places, the study points out, offer larger apartments and single-family homes that are attractive to families.[39]

In Denmark, for example, the fertility rates of suburbs and smaller towns were 50 percent higher than the rate in the central core, particularly in the capital of Copenhagen. The capital city reflects Danes' strong propensity to live alone. Overall, the percentage of single households exceeds 45 percent. The rise of the one-person home coincides with an aging population but also extends to younger generations—over twice as many Danes under 65 are living alone as those over 65.[40]

Similar patterns of "higher suburban fecundity" can be seen in the other European countries as well.[41] According to the French national statistical agency, the unaffordability of housing and the unsuitability of house sizes for families are the principal reasons for the exodus of families from the *ville de* Paris to the suburbs.[42] In many ways, Germany, the vital heart of Europe, has exemplified these changes in the continent's demography. Once again, urban centers are the epicenters of low fertility. Overall, one in three German households are single, and single dwellings house over 50 percent of the population in Berlin and over 45 percent of the populations in such cities as Hamburg, Munich, and Leipzig.[43]

These figures suggest that post-familial patterns will be stronger in the decades ahead. In a recent survey, some 30 percent of German women of child-bearing age said they do not intend to have children, and 48 percent of middle-aged German men agreed that a happy life is possible without children; only 15 percent of their fathers agreed with this idea when they were asked the same question at the same age.[44]

Until the last few decades, the childless trend was largely perceived as a northern European phenomenon. Yet Europe's southern
rim has also become decidedly less family-centric as it has urbanized. More than one-fifth of Italian women born around 1965 will
remain childless, notes one recent study by scholars at the University
of Pavia. Greek, Spanish, and Italian birth rates are among the lowest
in the world.[45]

EASTERN ASIAN CITIES TAKE THE LEAD

Surprisingly, the modern focal point for post-familial urbanism comes
from eastern Asia, where family traditionally exercised a powerful,
even dominant influence over society. The shift toward post-familialism arose first in Japan, the region's most economically and technologically advanced country. As early as the 1990s, sociologist Muriel
Jolivet unearthed a trend of growing hostility toward motherhood in
her work *Japan: The Childless Society?*—a trend that stemmed in part
from male reluctance to take responsibility for raising children.[46]

The trend has only accelerated since then. By 2010, a third of Japanese women entering their 30s were single, as were roughly one in
five of those entering their 40s—that is roughly eight times the percentage seen in 1960 and twice that seen in 2000. By 2030, according
to sociologist Mika Toyota, almost one in three Japanese males may be
unmarried by age 50.[47]

In Japan, the direct tie between low birth rates and dense urbanization is most expressed in Tokyo, which now has a fertility rate of
around one child per family, below the already depressed national
average. Some of the lowest rates on earth can be seen elsewhere in
eastern Asia, including those in Seoul, Singapore, and Hong Kong,
which are now roughly the same as the rate in Tokyo.[48] As more of Asia
becomes highly urbanized like Japan, this kind of ultra-low fertility
will spread to other parts of the continent.

Most critically, this dynamic has already spread to mainland China,
or at least to its larger cities, where fertility rates have dropped well
below 1.0. In 2013, Shanghai's fertility rate of 0.7 was among the lowest ever reported—well below the "one child" mandate removed in

2015 and only one-third the rate required to simply replace the current population. Beijing and Tianjin suffer similarly dismal fertility rates.[49]

This pattern of low fertility, notes demographer Gavin Jones, suggests that rapid urbanization has already made the notion of the "one child" policy antiquated. Now, even with fertility policies being loosened, many Chinese families are opting not to take advantage, due largely to the same reasons cited in other parts of the world: the high cost of living and high housing costs.[50]

SEOUL: CITY OF THE FUTURE?

Perhaps no city better reflects Asia's emerging urban paradigm than Seoul, the densest of the high-income world's megacities, outside of Hong Kong. The Korean capital is more than 2.5 times as crowded[51] as Tokyo, twice as dense as London, and five times as crowded as New York. No surprise then that retro-urbanist pundits love the place, as epitomized by a glowing report in *Smithsonian Magazine*[52] that painted Seoul as "the city of the future." Architects, naturally, joined the chorus. In 2010, the International Council of Societies of Industrial Design named Seoul the "world design capital." [53] Ultimately, Seoul epitomizes the retro-urbanist fantasy: a city that is dense and dominating, rapidly turning the rest of the country into depopulating backwaters. Seoul has monopolized population growth in Korea, accounting for nearly 90 percent of total growth since 1970. Seoul also currently holds nearly 50 percent of the country's population, up from 20 percent in 1960.[54]

Seoul's development has come at the expense of not just its own hinterlands but also its own humanity. Its formerly human-scaled form of housing, known as a *hanok,* that was one story and featured an interior courtyard has been largely replaced with tall, often repetitive towers that stretch even into the suburbs. While architects and planners celebrate this shift, they rarely consider whether this form of urbanization creates a good place for people, particularly families. When you consider the trends in similar cities, it's unsurprising that Korean sociologists have noted the shift to high-density housing as being unsuitable for families with children.[55]

Over time, the impact of these housing policies will be profound. By 2040, Korea's population will join those of Japan and Germany as one of the world's oldest.[56] This will occur despite determined government efforts to encourage childbearing, efforts that may well be doomed by the government's similar commitment to a dense, centralized urban form.

THE JAPANESE MODEL: THE CITY-NATION

What will happen to societies that are likely to retain extremely low rates of fertility? Japan, notes Canadian demographer Vaclav Smil, represents "an involuntary global pioneer of a new society."[57] Japan certainly exemplifies one way societies may evolve under diminishing birth rates. Projecting population and fertility rates is difficult, but the trajectory for Japan is unprecedented. The UN projects Japan's 2100 population to be 91 million, down from 2015's 127 million, but Japan's own National Institute of Population and Social Security Research projects a population of 48 million, nearly 50 percent lower than the UN's projection.[58]

Japan's urban centralization both feeds and accelerates this trend. Rather than disperse, Japan's population is "recentralizing." A country with a great tradition of regional rivalries, home to an impressive archipelago of venerable cities, is becoming, in effect, a city-nation, with an increased concentration on just one massive urban agglomeration: Tokyo.[59] This has, for the time being, allowed Tokyo to escape the worst of Japan's demographic decline, drawing heavily on the countryside and smaller cities, both of which are losing population. From 2000 to 2013, the Tokyo metropolitan area added 2.4 million residents, while the rest of the nation declined by 2 million.

Tokyo is now home to almost one in three Japanese. But its growth is likely to be constrained, as the last reservoir of rural and small-city residents seems certain to dry up dramatically. A projection for the core prefecture of Tokyo indicates a 50 percent population cut by 2100 to a number smaller than it was at the beginning of World War II; 46 percent of that reduced population will be over 65.[60]

This pattern of the city-nation, and its associated demographics, is also evident in other eastern Asian countries. Like Tokyo and Seoul,

Taipei, the capital of Taiwan, could also become a virtual city-country. Between 2001 and 2011, the Taipei metropolitan area attracted nearly 70 percent of Taiwan's growth, despite having less than 40 percent of the population.[61]

ONE PROBLEM WITH DIMINISHING BIRTH RATES: THE AGING POPULATION

The biggest challenge for these cities will not just be the smaller body count. As we've seen, relatively small places have thrived throughout history, such as Renaissance-era Venice or contemporary Hong Kong or Singapore. The most pressing challenge will be rapid aging, exacerbated by long national life spans. By 2050, according to UN estimates, Japan will have 3.7 times as many people aged 65 and older as aged 15 and under. By comparison, as late as 1975, there were three times as many children (15 and under) as people 65 and over. Even more troubling: In 2050, the Japanese cohort over 80 will be 10 percent greater than the 15-and-under population.[62]

This suggests it is time, in high-income countries at least, to shift our focus from concerns about overpopulation to a set of new and quite unique challenges presented by rapid aging and a steadily diminishing workforce. Even birth rates in developing countries are tumbling toward those of wealthy countries. As British environmental journalist Fred Pearce puts it, "the population 'bomb' is being defused over the medium and long term."[63]

Let's take a closer look at the "Four Asian Tigers"—Hong Kong, Singapore, South Korea, and Taiwan—that, like Japan, appear to be destined to become ever more urbanized, increasingly post-familial, and eventually, very old. Taiwan, for example, expects its over-65 population to pass its 15-and-under population by 2017;[64] for Singapore and South Korea, this will likely occur by the middle of the next decade.[65] By 2050, the 80-and-over population could exceed the under-15s by 75 percent in Hong Kong and by 30 percent in Taiwan.[66]

Some, like Pearce, see the Japanese model as an exemplar of a world dominated by seniors—with very slow and even negative population growth—that will be "older, wiser, greener." Following the adolescent ferment of the 20th century, Pearce looks forward to "the age of the old" that he claims "could be the salvation of the planet."[67]

Yet if the environmental benefits of a smaller, older, and less consumptive population may be positive, there may be other negative ramifications of a rapidly aging society. For one thing, there will be increasingly fewer children to take care of elderly parents. This has led to a rising incidence of what the Japanese call *kodokushi*, or "lonely death," among the aged, unmarried, and childless.[68] In Korea, Kyung-sook Shin's highly praised bestseller, *Please Look After Mom*, which sold 2 million copies, focused on "filial guilt" in children who fail to look after their aging parents and hit a particular nerve in the highly competitive eastern Asian society that seems to be drifting from its familial roots.[69] Additionally, an aging population will certainly diminish demand for both goods and services and likely would not promote a vibrant entrepreneurial economy.[70]

China is in a similarly dire situation. As the country gets richer and urbanizes, its demography increasingly mimics that of the Tigers and Japan. As we've seen, Chinese fertility rates have been dropping for decades and are now approaching among the lowest in the world. By 2050, China will suffer a net loss of 60 million people under 15 years of age, approximately the size of Italy's entire population. It will gain nearly 190 million people 65 and over, approximately the population of Pakistan, which is the world's sixth most populous country.[71]

Ultimately, China will face its own version of "demographic winter," although sometime later than Japan or the Tigers. The US Census Bureau estimates that China's population will peak in 2026 and then will age faster than any country in the world besides Japan.[72] Its rapid urbanization, expansion of education, and rising housing costs all will contribute to this trend. China's population of children and young workers between 15 and 19 will decline 20 percent from 2015 to 2050, while that of the world will increase nearly 10 percent.[73]

In China, the consequences of the rising number of elderly will be profound. Demographer Nicholas Eberstadt, for example, sees the prospect of a fiscal crisis caused by an aging and ultimately diminishing population. China, he notes, faces "this coming tsunami of senior citizens" with a smaller workforce, greater pension obligations, and generally slower economic growth.[74] It seems likely, as has occurred in Japan already, that rising costs associated with an aging population, and a dearth of new workers and consumers, will hamper wealth creation and income growth. Societies dominated by the old likely will become inherently backward-looking, seeking to preserve the existing wealth of seniors as opposed to creating new opportunities for the increasingly politically marginalized younger population.

The shift to an aging population also creates, particularly in Asia where urbanization is most rapid, the segregation of generations, with the elderly in rural areas and the younger people in cities. Around the world, the results of this shift are likely to resemble those seen in Japan, with cities becoming home to an ever-expanding part of the population, while people in the countryside are destined to grow older and ever more isolated. It is not clear how the expanding senior population, which was traditionally cared for by younger generations, will fare with fewer children to support them and in the absence of a well-developed welfare state.

The negative impacts of rapid aging and a diminished workforce are already being felt, even in such prosperous countries as Japan and Germany. By 2030, Germany's debt per capita could be twice as high as that of bankrupt Greece in 2014, and to help address the shortfall, officials have proposed more taxes. These would be effectively exacted from the working population, to create what German officials have labeled a "demographic reserve."[75] Even in traditional, thrifty Asian nations such as Japan and Singapore, savings rates have been dropping, and there is growing concern over whether these countries will be able to support their soaring numbers of seniors.[76]

Later this century, these same challenges will even be felt in many parts of the developing world. In rapidly urbanizing, relatively poor countries such as Vietnam, the fertility rate is already below replacement levels, and it is rapidly declining in other poorer countries such as Myanmar, Indonesia, and even Bangladesh. In parts of Latin America, especially Brazil, fertility rates are plunging to below those seen in the United States. Brazil's birth rate (now 1.9 from 4.3 in the late 1970s) has dropped not only among the professional classes but also in the countryside and among those living in the favelas. As one account reports, women in Brazil now say, "Afábrica está fechada"—the factory is closed.[77]

THE NEW URBAN VALUE SYSTEM

The shift toward post-familialism represents a significant breaking point in the history of cities. In the past, traditional beliefs and and kinship ties helped promote the idea of having at least two or three children, which is in line with the replacement birth rate. In contrast, the current era, particularly in cities, does not readily spawn a desire for family or children. Progress is, in part, a culprit: the ubiquity of mass education and communications has weakened many of the bonds that held families together and has worked to substitute societal values for those learned at home.[78]

Let's first examine the growing trend toward secularism. Some studies suggest that secularism reflects a society that is progressive, wealthy, and highly beneficial to the individual. Yet there is also a downside in how secularism affects the propensity for childbearing. As author Eric Kaufmann puts it, secularism appears to fail to "inspire the commitment to generations past and sacrifices for those yet to come."[79]

The impact of secularism has been particularly strong in our cities. Once centers of worship, urban cores have become pillars of secularism, with the exception of cities that cater to distinct minorities like Orthodox Jews, evangelical Christians, or observant Muslims. In the 20th century, religious and kinship ties suffered particularly under ideologies that required loyalty first to the state—such as Communism and National Socialism. This need, notes sociologist Robert Nisbet, served to turn family members into a "soulless, traditionless mass."[80]

If these vicious ideologues enjoyed, thankfully, limited success, the current material culture seems to be perhaps more effectively undermining interest in family. This can be seen worldwide. Increasingly childless Europe may boast some of the world's most impressive religious structures, but the moral influence that they once symbolized has diminished considerably.[81] In 1970, 40 percent of western Europeans went to church weekly; two decades later, that number had dropped to 16.6 percent. Critically, religion is particularly losing adherents among the young. Half of Britons aged 18 to 34 consider themselves non-religious, compared to just 20 percent of those over 55. For its part, eastern Asia, notes the Pew Research Center, is now the least religious place in the world, home to over three-quarters of the world's unaffiliated population, led by Japan and China.[82]

This secularizing trend is also developing, albeit less quickly, in the notably more religious United States. In 2007, barely 15 percent of baby boomers and 20 percent of Generation X said they were not religious; among the millennial generation, this proportion runs to roughly one-third.[83]

The tie between religiosity and fertility is very clear. Overall, an analysis of major US metropolitan areas showed that, essentially, those who believe in some higher spiritual value are far more likely to have children than those more secularly oriented. Increasingly, the heavy lifting of child-rearing appears to be falling on the religious.[84] Orthodox Jews, for example, produce an average number of children well above the average number produced by Jewish women overall (3.3 and over versus 1.9). Similarly, Salt Lake City, world center of the Mormon faith, has both the nation's highest rate of religious affiliation and the highest number of children per family. Three of the top six US cities in terms of birth rate are located along the Wasatch Front: Ogden, Salt Lake City, and Provo.[85]

Much larger groups, such as evangelical Christians, also marry and have offspring far more often than those who are only mildly religious.[86] Muslim birth rates tend to be higher in less urbanized and developed countries such as Afghanistan and Pakistan than in more educated, advanced countries such as Iran, Turkey, or Lebanon. The percentage of middle-aged women who have never had children in Lebanon is already 15 percent, and that number is far higher in its capital, Beirut. Singleness, among women, has also become somewhat accepted in such traditional societies as Iran, where women also account for 60 percent of university students.[87]

"URBAN TRIBES"

To some, the shift from kinship ties to largely post-familial arrangements represents a profound and largely positive advance in urban civilization. University of California psychology professor Bella DePaulo rightly rebuts the discrimination and stereotypes—from fecklessness to self-obsessiveness—often hurled at the unattached. But more provocatively, she asserts that they constitute an advantaged group in that they are more cyber-connected and "more likely to be linked to members of their social networks by bonds of affection." Unlike families, whose members, after all, are often stuck with each other, singles enjoy "intentional communities" and are thus more likely "to think about human connectedness in a way that is far-reaching and less predictable."[88]

These "singletons," as one urban scholar notes, enjoy a "rich social life" that is "anchored by themselves" through friendship networks and social media. "Living alone," he asserts, "might be what we need to reconnect."[89] Reliance on social media tends to emphasize further the primacy of post-familial relationships. A recent Australian study found, for example, that Facebook users were no less bonded to friends but tended to be far less tied to family compared to non-Facebook users.[90]

Like the trend toward secularism, the primary, and usually preferred, locale of this new social order is the large global city. DePaulo speaks about "urban tribes" made up of mostly single people "creating community ties that connect people to one another through work and leisure, holidays and crises."[91] For many individuals, she and others suggest, remaining single and childless makes logical sense. Some studies claim that US couples who choose not to have children enjoy higher net wealth, which certainly could prove persuasive.[92]

But this is more than a mere question of economics. Other singles simply feel they can get from friends and roommates what people used to seek from family members. "We've got all the benefits of family," explains one New York thirtysomething who has lived nearly two decades with his roommates, "with very little of the craziness that normally comes with them."[93]

It's important to note that many who eschew family formation today do so out of choice. In previous eras, people didn't have children because of factors such as extreme poverty, mass emigration, war, disease, or other major societal disruptions. In contrast, today's post-familialism has developed at a time of relative peace and prosperity in most high-income countries. This suggests that these trends are very powerful and not easily reversed, even by economic prosperity.

In his provocative 2012 book *Going Solo*, Eric Klinenberg points out that for "hip" urban professionals, living alone represents not only a way to cope with higher prices, particularly for housing, but also a "more desirable state." For young professionals, Klinenberg suggests, living alone in the city constitutes "a sign of success and a mark of distinction, a way to gain freedom and experience the anonymity that can make city life so exhilarating . . . it's a way to reassert control over your life."[94]

CHANGING SEXUAL MORES

Klinenberg states that this opportunity for freedom and control is particularly true for educated single women, who are more numerous than their male counterparts in the elite core areas of New York, Los Angeles, San Francisco, and Boston, particularly as they age into their 30s and 40s.[95] These same well-educated women, according to studies in both Germany and the Netherlands, are most likely to resist marriage and, particularly, childbearing.[96]

One reason is changing sexual mores. Middle-class women in their 20s and 30s, suggests Stanford sociologist Michael Rosenfeld, can enjoy "a second adolescence" seeking "new experiences" with a series of partners of considerable diversity.[97] Kate Bolick, writing in the *Atlantic*, believes that many of these accomplished women will do without long-term committed relationships, choosing instead "a room of one's own," a place where a single woman can live and thrive as herself.[98]

This altering of traditional relations between the sexes is acutely evident in the emerging exemplar of post-familialism, Japan. Many young Japanese are not marrying, and they increasingly show little sexual interest in each other. The percentage of sexually active female university students, according to the Japanese Association for Sex Education, has fallen to 47 percent, down from 60 percent a decade ago. These patterns seem to be taking hold even among older people; half of all adult Japanese admit to not having sex in a given month.[99]

And it's not just women, of course, contributing to Japan's post-familial culture. Many young Japanese males—sometimes labeled "herbivores"—appear more interested in comics, computer games, and socializing through the Internet than in seeking out the opposite sex. In a sense, Japanese males and females are even evolving into distinct races in terms of their physiques: while Japanese females are getting thinner, males are getting much heavier. Many are becoming increasingly autonomous. Academic surveys suggest that as many as 500,000 to 1.5 million Japanese, many of them young men in their 20s and 30s, remain isolated in their parents' homes, cut off from the workplace and society. The reasons for this are said to vary and include a weak economy, but this trend also illustrates a broad reconfiguration of familial arrangements, whose roots are not just based on opportunity and money.[100]

To say the least, none of these social changes is good for prospective family formation. What Johns Hopkins professor Andrew Cherlin described as "the deinstitutionalization of marriage" in America and other countries contributes to this trend.[101] Marriage is still linked with higher birth rates, even in countries where having children without a formal legal tie is widely acceptable. Cohabiting couples, notes Netherlands-based sociologist Theo Engelen, tend to produce fewer children, and the "family" tends to last for a considerably shorter time.[102]

Given recent trajectories, demographers Miho Iwasawa and Ryuichi Kaneko project that a Japanese woman born in 1990 stands less than even odds of getting married and staying married until age 50. Roughly one-sixth of Japanese women in their mid-40s are still single, and about 30 percent of all women that age are childless. Twenty years hence, they project, 38 percent of all Japanese women in their mid-40s could be childless, and an even higher share—just over 50 percent—would never have grandchildren.[103]

Similar trends can be found in other parts of highly urbanized, high-income eastern Asian countries. In Taiwan, 30 percent of women aged between 30 and 34 are single; only 30 years ago, just 2 percent of women lived unmarried so late. And this trend appears to be gaining. In a 2011 poll of Taiwanese women under 50, a strong majority claimed they did not want children.[104] Overall, demographer Gavin Jones suggests, up to a quarter of all eastern Asian women will remain single by age 50, and up to a third will remain childless.[105]

Demographer Wolfgang Lutz suggests that environments where marriage has declined, where childless or very small families predominate, create new "social norms" that establish childlessness as the new normative reality. This, he adds, also shapes the attitudes of children brought up in an environment dominated by adults and their concerns. Low birth rates and smaller families also mean that the young often grow up without siblings, cousins, and the extended family network that has been, as we've seen, critical to human life for much of our history as a species.[106]

In the past, the extended family made child-rearing easier. But without older siblings or relatively young grandparents, many families today have to pay for basic child care services, placing yet another burden on young couples. The days when a child could be watched by an aunt or older sister are gone when there are few or no siblings.

NEW CULTURAL NORMS

Although there have always been single people and couples without children, the post-familial society has achieved cultural influence that is unprecedented in urban history. Some of this has to do with the concentration of singles and the childless in key urban centers. In the United States, for example, influential media and information jobs generally are located precisely where levels of singleness and childlessness are highest. This is true as well for such cultural centers as Tokyo and London, which have well below-average numbers of families with children.[107] Of what are generally considered the six largest media companies in the United States—Comcast, Disney, News Corp, Time Warner Cable, Viacom, and CBS—four are headquartered in largely childless, heavily single Manhattan.

These heavily single and childless places, notes Eric Klinenberg, are inheritors of a culture that first emerged among the bohemians of the 1920s, who drifted to Paris's Left Bank and New York's Greenwich Village. These areas provided what Gertrude Stein described as "life without father." They created "the cradle of liberated personae" that could now "fully realize themselves," largely without the burden of monogamous marriages or children.[108] Increasingly, these values are embraced not only by the well-educated and affluent but also by other classes, particularly, as political scientist Charles Murray notes, by the less educated and poorer population.[109]

Post-familialism can be seen as the logical product of a culture that, in its passion to protect "rights," focuses on individual issues of self-empowerment, race, gender, and sexual orientation and leaves little room for obligations to one's immediate kin. "It is perverse," suggests *Financial Times* columnist Janan Ganesh, "to invest in this idea of individualism for so long and then go all squeamish when it reaches its logical conclusion: the childfree life, the ultimate expression of self-realisation above living for others."[110]

The new childless urbanites, notes Terry Nichols Clark, will identify less with their parents and grandparents, or even with their traditional cultural traditions, than with those who share their particular cultural and aesthetic tastes. They will have transcended the barriers of race and even country, embracing what Clark calls "a post-materialist" perspective that focuses on more abstract, and often important, issues such as human rights or the environment, as well as aesthetic concerns. No longer familial, as people have been for millennia, the urban singleton could be a harbinger of not only a "new race" but also of "new politics."[111]

There is also a kind of "Peter Pan" effect here, some argue. A hyper-individualist culture, notes Singapore pastor Andrew Ong, is "about not growing up—when you get married and have kids, you stop being cool."[112] The Asian variant of this first emerged in Japan with the rise of the so-called *shinjinrui* ("new race") in the 1980s, the emergence of which paralleled the trend toward childlessness.[113] Today, as we've seen, the *shinjinrui* culture's descendants can be found across the urban landscape of high-income countries.

In sharp contrast to their parents, who sacrificed for both their families and their countries, the "new race" prioritizes cultural pursuits, travel, and an almost defiant individualism. Now in their 30s and 40s, many of these people, indulge themselves in hobbies, fashion, or restaurants—personal pursuits not readily available to their homebound mothers or overworked fathers. Mika Toyota observes that "people's lifestyles are more important and their personal networks mean more than family. It's now a choice. You can be single, self-satisfied and well. So why have kids? It's better to go on great holidays, eat good food, and have your hobbies. A family is no longer the key to the city life."[114]

POST-FAMILIALISM AND THE URBAN FORM

Clustering in the urban core, these singles are creating not just a new culture but also a "new social environment" very different from that which existed in cities of the past, such as the world of my grandparents in Brooklyn. In the post-familial city, built around the needs of childless and often single professionals, the focus necessarily shifts to recreation, arts, culture, and restaurants. In other words, the preferences of this "new race" increasingly shape how we build our cities, and what things we choose to prioritize in them.

We know that families generally do not prefer dense housing, but those who advocate the emerging urban social order, not surprisingly, generally support densification. In the traditional cities, some of the most prized local amenities were low- to medium-density neighborhoods with schools, churches, and family-friendly shopping areas. In contrast, Eric Klinenberg strongly supports efforts to densify cities and discourages the building of single-family homes. To him, the 2,500-square-foot (232-square-meter) home in the suburbs represents both an environmental disaster and a threat to the affordability of small residences for "singletons."[115]

Nothing better illustrates the shift in the built environment of a post-familial society than the proliferation of plans for the construction of "micro-apartments" in cities like Singapore, Shanghai, Tokyo, New York, Seattle, and San Francisco. These residences of less than

300 square feet (28 square meters) would make even a two-bedroom co-op in Brooklyn, not to mention a single-family house like that of my Flatbush ancestors, seem like the Ponderosa Ranch and obviously are intended to house single young professionals; it is inconceivable for middle- or even working-class families to inhabit such spaces.[116]

PRICING OUT FAMILIES

As previously mentioned, middle-income housing affordability constitutes a huge constraint on family formation in many cities. High housing prices place particular burdens on young people interested in starting families. Being in the early years of their earning capacity, young households often can only afford to buy entry-level housing or may have to rent. Virtually all of the countries with ultra-low birth rates—Italy, Japan, China—suffer from very high housing prices.

The movement to the nation-city model—like we saw in Japan—where there is an extreme concentration of economic activity in one place, worsens these costs, as population clusters precisely where housing prices are highest.[117] Researchers Gavin Jones, Paulin Tay Straughan, and Angelique Chan report that in four eastern Asian countries, "a housing and urban environment unfriendly to children" was a principal reason for the reluctance of women to have children (or more children).[118]

Around the world, families need sufficiently spacious housing at affordable prices. By the 1960s, notes one Dutch researcher, families had come to recognize that "children became expensive in an urban setting." Housing prices were rising, particularly on a per-square-meter basis.[119] Recent studies from Europe reveal a direct connection between housing costs/availability and fertility/family formation. Women living in districts with highly affordable housing have their children sooner, while those living in expensive districts tend to have their children late or not at all.[120]

In the United States as well, greater middle-income housing affordability is strongly associated with more children. We measure middle-income housing affordability in terms of the price relative to household incomes—what demographer Wendell Cox calls the "median multiple."[121] Those metropolitan areas with the highest prices relative to incomes—such as New York, Los Angeles, the San Francisco Bay Area, Miami, Seattle, and Portland—all experienced explosive price inflation during the great housing bubble of the last decade (and earlier in some cases) and generally low rates of family formation.[122]

But perhaps the biggest challenges exist in land-scarce places like Hong Kong and Singapore. These markets have international border constraints (virtual or actual); there are no real opportunities for large-scale suburban development. Not surprisingly, prices have shot up, especially in Hong Kong.[123] This may explain, at least in part, the ultra-low birthrates in this special economic and political jurisdiction. Hong Kong's price increases have been attributed to its restrictive land-use policies[124] (in contrast to its fabled "free market" policies in other sectors) and to a huge increase in investors, especially from mainland China.

The link between house price and the decision whether to have children came up repeatedly among the younger people I interviewed in Singapore. As one young civil servant told me: "I feel Singapore is becoming more stressful—people are living in smaller spaces. There's no room for a child. The costs are tremendous. A generation ago, it was different. My father was a bus driver and could get a big HDB [Housing Development Board] flat. For my generation, it will be harder."[125]

BEYOND THE CASH NEXUS

We are entering an era for which there is no real precedent. Today's market system has created wonders and spread prosperity around much of the world, but it has not been too kind to the family. The ideal corporate executives of today, futurist Alvin Toffler noted over three decades ago, are those who have "dissolved" themselves from "their deep emotional attachments with their families of birth." But this represents just the beginning. To Toffler, the nuclear family represents "the second wave" of human existence, which is being replaced by a more flexible "third wave" lifestyle.[126] "Just as the nuclear family was promoted by the rise of the factory and office work," Toffler suggests, "any shift away from the factory or the office would also exert a heavy influence on the family."[127]

Family ties have also been undermined by the fierce competition of this highly globalized "third wave" economy. Firms often demand long hours of their workers in order to keep up with their rivals or to meet the demands of clients and customers. Increasingly, many of these workers are women.

This has an inevitable effect on birth rates and the nature of families. Women's growing involvement in the workforce, notes author Stephanie Coontz, has been necessary for decades in order for couples to afford children, but it also makes it more difficult for them to raise them.[128] This rise of female participation in the workforce has been widespread not only in the United States but also in Europe and most especially in eastern Asia. In 1970, less than half of women in Japan and Korea and only one-fifth of women in Singapore were working. By 2004, those numbers had increased to three-quarters in Japan and roughly three in five in South Korea and Singapore.[129]

This reflects what Harvard's Robert Putnam defines as the curse of "pervasive busyness" that now affects society in high-income countries.[130] Although intense work regimes may increase productivity today, it clearly makes matrimony and childraising more problematic. In this sense, businesses, by ignoring familial concerns, are setting into motion forces that will reduce both their future workforce and their consumer base.[131]

This is particularly true in eastern Asia, where job competition tends to be very intense. Singapore employers, notes Gavin Jones, remain "generally unforgiving of the divided loyalties inherent in the effort to combine childraising with working." They tend to be "unsupportive" of anything that does not focus on providing "maximum performance." Such pressures were repeatedly reported in my numerous interviews with younger Singaporeans. "People are consumed by their work," one young Singaporean told me. "There's a lack of time. You would expect nature will take care of this, but it doesn't."[132]

To reverse this pattern, companies, as well as the public sector, need to explore ways to extend flexibility in the workplace and find ways, particularly for mothers, to reenter "the fast track," if they so desire, as their children mature.[133] Some efforts in this direction have been made in Scandinavia, with some marginal impact on fertility rates.[134]

What may be even more necessary is a major reevaluation of values. Debbie Soon at the Institute of Policy Studies in Singapore suggests that societies need to reevaluate what constitutes success in order to gain an understanding that "a healthy family life is just as much a form of success as is good standing in one's chosen profession."[135]

Certainly an adjustment is needed if cities hope to develop future generations of urbanites. Demographer Wolfgang Lutz notes that Singapore, despite its host of pro-natalist policies, works at cross-purposes to these policies by insisting on long hours for employees, many of whom are women. Singapore's labor force participation rate for women is almost 60 percent. "In Singapore," Lutz points out, "women work an average of 53 hours a week. Of course they are not going to have children. They don't have the time."[136]

WHERE WILL FUTURE URBANITES COME FROM?
ELSEWHERE

Once fertility rates reach extremely low levels, Lutz notes, this trend could prove irreversible. In his estimation, the shift toward an increasingly childless society creates "self-reinforcing mechanisms" that help make single, childless, or one-child households increasingly predominant.[137] Lutz describes this as the closing of the "low fertility trap"— that is, the tendency for countries with very low birth rates to remain well below the replacement rate, even in the face of government efforts to increase marriage and birth rates.

If we continue to support high-density development in urban areas, cities will have to depend on the transfer of people from the countryside, the suburban periphery, and in many cases, other countries in order to combat their declining birth rates. Newcomers, particularly those from developing countries, are far more likely to have children than the existing urban populations in most high-income countries. This seems likely to be the one way these urban areas can maintain their economies and social programs and find the workforce to care for their aging populations.[138]

This is particularly true for cities in the United Kingdom, the United States, Canada,[139] Australia, Singapore, and to some extent, Germany. According to the United Nations, virtually all population growth in developed countries will be from migrants.[140]

Even economically distressed Italy has felt compelled to play the immigration arbitrage game and has started importing young workers from much poorer southeastern Europe. The Milan area, for example, added 634,000 foreign residents from 2000 to 2008, with the largest share coming from Romania, followed by Albania. Over that period, more than 80 percent of growth in Italy's Lombardy region came as a result of international immigration. With so few young native-born Italians, schools have been closed in many cities, and in others, half or more of the students come from other countries. "In Italy, they don't have children," observed one housecleaner from Ecuador. "They have dogs and cats."[141]

But migration may not be sufficient, or even feasible, as a long-term solution to a childless city. American demographer Phillip Longman compares Europe to a woman whose "biological clock is running down. It is not too late to adopt more children, but they won't look like her."[142] Germany, with its ultra-low birth rate and rapidly aging population, epitomizes the stakes of migration arbitrage. By 2025, Germany's economy will need 6 million additional workers, or an annual 200,000 new migrants, to keep its economic engine humming, according to government estimates.[143] The rationale for mass migration seems inexorable. Germany is unlikely to meet this demand internally due to a shrinking workforce.[144] Additionally, many migrants to Germany do not have the skills to participate in that country's high-end economy. They also threaten to inject many of their homelands' maladies, ranging from jihadism to street crime, into what have been fairly prosperous and peaceful places.

Indeed, as Europe's Muslim population continues to surge rapidly, particularly in northern Europe,[145] it poses a severe threat to old European values—not just religious but also civil. As the *Daily Mail*'s Peter Hitchens points out, when in relatively small numbers, immigrants to Anglophone countries generally adjust to the prevailing pluralistic values of these societies. Now, he suggests, Europe faces an "unstoppable demographic revolution in which Europe (including, alas, our islands) merges its culture and its economy with North Africa and the Middle East. If we let this happen, Europe would lose almost all the things that make others want to live there."[146]

In the process, the cultural life of the continent likely becomes more "multicultural" and global but ever less European. Its lodestar is no longer its own past or its common European dream but rather a future determined by affairs elsewhere and by people who, in many cases, are largely indifferent toward the continent's historical legacy and may even wish to demolish it.

This will occur more rapidly now even though, ironically, it was Germany's Chancellor Angela Merkel who, in 2010, proclaimed "multiculturalism had utterly failed" in her country.[147] Now, Merkel has become the chief enabler of a massive shift in population that can only—given the weakness of Europe's own culture—be essentially merged with, and even undermined by that of the Islamic world. Given the extremely secular nature of Europe's cities, the cultural conflict between them and a more religious and traditional population seems likely to fester in the decades ahead.

Ultimately, migration from abroad cannot fundamentally change a country's demographic trajectory. Indeed, even factoring in continued immigration, the European workforce is expected to decrease by as much as 10 to 25 percent by 2020, with much of the decline expected in northern and eastern Europe.[148] In some cases, the more prosperous parts of Europe are exhausting the fertility of the countries along its periphery. Eastern Europe, a major source of immigration to the more prosperous parts of the European Union, has lost so many young people that, in the future, these countries will have few left to offer their European partners. Non-EU Eastern Europe, excluding Russia, is expected to experience losses of 19 percent by 2050 and 34 percent by 2100. By 2050, Bulgaria could well lose 27 percent of its population, while Latvia, Lithuania, and Romania may see a drop of over 10 percent.[149] Estonia could see a reduction of more than half its current population by midcentury.[150]

The same patterns can be seen in Russia, another source of new migrants to European and North American cities. By 2050, Russia's population could fall from 2010's 142 million to as low as 126 million. President Vladimir Putin's regime has taken bold steps to reverse the issue, but it may be too late, according to some demographers.[151]

In the long run, slowing demographic growth also will affect migration from other developing countries that have traditionally sent workers to Europe, Australia, and North America. Tunisia, Morocco, and Turkey already are experiencing massive reductions in their birth rates.[152]

So, too, is Mexico, which has experienced a radical reduction in both its birth rate and its population growth rate. This has already helped slow Mexican immigration to the United States to levels about 33 percent less than those seen in 2005.[153] In Mexico, the low birth rate and declining rate of new family formation has inspired a joke in Mexico City about how Jesus was actually a Mexican. Why? "Because he lived at home till he was 33, he never had a job, his mother believed he was God, and he believed she was a virgin."[154]

TOWARD A BRAVE NEW URBAN WORLD?

In his brilliant and insightful 1932 novel, *Brave New World,* Aldous Huxley describes a future post-familial society where the words "mother" and "parent" are described as "smut," almost too embarrassing to mention.[155] Instead, society is made up entirely of unrelated—in terms of parentage—individuals, where over-strong attachment to others is discouraged in favor of a society built around the three principles of "community, identity, and stability."[156]

Today, we still stand far from Huxley's post-familial dystopia, but we seem to be moving—particularly in the high-income world—toward a new reality in which the concept of the family is supplanted by a new vision that embraces the lone individual, the networked single, and the childless couple. In this emerging world, as in *Brave New World,* pragmatic choices are made either by the individual to fulfill his or her particular needs or through what British writer Martin Earnshaw calls the "therapeutic intervention" of the state.[157]

Clearly, countries and cities cannot continue on this path without serious long-term ramifications. How can we change this trend and avoid such outcomes? It's unlikely we can return to any imagined "golden age" of traditional arrangements, particularly in urban centers. Instead, if it is to adapt even somewhat successfully, the family will continue to morph, becoming more egalitarian in its approach to child-rearing and, above all, more flexible, with perhaps an expanded role for the growing ranks of childless aunts and uncles.[158]

Ultimately, to thrive and expand in the coming decades, urbanism needs to restore the central role of families. To flourish in the long run, cities need to be more than "entertainment machines" or dense receptacles for those who wish to reduce their carbon footprint.[159] Cities are about people and about creating conditions for upward mobility, but they are also about the growth and development of the next generation. This means we need to place greater emphasis not on dense downtowns but rather on those remaining residential districts—like Ditmas Park and Flatbush—that can still accommodate families in areas not far removed from the historic urban center.

To be sure, any move to restore familialism cannot succeed by attempting to "turn back the clock" to the 1950s, as some social conservatives wish, or to some other idealized time.[160] Based on current trends, it's clear that globalization, urbanization, the ascendancy of women, longer life spans, and changes in traditional sexual relations will transform attitudes toward childraising. Ultimately a pro-family policy does not—and cannot—abandon the social gains made by women over the past half century. But there needs to be some accommodation for childraising, even if it takes place in more traditional or novel forms.

In the end, cities with few children and families will prove fundamentally unsustainable, deprived of a base from which they can draw new workers and consumers, as well as critical sources of both parental motivation and youthful innovation. In the coming decades, successful urban areas will be those that provide not only the vibrant districts that attract the young but also those, usually less dense, places that can help preserve the family's place, not as the exclusive unit in society but as one uniquely indispensable for the ages.

CHAPTER 6

The Case for Dispersion

■ ■ ■ ■

Cinco Ranch rises out of the flat Texas prairie 31 miles west of Houston. Formerly a cattle ranch, the development started in 1991 and now consists of several housing tracts, parks, and the town center.¹ It accommodates some 18,000 mostly middle-income people. Between 2000 and 2010, its population grew 63 percent.²

Bounded by the Grand Parkway that loops around the region's massive 1,700-square-mile urban footprint, the development stretches over 8,100 acres. The tracts range from small townhomes costing about $200,000 to what some might call McMansions that go for several times more. Nearly 60 percent of local residents who have moved there since 2014—over 1,100 households—are married couples with children, while less than 10 percent are single. "It's a pretty family-centric area," notes Ted Nelson, regional president of the central states for Cinco Ranch's primary developer, Newland Real Estate Group.

To some critics, Cinco Ranch—and other developments around Houston like Bridgeland, Sienna Plantation, The Woodlands, and Sugar Land—represents everything that is bad about suburban "sprawl," with leapfrogging development that swallows rural lands and leaves inner-city communities behind.³ The Grand Parkway, which will connect the community with the giant new Exxon campus rising to the north, has similarly been widely denounced as spurring "sprawling land development" that could hurt both the environment and the core city.⁴ Houston may be a uniquely "self-organizing city," in the words of Rice University's Lars Lerup, but this reality is deeply offensive to many planners and retro-urbanists.[5]

Yet to many residents of this burgeoning community, Cinco Ranch represents something else: an opportunity to enjoy the American dream with good schools, nice parks and a thriving town center. The area has a large nature preserve and even a "beach club" built around the pool.[6] Many find that Cinco gives them the sense of belonging and community that has historically been ascribed to the diverse, familial Manhattan neighborhoods described by Jane Jacobs, although she would no doubt be horrified by the comparison.

This form of development does face challenges if new families do not arrive to replace older ones or if few existing residents stay after their children leave. Changing demographics place a burden on these developments far different from that faced by communities built during the baby boom era and periods of more rapid population growth. These peripheral communities will need to offer more to their residents, particularly if they hope to keep them after their children have grown up.

One response to these challenges lies in making these places more culturally attractive. This has included building new town centers, entertainment venues, and shared open spaces, reducing the need to commute to the urban core for most recreational needs.[7] At the same time, as minorities have increasingly moved to the suburbs, many new communities have benefited from drawing on a more ethnically diverse population than previous suburban waves.[8] Roughly 40 percent of the area's residents are non-Hispanic white; one in five is foreign born, well above the Texas average. Barely half of the students at the local high school are Caucasian, and Asian students have been the fastest-growing group in recent years as their parents have been attracted to the area's high-performing schools.[9]

But much of the appeal also grows from a sense of living in a village amid an enormous urban area. "We have lived other places since we came to America 10 years ago," notes Priya Kothari, who moved to Cinco with her husband and two children in 2013. "We lived in apartments elsewhere in big cities, but here we found a place where we could put our roots down. It has a community feel. You walk around and see all the families. There's room for bikes—that's great for the kids."

In Houston, suburban growth is not taking place at the expense of inner ring density. The area has, in fact, enjoyed one of the strongest booms in core residential growth in the country. Yet this has come even as the city's outer suburban ring beyond Beltway 8 has also grown, last year attracting roughly 80 percent of all new homebuyers.[10]

Many residents have come from the inner rings of Houston, which like many urban cores have become both denser and less child-oriented in recent decades. These onetime inner-core residents may have enjoyed the pace and excitement closer to downtown or the Galleria edge city, but as they sought to settle down with their families, Cinco beckoned. "You look for a house when you have kids, and then you stay because this is what works for you," says Doug Bazzy, an IT consultant who moved to Cinco 14 years ago with his wife and three kids. "This is something that we were looking for, a more neighborly community—and that's why we are staying even as our kids leave the nest."

THE EVOLUTION OF TWO GEOGRAPHIES

In the past, the wealthy often headed to the countryside, creating elite communities on the periphery of great cities.[11] But as early as the 19th century, suburbs started to burgeon around the country's cities.[12] London, one observer noted in 1843, "surrounds itself with suburb clinging to suburb, like onions fifty to a rope."[13] But for Londoners, the middle-class aspiration was frequently to purchase a cottage with a small yard farther out in the periphery.

This shift to the periphery has been seen throughout the world. The classic Parisian dream may be to live comfortably in the middle of the city, leaving the surrounding *banlieues* dominated by grim working-class blocks of mostly dense apartments.[14] But since that time, outer Paris has increasingly embraced the detached house as well, predominantly in its *grande couronne* (second-ring suburbs), where most of the population lives, beyond the hardscrabble *petite couronne* (first-ring suburbs) just outside the city borders.[15]

This shift to the periphery was driven by many factors—cost, space, the desire for privacy, and an evolving divergence in social functions between the inner core and the widening periphery. By the turn of the last century, H. G. Wells could foresee this new division in the urban landscape, defined in large part by a divide between families with children and others:

> *The world of the coming time will still have its Homes, its real Mothers, the custodians of the human succession, and its cared-for children, the inheritors of the future, but in addition to this Home world, frothing tumultuously over and amidst these stable rocks, there will be an enormous complex of establishments, and hotels, and sterile households, and flats, and all the elaborate furnishing and appliances of a luxurious extinction.*[16]

Wells's notion of "luxurious extinction" is already upon us in many cities, particularly those in the "glamour zone" of global cities. As we've seen, residents of these cities generally tend to have considerably fewer children and are less likely to be married than those in less dense places where families, including married couples, predominate. Family households account for over 80 percent of the total in Cinco,[17] compared to 61.5 percent in the city of Houston, less than 60 percent in New York City,[18] and barely 43 percent in San Francisco.[19]

Wells proved remarkably prescient about the likely evolution of urban cores. These, he suggested, would evolve into "essentially a bazaar, a great gallery of shops and places of concourse and rendezvous." They would remain central to some industries, "an old nucleus" ideally suited to some specialized economic functions, and they would continue to attract portions of the upper classes.[20] Each of these descriptions closely resembles the dense cores of the great urban centers we've explored in previous chapters, notably New York, London, Chicago, and Tokyo.

However, the pattern of "luxurious extinction" can be found even in smaller, gentrifying, less expensive cities. In New Orleans, the movement of hipsters into old neighborhoods, notes geographer Richard Campanella, has created a dearth of families in its wake. Ten years ago, Campanella's increasingly "creative-class" neighborhood of Bywater was very family-oriented. Now, he notes, it's what he calls "a kiddie wilderness." In 2000, he found, 968 youngsters lived in the district, but only 285 lived there in 2010. When his son was born in 2012, he was the very first post-Katrina birth on his street, the sole child on a block that had 11 children when Campanella first arrived there from Mississippi in 2000.[21]

To be sure, suburban-style living has never been for everyone, and the denser, urban model will continue to exercise a powerful appeal, as we've already seen. The mystery novelist Raymond Chandler disdained suburban life with an "eight-room house, two cars in the garage, chicken every Sunday and the *Reader's Digest* on the living room table, the wife with a cast-iron permanent and me with a brain like a sack of Portland cement. You take it, friend. I'll take the big sordid dirty crooked city."[22]

But for many people, suburban living appeals to them at a certain stage of life, particularly as they age, start families, or seek a quieter life. Sociologist Herbert Gans, writing in the 1960s, identified the distinction seen by Wells between family-centric suburbanites and those inner-city dwellers he identified as "the rich, the poor, the non-white as well as the unmarried and childless middle class."[23] These divides still exist today, even as changing demographics have transformed suburbs into ever more diverse places by race, class, and marital status.

THE WAR AGAINST SUBURBIA

Suburban growth has long drawn the wrath of the intelligentsia, planners, and central city business interests. In his 1905 book, *The Suburbans*, the British poet T. W. H. Crosland launched a vitriolic attack on the "low and inferior species," the "soulless" class of "clerks" spreading into the new, comfortable houses in the suburbs, mucking up the aesthetics of the British countryside.[24] The gentlemen at *The (London) Times* were certainly less than impressed; suburban growth was exploding around London, which they feared would "produce a district of appalling monotony, ugliness and dullness."[25]

Much of the initial rejection of suburbia came from the right although in recent decades the criticism has become more widespread
among the progressive left. Some British Tories disparaged the suburbs
as ruinous to their bucolic settings, a tendency that exists to this day.
Even today, old-style conservatives like author-philosopher Roger Scruton openly detest suburbia and favor instead European-style planning
laws that Scruton claims force people to live "side by side." Densely
packed Paris and London, he points out, are clearly better places to
visit for well-heeled tourists than Atlanta, Houston, or Dallas.[26]

Left-leaning British intellectuals have long shared this disdain. In
1939, George Orwell described the new suburbs as "a prison with the
cells all in a row . . . semi-detached torture chambers." His colleague,
the editor Cyril Connolly, was not much kinder, describing middle-class
suburbs as "incubators of apathy and delirium."[27]

American intellectuals, for the most part, were generally no more
well inclined toward suburbs. Some suggested that suburbanites were
fundamentally deluded about their choice of residence. Architect Peter
Blake declared in God's Own Junkyard that the suburban pattern developing in the United States was "making life there only slightly less
tolerable than on tenement streets."[28] In reviewing the literature about
suburbia, urban historian Becky Nicolaides suggests that whatever
their other differences, intellectuals generally agreed about suburbia:
"the common denominator was hell."[29] Many who were most pas-
sionately committed to the city felt compelled to join the assault. Jane
Jacobs famously detested not only suburban Los Angeles but also the
bedroom communities of Queens and Staten Island. The 1960s social
critic William Whyte denounced suburbia as hopelessly stultifying and
boldly predicted, as many do today, that people would tire of such dull
places and eventually drift back toward the city core.[30]

Much like today, suburbs also elicited hostility from those whose
interests were most economically tied to the center city. In 1933, the
International Congresses of Modern Architecture—a group who made
their living off city growth—declared that the suburb was "a kind of
scum churning against the walls of the city" and that it was "one of the
greatest evils of the century."[31] In 1955, Manhattan developer William

Zeckendorf—who hired, among others, Le Corbusier to design his projects—joined the critics. Having profited greatly from high-density development in Manhattan, he even called for tight restrictions on fluid suburban development, which he claimed was dangerous and "against the nature of man."[32]

CLASS WARFARE IN SUBURBIA

Class has long played a major role in the assault on suburbs. Affluent urbanists often describe the suburbs as both environmentally irresponsible as well as culturally regressive. In 2014, Australian progressive columnist Elizabeth Farrelly haughtily described the suburbs as being "about boredom, and obviously some people like being bored and plain and predictable, I'm happy for them . . . even if their suburbs are destroying the world."[33]

The cultural and aesthetic aspect of anti-suburbanism is rarely far from the surface. One leading scholar, Paul Knox, has denounced suburbia as "vulgaria," a kind of "pathological condition of the American metropolis."[34] Another academic critic of suburbia attacked suburban sprawl in Southern California but advocated strong protections for the fashionable Connecticut countryside, where conflict between old money and new suburbanites has been going on for at least the last half century. "Magically," commented Arizona State University's Andrew Kirby, "sprawl becomes just plain wrong but the preservation of expensive enclaves just plain right."[35]

This combination of environmental zeal and cultural revulsion has produced increasingly strident efforts to limit, or stamp out, suburban development in several countries, such as Australia, the United Kingdom, and parts of the United States. Queensland University of Technology's Terry Flew[36] describes "a recurring tension between the desire of large sections of the population to own their own home (the fabled quarter-acre block) in the suburbs, and the condemnation of suburban life from an assortment of intellectuals, political radicals and cultural critics."[37]

Ninety percent of Australia's urban population lives more than three miles from the city center, but their lifestyle is largely derided by those, often wealthier, who can afford to live closer to the core. This, notes urban affairs writer Alan Davies,[38] "invite[s] the suspicion they're [the critics] implicitly class-based, whether consciously so or otherwise."[39] This also reflects distinctly different economic interests. Generally, restrictive "anti-sprawl" policies benefit the rich since such policies tend to make properties, whether in the city or the country, more expensive—something not helpful to the middle and lower classes.[40]

A similar class dynamic exists in the United States. Many of the expensive environmental fixes, such as solar power, expansion of open space, and other "sustainable" engineering, work well for "those who can afford them," notes Stony Brook University's Charles Sellers. They can then "glibly excoriate the rest of American society for environmental profligacy, but with utter complacency toward the advantages that enable their own 'greenness.'"[41]

ASPIRATIONAL GEOGRAPHY: THE BRITISH EXPERIENCE

Under a regime hostile to suburban growth, the middle and working classes would have little alternative but to live in the denser and somewhat more hierarchical world that existed before the Industrial Revolution. Leading retro-urbanists like Britain's Richard Rogers speak directly to the ideal of "medieval" cities and towns. An advocate of ultra-high densities, Rogers views suburban communities as aesthetically unpleasant and socially destructive. "Do you really want to be living in the suburbs with five cats, four dogs, a cabbage patch and five rooms?" he asks.[42]

His vision for the future is built around what the British call "cramming," increasing density by such means as converting houses to flats as well as building on gardens. With this approach, planners and their allied developers seek to overturn the aspirations of the vast majority who live in suburban settings and have done so in most high-income countries throughout the last half century.[43] Many modern progressives support this approach, but this marks a major departure from what used to fit comfortably with older social democratic aspirations. The influential London socialist Herbert Morrison, for example, embraced the very opposite of the density gospel when he embraced the slogan "Up with the houses! Down with the slums!"[44]

In the Britain of the 1930s, this meant not only new council flats built on the periphery but also more small- and medium-sized houses for purchase. Of the nearly 4 million houses built in England between 1919 and 1939, the vast majority—nearly 3 million—were for sale. The number of owner-occupied houses in Britain soared from around 750,000 in the early 1920s to more than 3.25 million by 1938. Not only were British middle- and working-class people escaping the crowded, and often unsanitary, conditions in the inner city but they were also becoming an increasingly landed class.[45]

After the war, this trend accelerated. As per capita income in Britain jumped a remarkable 33 percent between 1948 and 1960,[46] more British families had the wherewithal to move to places such as Milton Keynes, a sprawling new town to the northwest of London where even a household of modest means could find a place. Historian Mark Clapson notes that the reasons for Milton Keynes's success—safety, privacy, and a spot of lawn—"would have occurred to an estate agent if not to urban pundits, planners, or those who could afford to live well closer to London's heart."

Clapson adds that Milton Keynes, now home to over 160,000 people, delivered to a broad swath of professionals, skilled workers, and even manual laborers a preferred "Englishness" of tidy homes and greenery that was once the exclusive province of the upper class and their dependent peasantry.[47] "Was there ever such a stealthy social revolution as the rise of this semi-detached suburbia?" asks English filmmaker John Boorman in his memoir, *Adventures of a Suburban Boy.*[48]

THE AMERICAN EXPERIENCE

Suburban development in the United States reflected a similar aspiration toward lower-density development and homeownership. By the 1870s, prominent Philadelphia families were already escaping the crowded streets of William Penn's old city for the leafier districts outside city boundaries. The ensuing development of suburban railroads carried much of the city's business and professional establishments away from the central Rittenhouse Square area to residences in various Main Line communities along the train routes.[49]

By the 1920s, suburbs nationwide were growing at twice the rate of cities and increasingly accommodating middle- and even working-class families, including many from the depopulating countryside.[50] As in Britain, the shift to the suburbs reflected the cherished aspirations of the middle class. Such desires may have seemed misplaced or even tawdry to critics, but they seemed self-evident to many, including one Chicago meat cutter who, in the 1920s, exchanged a small apartment on the second floor of an apartment house for "a six-room house with a big yard" in the far western suburbs.[51] For such people, the suburban option represented, in architecture historian Robert Bruegmann's words, "a revolution in expectations."[52]

As in Britain, many progressives supported this movement. During the Great Depression, New Dealers encouraged both dispersion of population and increased homeownership. Initially, suburban development was warmly embraced by liberals who supported the old Jeffersonian ideal of dispersed property ownership. "A nation of homeowners," President Franklin D. Roosevelt believed, "of people who own a real share in their land, is unconquerable."[53]

That generation of progressive politicians wanted more Americans to own homes—and they encouraged this through various legislative actions, including the creation of the Federal Housing Administration and the Federal National Mortgage Association, or Fannie Mae. Particularly effective was the 1944 GI Bill of Rights, which provided low-interest loans with only nominal down payments to returning veterans, who were then returning to a country where 98 percent of American cities were experiencing significant housing shortages. Almost half of suburban housing, notes historian Alan Wolfe, depended on some form of federal financing.[54]

In recent decades, sadly, many progressives have become increasingly strident in their opposition to suburbia, some of them even suggesting that suburbs reflect something of a dangerous addiction foisted on America by the likes of Ronald Reagan.[55]

Yet in some ways, this hostility runs against a population that, for the most part, lives a suburban lifestyle and overwhelmingly prefers single-family houses.[56] The massive postwar shift to suburbia is now well over a half century old. In 1950, only half of the residents of to-day's major metropolitan areas lived in suburbs,[57] but since that time, 90 percent of metropolitan growth has been in the suburbs.[58]

The move to suburbia in America has been, as in Britain, closely aligned with the rapid expansion of homeownership. By 1962, over 60 percent of Americans owned their own homes, an increase from the 41 percent who did before World War II. The increase in homeownership between 1946 and 1956, notes author Stephanie Coontz, was greater than that achieved in the preceding century and a half.[59]

Homeownership was widely seen as a critical factor in America's experiment with self-government. As sociologist Robert Lynd notes, "the characteristic thing about democracy is its diffusion of power among the people."[60] This movement continued, notes economist Ed Glaeser, despite widespread suggestions that "a New Urbanism"— associated with higher-density housing and greater transit use—was generally gaining at the expense of suburbs.[61] Indeed, before the 2008 financial crisis, the homeownership trend actually accelerated. According to the 2010 census, covering the decade from 2000, inner cores gained 206,000 residents, reversing years of losses. However, this downtown growth was more than negated by a loss of 272,000 residents living between two and five miles from the urban core. In contrast, the communities 10 miles and more from the core gained approximately 15 million people.[62]

AFTER THE FALL: HAS EVERYTHING CHANGED?

The Great Recession, which saw millions of homes foreclosed upon, many in suburbia, suggested to some that the mass movement to the periphery was ending.[63] As homeownership rates dropped from histor-ical highs during the Great Recession, some, like American economist Paul Krugman, envisioned a historical shift from an age of owning a home to an age of renting an apartment, which was more likely to occur close to the city core.[64] Urban pundit Richard Florida saw the emergence of a new paradigm that would toss out not only the "subur-ban myth" of homeownership itself but also its "long-privileged place" at the center of the US economy.[65]

To be sure, homeownership dropped during the recession, as it had during the Great Depression. Yet the home values in suburbs around the country were not the only victims of the bubble; condo projects, including those in major cities such as Los Angeles, San Diego, Chicago, Atlanta, Miami, and Vancouver, also suffered major declines, with many residents forced into rentals.[66]

These reversals did not mean the rebound of the urban core was over any more than it suggested the death of suburbs, but the latter notion gained great currency in the media. Jay Bookman, an outspoken New Urbanist and *Atlanta Journal-Constitution* columnist, pronounced in 2009 that "the phenomenon of sprawl has passed into history," becoming the equivalent of "roadkill" doomed by changing economics and demographics.[67] Another account, this one in the *Daily Mail*, suggested that the suburbs would end up as the "ghost towns" of the future as people departed suburbia for downtown.[68] How to carve up the suburban carcass was widely discussed, with some envisioning that suburban three-car garages would be "subdivided into rental units with streetfront cafés, shops and other local businesses," while abandoned pools would become skateboard parks.[69]

In their passion to promote the "renaissance of the traditional city" and the inevitable decline of suburbia, retro-urbanists seem to have forgotten one major thing: the preferences of most people in high-income countries, particularly the United States, which include lower-density living.[70] In fact, after a brief period of slightly more rapid urban growth immediately following the recession, US suburban growth rates again began to surpass those of urban cores. By 2014, growth was faster not only in traditional suburbs but also in the exurban areas—broadly predicted to be the most doomed by demographic trends and high energy costs.[71] At the same time, the fastest *city* growth, notes Trulia economist Jed Kolko, was largely taking place in the most "suburbanized" places like Phoenix, San Antonio, and San Diego.[72]

Further, the single-family house did not lose its appeal in the last decade, as was commonly suggested. Between 2000 and 2011, detached houses accounted for 83 percent of the net additions to the US occupied housing stock. Within the major metropolitan areas, counties that gained domestic migrants had a larger detached housing share (60 percent) than those that lost domestic migrants (51 percent). In the last decade, detached housing has grown far faster than multiunit housing and at a greater pace than in previous decades. In the 2000s, 75 percent of building permits were for detached housing, nearly equal to the 1990s rate of 77 percent. This is more than one-fifth higher than the detached housing shares in the 1960s, 1970s, and 1980s—eras associated with rapid suburban growth.[73]

This also reflects Americans' continued attachment to homeownership. Whereas roughly 40 percent of urban-core residents own their homes, over three-fifths of residents in older suburbs and more than seven in ten residents in newer suburbs and exurbs are homeowners.[74] No, this attachment isn't fading, as some have insisted. A 2012 study by the Joint Center for Housing Studies at Harvard found "little evidence to suggest that individuals' preferences for owning versus renting a home have been fundamentally altered by their exposure to house price declines and loan delinquency rates, or by knowing others in their neighborhood who have defaulted on their mortgages."[75] A 2013 survey by the University of Connecticut found that 76 percent of those polled believe that being able to own your own home is necessary to be considered middle class.[76]

THE GLOBALIZATION OF DISPERSION

Suburbanization is now a global phenomenon. In Tokyo, like other large cities, the movement to the suburbs began with the expansion of commuter railways, most of which were privately owned. Some Tokyo suburbs were designed, at least in part, with notions borrowed from planner Ebenezer Howard's "garden cities" concept. Most of the rapid development, however, took place in less dense "suburban development areas" within 50 kilometers (30 miles) of Tokyo station.

This movement outward reflects the extreme costs of housing and office space closer to the core of Japan's many cities, particularly Tokyo. Since 1960, over 90 percent of all growth in Tokyo and Osaka-Kobe-Kyoto has been on the periphery; 83 percent of the population increase in Nagoya has also been suburban.[77] Long a nation with a strong feudal tradition, Japan saw its "homeowner society" largely forged in the suburban tracts outside its great cities after World War II, and by 2013, suburbia accounted for almost 62 percent of all households.[78]

Nowhere has the suburban allure been more pervasive than in Australia, where 69 percent own their own homes.[79] Indeed, despite strong planning policies designed to increase density, Australia's largest cities became significantly *less* dense between 2006 and 2011, with particularly strong growth in newer suburbs.[80] Australians continue to seek out homes—upward of 90 percent of Australians surveyed in a recent poll felt it was worthwhile to buy a house. Not surprisingly, this was particularly marked among people with children.[81]

Similarly, nearly two-thirds of Canadians live on the outskirts of core cities, and 69 percent own their own homes.[82] Roughly 95 percent of growth in the country's 33 metropolitan areas took place in the suburbs and exurbs between 2006 and 2011,[83] something rarely discussed among the country's city-centric planners and development community. "There's a heck of a lot more happening on the edge," notes David Gordon, a dedicated but data-driven New Urbanist and director of the School of Urban and Regional Planning at Queen's University in Kingston, Ontario. "You just don't notice it."[84]

In Europe, oft-cited as a paragon of dense development, lower densities continue to attract the bulk of domestic migrants, even as newcomers flock to the urban cores.[85] Since the end of World War II, suburban growth has outpaced growth in such venerable cities as Antwerp, Copenhagen, Hamburg, Milan, Paris, and Rotterdam; in many cases, urban density has dropped in these metropolitan areas as they become ever more suburbanized.[86]

Overall, a survey of 24 large European urban areas found that between 1971 and 2011, suburban areas grew by over 9.7 million people, while the core areas lost 600,000 people. In 1971, European cores and suburbs had about the same population. By 2011, the suburbs had grown to have 60 percent more residents. Virtually every major European metropolitan area—37 out of 40 large ones—grew more in their suburban peripheries than in their cores. Some of the disparities were large. In Madrid, the suburbs grew 450 percent between 1971 and 2011, compared to only 5 percent in the core. In Toulouse, the suburbs grew 327 percent, while the core edged up only 20 percent. In Zurich,[87] the suburbs grew 186 percent, compared to the core *decline* of 12 percent.[88]

At the same time, some notable cores have reversed their previous loss patterns in recent years, though most remain well below their much earlier peaks. The *ville de* Paris has regained little more than 100,000 of its 800,000 lost since 1921. This is true not only in smaller cities but also in ones with vibrant cores, such as London and Amsterdam, as well as Paris, where the core lost 250,000 residents over 40 years, but the suburban rings gained 2.5 million residents. Inner London[89] has regained much more—800,000 residents—but still needs another 1.3 million to restore its 1901 peak. (Outer London is so suburban that it provided much of the ammunition for the British anti-suburban movement.) Others cores, like Stockholm and Madrid, have risen above previous peaks.[90]

What this suggests is that when they focus on promoting density, planners in Europe, the United States, and Australia are working against the preferences of most consumers. In Sweden, planners have spent a half century pushing this model on their citizens but with little success, as 90 percent of Swedes prefer single-family homes.[91]

Dispersion is also rising in developing countries. In the last decade, 99 percent of Beijing's growth took place outside the historic core; in Shanghai, the central area actually *lost* population. Between 2000 and 2010, only 1 percent of Beijing's total population increase was in the inner city.[92] China is clearly urbanizing but in a highly dispersed, albeit still dense, manner.[93]

In China today, there are even attempts to duplicate American, Canadian, and Australian suburbs, with names such as Orange County, Vancouver Forest, Sydney Coast, or Yosemite.[94] A trend toward the periphery also can be seen in virtually all of the world's 34 megacities, with some of the largest declines reported in the fast-growing conurbations of the developing world.[95] This trend is the organic process by which cities have grown from virtually the beginning of time: unless forced elsewhere, growth tends to occur principally on the periphery.[96]

NEWCOMERS TO AMERICA'S "UNIVERSAL ASPIRATION"

None of this suggests that suburbs have not changed. Over time, suburbs have become more ethnically diverse, which is in sharp contrast to the past. As late as 1970, some 95 percent of US suburbanites were white.[97] Levittown, the quintessential middle-income suburb, excluded African Americans in its early years.[98] Government policies often supported such discrimination, notes historian Kenneth Jackson, and later, the integration of city schools hastened the exodus of whites from cities.[99]

In recent decades, the old notion of "white" suburbia—one of the legitimate bases for suburban criticism—has become increasingly archaic. Between 1970 and 1995, the number of African Americans in suburbia grew from 3.6 million to over 10 million. Indeed, the last two decades of the 20th century showed that more African Americans moved into the suburbs than in the previous 70 years, a trend that has continued unabated.[100] Brookings Institution research indicates that in the 100 largest US metropolitan areas, more than one-half of the African American population lives in the suburbs. This movement was particularly marked among families with children; the number of black children living in cities like New York, Oakland, Atlanta, and Los Angeles dropped precipitously as families sought out safer streets, better schools, and more affordable space.[101]

Overall, notes a Harvard research paper, suburbs now are generally far less segregated than traditional, denser urban areas.[102] This is driven not only by African Americans but also by the country's fastest-growing minority groups, Asians and Latinos. Roughly 60 percent of Hispanics and Asians, notes Brookings, already live in suburbs.[103] Between 2000 and 2012, the Asian population in suburban areas of the nation's 52 biggest metro areas grew 66.2 percent, while that in the core cities expanded by only 34.9 percent.[104] Of the top 20 cities over 50,000 in terms of Asian population, all but two are suburbs.[105]

In some cases, this may reflect the growing popularity of certain elite cities, which has served to displace some minorities. As the National Urban League, a prominent American civil rights organization, points out, some cities that most epitomize urban revival—San Francisco, Chicago, and Minneapolis—also suffer the largest gaps between black and white incomes.[106] Notwithstanding the impassioned rhetoric about the blessings of diversity, the most thoroughgoing form of "ethnic cleansing" now occurs in the "hippest" urban zones, which increasingly consist of monotonic "white cities" with relatively low, and falling, minority populations.[107] For instance, San Francisco, Portland, and Seattle, though achingly politically correct in theory, are actually becoming whiter and less ethnically diverse, while the rest of the country, particularly suburbia, is diversifying.[108]

The overall trend toward dispersion has also been accelerated by the movement of immigrants. In the early 20th century, only one-third of Americans lived in cities, but 72 percent of immigrants did. In the last half century, that has changed radically.[109] Edgardo Contini, a prominent Los Angeles architect and planner, observed in the 1960s:

> *The suburban house is the idealization of every immigrant's dream—the vassal dream of his own castle. Europeans who come here are delighted by our suburbs, even by the worst sprawl. Not to live in an apartment! It is a universal aspiration to own your own home.*[110]

Contini, for one, would not have been surprised that the fastest growth in immigrant populations now overwhelmingly takes place in the suburbs; between 2000 and 2013, suburbs accounted for three-quarters of the growth among newcomers.[111] More than 40 percent of non-citizen immigrants now move directly to suburbs.[112] For minorities, notes a study by Arizona State University geographer Deirdre Pfeiffer, the fastest integration into the middle class and American norms comes in the most disdained geography of all—the farthest-flung, newly minted suburbs. An examination of this phenomenon in Houston confirmed it there as well; a Rice University researcher found that minorities and lower-income residents did better in terms of education, income levels, and homeownership in newer "post-civil rights" suburbs like Katy (including Cinco Ranch) and Sugar Land.[113]

Suburbia, of course, faces many challenges—from the environment to demographic shifts—but more and more, a lack of diversity is not one of them. Indeed, in the decade ending in 2010, the percentage of suburbanites living in "traditional," predominantly white suburbs fell from 51 percent to 39 percent.[114] According to a University of Minnesota report,[115] in the 50 largest US metropolitan areas, 44 percent of residents live in racially and ethnically diverse suburbs, defined as being between 20 and 60 percent non-white.[116]

MULTIRACIAL SUBURBS IN OTHER COUNTRIES

Similar shifts have occurred in the United Kingdom, Canada, and Australia.[117] Immigrants continue to move out of British cities, notes Professor Philip Rees from the University of Leeds. As they seek out more housing space, minorities are moving from urban cores to the suburbs.[118] Some of the most integrated places in the United Kingdom are working-class suburbs and commuter towns such as Southend-on-Sea.[119] Overall, more than one in seven British suburban residents are classified as non-white, compared with the national average of less than one in twelve.[120]

The suburbs of Canada have also seen a significant movement of immigrants. Toronto, in particular, boasts an archipelago of multiethnic suburbs, notably Mississauga, Richmond Hill, and Markham. With more than 70 percent of its residents being "visible minorities," Markham is now widely considered the most diverse city in Canada. As in the United States, this trend has been accelerated by the rapid gentrification of the city's inner core, which has become both more expensive and denser as apartments have replaced the more preferred single-family house.[121]

Similar patterns can be found in Australia's major metropolitan regions. The western suburbs of Sydney, for example, are home to some of the country's most diverse suburbs, including Cabramatta, whose population is 87.7 percent non-English speaking. This is the highest non-English-speaking population of any urban area in Australia, followed by those in other Sydney suburbs, such as Bankstown and Canley Vale.[122] Like their Sydney counterparts, the suburbs of Melbourne now contain the most diverse populations in the metropolitan area. In the community of Sunshine, some 50 percent of the population was born outside Australia.[123] The largest share of immigrants in Australia's capital cities is found in largely suburban Perth, in the far west of the country, where over one-third of the population is foreign born.[124]

FROM WHITE BASTIONS TO THE "NEW SLUMS"?

In the past, suburbs were widely attacked, and rightfully so, for being racially "uniform."[125] But now that they have become more diverse, critics claim they are now becoming the "new slums," much like the poorer Paris *banlieues* and similarly poor areas around other European cities.[126] In the United States, the Brookings Institution's Christopher Leinberger suggests that the people headed to suburbs and especially exurbs will be poor, heavily minority families. Rather than stay in gentrifying cities, these people will be crowding into dilapidated former McMansions in the "suburban wastelands."[127]

It is true that, even in the United States, suburbs have experienced a rapid growth in poverty as some historically neglected populations have spilled into suburban areas, particularly longer-settled communities. These include the southern and eastern parts of Los Angeles, the northern periphery of St. Louis, or along the West Side of Chicago, closer to the urban core. Still, the average poverty rate in the historical core municipalities[128] in the 52 largest US metro areas, according to the last decennial census, was 24.1 percent, more than double the 11.4 percent rate in suburban areas. In addition, notes the 2010 census, many among the suburban "poor" are far from destitute or emblematic of multigenerational poverty but rather are people with smaller paychecks, often elderly residents with savings and paid-off mortgages.[129]

But overall, suburbs are not primary generators of inequality. According to University of Washington professor Richard Morrill's examination of 2012 American Community Survey data, less dense, suburban-dominated areas tend to have "generally less inequality" than the denser core cities. For example, in California, Riverside-San Bernardino is far less unequal than Los Angeles, and Sacramento is less unequal than San Francisco.[130] In the 51 metropolitan areas with a population greater than 1 million, notes demographer Wendell Cox, suburban areas are less unequal (as measured by the Gini coefficient)[131] than the core cities in 46 cases.[132] This is also the case in Australia, where suburbs still retain, as noted in a 2015 report, "a remarkable level of universality and equality."[133]

The suburban detached house—detested by many planners—remains the linchpin of middle-class economics. The house is easily the largest asset of most households, usually about two-thirds of a family's wealth.[134] Some on Wall Street have eagerly embraced the idea of a "rentership society," in which people are forced to rent their domicile from the investor class rather than own their own homes. But for the middle class, whatever their ethnicity, this would be a major setback, a return to conditions that existed before World War II, when it was largely the well off or those living in rural areas who owned their own homes.[135] On average, some 71 percent of Anglo households in the major metropolitan areas own their own homes, compared to only 43 percent for Latinos, 38 percent for African Americans, and 59 percent for Asians.[136] But the importance of property ownership extends well beyond race. A 2015 Massachusetts Institute of Technology report suggests that much of the reason for growing inequality in both Europe and America has been the rise of housing prices, which has made current homeowners wealthier but kept newcomers out of the market. Draconian attempts to limit or even eliminate suburban growth would guarantee that minorities, the next generation, and other people without inherited wealth will be hard-pressed to achieve upward mobility or even their parents' level of wealth.[137]

LIFE IN HELL

For almost a century, critics have painted the suburbs as a threat to social stability and cohesion. Historian Lewis Mumford saw "mass Suburbia" as lacking both the vibrancy of a city and the neighborliness of a small town. Although he had some sympathy for the ideal of the "garden city," he maintained that most suburbs grant their denizens only "an encapsulated life," in which each resident is a prisoner of his car, his home, and his isolation—so much so that "even the advantages of the primary neighborhood group disappear."[138]

More recently, John Norquist, a former Milwaukee mayor and leading New Urbanist, contended, as is often asserted, that people have "grown tired of the cul-de-sacs, isolation and sterility of edge cities."[139] In much the same way, New Urbanist guru Andrés Duany insists that largely suburbanized cities such as Phoenix are places "where civic life has almost ceased to exist," although this assertion is not backed up with any data.[140] The suburb, according to the Congress for the New Urbanism, "spells the end of authentic civic life."[141] The more hyperbolic social critic James Howard Kunstler goes even further. "The state-of-the-art mega-suburbs of recent decades," he suggests, "have produced horrendous levels of alienation, anomie, anxiety, and depression."[142]

New Urbanist theorists and "smart growth" advocates claim that by using more traditional architecture and increased densities, we can once again enjoy the kind of "meaningful community" that existed in the past but is supposedly unachievable in conventional suburbs.[143] Yet these claims that social comity can be created by architecture are somewhat exaggerated, to be charitable. New Urbanist Léon Krier, for example, claims that New Urbanism can bring together "diverse ages, races and incomes," citing Seaside and Celebration, Florida, as his examples. This is certainly an odd choice, given that most of the homes in these developments are upward of $600,000, and many are around $1 million.[144]

To be sure, some ideas proposed by New Urbanists—such as offering more options for walking and biking, as well as the need for town centers—can improve the quality of suburban communities. Yet rather than merely suggest improvements or prove the appeal of New Urbanist designs in the competitive marketplace, there is a growing tendency among New Urbanists to impose, as one critic puts it, "proscriptive policies and social restraint."[145] One strong smart growth advocate has even suggested siphoning tax revenues from suburbs to keep them from "cannibalizing" jobs and retail sales. There is a need to "curb sprawl," he says, in order to create the conditions needed for an idealized high-density community with heavy transit usage and main streets with housing over the shops.[146]

This sentiment is often couched in the notion that such sweeping adjustments would be welcome by people stuck in what seems to be, to many critics, a suburban dystopia. Some retro-urbanists even suggest that the desire for lower-density living is not a matter of preference but largely the product of government subsidies, which discounts the massive role the federal government has tried to play in urban core areas.[147] Yet to suggest that these places are dystopian and disliked by their denizens is misleading at best.

To be sure, with slowing population growth and delayed child-bearing, it is likely that in the United States, and other countries, rapid dispersion and ever-lower urban density may be slowing down, in part due to regulatory policies that result in escalating land costs. But it is absurd to suggest, as does author Roberta Brandes Gratz, that most Americans actually pine to live in the dense environments of places like Prague and away from their automobile-dominated communities. To be sure, Prague is a wonderful place to visit, but it's doubtful that most American families would like to live in the 753-square-foot apartments that accommodate the average household in that city.[148]

People generally don't move to suburbs because they love to drive but rather because they long for the more basic elements that affect everyday life—good schools, parks, safety, and more privacy. "I don't think most people buy into the generally negative image of suburbs most academics, most planners would articulate," notes McMaster University professor Richard Harris.[149]

The ultimate reality is that suburbs are generally far more cohesive than the critics suggest. Indeed, in 2006 when University of California at Irvine's Jan Brueckner and Ann Largey conducted 15,000 interviews across the country, they found that for every 10 percent drop in population density, the likelihood of people talking to their neighbors once a week increased 10 percent, regardless of race, income, education, marital status, or age.[150] These findings were confirmed in later surveys from the Pew Research Center, which found that suburbanites were considerably more satisfied with their communities than their urban core counterparts.[151]

Some retro-urbanists argue that the key to suburban social cohesion lies with homogeneity, although this is clearly an outdated idea. Urban author Paul Knox, a writer deeply hostile to "contemporary suburbia,"[152] suggests that suburbs may not be inspirational, but they do evidence "high levels of neighborliness." He also claims suburbanites tend to be more active in their communities, but unlike city residents, "they lack something in *feelings* of mutuality," although he offers no real support for this view.[153]

One common notion among planners and academics is that suburbs often lack the traditional public spaces they consider critical to social cohesion. American sociologist Melvin Webber, however, suggests that urban public spaces as they are commonly understood—piazzas, High Streets—do not necessarily make for cohesive communities. "The non-place urban realm," connected by a network of roads—such as in Milton Keynes—has managed to create a "civilized, urbane and connected place" with a strong "civic identity." In contrast, some places with highly developed public spaces, such as the Brazilian capital of Brasília, have much less social cohesion. "We should separate our desire for public space from our desire for community," notes British author Richard Williams. "They are only loosely connected, if at all."[154]

Perhaps the biggest reason for greater social cohesion in suburbs stems from the preponderance of homeowners. By their investment, owners tend to have a much greater financial stake in their neighborhoods than renters do.[155] One study found that 77 percent of homeowners had at some point voted in local elections, compared with 52 percent of renters. About 38 percent of homeowners knew the name of their local school board representative, compared with only 20 percent of renters. The study also showed a higher incidence of church attendance among homeowners.[156] A 2011 Georgetown University study suggests that homeownership also increases volunteering hours by 22 percent. These constitute building blocks for community, with greater grassroots participation.

The allure of suburban life remains powerful, even in places like Toronto, which is generally seen as one of the world's most livable cities.[157] Even so, for every person who moved from the suburbs of

Toronto to the city in recent years, 3.5 people moved toward the periphery, according to Statistics Canada. The people most likely to move out were 25- to 44-year-olds, people entering the stage of family formation. As one Torontonian who recently moved to the suburbs observed:

> *Bigger houses and wide open yards are only two reasons people are leaving for the new suburbs. They're also leaving because they feel Toronto is becoming less and less livable. The evidence is in school closures, the daily battle to get to work, and rising user fees and long waiting lists for daycares, hockey rinks and other community amenities. . . . The big city has its uses. It served me well, and I served it back. Living in Toronto enabled me to transform my life in ways I dearly wanted: marriage, fatherhood, career advancement. That transformation has brought with it needs that Toronto cannot adequately provide: personal space, affordability, an emphasis on community over privacy. The intensity and the anonymity of the city now hinder my life more than they help. Simple as that. I'm outta here.*[158]

THE PLACE FOR FAMILIES

Perhaps most critically, suburbs continue to function as something akin to "nursery of nations." As sociologist Herbert Gans noted in the 1960s, suburbanites approach community with very different goals and aspirations than their urban counterparts. Rather than street-level vibrancy and lifestyle innovations, he noted, suburbanites prioritize more mundane things such as privacy, good schools for their kids, nice parks, and friendly, stable neighborhoods—prosaic but fundamentally critical determinants in their choice of community.[159]

In contrast, families have not been a primary focus of New Urbanist thinkers, although they are quick to denounce suburbs for the decline in families, citing the difficulties of paying mortgages, long commutes, and chauffeuring children. Yet they generally do not bother to make a compelling case for families to return to the city.[160] In the 10 principles of urbanism listed on NewUrbanism.org, families, in fact, are barely mentioned, while the terms "pedestrian" and "resident" are widely employed.[161] For the most part, admits Douglas Porter, author of *Making Smart Growth Work*, dense development appeals primarily to young people, couples, and empty nesters looking to live in city and urban centers "because they prefer to be near their workplaces and urban amenities."[162] Clearly, as we have seen before, the dense city is an ideal place for certain sections of the population, but it is not so conducive to many others.

Most projections of suburban decline reveal a lack of appreciation for the impact of changes in life stages—a consideration that is crucial to the human city. Young people are more likely to move to the core city, but as a British study demonstrates, they don't stay long—city center populations are far more likely to move annually than the rest of the British population.[163] Similarly, an analysis of US census data by Wendell Cox finds that people tend to move to dense urban areas in their 20s and then leave when they begin to seek out housing to buy or start families.[164]

These sentiments are often not recognized by retro-urbanists, who believe that somehow, young urbanites will stay in core cities forever. In reality, 36 percent of New Yorkers under 35 said they planned to leave within five years, according to a 2011 poll. Even Brooklyn, the epicenter of the urban renaissance, has seen more college-educated citizens leave than arrive in recent years.[165]

The simple reality is this: once a person starts a family, he or she has a tendency to move out of the city because, despite the city's many allures, suburbs offer the factors we know parents want: more freedom of movement, safety for their children, and generally less expensive housing—not to mention another critical factor: better childhood education.[166] Overall, only 53 percent of students in city schools graduate, compared to 71 percent in suburbs.[167] Where gaps are most extreme, mostly in large core cities, the percentage of children in private schools can reach 20 percent or more, which is at least four times greater than in districts with good education systems.[168] Dropout rates in most large US metropolitan areas tend to be 20 to 40 percent higher in the inner cities. Even poorer children tend to perform better in suburban or exurban schools than those in the inner city, according to one recent study.[169]

The educational gap affects almost all great cities, including London, where the lack of decent secondary schools has been found to push middle-class families out, and New York.[170] "You really have to worry about the schools in New York," says Brooklyn resident Jason Walker, whose two children are six and eight. "If you have to go to private schools, this makes it a struggle to stay here."

Some retro-urbanist thinkers, like Peter Katz, hope that families will begin to stay in urban centers as schools improve.[171] But to date, there seems to be no new proliferation of good city schools. Most public schools in cities fail to perform even to minimal standards.[172] Suburban schools, although not always great, consistently out-perform those of inner cities in terms of achievement, graduation and college entrance.[173]

In contrast to the challenges schools present to urban parents, places like Cinco Ranch, located in the high-performing Katy Independent School District, possess a magnetic attraction for families. Irvine, California, with its broad streets and massive shopping centers, may lack the urban charms of Flatbush or even west Los Angeles, but its schools are critically important to those with children. "Everything stems from education," notes Irvine resident Eveleen Liu, a manager with Salesforce.com. "The city draws people who are impassioned about their kids and their school. Everyone volunteers. It's the glue that holds this place together."

According to 2010 census data, the proportion of city households with children ages 5 to 17 was twice that of suburbs and almost three times higher than newer developments and exurbs. This difference exists even in relatively dense places like Southern California. Irvine has far larger households than more traditional urban places like Santa Monica, where households tend toward childlessness. The median household size in Irvine was 2.61, while for Santa Monica, it was 1.87.[174] Irvine's other big allure is safety. The city consistently rates among the safest American cities with over 100,000 residents.[175] To be sure, many cities, notably New York, have become much safer and some suburbs less so, but the overall picture still strongly favors suburbs. A review of 2011 crime data, as reported by the FBI, indicates that the violent crime rate in the core cities of major US metropolitan areas was approximately 3.4 times that of the suburbs.[176] Although there are pockets of higher crime in Britain's suburbs, overall, they also show considerably lower crime rates than cities.[177]

WHY WE NEED BOTH GEOGRAPHIES

Ultimately, urban policy should be about choices, and developers should respond to market signals and preferences rather than government edicts that suggest how people should live. If people choose to move into the city and the market supports it, that, too, should be encouraged.

But the notion that development be "steered" into ever-denser pockets violates, as we've seen, the wishes of the vast majority. These attitudes reflect a remarkable degree of disrespect and even contempt toward the choices people make. If people move to the periphery, it is not because they are deluded or persuaded by advertising but because they perceive that is where their quality of life is higher.[178]

As we've seen, suburban and urban expansion are nothing new. New archeological evidence points to the earliest cities being formed by combining several discrete small communities; even the ancient Maya had what researchers described as "urban sprawl," complete with large houses and even an archaic version of strip malls. For his part, Aristotle spoke about cities as the union of "several villages." Suburbs and small communities are not new phenomena but instead are woven into the history of urban life.[179]

Rather than demonizing and belittling the suburbanite, urbanists would be far better off taking a more human-city approach and focusing on how to improve life not only in the city cores but also in extensive areas that have developed around them. As American sociologist Herbert Gans noted:

> *I have never seen any persuasive evidence that sprawl has significant bad effects, or high-density development significant virtues. Indeed I doubt that density itself has much*

impact on people, except at levels which create overcrowding or isolation. I therefore believe that people should be able to choose the density levels they prefer. Since most Americans who are able to choose have long preferred low-density housing, I favor urban policies that respect that preference, while not ignoring the minority preferring high-rise housing.[180]

This is not to say that dense urbanity is bad, for it is not, but it simply does not fit the needs of much of the population, particularly as they enter their 30s and 40s. The real issue here is not the urban form but what locales best provide a better life for most citizens. What is needed now is recognition that cities need to nurture both geographies—the largely childless inner districts and those areas likely to attract middle-class families: the suburbs and less dense urban neighborhoods. Cities can be ideal for younger people and those in the early stages of their careers. For them, living in a dense city might actually prove more healthful due to both the greater prevalence of walking or biking and the stimulation that comes from city life. It also can appeal to a small but significant population of empty nesters, childless couples, and the super-affluent, who can afford the blessings offered by dense urbanity.

The notion that suburban, or dispersed, living is something to be limited—or even banned as fundamentally unhealthy—ultimately deprives the city of both an alternative for its maturing citizenry and a future source of young people. Attempts to restrain, or even eliminate, urban expansion will almost certainly have a direct impact on family formation. In the long run, to be both socially and demographically sustainable, the city needs to embrace both geographies, playing not only to the wealthy, young, or very poor but also to families who seek out less density and a better environment. As much as a society wants to replace itself and have places for families and the young, it needs to pay attention to the needs of suburbanites as well as inner-city dwellers. In the long run, these geographies need each other.

CHAPTER 7

How Should We Live?

■ ▤ ■ ■

THIS BOOK STARTED with the simple question: What is a city for? In exploring this issue, it seems clear that the policy being advocated for our urban centers often fails to address the basic issues that concern most people: the need for affordable space, privacy, and for a large share of the population, the ability to raise a family in a healthy manner without facing enormous financial constraints.

With its emphasis on density and centralization, today's dominant approach to urban growth leads us toward a future that we may want to avoid. It will, inevitably, reduce individual options, decrease family formation in places that will be running low on workers and consumers, exacerbate class divisions, and make life more unpleasant for city dwellers of all kinds.[1] In the high-income world, shrinking personal space and raising its cost means many cities will be forced to accept large-scale immigration to maintain their workforces, often at a high social cost. Under any circumstances, cities are likely to suffer both from a shortage of young people and a growing class bifurcation, conditions similar to those seen during the centuries leading to the eventual dissolution of the Roman Empire.

Enforced densification, heralded by the rise of megacities, will also negatively impact urban areas in the developing world, where the vast majority of urban growth is taking place. People leave the countryside to escape poverty but then find themselves unable to support themselves in the urban environment and are left to poverty in a different setting.[2] The prospect of a totally dystopian future of almost unimagined densities is far from inconceivable. In Mumbai, there are neighborhoods where the population reaches 1 million per square mile; two-thirds of city residents live in a mere 5 percent of its space.[3]

As British author James Heartfield suggests, the question we must address is, how should we live? The answer must be one that offers a broad array of choices, which historian Robert Fishman described nearly three decades ago as "urban pluralism," and that encompasses the city center as well as close-in suburbs, new fringe developments, and exurbs.[4]

In this approach, suburbs and exurbs are not seen as unfortunate manifestations but as natural products of urban growth and affluence. After all, urban expansion did not emerge when the first freeway was built or when the Levitt brothers started adopting the mass production techniques of the American Seabees.[5] Every town "has its suburbs," observed Fernand Braudel. "Just as a strong tree is never without shoots at its foot, so towns are never without suburbs."[6]

This book argues for a broader definition of what constitutes a city. Urbanity's future extends from the densest parts of Mumbai, or Manhattan, or Marunouchi to the far-flung suburban expanses of Navi Mumbai,[7] massive developments outside Houston, or the housing estates of Essex. To succeed, urbanism needs to encompass not only different forms but also people in all their variety and various life stages—from birth to young adulthood to retirement.

This extends the urban debate well beyond the usual focus on hipsters or wealthy retirees to include those broad sections of society—including most millennials, immigrants, seniors, and families—whose long-term interests are often ignored. The interests of these populations, and what they prefer and aspire to, should be front and center in our consideration of the future of cities.

THE MILLENNIAL CITY

The urban future will be shaped, and rightfully so, by the rising millennial generation, born after 1983, who number over 1.7 billion worldwide.[8] In the United States, millennials are the largest cohort in the country and by 2020, they will constitute one-third of the adult population.[9] In the next five years, this generation will spend more on a per-household basis than any other generation, including an estimated $2 trillion on rent and home purchases combined.[10]

Some believe that most millennials will adopt urban life and put an effective end to the decades-long process of suburbanization.[11] Urban theorist Peter Katz, for example, suggests that millennials have little interest in "returning to the cul-de-sacs of their teenage years."[12] We are entering a new era, one planner predicts, where the move to suburbia ends as "young professionals and empty nesters" pay a premium to crowd into the inner city.[13]

Do millennials actually "hate the burbs" so much, as one *Fortune* editor confidently claimed, that they will choose to remain in the core city as they reach their 30s and beyond?[14] This seems unlikely. For one thing, most young Americans lack, if not the inclination, the resources to reside comfortably in pricey places like Brooklyn or San Francisco. Indeed, only 20 percent of millennials live in urban-core districts.[15] Between 2000 and 2010, nearly 90 percent of millennial growth in major metropolitan areas took place in the suburbs and exurbs.[16]

As a group, young people have long tended to prefer city cores—certainly in comparison with older people and especially families. This was evident, for example, in the 1970s and 1980s, when the new urban pioneers were called yuppies, the predecessors of today's hipsters.[17] In 2011, people in their 20s made up roughly 24 percent of the population of central business districts, injecting vitality and a renewed fashionability. But these much-reported CBD-dwelling, inner-city millennials represent less than 3 percent of their overall population.[18]

More important still is the question of where millennials plan to settle later in life. Extensive generational survey research by Frank N. Magid Associates reveals that 43 percent of millennials describe suburbs as their "ideal place to live," compared to just 31 percent of older generations. Only 17 percent of millennials identify the urban core as their preferred long-term destination.[19] A 2014 survey by the Demand Institute came up with similar findings, with most millennials expressing a desire for more space and suburban locations.[20]

The following year, according to a National Association of Home Builders survey, roughly two-thirds of millennials said they ultimately desired a home in the suburbs. Perhaps even more remarkably, a study from the Urban Land Institute, historically less than enthusiastic about suburbs, found that some 80 percent of current millennial homeowners live in single-family houses, and 70 percent of the entire generation expects to be living in one by 2020. The suburbs will change, in large part due to their influence, but the single-family house itself and the general lifestyle associated with it seem likely, barring an economic catastrophe, to persist over the coming decades.[21]

If some millennials are staying in the city longer than previous generations,[22] much of this has to do with economic pressures that have made changing locations or buying a house very difficult.[23] But as the majority of the millennial population enters their 30s by 2018, the demand for suburban houses is likely to increase dramatically, according to economist Jed Kolko. Faced with huge student debt,[24] a weaker job market, and often-high housing prices, millennials face tougher challenges than previous generations but maintain remarkably similar aspirations.[25] Canadian millennials share many of the same tastes, and most seek suburban locations in large part for the same reasons as other groups: urban congestion, lack of living space, and in many cases, prohibitively high prices.[26]

MILLENNIALS ABROAD

Millennials in Europe face even greater challenges related to achieving their aspirations. Throughout southern Europe, due to weak economies and high housing prices, more than 50 percent of young people aged 18 to 34 live with their parents.[27] Yet like their counterparts across the Atlantic, they still prefer to own homes. This is particularly true among British millennials, of whom almost nine in 10 said they were interested in purchasing a home in the next 10 years, according to a study by the progressive Institute for Public Policy Research. Nick Pearce, the group's director, found that young people wanted to own homes in part to enhance a "sense of belonging to their neighborhood," and they felt ownership would commit them to the area for the long run.[28]

Financial challenges are even emerging in such traditionally egalitarian societies as Australia. Ownership at a relatively early age was once commonplace there, and younger Australians still prefer single-family housing[29]—indeed, between 70 and 90 percent of 15- to 29-year-olds would like to own their own home by the age of 30. But, largely due to high prices, only four in 10 believe they will ever achieve this goal.[30] Rising house prices, in large part caused by restrictive land-use policies, have already cost roughly 1.5 million residents—most of them young—the chance to own a home.[31]

Young people also still aspire to own their own homes in a host of other countries, including China, Taiwan,[32] and Sweden.[33] In China, notes scholar Yapeng Zhu, homeownership now constitutes "a Chinese dream for young people, including both college graduates and migrant workers."[34] Perhaps even more than Europeans or Australians, the inheritors of Asia's boom, faced with dramatically higher housing prices, are struggling to achieve homeownership.[35] According to a recent survey, a growing segment of young Koreans, for example, believe they will never own a home, get married, or have children. Caught in a high-density, high-competition environment with housing prices well above what they are able to pay, young Koreans are, not surprisingly, very pessimistic about their long-term prospects.[36]

THE GLOBAL HOUSING SHORTAGE

The predicament facing millennials is primarily rooted in an evolving global housing shortage, particularly for the kinds of affordable, spacious accommodations sought by families. In America and elsewhere, this shortage has been exacerbated by a regulatory and economic environment that has made it much tougher to build houses. Aimed at limiting suburban growth and fostering urban densities, these policies have broken the long, consistent relationship between housing prices and incomes.

William Fischel, an economist at Dartmouth College, has demonstrated how stringent land-use regulations in places like California have driven up house prices substantially in relation to prices elsewhere.[37] Given the extraordinary costs of land in places like California, many developers only find it worthwhile to build homes largely for the affluent, making the era of the Levittown-style "starter home" all but defunct.[38] Overall, US housing production has dropped not only since the 2007 recession but again since 2011. In California, production has fallen so far that Houston—a single Texas metropolitan area—produced as many new homes in 2014 as the entire Golden State.[39] These high housing prices also affect rents, and they hurt the poor most of all. In New York, Los Angeles, and San Francisco, for example, renters spend 40 percent of their income on rent, well above the national average of under 30 percent.[40]

This growing divergence in prices has spurred migration from places like California and the Northeast to the Sun Belt[41] and has even created opportunities for less expensive, and generally less wealthy, older cities like those along the Rust Belt. For years, Rust Belt cities have pegged their aspirations on developing a coastal-like cultural of "coolness." Increasingly, though, notes Cleveland State University's Richey Piiparinen, lower costs and a more family-friendly appeal have already helped Cleveland and Pittsburgh enjoy faster migration of young, educated people than places like Portland, Chicago, Los Angeles, or New York.[42]

The impact of housing shortages is, if anything, even greater in other countries, which generally lack the "safety valve" of less regulated environments that Texas and other states provide in the United States. In Great Britain, a lack of new construction, particularly that of single-family houses, has driven up prices well beyond those seen in the United States, relative to income. To keep up with demand, Britain needs roughly 500,000 new homes a year, but it produces barely one-fifth that number, on average.[43]

Mark Carney, governor of the Bank of England, believes this shortage of housing constitutes the "biggest risk" to the UK economy.[44] People are as keen as ever to buy,[45] but high housing prices and surging rents are forcing a fifth of 18- to 34-year-olds to live with their parents,[46] while private renters spend 40 percent of their income on housing. Carney found it "shocking" that "many people in their 20s now regard it as an accepted fact that they will never have much by way of a home."[47] Housing needs in Britain are so underserved, notes author

James Woudhuysen, that at current rates of building, the average dwelling in the United Kingdom would have a 1,000-year lifetime before it could be replaced.[48]

Canada and Australia, countries with extensive land but tough regulations against single-family homes, also face a growing shortage of affordable housing. Over the past 40 years, housing completions in Australia, adjusted to population, have dropped off by roughly 50 percent,[49] while prices have risen by almost twice the rate of incomes since the 1970s.[50] Australia has seen the value of its housing stock, relative to GDP, rise 85 percent, according to the Reserve Bank of Australia, while it has remained stable in the United States, where housing regulations vary by region.[51]

The housing shortage is even more severe in rapidly developing countries. By 2025, cities in India and China will require an estimated 16 trillion square meters of new housing.[52] China's main cities have arguably suffered the most rapid growth of property prices relative to income in the world. According to Credit Suisse estimates, median prices for housing in Beijing have increased threefold since 2000 and now cost 23 times wages. In Shanghai, prices are over 17 times median wages, and in Shenzhen, prices are 12.7 times wages. This is higher than even ultra-expensive cities such as Hong Kong, London, Sydney, San Francisco, and New York.[53]

A WORLD OF VILLAGES

Only a policy that embraces some form of urban expansion can hope to relieve the housing needs of future generations. As people start looking to establish households, they seek out affordable, family-friendly communities, according to millennial chroniclers Morley Winograd and Michael Hais. Inevitably, they will then reshape their communities in their own way. For example, millennials may seek to customize their residences for greater energy efficiency or place greater emphasis on "technology capabilities" than on larger living rooms or other traditional suburban amenities.[54]

Some millennials may be attracted to the notion of a village-like development that differs from the traditional bedroom suburb, a concept that draws on the pioneering work of Ebenezer Howard and his 20th-century "garden cities." Recall that these spaces sought to combine the best of urban living (e.g., convenience and walkability) with the best of suburban living (e.g., good schools and more space).[55]

This approach has roots that extend back at least a century and a half. Some early suburban developments in the United States anticipated Howard's garden cities, such as Llewellyn Park, New Jersey, which was started in the 1850s. Riverside, Illinois, nine miles from Chicago, was designed as a "picturesque enclave" but also included a town center near the train station. These developments appealed to such figures as Frederick Law Olmsted, the creator of Central Park, who remarked that "no great town can long exist without great suburbs."[56]

In Southern California, the great growth center of the mid-20th century, dispersed urbanity emerged as the predominant form in a great world city for the first time. From early in its 20th-century development, the Los Angeles ideal was not to mimic centralized cities like New York but to become "a federation of communities coordinated into a metropolis of sunlight and air." Some civic leaders, like Methodist minister Dana Bartlett, envisioned building a "better city"—the City Beautiful amid a paradisaical setting—that would be "nearer to nature's heart" with many parks and open public spaces, as well as employment near residences.[57]

Southern California never fulfilled Bartlett's ideals, in large part due to the desire of corporate interests to cash in on a seemingly insatiable market for small-plot houses.[58] Yet the notion of a region of dispersed communities and businesses appealed to millions who made Los Angeles one of the fastest-growing metropolitan areas in the high-income world.[59] Between 1950 and 2000, Los Angeles grew faster than all but three of the world's 19 high-income urban areas that were rated among the 30 largest by the United Nations (there was greater growth in Seoul, Tokyo, and Nagoya).[60]

The drive to build garden cities gained momentum during the New Deal, which fostered "green belt towns" outside Cincinnati, Milwaukee, and Washington, DC. These communities were seen as "the blueprint for the future" by some New Dealers; Rexford Tugwell, a leading adviser to President Franklin Roosevelt, envisioned 3,000 such communities across the country that would rearrange "the physical face of America."[61]

The war and eventual opposition to such federal planning stopped this program. But starting in the 1960s, private developers began to revive the garden city, albeit in a radically different form. This included new communities such as the Woodlands outside Houston, as well as Reston and Columbia outside Washington, DC, and Irvine and Valencia in Southern California.[62]

REVIVING OLDER SUBURBS

The "village" model is not exclusive to new developments. Many older suburbs have developed "lifestyle centers"—walkable developments that are seen as the modern-day equivalent of an old Main Street or British High Street. These often feature narrow streets and small storefronts mixed with housing and office space. Parking is mostly hidden underground or in the interior of faux city blocks. These are built around what are relatively low-density communities to serve as a "satellite city core" that is essentially a cultural center for the surrounding region.[63]

This shift in suburban form is also occurring in traditional New York suburbs such as Brookhaven, Islip, and North Hempstead on Long Island, as well as in communities as far flung as Naperville outside Chicago, or the city of Orange south of Los Angeles.[64] These developments often seek to appeal to millennials and young families, who increasingly, notes one researcher, seek to balance work and life far more than earlier generations.[65]

In recent years, the suburbs have even started to attract some of the urban avant garde, who are now moving to what the *New York Times* labeled "hipsturbia."[66] The *Observer* even suggested that "hipsturbia"—for all its pretense of vegan restaurants, tattoo parlors, and trendy boutiques—represents a continuation of the trend that first saw young people, many originally from the suburbs, move from Manhattan to less crowded Brooklyn. It added that hipsturbia "is not really a reverse migration. It's a homecoming."[67]

SUBURBS WILL LIKELY RESIST MOST DENSIFICATION

Some, including Jane Jacobs, have suggested that these moves will make suburbs more city-like, with more amenities and common places.[68] To be sure, the pattern of rapidly increasing dispersion has slowed, in large part due to reduced population growth, but it still remains the dominant trend.[69] Suburbanites may have evolving views on the environment and diversity, but most are unlikely to welcome wide-ranging densification or give up on such privacy-enhancing amenities as cul-de-sacs, for which they will often pay a premium.[70]

Historically "reluctant" to become cities, suburbs generally can be expected to, for the most part, resist high degrees of densification, except sometimes in already developed or specially zoned commercial districts.[71] More ambitious attempts by planners to impose strict regulations on construction and mandate higher densities have sparked widespread opposition in states such as New Jersey and in parts of California.[72] This can be seen, ironically, even in the "greenest" areas, such as Marin County north of San Francisco, where residents have objected to densification schemes that would undermine the "small-town, semi-rural and rural character of their neighborhoods," the very things that drew them there in the first place.[73]

As author Fred Hirsch explained, suburbanites usually move to these communities in order *not* to live in a crowded place, and if forced to by a growing population, they tend to "leapfrog" to less dense areas. They often look to their governments to act as a "shield" that protects them from the encroaching urban world that they left for a reason.[74] They are not so much anti-social, as is sometimes alleged, but are seeking a level of "self-determination," that they could not hope to receive from larger units of government, according to Notre Dame Law School professor Nicole Stelle Garnett,[75] Aroused by what they perceive as threats to their preferred way of life, suburbanites can prove very effective in their opposition, particularly when they are affluent, educated, and provoked to act. "There's nothing like being a NIMBY with clout," notes one Oregon newspaper.[76]

Future suburbs may not look as physically different as some imagined, but they will be very different in terms of who lives there.

Peripheral communities will be increasingly diverse not only by race and ethnicity but also by age and sexual orientation. In the United States, nearly two-thirds of single-person households live in the suburbs of the major metropolitan areas, and gay households have been heading out to suburbs as well. Even in metropolitan San Francisco, 40 percent of same-sex couples live outside the city proper.[77]

THE PERSISTENCE OF FAMILIALISM

The aging of society and the decline in childbearing rates are widely suggested to be driving ever-greater densification.[78] The shrinking of households with children as a percentage of the population, the Brookings Institution's Chris Leinberger suggests, will cause "the death of the fringe suburb" as more people flock closer to the urban core. With the demise of the "stereotypical household," it is widely maintained that demography will undermine and even eradicate the "suburban dream" as people desert larger single-family homes in favor of cozy urban apartments.[79]

Yet hopefully these shifts may be exaggerated. For one thing, houses are not getting smaller, as widely predicted. After several years of downsizing, house sizes began to expand again by 2011, although often on smaller lots.[80] House sizes set a new record in 2012, becoming 300 square feet larger than they were in 2000.[81] In Canada and Australia, house sizes also have expanded in recent years, while preferences for larger single-family houses have barely shifted. One reason for this, notes an Australian survey, is that "empty nester" households frequently need extra rooms for visiting children or grandchildren.[82]

Given the terrific pressures against family formation in many urban areas around the world, it is incumbent on planners to find ways to ease the process for those who wish to have children. This may present a challenge in many places but will not, as some suggest, work against the social mores of the new generation.

Millennials, according to US surveys, can be very liberal in their social views, particularly regarding race, gender equality, and gay rights, but they often hold surprisingly traditional views on the issues of teenage sex, abortion, and the importance, if not of marriage, of family.[83]

Pew Research Center surveys found that rather than being committed to perpetual singlehood, a majority of American millennials ranked being "good parents" as their highest priority, while a third said their top priority is to have a successful marriage. In contrast, having a "high-paying career" was named by only 15 percent.[84] The latest Monitoring the Future report found that 78 percent of female high school seniors and 70 percent of males said that having a good marriage and family life is "extremely important" to them—numbers that are virtually unchanged since the 1970s.[85]

Indeed, despite changing social norms, most young people, even in high-income societies, still appear to yearn for the comforts and rewards of family life, however delayed by high housing costs, a weak economy, and high-density development. In Europe, the ideal number of children in a family, according to surveys, stands close to two, well above the actual fertility rate.[86] Similarly, in Singapore, most young people express a strong desire to get married and have children, preferably more than one.[87]

This pattern is even more evident in the United States, where in the years before before the Great Recession, the number of women having more than two children actually increased from previous decades.[88] In a survey conducted by the Pew Research Center, nearly half of adults surveyed identified two as the "ideal" number of children—a number that has been consistent since the early 1970s—while over a quarter preferred three children and nearly 10 percent preferred four. In contrast, barely 3 percent opted for one, while a similar number chose none.[89] People may well be delaying childbearing or having fewer children, but for most, childlessness is not a preferred option.

SENIORS AND SUBURBIA

The rapid aging of societies—the US population over 65 will double to 80 million by 2050—also has been seen as fostering the "back to the city" trend. Some news reports have claimed that "millions" of aging boomers, now relieved of their children, are leaving their suburban homes for city apartments.[90]

Such assertions are simply in conflict with both the preferences and the actual behaviors of US seniors. During the past decade, more than

99 percent of population growth among people aged 65 in major metropolitan areas took place in counties with densities of less than 2,500
residents per square mile, well below traditional urban densities,which
average at least two to four times as much. Seniors, according to industry research, are seven times more likely to buy a suburban house
than move to a more urban location. Not surprisingly, nine of the top
10 counties for active senior housing are in suburban locations.[91] This
trend is unlikely to change in the future. A National Association of
Realtors survey found that the vast majority of buyers over 65 looked
in suburban areas, followed by rural locales.[92]

In contrast, relatively few seniors are likely to give up their homes
for condos in the city center; a study by the Research Institute for Housing America suggested that barely 2 percent of all "empty nesters" seek
an urban locale. A 2011 survey by a real estate advisory firm estimated
the empty nester "back to the city" condominium demand at 250,000
households nationwide, a lucrative but small market compared to the
size of the aging population.[93]

Similar patterns can be seen in Australia, where the census has
seen a steady movement of seniors away from the central districts of
the country's main cities. Seniors, one report suggests, overwhelmingly want "to remain within their local communities . . . where they
want to be." Many others are heading out to the far periphery, 20 or
30 kilometers (about 12 to 19 miles) from the central business districts
of Australia's large cities.[94] Canadian boomers are similarly inclined,
with more than two-thirds favoring retirement in the countryside,
small towns, or suburbs.[95]

Why are seniors, like millennials, not acting as many retro-urbanists have predicted? Some of the reasons have to do with seniors' inclination to continue working. In 2013, nearly 40 percent of men and 30
percent of women between the ages of 65 and 69 in the United States
were still working, almost twice as large a segment as in the 1980s.[96]
This is also true in Australia, where one in three men aged 65 to 69
were still working in 2012, compared to just one in six a decade earlier.[97] Canadian seniors are also twice as likely to be in the workforce
today than a decade ago.[98]

But whatever the reason, most seniors will likely remain in their current residence or neighborhood for decades to come. AARP studies have found that only one in four seniors expresses any desire to move, even at the last stages of life. Some 85 percent would prefer to get long-term care at their homes as opposed to nursing homes or assisted living facilities.[99] Rather than try to force seniors out of their homes and neighborhoods, notes a report from the American College of Physicians, it might be better to focus on serving those "aging in place," which is not only what seniors prefer but is also generally far less expensive than care facilities.[100] This suggests that suburbs, originally built for families, may need to "retrofit" to accommodate older people by offering new modes of transportation and housing options as people age.[101]

Critically, seniors, the vast majority of whom are without children at home, remain very familial; the estimated portion who have offspring is roughly 80 percent.[102] Families with children in the home constitute a smaller share of the population than in the past—about one-fourth in the United States, or roughly half the percentage seen a half century ago—but kinship ties now increasingly extend to grandparents and even great-grandparents as life spans increase.[103] In many ways, notes author Stephanie Coontz, the family is simply shifting away from the 1950s paradigm dominated by the nuclear family and toward "blended" family patterns associated with the more distant past.[104]

The preeminence of family considerations among seniors can be seen in a 2014 study by the US moving company Mayflower, which found that the biggest reason seniors move is to be closer to their children and grandchildren. Similarly, as many as one in four millennials have moved to be closer to their parents, often to enjoy life in more affordable communities and receive help with raising their kids.[105] Grandparents are the primary caregivers for one in five children, and overall, family members provide some regular child care for nearly half of the country's preschoolers.[106]

THE RETURN OF THE MULTIGENERATIONAL HOUSEHOLD

For much of the postwar period, Americans increasingly shifted from multigenerational to nuclear family–dominated homes. But in recent years, this process has reversed. The number of people over 65 living with their children grew 50 percent between 2000 and 2007, according to the US Census Bureau.[107] Overall, the percentage of multigenerational homes has risen from a low of 12 percent of all households in 1980 to 16.7 percent of all households in 2009. The last time multifamily households stood at this level was in the 1950s.[108] In a 2015 report by the National Association of Realtors, over 13 percent of all new homes purchased were multigenerational.[109]

Many major developers have recently targeted this growing market segment. New England's largest homebuilder have all created houses—some with separate entryways and kitchens—that appeal to multigenerational households.[110] Homebuilder Toll Brothers has started incorporating a guest suite with a kitchenette in lieu of the traditional family room.[111]

These trends can also be seen elsewhere in the world. In Australia, a country with some of the highest housing costs in the world, some people are building "granny flats" in the backyards of their parents' houses—not only to house their parents but also themselves.[112] Chinese planners, preparing for what will be a veritable tsunami of older persons, also are looking at expanded suburban housing for the country's senior population.[113] Given the rising prices in key core cities and the likely movement of families to the periphery, the future of Chinese extended families might involve their living on the periphery or in smaller cities.

THE ECONOMICS OF DISPERSION

Some claim that dispersing work from the cores "undermines" prosperity.[114] However, most of the densest cities—notably in the third world—are also consistently the poorest, with very low levels of GDP per capita. Among the high-income world's metropolitan areas, only one, Macau, is dense. Hartford is the second most affluent city in the high-income world, and it has very low urban density. The other eight in the top 10 are also in the United States and include five with lower-than-average urban density (for the United States): Boston, Houston, Bridgeport, and Seattle.[115]

It is widely asserted that most future economic growth will take place in and around the core city.[116] But in the United States, for example, only 9 percent of employment is in the central business districts, with an additional 10 percent in the balance of the urban cores. Twice as many Americans work 10 miles from the urban core as in the core itself, with suburbs accounting for some 65 percent of all employment in metropolitan areas.

Suburban economies were widely dismissed after the housing crash, but even with a weak recovery, these areas rebounded smartly. Between the tough employment years of 2010 and 2013 (the latest available data), suburbs and exurbs accounted for 80 percent of all new jobs created.[117] Since 2013, the suburbs experienced more rapid growth in office occupancy than their inner-city counterparts, according to the office consultancy CoStar.[118]

Many suburbs are no longer bedroom communities but major job centers.[119] In 2013, the Los Angeles suburb of Irvine had 2.1 jobs for every resident worker. Santa Clara, a San Jose suburb, had 1.7 jobs per resident worker, while Bellevue, a Seattle suburb, had 1.8, and Irving, a Dallas suburb, had 1.6.[120] Each of these suburbs had a higher jobs-to-resident-worker ratio than its core municipality. Other areas, such as Westchester County outside New York, began showing a greater surplus of employees over working-age residents as early as 1990.[121] This dispersion of employment has occurred even in Portland—the oft-cited model for urban density—where all job growth was clustered in the suburbs and exurbs between 2000 and 2013.[122]

A similar dispersion of work is taking place throughout the world. Since 2012, Australian job growth in suburban areas has surpassed that in the urban core, despite the strong preferences of planners for higher-density development.[123] Germany, for its part, has long been characterized by regional dispersion of its key companies and industries, or what one government report refers to as "a tiered system of central places."[124] This has led some firms located in backwaters to place some of their key facilities in larger cities, even though their corporate headquarters remain in place.[125]

But overall, Germany's dispersed cities do well compared to its capital, Berlin, and reveal how the market vitality of a place, particularly in the global context, can be far more decisive than size, especially in advanced economies.[126] Other European countries are increasingly focusing on ways to connect their various regions in an effort to reduce greenhouse gases and extend the range of employment options for residents.[127] This strategy has already been widely implemented in the Netherlands, where a network of smaller cities across the country allows for a dispersion of economic activities.[128]

Perhaps the most transformative changes can be seen in the technology industry, whose origins lay largely in suburbs. Some now assert that this pattern has been reversed as employers respond to changing preferences among young workers who desire a more urban lifestyle,[129] suggesting that core cities will now dominate technological innovation.[130] Yet, most tech employment remains firmly in suburbanized areas—with lower-density development and little in the way of transit usage[131]—such as Silicon Valley, Raleigh-Durham, Orange County, and Dallas-Fort Worth.[132]

This trend can be seen in other tech developments around the world. Cambridge Science Park (UK) now holds 100 companies and has sparked development throughout that region. Similar projects have been established elsewhere in the United Kingdom, as well as in France, China, Taiwan, Korea, and India.[133] In Mexico City, where densities have dropped two-thirds over the past century, tech businesses cluster in the Santa Fe development on the city's outskirts.[134] In India, much of Mumbai's new tech development is occurring on the city's fringe. Like their counterparts elsewhere, the vast majority of the over 1 million residents in Navi Mumbai, the city's large planned suburb, work in that community, while future tech development is expected to take place in smaller "second-tier" cities scattered throughout the subcontinent.[135]

THE FUTURE ECONOMIC ROLE OF THE CENTRAL CITY

If economic dispersion continues, what is the future role of the core city? Although its dominion will be far less powerful than in the past, its prospects are far from "bleak," as was commonly believed in the 1970s.[136] That era was particularly tough for inner cities, which were still reeling from the massive loss of manufacturing and retail jobs that took place after World War II.[137]

Yet as historian Robert Bruegmann points out, the loss of these industries helped create the pre-conditions for a new, dynamic core economy. Deindustrialization curbed congestion and pollution and chased working-class families away from the core. The hip city of today rests on the wreckage of the old industrial version.[138] This transformation has allowed city cores to maintain or even slightly expand their shares of metropolitan jobs, even if overall, suburbs accounted for more than 80 percent of all employment gains.[139]

As previously mentioned, certain core geographies, rid of the detritus of their past, have proved well suited for particular industries—high finance, media, and fashion—where regular face-to-face meetings, social connections, and access to privileged information remain critical.[140] Analyst Aaron Renn has also noticed a recent rise in the number of "executive headquarters" located in cities. These headquarters may move away from suburban areas or smaller cities, but they usually consist of only a small number of very senior leaders and support staff. Moving one of these headquarters to the city involves the movement of sometimes fewer than a hundred employees, as opposed to the thousands who might have been relocated to a downtown headquarters decades ago.[141]

This increasingly elite role for cities also can be seen in fields like finance, one of the primary drivers of office expansion during the 1980s. Although the high-end jobs tend to remain in New York, overall financial employment there has experienced a 7 percent reduction since 2008. Other traditional business-service sites like San Francisco, Boston, and Chicago have also created few financial jobs, while growth has been most rapid in second-tier cities such as Richmond, Salt Lake City, and St. Louis. Big money and financial power may remain concentrated in Gotham, but jobs, particularly for the middle-income worker, increasingly are not.[142]

JOB DECENTRALIZATION AND COMMUTING PATTERNS
The success of dispersion rests on reducing or at least containing commute times. Contrary to popular myth, suburbanites already endure shorter commutes than their urban-core counterparts.[143] In fact,

one reason California commuting times dropped 9 percent between 1990 and 2004 was that suburb-to-city commutes were replaced with suburb-to-suburb and even city-to-suburb commutes. A Public Policy Institute of California report concludes that "job decentralization has a moderating impact on commuting times."[144]

In contrast, high-density communities often suffer the longest commutes. In Tokyo, which arguably boasts the world's most extensive transit system, commutes average 60 minutes. This is more than double the average commute time in the United States. Developed mass transit does not mean less traffic. Seoul, Athens, Rome, Tokyo, and Paris, note urban scholars Peter Gordon and Harry Richardson, all have extensive transit systems but suffer horrific traffic.[145]

Overall, public transit, widely seen as a way of reversing dispersion, has had little effect in all but a handful of American cities, although it does provide an important option for those who cannot or do not wish to drive. But in the United States, at least, massive new funding and scores of new transit lines have generated very little growth in the share of people using transit.[146] What has occurred, notes author William Bogart, is that greater mobility has allowed increased "spatial reach" in cities but in ways that have kept commute times, overall, fairly stable.[147]

Improvements in commuting could eventually be enhanced by the gradual introduction of new autonomous driving systems, which could reduce accidents, traffic congestion, and the stress of dealing with traffic. These cars are likely to make suburbs, if anything, more accessible with less hassle. Along with providing improvements in fuel efficiency and reducing greenhouse gas emissions, these vehicles would allow dispersion to continue along with market demands.[148]

THE RISE OF THE HOME-BASED ECONOMY

The development of the periphery, historian Robert Fishman wrote over a decade ago, creates "a new city" whose true center "is not in some downtown business district but in each residential unit."[149] Communications technology has enhanced this, raising the prospects for what futurist Joseph Pelton described as "telecities," which would link jobs not to highways or transit but to the Internet, diminishing the need for massive new office buildings that have historically dominated city centers.[150] Indeed, the increasing speed and ubiquity of communications technology, notes Claremont Graduate University's Thomas Horan, "allows a closer knitting of home and work environments."[151]

In the United States, opportunities to work at home are growing rapidly, at nearly double the rate of transit. Working at home has replaced transit as the principal commuting alternative to the automobile in the vast majority of American cities. In 2013, according to data in the American Community Survey, working at home led transit in 37 of the 52 major metropolitan areas with over 1 million in population.[152]

In the United Kingdom, the number of telecommuters has also grown rapidly, rising more than 30 percent in a 10-year period. One-tenth of the British workforce, some 2.8 million people, telecommuted at least part time over the past decade. Although the United States leads in companies that offer this option—some 90 percent—a 2012 study by Citrix Systems found that the vast majority of companies in countries as diverse as China, India, France, and Germany also offered opportunities for telework.[153]

Over time, these shifts will impact the shape and manner of cities and expand the options for both workers and managers. One harbinger could be communities like Ladera Ranch in Orange County, where high-speed Internet connections and home workspaces, as well as separate doors for customers, are essential parts of the development.[154] Large numbers of home-based businesses have risen in resort areas such as Steamboat Springs, Nantucket, Jackson Hole, and the Upper Peninsula of Michigan, where professionals, taking advantage of the new technology, can operate their businesses from what was once a vacation home or from a small office park in the area.[155]

Frederick Pilot, author of the 2015 book *Last Rush Hour,* envisions telecommuting as the linchpin of an "emerging Information Everywhere Age" that may render future offices increasingly "obsolete." The Cisco Connected World Technology Report surveyed 2,600 information technology professionals in 13 countries in 2010 and found that *three of five workers* said it's unnecessary to be in the office to be productive. The same number said they would choose jobs with lower pay if it meant avoiding the regular commute. In his book, Pilot cites a 2012 survey of 3,000 millennial-generation business owners, which found that 82 percent believe many businesses will be built entirely with virtual teams of online workers by 2022.[156]

Millennials, in particular, may be attracted to the environmental savings that can result from reduced office energy consumption, roadway repairs, urban heating, office construction, business travel, and paper usage (as electronic documents replace paper).[157] Overall, according to a 2007 survey, greater use of telecommuting in the United States alone could save 1 billion tons of emissions over 10 years.[158]

Yet for most, the real benefit of telework is smashing the great barrier between work and home life. We may well be on the verge of the home-centered urban paradigm first envisioned by futurist Alvin Toffler more than four decades ago. In his vision, the house becomes "the electronic cottage," the center of a new economy, with benefits not only for the environment but also for families, partly from allowing mothers and fathers to work while being active parents.[159] The implication for housing forms is fairly obvious: as people use houses for work, they are likely to look for larger—not smaller—and more comfortable places to live.

CAN SUBURBS BE GREENER?

Preferences and market changes point to continued urban expansion, but such a trend is certain to engender opposition from the influential environmental movement. A decade ago, many environmentalists insisted that suburbs would collapse by themselves due to "peak oil," a theory that maintained that fossil fuel supplies were running dangerously low. Author James Howard Kunstler boldly predicted that high energy costs would make "the logistics of daily life impossible" in the suburbs.[160] Yet the prospect of an energy-driven suburban collapse has become increasingly unlikely, in large part due to recent advances in US oil and gas production that have driven prices down.[161]

Unable to wait for energy shortages to do their work, retro-urbanists increasingly base their opposition to suburbs on concerns over climate change instead.[162] Densification, claims influential architect

Peter Calthorpe, is no less than "a climate change antibiotic."[163] This strong linkage of suburbs to climate change proves somewhat extravagant and perhaps more than a little self-serving. In reality, carbon emissions in low-density America are falling, largely due to the use of natural gas over coal, while much of the world's increases in carbon emissions are occurring in densely packed places like India, China, and even supposedly ultra-green Europe.[164]

Cramming, notes a recent National Academy of Sciences report, can do relatively little to reduce US greenhouse gas emissions—perhaps as little as reducing them by only 2 percent.[165] Implementing less intrusive policies such as those requiring better mileage on cars—including electric-, natural gas-, or hydrogen-propelled cars—would be far more impactful, not to mention practical.[166] These steps, suggests a report from McKinsey & Company and The Conference Board, could ensure significantly reduced greenhouse gas emissions without any "downsizing of vehicles, homes or commercial space" and without any changes in the number of miles traveled. There is, McKinsey and The Conference Board also conclude, simply no strong environmental case for "a shift to denser urban housing."[167]

Indeed, a 2013 New Zealand paper suggests that, with the proper design that offers a greater surface area for solar panels, single-family homes are actually better for the environment than multifamily houses. It may be time, notes researcher Hugh Byrd, to challenge "conventional thinking that suburbia is energy inefficient," a belief that has become so enshrined in architectural policy.[168] Byrd notes that there are numerous ways to make lower-density environments more environmentally friendly, such as planting trees.[169]

Research also shows that compact, dense cities are not necessarily better for the environment. The packing of people into an ever-expanding environment of concrete, steel, and glass creates what is known as "the urban heat island effect."[170] In Japan, researchers found higher-density areas create more heat than less dense areas.[171] NASA similarly has found greater heat island effects in the densely populated cities of the Northeast than in more sprawling, less dense metropolitan areas elsewhere. "Densely developed, aggregated cities," NASA found, "produce stronger urban heat islands than sprawling cities with less development density."[172]

There are other unintended but negative environmental consequences to densification. Increased densities, for example, increase congestion and create more "stop and go" conditions that ultimately add to emissions. Transport Canada research indicates that fuel consumption per kilometer (and thus GHG emissions) rises nearly 50 percent as arterial street traffic conditions deteriorate.[173]

Still, some areas, such as California, continue to restrict suburban growth in an effort to combat climate change. California's policies have had mixed results. Attempts to promote "transit-oriented" developments have proven notably ineffective in reducing automobile travel, a *Los Angeles Times* report found. Relatively few of those living in these buildings actually took transit.[174] In addition, these strict policies may have the unintended effect of driving people, jobs, and factories from California's mild climate to areas in the United States and abroad where extreme weather, as well as weaker regulations, lead to greater energy consumption, all but wiping out any greenhouse gas reductions achieved by California's policies.[175]

BACK TO THE ROOTS: RECONNECTING WITH NATURE

Suburbia's poor image among environmentalists belies the fact that suburbanization, at least initially, was driven by what H. G. Wells described as a "passion for nature," particularly among parents interested in "the healthfulness of the countryside." During the first suburban waves, many working-class families, whose homes were frequently self-built, even supplemented their meager earnings by planting vegetables and raising farm animals on their small plots while the more affluent often worked their yards for fun and exercise.[176]

Suburbanites, suggests author Christopher Sellers, sought to fuse the natural environment with the human one; they found a way of life they liked and often fought to protect it. As something of an ironic footnote, much of the initial drive to regulate housing development came from suburban residents eager to protect the surrounding countryside for their own and their families' benefit.[177]

In the rush to build suburbia during the last decades of the 20th century, these values were often sacrificed. But given the slower population growth in most countries, there may be opportunities to build more environmentally friendly communities with adequate open space, attention to natural land contours, and climate-appropriate landscaping.[178] One unappreciated benefit of suburban development can be the proliferation of wildlife in those areas. In many cases, densification can be very hard on natural systems, eliminating the sort of interstitial spaces that allow animals to thrive in less dense areas; suburban gardens often serve well for certain insect, bird, and small mammal species.[179]

As agricultural lands in America's northeast have been turned into forests and suburban developments, many animal species have started coming back, including coyotes, cougars, and even black bears. Although there are rare coyote or even bear sightings close to city cores,[180] the suburbs have the highest proliferation of wild animals. Environmental essayist Donald Worster suggests that suburban development is generally even more animal friendly than the agricultural monoculture it replaced.[181]

The maintenance of small, accessible green spaces, including backyards, has clear benefits. As journalist and author Richard Louv suggests, people living unconnected to natural space suffer what he calls a "nature deficit" disorder, which impacts their moods, health, and intellectual development.[182] Studies in the United States, the Netherlands, Japan, Australia, the United Kingdom, and other countries have found a strong relationship between good health and access to green spaces.[183]

MALTHUSIAN URBANISM

Technology and social change should allow us to shape an urban future that improves the life of most residents and families rather than conforms to a policy that favors the ever-denser cramming of humans into ever-smaller spaces.[184] In many ways, this unfortunate impulse increasingly stems from what might be seen as a neo-Malthusian worldview, which may not be based entirely on science but, as one critic suggests, reflects "a deeply held misanthropy that continually overlooks mankind's ability to overcome problems and create new worlds."[185]

The essence of the Malthusian approach, as historian Edward Barbier notes, assumes the economy has no "access to new sources of land and natural resources" and is "unable to innovate," thus making it "vulnerable to collapse."[186] In this worldview, humanity is increasingly seen as a "cancer on the environment" whose influence needs to be curbed and restrained into as small a footprint as possible.[187] Urban expansion is particularly looked down upon, not only for its alleged impact on greenhouse gas emissions but also for its encroachment upon farmland. Suburbs are purportedly bad, in part because they reduce the ability of farmers to grow food.[188]

As has been the case in so many retro-urbanist assertions, this one is widely off the mark. Massive farmland losses in the United States—which, since 1950, represent an area larger than the states of Texas and Oklahoma together—have been more than compensated for by total agricultural productivity, which has increased 160 percent.[189] Expanding cities are not the primary cause for the loss of most US farmland—overall, urban areas account for only 3 percent of the country's land area—but instead, such things as market forces, technological changes, and the business decisions of farmers themselves seem to be the primary cause.[190] This is also true in Canada, where urban development covers only 3 percent of the land in the country's agricultural belt.[191]

The Malthusian idea is even more absurd in Australia, where the built environment covers only 0.2 percent of the country's total area.[192] Since 1981, Australia's agricultural land has shrunk by an area double the size of the state of Victoria. Urbanization is not a factor. The agricultural land taken out of production since 1981 is more than 50 times the land area of all the urbanization that has developed in Australia since western colonization *began.*[193]

Indeed, the world is not facing a crisis of too little arable land or too poor food production, as commonly asserted by neo-Malthusians. Instead, scholar Shlomo Angel has shown that, worldwide, there are adequate reserves of cultivable land sufficient to feed the planet—particularly given slower population growth—in perpetuity.[194] Given the huge increases in agricultural productivity and the development of energy resources, it seems that the much-predicted "era of ecological scarcity" may not be as imminent as often suggested.[195]

CITIES AS THE ULTIMATE CONTRACEPTIVE

Not surprisingly, neo-Malthusians often embrace densification and oppose urban expansion due to concerns over the population and greater consumption. Fear of rapid population growth has fueled the green movement since the days of Paul Ehrlich's 1968 bestseller, *The Population Bomb*. In the book, Ehrlich predicted that by the late 1970s, we would witness mass starvation as the population would outstrip food supply. Ehrlich espoused draconian steps to limit fertility, imposed by what he saw as a "relatively small group" of enlightened individuals. He even raised the possible feasibility of placing "sterilants" in the water supply and advocated tax policies that discouraged childbearing.[196]

Although few of his more dire predictions actually occurred, these notions have been deeply entrenched within the environmental movement. Ernest Callenbach's 1975 cult novel, *Ecotopia*, describes a future green republic based in the San Francisco region where childbearing is discouraged and the nuclear family has become largely supplanted by communal arrangements. In Ecotopia, a gradually reduced population is celebrated at a time when mass starvation has swept the developing world.[197]

Of course, the slowdown of global population growth is a net positive, particularly in the developing world. But as we've explored, in many countries, including China, the impending demographic crises will be less about overpopulation and more about low fertility rates, rapid aging, and a potentially devastating decline in economic opportunities. Many of these threats are tied to rising pension costs for an older population poorly balanced by a declining workforce.[198] But these concerns seem to take second place among neo-Malthusians, who appear to see the city as a kind of geographic contraceptive.

RESTORING HUMANITY TO URBANITY

Already, almost half the world's population lives in places with be-low-replacement-rate fertility. Demographer Wolfgang Lutz projects that the global population will peak at 9.6 billion as early as 2075 and drop to 9 billion by 2100. The United Nations projects that the population will rise faster, hitting 10.9 billion by 2100. Both projections, however, indicate a substantial slowing of the growth rate.[199]

Rather than embrace an urbanity that discourages family formation and the prospects of wider prosperity, we should—in higher-income countries at least—be looking for policies that actually encourage childbearing and the continued growth of middle-class households. Urban policy should not simply try to preserve the structures of the past, but it should find ways to cultivate the affordability, mobility, and family-friendliness of cities.

There have been widespread attempts to address falling fertility rates. Japan, Singapore, France, Germany, Hong Kong, and Sweden have all tried to adopt family-friendly policies, such as offering subsidies and tax breaks to encourage family formation.[200] Yet these policies have not worked well, in large part because the cost of space has become too high for most couples.[201] Places such as Hong Kong[202] and Singapore[203] offer generous benefits to young families, but as Yap Mui Teng of the Institute of Policy Studies notes, fertility rates remain very low in both countries.[204]

There may be no effective way to raise fertility rates unless we create affordable housing alternatives that offer breathing room for families. The United States, for example, does not have specific policies aimed at increasing fertility, but it has many areas where housing costs are reasonable, making them attractive to families.[205] Among the major metropolitan areas covered by the *Demographia International Housing Affordability Survey*, all areas with "affordable" ratings are in the United States, and these tend to have a more robust presence of families.[206]

Taking advantage of its vast land resources, Russia has developed plans to grant families land for home building in the area around Moscow upon the birth of their third child.[207] Further, the national government has implemented a 140 percent expansion of the Moscow city limits into rural areas that is intended to reduce overcrowding and provide more living space.[208]

Within the limitations of its vastly larger population and more constrained land area, China has adopted an urban policy encouraging people to move to more affordable regions.[209] But even at lower prices, increasingly dense urban lifestyles have been undermining the strong family ties that have long underpinned Chinese societies. Authorities are concerned that the new generation, with their much-smaller family sizes than those of their parents, lacks sufficient "filial piety," a surprising embrace of Confucian ideals from a nominally Marxist regime that previously attempted to liquidate China's historic traditions.[210]

EXPAND THE CITY OR "SAVE THE SLUMS"?

The notion that urban expansion must be curtailed, and even eliminated, ignores, to a large extent, the historic ability of our species—and particularly the urbanized portion of it—to adjust to environmental change. After all, the earliest cities of Mesopotamia and Egypt arose, in part, from a change in climate that turned marshes into solid land, which could then be used for intensive, irrigated agriculture.[211]

Later, in the industrial era, pollution and haze covered most cities—St. Louis, Pittsburgh, Los Angeles, Düsseldorf, Osaka—in the high-income world. However, this has been greatly reduced by the implementation of new technologies. Emissions controls helped reduce high-pollution days in Los Angeles from 33 days in the 1970s to 5 by the beginning of the new century.[212] At the same time, the many waterways that had been used as dumping grounds for manufacturers since the onset of the Industrial Revolution were once considered hopelessly polluted but have come back to life, often as prized urban real estate.[213]

Ultimately, the best way to address the future of cities is to build more of them and expand people's options for a better life. This is quite different from turning our communities into "sim cities," where planners can not only essentially pick the kind of housing they prefer but also force communities to have the proper quotas for racial and economic diversity. Like top-down planning during the Soviet era, this approach often ends up with policies that do not align with human needs.[214]

We need to create the communities that people prefer and can afford. This may well include more mid- and even high-density housing close to urban cores, but for the most part, it means once again building communities that are affordable and meet both the needs and preferences of the vast majority.[215] To accomplish this, we must overcome what author Austin Williams calls the "poverty of ambition" among many planners, political leaders, and developers today. We suffer from constraints based on "no real belief in the transformative capacity of society"; in the neo-Malthusian tradition, the solution generally adheres to constraint and lessening of opportunity.[216]

New peripheral development faces powerful opposition from wealthy country dwellers, some planners, and most environmentalists, as they are unable to imagine a better future for the middle and working classes. "Successive attempts have been made to keep the proles in the towns," James Heartfield notes, "where they belong, reserving the green and pleasant land for the nobs."[217]

Britain, for example, is likely to be a major battleground in this conflict over future growth. Some suggest that Britain needs to return to something closer to the policies of the 1950s and 1960s when Labour and Conservative governments competed to prove who could build more homes. Today, that approach is necessary again; the best way to address Britain's housing problems would be not to "cram" but to construct new communities like Milton Keynes, such as the one that was completed in Ebbsfleet.[218] The notion here is less a continuation of "sprawl," as is often implied, but more the creation of new, albeit smaller, job-rich cities that would be both more family friendly and affordable.

"If we get this right, it should be a really good model community," one local councillor explains. "The notion that a resident would say, 'My dream is to commute back and forth to Canary Wharf' is nonsense. It shouldn't be a dorm; it should be an importer rather than an exporter of people during the day."[219]

It is in the developing world, of course, that the need to build more housing is most pressing.[220] Increasingly, the best hope for India, notes a 2013 World Bank study, lies in the growth of smaller cities as well as suburban areas on the outskirts of larger ones.[221] These are places where India's growing urban population may find more space, homeownership, and upward mobility. This is particularly true in a country where many people still find village life too stifling and without adequate opportunity.

The necessity of building and expanding housing options in the developing world conflicts with the notion that these cities should become ever denser, even if they are already far more tightly packed than the average city in the high-income world. Packing people in slums appeals to some in the West, as discussed earlier,[222] with groups such as Friends of the Earth applauding the massive slum of Dharavi, as an "inspiration" for the urban future.[223] But those who have seen, and smelled, the results of this overcrowding, and particularly those who have to endure it every day, may be less inspired and more interested in finding a more pleasant alternative.

SAVING THE FUTURE FOR THE NEXT GENERATION

These pro-density views also work to create what has become a hard but permanent reality for future city dwellers: high housing costs. In higher-income countries, baby boomers, who have enjoyed considerable access to lower-density, affordable housing, may see this option slip away for their children.

Higher housing prices, in part the product of harsh building restrictions in city peripheries, may have enriched older homeowners, but they have reduced the earnings and assets of younger generations who actually possess less wealth than their counterparts enjoyed a decade earlier, according to a recent report by Australia's Grattan Institute.[224] Due largely to lesser degrees of homeownership among the young, the net worth of those over 65 compared to those under 35 has shifted from being 10 times greater to being over 50 times greater.[225]

Essentially, today's young people—facing weak economic opportunities and diminished prospects of homeownership—are being asked both to accept lower living standards and to help pay, particularly in Europe, for the comfortable retirements of their parents and grandparents.[226]

These burdens are imposed on people whose chances of living comfortably, owning a home, and starting a family are under serious assault.[227] Some might suggest that young people would be better off renting a smaller space—as well as renting cars and even furniture—and living a nomadic existence.[228] But such an existence is, as we've seen, hardly compatible with family formation—not to mention social stability and asset accumulation.

ALLOWING THE ORGANIC EXPANSION OF CITIES

As Frank Lloyd Wright suggested, cities are best treated as "organic" entities; the city, he said, should not be a device to "destroy the citizen" and his affiliations, but rather, it should serve as a "means of human liberation." Cities, he suggested, can be extended and improved to meet the needs of citizens in terms of privacy, space, and the ability to shape their communities, both inside the political realm and, perhaps more importantly, through associations, churches, and family ties.[229]

Such organic development, as sociologist Herbert Gans noted, rests on planners' and developers' willingness to "understand and respect the existing predispositions" of people before concocting solutions.[230] Finding ways to improve both the core and peripheral geographies, where the vast majority live, should engage the energies of planners, pundits, and developers. Sadly, this would represent something of a revolution in thinking. Over the past 40 years, suggests architect John Kaliski, density advocates have amassed "a coterie of academic, professional, and populist boosters" while paying little attention to the suburbs except to excoriate them or seek ways to hasten their demise.

Kaliski, who has worked in places like the San Fernando Valley north of Los Angeles, observes that suburbanites are not the anti-social misfits often portrayed in media or academic accounts. Most seek "to build upon the affirmative choice of suburban, not neo-urban, lifestyles."[231] In trying to preserve their preferred way of life, they have a great deal in common with denizens of large cities—including Istanbul, New York, Toronto, and London—who have objected to new densification schemes in their own areas.

People—in either traditional cities or suburbs—generally do not want to see their often unique and human-scaled neighborhoods transformed into monotonic high-rise blocks. They rarely embrace modern architecture that, in the tradition of Corbusier, tramples over local forms, standing as massive urban sculptures resembling anything from a sponge to a pickle.[232] There's little nostalgia for the kind of stark towers developed by Japanese architect Minoru Yamasaki, designer of the World Trade Center and the Pruitt-Igoe housing project in St. Louis; both were inhuman in scale, and one was destroyed by terrorists while the other, something of an "instant slum," was razed by the city just 17 years after completion.[233]

PAYING ATTENTION TO THE "SMALL UNIT"

We have a tendency to see history, including urban history, in terms of large-scale ideas about place, beauty, economic efficiency, and the natural world. From the viewpoint of an investment banker, academic, or planning official, the logic for densification may seem self-evident and useful. But if this approach gets in the way of people who want to live decently and affordably, what use are these grand ideas?

Urban historian Lewis Mumford roundly lamented that modern cities employed "highly advanced technical means"—expanding transportation, ever-wider lanes, more congestion, ever-taller structures—to develop what he described as the "obsolete forms and ends of a socially retarded civilization." Far better, he suggested, to use our technical prowess to design a city that lends itself "to decentralization in a life-centered order."[234]

No friend of mass suburbs, Mumford was an admirer of Ebenezer Howard's "garden cities" as well as the human-scaled neighborhoods that were common throughout New York earlier in the last century. Yet his most important insight for today says to focus less on the gargantuan and more on the small—but most essential—units of society:

> We shall never succeed with dealing with the complex problems of large units and differentiated groups unless at the same time we rebuild and revitalize the small unit. We must

begin at the beginning; it is here where all life, even in big communities and organizations, starts.[235]

This is one reason why I have put such emphasis on what people actually do—where they move, how they live—as well as their aspirations. History, Fernand Braudel reminds us, "is present at this level too."[236] Planners and developers often want to impose their visions from above; there is a general tendency not to encourage diverse forms but rather a one-size-fits-all model. A better approach would be to listen more both to the market and to local residents—what Houston's Lars Lerup defines as "a motley crew that motors self-organization."[237]

Such a grassroots approach can be messy, of course, and it will need to be constrained by the necessities of the common good and the environment. Yet it is time to recognize that the much-praised model of highly stratified, dense urban culture—so attractive to the global rich, some young people, and childless professionals—ultimately offers little for the vast majority. A new approach to urbanism is desperately needed, one that sees people and families not as assets or digits to be moved around and shaped by their superiors but as the essential element that shapes the city and constitutes its essence.

ACKNOWLEDGEMENTS

■ ■■■

Writers, like other human beings, may be born alone, but they don't write books that way. This book would never have seen the light of day if it were not for the interventions of several people and organizations, as well as the support of my family.

Given that the ideas in this book are at least controversial—and, perhaps to some, heretical—finding a publisher for this effort was no easy task. Fortunately, through my friend Ted Fishman in Chicago, I met Doug Seibold, the president of Agate Publishing in Evanston. Doug was willing to take the risk, and he also assigned his excellent staff, including editor Jessica Easto, to help put the book through its final paces. Their efforts are greatly appreciated.

Among the organizations that I would like to thank for their help with this book are Civil Service College Singapore and the Singapore University of Technology and Design (SUTD) for their original inspiration and for publishing some of the initial work that has been knitted into the book. I would like to thank in particular former Singapore ambassador to the United States, Chan Heng Chee, now at SUTD, as well as Belinda Yuen and Poon King Wang. At Civil Service College, where much of the initial work on the chapters concerning megacities and post-familialism took place, I was greatly assisted by editor Sheila Ng, Toh Boon Kwan, Anuradha Shroff, Sim Hee Juat, and Tan Li San. But I owe much of my understanding of Singapore to my longtime friend and veteran civil servant Peter Ho, entrepreneur Calvin Soh, and demographer Gavin Jones.

None of this, of course, would have been possible without the stalwart support of Chapman University and its Center for Demographics and Policy. This includes backing from Chapman president James Doti and chancellor Daniele Struppa, as well as from Sociology Department chairman Ed Day and associate dean of Wilkinson College of Arts, Humanities, and Social Sciences Ann Gordon. I also want to thank Ken Murphy of the Chapman University Argyros School of Business and Economics, which provided many of the students who worked on this project. Christina Marshall in the Chancellor's office and Lenae Reiter in the Sociology Department both helped greatly with the logistics of the project.

Chapman students contributed greatly to various reports that later helped support the book. I was fortunate to get excellent help from Haley Wragg, Clinton Stiles-Schmidt, Grace Kim, Charlie Stephens, Nate Kaspi, Grace Xu, Zohar Liebermensch, Dylan Cox, and Jordan Taffet. Recent graduate Alicia Kurimska helped not only with the research but also with editing and endnotes.

Over the last year, the ideas in this book received significant validation from the board of the Center for Opportunity Urbanism, which is based in Houston and for which I am executive director. The board members, led by Chairman Leo Linbeck and Richard Weekley, have embraced and been willing to promote a more human-based, family-friendly, and egalitarian approach to urbanism. Their support has been critical throughout the time that this book was being completed.

Ultimately, this book would not have been possible without the financial and spiritual support of Fieldstead and Company in Irvine, California. I remain in debt to Howard and Roberta Ahmanson, Doug Swardstrom, Steve Ferguson, Joe Gorra, and the rest of their staff for helping fund the research phase of the book.

This effort was greatly enhanced by participation in the Infinite Suburbia project of the Massachusetts Institute of Technology. I have been honored to work with MIT's Center for Advanced Urbanism and its director, Alan Berger, as well as his excellent staff, including Celina Balderas-Guzmán. I also want to thank my own longtime editor, Zina

Klapper of Los Angeles, who helped with many of the essays, includ-ing my own, in the upcoming Infinite Suburbia book.

In terms of editing and input, I owe much to Aaron Renn, formerly of Chicago and now residing at the Manhattan Institute in New York. I also received valuable insight from Bob Bruegmann, Fred Siegel, and Michael Lind, as well as from my colleagues at the Center for Opportu-nity Urbanism, Wendell Cox and Tory Gattis. Wendell's globe-circling demographic work is one of the pillars upon which this book stands. In particular, I want to thank Ali Modarres, head of the Urban Stud-ies Program at the University of Washington-Tacoma, who helped me think through the initial ideas that form this book.

Much of the material in this book started off as articles for news-papers and magazines. I want to thank in particular Brian Calle and Mike Tipping at the *Orange County Register*, where I have a weekly column, as well as Jeremy Bogaisky at *Forbes*, where I write the weekly "New Geography" column. Other editors who helped shape this book include Malcolm Jones and John Avlon of the Daily Beast, Harry Siegel at the *New York Daily News*, Carl Cannon and Tom Bevan at RealClear-Politics.com, and Brian Anderson at *City Journal*.

Finally, but hardly least, is the huge contribution of my wife, Mandy, who runs the business side of things. Without her, neither this book nor much else would get done around here. Mandy also engineered our recent move to Orange County after, for me at least, 40 years in Los Angeles. My fundamental inspiration comes from her and our two wonderful daughters, Ariel and Hannah. It is for them, and their gen-eration, that I hope these ideas can be turned into reality.

BIBLIOGRAPHY

■■■■

ABBEY, Philip R. (2005, April 9). "Treaty Ports & Extraterritoriality in 1920s China." http://www.chinapage.org/transportation/port/treatport1.html.

ABBOTT, Carl. (1999) *Political Terrain: Washington, DC From Tidewater Town to Global Metropolis*, Chapel Hill: University of North Carolina Press.

ABC7 NEWS. (2013, November 5). "Voters reject condo complex project on San Francisco waterfront," http://abc7news.com/archive/9315343/.

ABKOWITZ, Alyssa. (2015, April 2). "A High-Rise Race in Mumbai," *Wall Street Journal*, http://www.wsj.com/articles/a-high-rise-race-in-mumbai-1427988257.

ABLEY, Ian. (2009, July 26). "UK Green Path Leads to Deindustrialization and Worsening Housing Shortage," *New Geography*, http://www.newgeography.com/content/00928-uk-green-path-leads-deindustrialization-and-worsening-housing-shortage.

ABRAHAMSON, Eric John. (2013). *Building Home: Howard F. Ahmanson and the Politics of the American Dream*, Berkeley: University of California Press.

ADACHI, Sachiho A., et al. (2014, August). "Moderation of Summertime Heat Island Phenomena via Modification of the Urban Form in the Tokyo Metropolitan Area," *Journal of Applied Meteorology & Climatology*, vol. 53, 1886–1900, doi: http://dx.doi.org/10.1175/JAMC-D-13-0194.1.

ADES, Alberto and Edward L. GLAESER. (1995). "Trade and Circuses: Explaining Urban Giants," *The Quarterly Journal of Economics*, vol. 110, 195–227.

AGENCE FRANCE PRESSE. (2013, August 6). "China's Young Adults Are Becoming More Obese," *The Huffington Post*, http://www.huffingtonpost.com/2013/08/06/china-young-adult-obese_n_3711059.html.

AHMED, Samir Naim. (2010, December 3). "Impact of Globalization On A Southern Cosmopolitan City (Cairo): A Human Rights Perspective," *Countercurrents.org*, http://www.countercurrents.org/ahmed031210.htm.

AKBARI, Hashem. (2005, August 23). "Energy Saving Potentials and Air Quality Benefits of Urban Heat Island Mitigation," *SciTech Connect*, http://www.osti.gov/scitech/biblio/860475.

AKHTER, Shahin and Ferdous ARA. (2014, September 1). "Dhaka braces for sewage mess," *New Age*, http://newagebd.net/44180/dhaka-braces-for-sewage-mess/.

ALCANTARA, Krisanne. (2012, November 16). "Multigenerational Homes: Real Estate's Next Big Thing as More Families Share a Space," *AOL Real Estate*, http://realestate. aol.com/blog/2012/11/16/multigenerational-homes-real-estates-next-big-thing-as -more-fa/.

ALTER, Lloyd. (2014, January 3). "It's time to dump the argument that density and height are green and sustainable," *treehugger*, http://www.treehugger.com/urban-design/its -time-dump-tired-argument-density-and-height-are-green-and-sustainable.html.

———— (2007, October 2). "To Go Green, Live Closer to Work," *treehugger*, http://www .treehugger.com/sustainable-product-design/to-go-green-live-closer-to-work.html.

ANDERLINI, Jamil. (2015, April 30). "China's Great Migration," *Financial Times*, http://www.ft.com/intl/cms/s/2/44096ed2-eeb0-11e4-a5cd-00144feab7de.html.

ANGEL, Shlomo. (2012). *Planet of Cities*, Cambridge: Lincoln Institute of Land Policy.

ANTON, Mike. (2012, June 11). "Southern California—This Just In," *Los Angeles Times* http://latimesblogs.latimes.com/lanow/2012/06/irvine-safest-city.html.

APPLEBAUM, Anne. (2012). *Iron Curtain: The Crushing of Eastern Europe 1944–1956*, New York: Anchor Books.

APPLESEED. (2011, May). "The Economy of Greenwich Village: A Profile," New York University, http://www.gvshp.org/_gvshp/preservation/nyu/doc/nyu-report-05-2011 .pdf.

ARENDT, Randall G. (1996). *Conservation Design for Subdivisions*, Washington, DC: Island Press.

ARIEFF, Allison. (2009, January 11). "What Will Save the Suburbs?," *New York Times*, http://opinionator.blogs.nytimes.com/2009/01/11/what-will-save-the-suburbs/.

ARIES, Phillippe. (1962). *Centuries of Childhood: A Social History of Family Life*, trans. by Robert Baldick, New York: Vintage.

ARISTOTLE. (1984). *The Politics*, trans. by Carnes Lord, Chicago: University of Chicago Press.

ASSOCIATED PRESS. (2006, December 7). "U.S. Suburban Poverty Tops City Poverty for 1st Time."

ASTONE, Nan Marie, Steven MARTIN, and H. Elizabeth PETERS. (2015, April 28). "Millennial Childbearing and the Recession," *Urban Institute*, http://www.urban.org /research/publication/millennial-childbearing-and-recession

AUSLIN, Michael. (2015, February 26). "Japan's Gamble on 'Womenomics'," *Wall Street Journal*, http://www.wsj.com/articles/michael-auslin-japans-gamble-on-womenomics-1424998266.

AUSTRALIAN GOVERNMENT DEPARTMENT OF THE ENVIRONMENT. (2011). "Built Environment," http://www.environment.gov.au/science/soe/2011-report/10-built-environment/2-state-and-trends/2-2-urban.

AZEVEDO, Viviane and Cesar P. BOUILLON. (2009, August). "Social Mobility in Latin America: A Review of Existing Evidence," *Inter-American Development Bank*.

BADGER, Emily. (2015, May 4). "In the shadows of booming cities, a tension between sunlight and prosperity," *Washington Post*, http://www.washingtonpost.com/blogs /wonkblog/wp/2015/05/04/in-the-shadows-of-booming-cities-a-tension-between-sunlight-and-prosperity/

———— (2015, March 26). "New Census data: Americans are returning to the far-flung suburbs," *Washington Post*, http://www.washingtonpost.com/blogs/wonkblog/wp/2015/03/26/new-census-data-americans-are-returning-to-the-far-flung-suburbs/.

BAILEY, Ronald. (2014, August 22). "Environmentalism and the Fear of Disorder," *reason.com*, http://reason.com/archives/2014/08/22/environmentalism-and-the-fear-of-disorde.

BAJPAI, Kanti. (2012, June 23). "Why we need more cities," *Times of India*, http://timesofindia.indiatimes.com/edit-page/Why-we-need-more-cities/articleshow/14344501.cms.

BAKER, Alden. (1981, March 24). "U.S. cities left on their own," *The Globe and Mail*, Canada.

BALAKER, Ted and Sam STALEY. (2006). *The Road More Traveled: Why the Congestion Crisis Matters More than You Think and What We Can Do About It*, Lanham, Maryland: Rowman and Littlefield.

BALSDON, J.P.V.D. (1969). *Life and Leisure in Ancient Rome*, New York: McGraw Hill.

BALTZELL, A. Digby. (1950). *Philadelphia Gentlemen*, New Brunswick, New Jersey: Transaction Press.

BARBER, John. (2007, December 20). "Toronto Divided: A tale of three cities," *Globe and Mail*, http://www.urbancentre.utoronto.ca/pdfs/researchbulletins/RB41Media_Release2.pdf.

BARBIER, Edward B. (2011). *Scarcity and Frontiers: How Economies Have Developed Through Natural Resource Exploitation*, Cambridge: Cambridge University Press.

BARBOUR, Elisa. (2006, February). "Time to Work: Commuting Times and Modes of Transportation of California Workers," *Public Policy Institute of California*, http://www.ppic.org/main/publication.asp?i=660.

BARKHAM, Patrick. (2014, October 1). "Britain's housing crisis: are garden cities the answer?," *The Guardian*, http://www.theguardian.com/politics/2014/oct/01/britains-housing-crisis-are-gaden-cities-the-answer-ebbsfleet-kent-green-belt.

BARRAGAN, Bianca. (2014, April 2). "Los Angeles is the Biggest Anti-Sprawl Success Story in the US," *Curbed Los Angeles*, http://la.curbed.com/archives/2014/04/los_angeles_is_the_biggest_antisprawl_success_story_in_the_us.php.

BARRIONUEVA, Alexei. (2010, September 5). "Educational Gaps Limit Brazil's Reach," *New York Times*, http://www.nytimes.com/2010/09/05/world/americas/05brazil.html.

BARTA, Patrick and Paul HANNON. (2009, July 1). "Economic Crisis Curbs Migration of Workers," *Wall Street Journal*, http://www.wsj.com/articles/SB124636924020073241.

BARTA, Patrick and Krishna POKHAREL. (2009, May 13). "Megacities Threaten to Choke India," *Wall Street Journal*, http://www.wsj.com/articles/SB124216531392512435.

BARTLETT, Dana.(1907). *The Better City: A Sociological Study of a Modern City*, Los Angeles: Neuner Press.

BASU, Radha. (2012, March 21). "Retire on CPF Savings? Think Again," *Straits Times*, http://newshub.nus.edu.sg/news/1203/PDF/RETIRE-st-21mar-pA11.pdf.

BASULTO, Dominic. (2014, October 28). "The future of innovation belongs to the mega-city," *Washington Post*, http://www.washingtonpost.com/blogs/innovations/wp/2014/10/28/the-future-of-innovation-belongs-to-the-mega-city/.

BATALOVA, Jeanne. (2015). "Data Hub," *Migration Policy Institute*, http://www.migrationinformation.org/DataHub/gcmm.cfm#map1.

BATT, Andrew. (2013, November 19). "Asians buying two-thirds of London new-build homes," *PropertyGuru.com.sg*, http://www.propertyguru.com.sg/property-management -news/2013/11/36937/asians.

BAUCHAM, Voddie, Jr. (2012, June). "What About the Fatherless Families?," *FamilyLife*, http://www.familylife.com/articles/topics/faith/essentials/reaching-out/what-about -the-fatherless-families.

BBC NEWS. (2013, October 15). "More than a quarter of Londoners 'in poverty'," http://www.bbc.com/news/uk-england-london-24517391

BEAVERSTOCK, J.V., P.J. TAYLOR, and R.G. SMITH. (1999). "A Roster of World Cities," *Cities*, vol. 16, 445–458. doi: 10.1016/S0264-2751(99)00042-6.

BECERRIL, J.E. and B. JIMENEZ. (2007). "Potable water and sanitation in Tenochtitlan: Aztec culture," *IWA Publishing*, http://ws.iwaponline.com/content/7/1/147.

BECKERT, Sven. (2001). *The Monied Metropolis: New York City and the Consolidation of the American Bourgeoisie*, Cambridge: Cambridge University Press.

BELL, Daniel. (1973). *The Coming of Post-Industrial Society: A Venture in Social Forecasting*, New York: Basic Books.

BELL, Daniel A. and Avner DE-SHALIT. (2011). *The Spirit of Cities: Why the Identity of a City Matters in a Global Age*, Princeton, New Jersey: Princeton University Press.

BELLMAN, Eric. (2010, July 9). "A New Detroit Rises in India's South," *Wall Street Journal*, http://www.wsj.com/articles/SB10001424052748704111704575354853980451636.

BELVEDERE, Matthew J. (2013, October 8). "'End of suburbia' may nearly be upon us: Sam Zell," *CNBC*, http://www.cnbc.com/id/101095397#.

BENDAVID, Naftali. (2015, January 2). "Europe's Empty Churches Go on Sale," *Wall Street Journal*.

BENNETT, Oliver. (2012, March 16). "In the shadow of the Shard: Why the next generation of skyscrapers is struggling to get off the ground," *Independent*, http://www .independent.co.uk/property/house-and-home/in-the-shadow-of-the-shard-why-the -next-generation-of-skycrapers-is-struggling-to-get-off-the-ground-7574496.html.

——— (2015, February 26). "London's galloping high-rise developments face a backlash from protest movement," *Independent*, http://www.independent.co.uk /arts-entertainment/architecture/londons-galloping-highrise-developments-face -a-backlash-from-protest-movement-10073657.html.

BERGER, Martine. (1996). "Trajectories in Living Space, Employment and Housing Stock: The Example of the Parisian Metropolis in the 1980s and 1990s," *International Journal of Urban and Regional Research*, vol. 20, 240–254. doi: 10.1111/j.1468 -2427.1996.tb00314.x

BERNSTEIN, Sharon and Francisco VARA-ORTA. (2007, June 30). "Near the rails but on the road," *Los Angeles Times*, http://articles.latimes.com/2007/jun/30/local /me-transit30.

BERUBE, Alan. (2014, February 20). "All Cities Are Not Created Unequal," *Brookings*, http://www.brookings.edu/research/papers/2014/02/cities-unequal-berube.

BEVINS, Vincent. (2010, December 16). "Working to a Different Beat," *Financial Times*, http://www.ft.com/cms/s/0/03f66d2e-0899-11e0-b981-00144feabdco.html.

BHAGAT, R.B. (2011). "Emerging Pattern of Urbanisation in India," *Economic and Political Weekly*, vol. 46, 10–12, http://suburbin.hypotheses.org/files/2011/09 /RBBhagatUrbanisation.pdf.

BHAGAT, Simit. (2010, April 1). "How Mumbai lost its animal instinct," *Times of India*, http://timesofindia.indiatimes.com/city/mumbai/How-Mumbai-lost-its-animal -instinct/articleshow/5854425.cms.

BHAUMIK, Sumon Kumar, Shubhashis GANGOPADHYAY and Shagun KRISHNAN. (2009). "Reforms and Entry: Some Evidence from the Indian Manufacturing Sector," *Review of Development Economics*, vol. 13, 658–672. doi: 10.1111/j.1467-9361.2009.00519.x.

BIDOUX, Pierre-Emile, Emilie MOREAU and Sandra ROGER. (2010, January)."Paris gagne à nouveau des familles," *INSEE*, http://www.insee.fr/fr/themes/document .asp?reg_id=20&ref_id=15800&page=alapage/alap326/alap326.htm.

BINKOVITZ, Leah. (2015, April 18). "Study: Newer Houston suburbs offer best opportunities for minorities," *Houston Chronicle*, http://www.houstonchronicle.com /neighborhood/katy/news/article/Study-Newer-Houston-suburbs-offer-best-6209145 .php.

――――― (2015, January 10). "Suburbs look to become cultural centers," *Houston Chronicle*, http://www.houstonchronicle.com/neighborhood/katy/news/article/Suburbs-look-to -become-cultural-centers-6007080.php.

BISSINGER, Buzz. (1997). *A Prayer for the City*, New York: Random House.

BIVINS, Ralph. (2014, April 2). "Boom on! Houston notches more new home starts than the entire state of California," *CultureMap*, http://houston.culturemap.com/news /real-estate/04-02-14-boom-on-houston-notches-more-housing-starts-than-the-entire -state-of-california/.

BLAKE, Peter. (1979). *God's Own Junkyard: The Planned Deterioration of America's Landscape*, New York: Holt, Rinehart and Winston.

BLANCHFLOWER, David G. (2010, January 21). "Credit Crisis Creates Lost Generation: David G.Blanchflower," *bloomberg.com*, http://www.bloomberg.com/apps /news?pid=newsarchive&sid=aJ62ylOdJaAI (webpage discontinued).

BOARD ON ENERGY AND ENVIRONMENTAL SYSTEMS. (2009). *Driving and the Built Environment: The Effects of Compact Development on Motorized Travel, Energy Use, and CO2 Emissions*.

BOCK, Arthur E.R. (1955). *Manpower Shortage and the Fall of the Roman Empire in the West*, Ann Arbor: University of Michigan Press.

BOGART, William. (2006). *Don't Call It Sprawl: Metropolitan Structure in the 21st Century*, Cambridge: University Press.

BOLAND, Leo and Joe SIMPSON. (2010, July 4). "State of the Suburbs," *Local Futures Group for the Successful City-Suburbs Project*, http://www.localleadership.gov.uk/docs /suburbs.pdf.

BOLICK, Kate. (2011, November). "All the Single Ladies," *The Atlantic*, http://www .theatlantic.com/magazine/archive/2011/11/all-the-single-ladies/308654/.

BOOKMAN, Jay. (2009, November 23). "Sprawl has passed into history," *Houston Tomorrow*, http://www.houstontomorrow.org/commentary/story/jay-bookman/.

BOONE, Christopher C. and Ali MODARRES. (2006). *City and Environment*, Philadelphia: Temple University Press.

BOOTH, Robert. (2009, February 5). "Charles declares Mumbai shanty town model for the world," *The Guardian*, http://www.theguardian.com/artanddesign/2009/feb/06 /prince-charles-slum-comments.

BORUFKA, Sarah. (2010, May 23). "A Look Behind the Thin Walls of Czech *Panelák* Apartment Buildings," *Radio Prague*, http://www.radio.cz/en/section/czech-life /a-look-behind-the-thin-walls-of-czech-panelak-apartment-buildings.

BOSELEY, Sarah. (2014, March). "Sanitation, swift action when battling pandemics in megacities," *Taipai Times*, http://www.taipeitimes.com/News/editorials /archives/2014/03/02/2003584664.

BOSKER, Biana. (2014, August 20). "Why haven't China's cities learned from America's mistakes?," *The Guardian*, http://www.theguardian.com/cities/2014/aug/20/why -havent-chinas-cities-learned-from-americas-mistakes.

BOUCHER, Bernice. (2014, April 21). "14 Ways the Workplace is Evolving," *GlobeSt.com*, http://www.globest.com/commentary/office/14-Ways-the-Workplace-is-Evolving -345133.html.

BOWRING, Philip. (2012, July 5). "South Korea's Population Vacuum" *Asia Sentinel*, http://www.asiasentinel.com/society/south-koreas-population-vacuum/.

BRADSHER, Keith. (2002, December 27). "A High Tech Fix for One Corner of India," *New York Times*.

BRAND, Stewart. (2005, April 8). "Cities & Time," *The Long Now Foundation*, http://longnow.org/seminars/02005/apr/08/cities-and-time/.

———— (n. d.). "Urban squatters save the world," *McKinsey & Company*, http://voices .mckinseyonsociety.com/urban-squatters-save-the-world/.

BRANIGAN, Tania. (2011, October 2)."China becomes an urban nation at breakneck speed," *The Guardian*, http://www.theguardian.com/world/2011/oct/02/china -becomes-an-urban-nation.

———— (2011, October 3) "China's rural poor left stranded as urbanites race ahead," *The Guardian*, http://www.theguardian.com/world/2011/oct/03/china-rural-poor-left -stranded.

BRAUDEL, Fernand. (1979). *The Perspective of the World: Civilization and Capitalism: 15th -18th Century*, vol. 3, translated by Sian Reynolds, New York: Harper and Row.

———— (1992). *The Structures of Everyday Life*, Berkeley: University of California.

BREEN, Matthew. (2013, January 9). "Gayest Cities in America, 2013," *Advocate.com*, http://www.advocate.com/print-issue/current-issue/2013/01/09/gayest-cities -america-2013.

BREEN, Tom. (2013, February 11). "UConn/Hartford Courant Poll: Middle Class Dream Persists, Though Harder to Attain," *UConn Today*, http://today.uconn.edu /blog/2013/02/uconnhartford-courant-poll-middle-class-dream-persists-though -harder-to-attain/.

BRINKLEY, Joel. (2013, March/April). "China's Looming Crisis: Daunting Troubles Mount," *World Affairs*, http://www.worldaffairsjournal.org/article/china%E2%80%99s -looming-crisis-daunting-troubles-mount.

BROOK, Daniel. (2013). *A History of Future Cities*, New York: Norton.

BROWN, Eliot. (2012, July 12). "New York Lays Groundwork to Reshape Skyline," *Wall Street Journal*, http://www.wsj.com/articles/SB10001424052702303919504577523182 567585366.

———— (2013, October 11). "Chinese Builder Charges Into Brooklyn," *Wall Street Journal*, http://www.wsj.com/articles/SB10001424052702304520704579127822887005590.

―――― (2015, January 2). "Young Drive an Urban Rebound," *Wall Street Journal*, http://www.wsj.com/articles/young-drive-an-urban-rebound-1420250736.

BROWN, Patricia Leigh. (2004, June 17). "Defining Sprawl: From A to Z," *New York Times*, http://www.nytimes.com/2004/06/17/garden/design-notebook-defining -sprawl-from-a-to-z.html.

BRUECKNER, Jan K. and LARGEY, Ann G. (2006, October). "Social Interaction and Urban Sprawl," *Department of Economics, UC Irvine*, http://www.economics.uci.edu /files/economics/docs/workingpapers/2006-07/Brueckner-07.pdf.

BRUEGMANN, Robert. (2005). *Sprawl: A Compact History*, Chicago: University of Chicago Press.

BUFFALO BAYOU PARTNERSHIP. (2015). "Buffalo Bayou Park," *Buffalo Bayou Partnership*, http://buffalobayou.org/visit/.

BULA, Frances. (2009, April 10). "Vancouver building permits fall with economy," *The Globe and Mail*, http://www.theglobeandmail.com/news/national/vancouver-building -permits-fall-with-economy/article20441374/.

BURBANK, Jeremy and KEELY, Louise. (2014, September 16). "Millennials and their Homes," *Demand Institute*, http://demandinstitute.org/blog/millennials-and -their-homes.

BUREAU OF LABOR STATISTICS. (2012, November 7)."International Comparisons of GDP per Capita and per hour, 1960–2011," http://www.bls.gov/fls/intl_gdp_capita _gdp_hour.pdf.

BURKE, Peter. (1994). *Venice and Amsterdam*, Cambridge: Polity Press.

BUTLER, Chris. (2007). "The Rise of the Dutch Republic in the 1600's," *The Flow of History*, http://www.flowofhistory.com/units/west/14/FC93.

BYRD, Hugh, et al. (2013, October). "Measuring the Solar Potential of a City and Its Implications for Energy Policy," *Energy Policy*, vol. 61, 944–952, doi:10.1016 /j.enpol.2013.06.042.

CALLENBACH, Ernest. (1975). *Ecotopia*, Berkeley: Heyday Books.

CALTHORPE, Peter. (2011, February 1). "Urbanism in the Age of Climate Change: Urbanism Expanded," *Streetsblog SF*, http://sf.streetsblog.org/2011/02/01/urbanism -in-the-age-of-climate-change-urbanism-expanded/.

CAMPANELLA, Richard. (2013, March 1). "Gentrification and its Discontents: Notes from New Orleans," *New Geography*, http://www.newgeography.com/content/003526 -gentrification-and-its-discontents-notes-new-orleans.

CAMPO-FLORES, Arian and DOUGHERTY, Conor. (2013, December 1). "Overseas Money Pours Into Miami Real Estate," *Wall Street Journal*, http://online.wsj.com /news/articles/SB10001424052702303329045792238632032080576.

CANNUSCIO, Carolyn, BLOCK, Jason, and KAWACHI, Ichiro. (2003, September 2). "Social Capital and Successful Aging: The Role of Senior Housing," *American College of Physicians*, vol. 139, doi: 10.7326/0003-4819-139-5_Part_2-200309021-00003.

CAPUANO, Glenn. (2015, February 10). "Western Sydney profile, a region of diversity and growth," *.id*, http://blog.id.com.au/2015/population/local-government/western -sydney-diverse-and-growing-rapidly/.

CARCOPINO, Jerome. (1940). *Daily Life in Ancient Rome*, New Haven: Yale University Press.

CARLSON, Allan. (2006, January/February). "The Family Factors," *Touchstone,* http://www.touchstonemag.com/archives/article.php?id=19-01-023-f.

CARMONA, Michael (2002). *Hausmann: His Life and Times and the Making of Modern Paris,* Chicago: Dee.

CASTELLS, Manuel. (1999) "The Informational City is a Dual City: Can It Be Reversed," *High Technology and Low Income Communities: Prospects for the Positive Use of Advanced Information Technology,* Cambridge: MIT Press, 30–31.

——— (1989). *The Informational City,* London: Blackwell.

CBC NEWS. (2013, April 29). "Carbon footprint assumptions do not hold true for Halifax." http://www.cbc.ca/news/canada/nova-scotia/carbon-footprint-assumptions -do-not-hold-true-for-halifax-1.1371095.

——— (2014, August 19). "Top 10 most livable cities include Vancouver, Calgary and Toronto," http://www.cbc.ca/news/business/top-10-most-livable-cities-include -vancouver-calgary-and-toronto-1.2740493.

CELORIO, Gonzalo. (2004). "Mexico: City of Paper," *The Mexico City Reader,* Madison: Wisconsin University Press, 33–34.

CEOS FOR CITIES FACEBOOK PAGE. https://www.facebook.com/CEOsforCities/.

CHA, Ariana Eunjung. (2008, October 1). "Financial Hubs See an Opening Up at the Top," *Washington Post,* http://www.washingtonpost.com/wp-dyn/content/article /2008/09/30/AR2008093002718.html.

CHAMIE, Joseph and MIRKIN, Barry. (2012, March 8). "Childless by choice," *Khaleej Times,* http://www.khaleejtimes.com/article/20120308/ARTICLE/303089865/1098.

CHANG, Pao-Chi. (2014, December 9). "Building Construction," Encyclopedia Britannica, http://www.britannica.com/EBchecked/topic/83859/building-construction/60133 /Early-steel-frame-high-rises.

CHARRIER, J.B. (1988). *Villes et Campagnes,* Paris: Masson.

CHELALA, Cesar. (2012, June 6). "Demographic threat shadows a world power," *Japan Times,* http://www.japantimes.co.jp/opinion/2012/06/26/commentary /demographic-threat-shadows-a-world-power/.

CHEN, Te-Ping. (2012, March 27). "Hong Kong Frets Over Low Fertility Rate," *Wall Street Journal,* http://blogs.wsj.com/chinarealtime/2012/03/27/hong-kong-frets-over-low -fertility-rates/.

——— (2013, August 12)."Hong Kong's High Cost of Living Deters Would-Be Parents," *Wall Street Journal,* http://blogs.wsj.com/chinarealtime/2013/08/12/hong-kongs -high-cost-of-living-deters-would-be-parents.

——— (2013, October 3). "In Hong Kong, Retail Rents Lose Their Shine," *Wall Street Journal,* http://online.wsj.com/news/articles/SB1000142405270230349250457911115 41926639228.

CHEN, Te-Ping and YUNG, Chester. (2013, August 21). "Politics, Cost of Living Push Hong Kong Residents Overseas", *Wall Street Journal,* http://blogs.wsj.com /chinarealtime/2013/08/21/politics-cost-of-living-pushes-hong-kong-residents -overseas/.

CHERLIN, Andrew. (2013, January 25). "The deinstitutionalization of marriage," *The National Council on Family Relations,* https://www.ncfr.org/news/zippy-weekly-videos /deinstitutionalization-marriage.

CHESTERTON, G. K. (2013). *Orthodoxy,* London: Catholic Way Publishing.

CHEVREAU, Jonathan. (2015, March 24). "Urbs or Burbs? TD Survey finds generational divide on housing preferences," *Financial Independence Hub*, http://findependencehub .com/urbs-or-burbs-td-survey-finds-generational-divide-on-housing-preferences/.

CHIA, Arthur. (2013, August 17). "Singapore seeks its home," *New Geography*, http://www.newgeography.com/content/003881-singapore-seeks-its-home.

CHILD POLICY INTERNATIONAL. (2009, April). "France," Columbia University, http://www.childpolicyintl.org/countries/france.html (webpage discontinued).

CHILD POVERTY ACTION GROUP. "Child poverty in London," http://www.cpag.org.uk /campaigns/child-poverty-london.

CHO, Mihye. (2010, September). "Envisioning Seoul as a World City: The Cultural Politics of the Hong-dae Cultural District," *Asian Studies Review*, vol. 34, 329–347.

CHRISTIE, Joel. (2015, January 24). "Multi-billionaire who gave a lecture about American's 'needing to have less things and live a smaller existence' owns a staggering FIVE mansions . . . including the nation's most expensive home," *Daily Mail*, http://www.dailymail.co.uk/news/article-2924457/He-said-Multi-billionaire -gave-lecture-American-s-needing-things-live-smaller-existence-owns-FIVE-mansions -are.html.

CHRISTIE, Les. (2012, April 3). "The New American household: 3 generations, 1 roof," *CNN Money*, http://money.cnn.com/2012/04/03/real_estate/multi-generation -households/index.htm.

CHRISTOPHER, A.J. and TARVER, James D. (June 1994). "Urbanization during Colonial Days in Sub-Saharan Africa," *Urbanization in Africa: A Handbook*, Westport: Greenwood Press, 46–7.

CHU, Ben. (2014, February 9). "Britain is suffering from a housing crisis—who is to blame and how can we fix it?," *Independent*, http://www.independent.co.uk/property /house-and-home/property/britain-is-suffering-from-a-housing-crisis—who-is-to -blame-and-how-can-we-fix-it-9113329.html.

CINCO RANCH LIFE. "Cinco Ranch History," http://www.cincoranchlife.org/page /20251~312161/Cinco-Ranch-History.

CITY LIFE. (2014, April 25). "Micro Units—The Newest Trend in Real Estate," *CitiesJournal*, http://www.citiesjournal.com/micro-units-newest-trend-real-estate/.

CITY OF MELBOURNE. "Multicultural communities," http://www.melbourne.vic.gov.au /about-melbourne/melbourne-profile/Pages/multicultural-communities.aspx.

CITY-DATA.COM. "Cinco Ranch, Texas," http://www.city-data.com/city/Cinco-Ranch -Texas.html.

———— "New York, New York," *City-Data.com*, http://www.city-data.com/city/New-York -New-York.html.

———— "San Francisco, California," *City-Data.com*, http://www.city-data.com/city /San-Francisco-California.html.

CLAPSON, Mark. (1998). "Community and Association in Milton Keynes Since 1970," *The Best Laid Plans: Milton Keynes since 1967*, Luton: University of Luton Press, 101–106.

———— (2000). "The Suburban Aspiration in England Since 1919," *Contemporary British History*, vol. 14, 151–174. doi: 10.1080/13619460008581576.

CLARK, Frank. (2012, December 10). "The future of Chicago's schools," *Chicago Tribune*, http://articles.chicagotribune.com/2012-12-10/opinion/ct-oped-1210 -schools-20121210_1_shutter-schools-public-school-district-charter-schools.

CLARK, Gregory. (2007). *A Farewell to Alms: A Brief Economic History of the World*, New Jersey: Princeton University Press.

CLARK, Jeff. (2013). "Toronto: Visible Minorities," *Neoformix*, http://neoformix.com /Projects/DotMaps/TorontoVisMin.html.

CLARK, John G., et al. (1982). *Three Generations in Twentieth Century America*, Homewood: The Dorsey Press.

CLARK, Terry Nichols. (2004). "Urban Amenities," *The City as Entertainment Machine*, Amsterdam: Elsevier.

CLARK, Terry Nichols, et al. (2004). "Amenities Drive Urban Growth: A New Paradigm and Policy Linkages," *The City as Entertainment Machine*, Amsterdam: Elsevier, 291–318

CLARK, Terry Nichols and INGLEHART, Ronald. (1998). "The New Political Culture," *The New Political Culture*, Boulder: Westview Press.

COHEN, Abraham. (1975). *Everyman's Talmud*, New York: Schocken Books.

COHEN, Steven. (2014, June 16). "Individual Material Consumption, Guilt and the Crisis in Global Sustainability," *Huffington Post*, http://www.huffingtonpost.com/steven -cohen/individual-material-consu_b_5498831.html.

COLEBATCH, Tim. (2012, February 9). "Working longer, retiring stronger," *Sydney Morning Herald*, http://www.smh.com.au/federal-politics/political-news/working -longer-retiring-stronger-20120208-1rfog.html.

COLIN BUCHANAN AND PARTNERS. (2008, September). "The Economic Impact of High Density Development and Tall Buildings in Central Business Districts," *British Property Federation*.

COLLINS, Lois M. (2014, May 23). "The potential impact of falling fertility rates on the economy and culture," *Deseret News National*, http://national.deseretnews.com /article/1522/the-potential-impact-of-falling-fertility-rates-on-the-economy-and -culture.html

CONFESSORE, Nicholas. (2006, August 6). "Cities Grow Up, and Some See Sprawl," *New York Times*, http://www.nytimes.com/2006/08/06/weekinreview/06confessore .html.

CONN, Steven. (2004, August 17)."Let's make suburbs into cities: New urbanism, car culture and the future of community," *Salon*, http://www.salon.com/2014/08/17 /lets_make_suburbs_into_cities_new_urbanism_car_culture_and_the_future_of _community/.

CONSTANTINEAU, Bruce. (2014, March 17). "'Huge demand' for tiny rental units in Vancouver," *Vancouver Sun*. http://www.vancouversun.com/Huge+demand+tiny +rental+units+Vancouver/9628610/story.html.

COONTZ, Stephanie. (1992). *The Way We Never Were: American Families and the Nostalgia Trap*, New York: Basic Books.

COOPER, James Fenimore. (2002). "From Notions of the Americans and New York," *Empire City: New York Through the Centuries*, New York: Columbia University Press.

CORTRIGHT, Joe and MAHMOUDI, Dillon. (2014, December). "Lost in Place: Why the persistence and spread of concentrated poverty—not gentrification—is our biggest urban challenge," *CityReport*, http://cityobservatory.org/wp-content/uploads/2014/12 /LostinPlace_12.4.pdf.

COSCARELLI, Joe. (2013, September 20). "Michael Bloomberg Thinks He's a 'Godsend'," *NYMAG*, http://nymag.com/daily/intelligencer/2013/09/michael-bloomberg -billionaires-are-a-godsend.html.

COX, Wendell. (2015, February 21). "10 most affluent cities in the world: Macau and Hartford top the list," *New Geography*, http://www.newgeography.com /content/004853-10-most-affluent-cities-world-macau-and-hartford-top-list.

———— (2010). "2010 Major Metropolitan Area & Principal Urban Area (Urbanized Area) Population & Density," *Demographia*, http://demographia.com/db-msauza2010.pdf.

———— (2011, February 9). "Australia's Housing Affordability 'Outrage'," *New Geography*, http://www.newgeography.com/content/002038-australias-housing-affordability -outrage.

———— (2014, August 22). "Beyond polycentricity: 2000s job growth (continue to) flow population," *New Geography*, http://www.newgeography.com/content/004486 -beyond-polycentricity-2000s-job-growth-continues-follow-population.

———— (2012, April 18). "California declares war on suburbia II: The cost of radical densification," *New Geography*, http://www.newgeography.com/content/002781 -california-declares-war-suburbia-ii-the-cost-radical-densification.

———— (2012, June 1). "China's Top Growth Cities," *New Geography*, http://www .newgeography.com/content/002873-chinas-top-growth-centers.

———— (2011, July 8). "The Costs of Smart Growth Revisited: A 40 Year Perspective," *New Geography*, http://www.newgeography.com/content/002324-the-costs-smart-growth -revisited-a-40-year-perspective.

———— (2010, June 11). "The Declining Human Footprint," *New Geography*, http://www .newgeography.com/content/001615-the-declining-human-footprint.

———— (2015, January). "Demographia World Urban Areas," 11 ed., *Demographia*, http://www.demographia.com/db-worldua.pdf.

———— (2012, July 30). "Density is not the issue: The urban scaling research," *New Geography*, http://www.newgeography.com/content/002987-density-not-issue-the -urban-scaling-research.

———— (2014, July 9). "Dispersing Millennials," *New Geography*, http://www .newgeography.com/content/004410-dispersing-millennials.

———— (2015, May 13). "Dispersion and Concentration in Metropolitan Employment," *New Geography*, http://www.newgeography.com/content/004921-dispersion-and -concentration-metropolitan-employment.

———— (2013, February 6). "Dispersion in the World's Largest Urban Areas," *New Geography*, http://www.newgeography.com/content/003468-dispersion-worlds -largest-urban-areas.

———— (2011, August 29). "The Evolving Urban Form: Beijing," *New Geography*, http://www.newgeography.com/content/002406-the-evolving-urban-form-beijing.

———— (2012, August 8). "Evolving Urban Form: Dhaka," *New Geography*, http://www .newgeography.com/content/003004-evolving-urban-form-dhaka.

———— (2011, September 14). "The Evolving Urban Form: Milan," *New Geography*, http://www.newgeography.com/content/002441-the-evolving-urban-form-milan.

———— (2011, February 17). "The Evolving Urban Form: Seoul," *New Geography*, http://www.newgeography.com/content/002060-the-evolving-urban-form-seoul.

———— (2011, June 16). "The Evolving Urban Form: Shanghai," *New Geography,* http://www.newgeography.com/content/002283-the-evolving-urban-form-shanghaiData.

———— (2012, June 20). "The Evolving Urban Form: Tokyo," *Newgeography.com,* http://www.newgeography.com/content/002923-the-evolving-urban-form-tokyo.

———— (2014, December 29). "Exodus of the School Children," *New Geography,* http://www.newgeography.com/content/004815-exodus-school-children.

———— (2012, October 1). "Flocking Elsewhere: The Downtown Growth Story," *New Geography,* http://www.newgeography.com/content/003108-flocking-elsewhere-the-downtown-growth-story.

———— (2009, April 8). "Greenhouse Gas Emissions and Reality: Residential Emissions," *New Geography,* http://www.newgeography.com/content/00728-greenhouse-gas-emissions-and-reality-residential-emissions.

———— (2010). "Home Ownership by Type of Urban Sector," *Demographia,* http://www.demographia.com/db-csm-own.pdf.

———— (2014, November). "Housing Affordability and the Standard of Living in Toronto," *Frontier Centre for Public Policy,* http://archive.fcpp.org/sites/default/files/toronto-housing.pdf.

———— (2006, January). "How the Suburbs Made Us Rich," *PA Townships,* http://www.demographia.com/psats-suburbsrich.pdf.

———— "Major Metropolitan Area & Core Municipality Population: 1950 & 2010," *Demographia,* http://www.demographia.com/db-19502010mmsa.pdf.

———— "Major Urban Area Densities: Australia," *Demographia,* http://www.demographia.com/db-ucentres0611.pdf.

———— (2010, August 5). "Melbourne: Government Seeking Housing Affordability," *New Geography,* http://www.newgeography.com/content/001708-melbourne-government-seeking-housing-affordability.

———— (2014, June 25). "New York, Legacy Cities Dominate Transit Urban Core Gains," *New Geography,* http://www.newgeography.com/content/004384-new-york-legacy-cities-dominate-transit-urban-core-gains.

———— (2012, July 2). "Pakistan: Where the Population Bomb is Exploding," *New Geography,* http://www.newgeography.com/content/002940-pakistan-where-population-bomb-exploding.

———— (2014, September 17). "Paving over Hunan? The Portland Model for China," *New Geography,* http://www.newgeography.com/content/004525-paving-over-hunan-the-portland-model-china.

———— (2013, August 28). "Plan Bay Area: Telling People What to Do," *New Geography,* http://www.newgeography.com/content/003899-plan-bay-area-telling-people-what-do.

———— (2011, September 29). "Smart growth (livability), air pollution and public health," *New Geograhpy,* http://www.newgeography.com/content/002462-smart-growth-livability-air-pollution-and-public-health.

———— (2012, February 14). "Special Report: Census 2011: Urban Dispersion in Canada," *New Geography,* http://www.newgeography.com/content/002672-special-report-census-2011-urban-dispersion-canada.

———— "Southeast England Population by Area from 1891," *Demographia,* http://www.demographia.com/db-seuk1891.pdf.

—— (2013, October 23). "Suburban & Urban Core Poverty: 2012: Special Report," *New Geography*, http://www.newgeography.com/content/004006-suburban-urban-core -poverty-2012-special-report.

—— (2014, August 1). "Urban Cores, Core Cities, and Principal Cities," *New Geography*, http://www.newgeography.com/content/004453-urban-cores-core-cities -and-principal-cities.

—— (2015, March 6). "Urban Core Millennials? A Matter of Perspective", *New Geography*, http://www.newgeography.com/content/004864-urban-core-millennials -a-matter-perspective.

—— (2013, July). "Urban Policy: A Time for a Paradigm Shift," *Frontier Centre for Public Policy*, https://www.heartland.org/sites/default/files/cox_urban_shift.pdf.

—— (2013, June 15). "U.S. Sets New House Record in 2012," *New Geography*, http://www.newgeography.com/content/003772-us-sets-new-house-size-record-2012.

—— (2012, November 21). "What is a Half-Urban World", *New Geography*, http://www .newgeography.com/content/003249-what-a-half-urban-world.

—— (2015, January 27). "World Megacities: Densities Fall as they become Larger," *New Geography*, http://www.newgeography.com/content/004835-world-megacities -densities-fall-they-become-larger.

—— "World Megacities: Growing & Becoming Less Dense," *New Geography*, http://www .newgeography.com/content/004823-megacities-growing-and-getting-less-dense.

COX, Wendell and PAVLETICH, Hugh. (2014). "11th Annual Demographia International Housing Affordability Survey: 2015," *Demographia*, http://www.demographia.com /dhi.pdf.

COY, Peter. (2012, November 16). "The Death of the McMansion Has Been Greatly Exaggerated," *Bloomberg Business*, http://www.bloomberg.com/bw/articles /2012-11-16/death-of-the-mcmansion-has-been-greatly-exaggerated.

CRITSER, Greg. (2010, September 2). "A Pill For Los Angeles? Medicating the Megacities," *Newgeography.com*, http://www.newgeography.com/content/001742-a -pill-for-los-angeles-medicating-megacities.

CROSSLEY, David. (2009, October 12). "Is the Grand Parkway out of sync with community priorities?,"*Chron*, http://blog.chron.com/thelist/2009/10/is-the-grand -parkway-out-of-sync-with-community-priorities/.

CURTIN, Philip D. (1984) *Cross-Cultural Trade in world history*, Cambridge: Cambridge University Press.

CZEKALINSKI, Stephanie. (2012, July 19). "Suburbs Diversify but Many Areas Still Segregated, Report Says," *National Journal*, http://www.nationaljournal.com /thenextamerica/demographics/suburbs-diversify-but-many-areas-still-segregated -report-says-20120719.

DAILY MAIL REPORTER. (2012, April 5). "American suburbs turning into ghost towns: How homeowners are ditching out of town areas to live in city areas," *Daily Mail*, http://www.dailymail.co.uk/news/article-2125507/American-suburbs-turning-ghost -towns-How-homeowners-ditching-town-areas-live-big-cities.html.

DALEY, John and WOOD, Danielle. (2014, December 9). "The wealth of generations," *Grattan Institute*, http://grattan.edu.au/report/the-wealth-of-generations/.

DARROCH, Gordon. (2014, October 19). "Dutch battle surge of desperate, violent Muslim refugees," *Washington Times*, http://www.washingtontimes.com/news/2014 /oct/19/dutch-battle-surge-of-desperate-violent-muslim-ref/.

DAS, Gurcharan. (2009). "At last, good news about poverty," *Times of India Blogs*, http://blogs.timesofindia.indiatimes.com/men-and-ideas/at-last-good-news-about/.

DAVID, Quentin, et al. (2013). "Is Bigger Better? Economic Performance of European Cities, 1960–1990," *Cities*, vol. 35, 237–254.

DAVIDSON, Jacob. (2014, August 13). "You'll Never Guess the City Where Private School Is Most Common," *Time*, http://time.com/money/3105112/private-school-enrollment -cities-highest/.

DAVIES, Alan. (2012, March 20)."Is suburban living a neurotic condition?," *Crikey*, http://blogs.crikey.com.au/theurbanist/2012/03/20/is-suburban-living-a-neurotic -condition/.

DAVIES, Alex. (2015, March 9). "Self-Driving Cars Will Make Us Want Fewer Cars," *Wired*, http://www.wired.com/2015/03/the-economic-impact-of-autonomous -vehicles/.

DAVIS, Bob and PAGE, Jeremy. (2011, March 7). "China's Focus Turns to its Poor," *Wall Street Journal*, http://www.wsj.com/articles/SB10001424052748703362804576184364 247082474.

de BARY, William Theodore, CHAN, Wing-Tsit and WATSON, Burton. (1960). *The Sources of Chinese Tradition*, New York: Columbia University Press.

de CASTELLA, Tom. (2011, October 25)."Eight radical solutions to the housing crisis," *BBC News Magazine*, http://www.bbc.com/news/magazine-15400477.

de LACEY, Martha. (2012, September 25). "The REAL Story of Britain's servant class," *Daily Mail*, http://www.dailymail.co.uk/femail/article-2207935/Downton-Abbey -servants-New-BBC-series-Servants-The-True-Story-Life-Below-Stairs.html.

de PAULO, Bella. (2006). *Singled Out: How Singles are Stereotyped, Stigmatized and Ignored, and Still Live Happily Ever After*, New York: St. Martins/Griffin.

de VRIES, Jan. (1984). *European Urbanization 1500-1800*, London: Routledge.

DEAN, Jason. (2006, December 18). "How Capitalist Transformation Exposes Holes in China's Government," *Wall Street Journal*, http://www.wsj.com/articles /SB116639648334652910.

DEMAND INSTITUTE. (2013). "Millennials and Their Homes: Still Seeking the American Dream," http://demandinstitute.org/demandwp/wp-content/uploads /2015/01/millennials-and-their-homes-final.pdf.

DePARLE, Jason, GEBELOFF, Robert, and TAVERNISE, Sabrina. (2011, November 18). "Older, Suburban and Struggling, 'Near Poor' Startle the Census," *New York Times*, http://www.nytimes.com/2011/11/19/us/census-measures-those-not-quite-in-poverty -but-struggling.html.

DESAI, Rajiv. (2009, November 16). "Incredible India Indeed," *Times of India*, http://timesofindia.indiatimes.com/home/opinion/edit-page/Incredible-India -Indeed/articleshow/5232986.cms.

DESOUZA, Kevin C. (2014, February 18). "Our Fragile Emerging Megacities: A Focus on Resilience," *Planetizen: The Urban Planning, Design, and Development Network*, http://www.planetizen.com/node/67338.

DEWAN, Shaila. (2013, December 4). "Home Buyers Are Scarce, So Renters Take Their Place," *New York Times*, http://www.nytimes.com/2013/12/05/business/first-time -buyers-are-scarce-so-in-some-cities-renters-move-in.html.

DILLON, Sam. (2009, April 22). "Large Urban-Suburban Gap Seen in Graduation Rates," *New York Times*, http://www.nytimes.com/2009/04/22/education/22dropout.html.

diPASQUALE, D. and GLAESER, E. (1998). "Incentives and Social Capital: Are Homeowners Better Citizens?," *Journal of Urban Economics*, vol. 45.

DIVERSITY OFFICER MAGAZINE. (2008, November 3). "Higher birthrates among Sweden's foreign-born," http://diversityofficermagazine.com/diversity-news/hot-diversity-news/.

DOBBS, Richard. (2010, August 16). "Megacities," *Foreign Policy*, http://foreignpolicy.com/2010/08/16/megacities/.

DOBBS, Richard, et al. (2012, June). "Urban world: Cities and the rise of the consuming class," *McKinsey & Company*, http://www.mckinsey.com/insights/urbanization/urban_world_cities_and_the_rise_of_the_consuming_class.

DOBBS, Richard, REMES, Jaana, SMIT, Sven, MANYIKA, James, ROXBURGH, Charles, and RESTREPO, Alejandra. (2011, March). "Urban world: Mapping the economic power of cities," *McKinsey & Company*, http://www.mckinsey.com/insights/urbanization/urban_world.

DOBRINER, William N. (1963). *Class In Suburbia*, Englewood Cliffs: Prentice Hall.

DOMINICZAK, Peter. (2014, December 1). "Bicester announced as new garden city," *Telegraph*, http://www.telegraph.co.uk/finance/autumn-statement/11266801/Bicester-annouced-as-new-garden-city.html.

DONALD, Alastair. (2008). "A Green Unpleasant Land," *The Future of Community: Reports of a Death Greatly Exaggerated*, London: Pluto Press.

———— (2011) "The Emerging City," *The Lure of the City: From Slums to Suburbs*, London: Pluto Press.

DONALDSON, Scott. (1977). "City and Country: Marriage Proposals," *New Towns and the Suburban Dream*, Port Washington: Kennikat Press.

DONG, Liu. (2012, November 1). "Public outrage derailing China's growing number of needed plants," *Global Times*, http://www.globaltimes.cn/content/803913.shtml.

DOSICK, Jonathan. (2012, September 17). "Common Sense, Deferred: Lessons from the 'Fresh Air' Fight, Part One," *Made in America*, https://www.madinamerica.com/2012/09/common-sense-deferred-lessons-from-the-fresh-air-fight/.

DOUGHERTY, Conor. (2009, July 1). "Cities Grow at Suburbs' Expense During Recession," *Wall Street Journal*, http://www.wsj.com/articles/SB124641839713978195.

———— (2009, March 31). "In the Exurbs, the American Dream Is Up for Rent," *Wall Street Journal*, http://www.wsj.com/articles/SB123845433832571407.

DOUGHERTY, James. (1986). "Exiles in the Earthly City," *Civitas: Religious Interpretations of the City*, Atlanta: Scholar Press.

DOWNS, A. (1994). *New Visions for Metropolitan America*, Washington, DC: Brookings Institution Press.

DPCD SPATIAL ANALYSIS AND RESEARCH BRANCH. (2009, July). "Demographic characteristics of communities within the Melbourne Investigation Area," Victorian Environmental Assessment Council and Metropolitan Melbourne Investigation, http://www.veac.vic.gov.au/reports/VEAC%20demographics%20report%20Final%2014.7.09.pdf.

DR. HOUSING BUBBLE. (2012, August 5). "Rental Nation: US Home ownership rate continues to decline to multi-decade lows while rental vacancies continue to decline. Record prices in few areas," http://www.doctorhousingbubble.com/rental-nation-rental-vacany-rate-home-ownership-rate-number-of-renters-increases/.

DRAPER, Robert. (2013, September). "Kinshasa, Urban Pulse of the Congo," *National Geographic*, http://ngm.nationalgeographic.com/2013/09/kinshasa-congo/draper-text.

DREIER, Peter, MOLLENKOPF, John, and SWANSTROM, Todd. (2002). *Place Matters: Metropolitics for the Twenty-first Century*, Lawrence: University Press of Kansas.

DREILING, Martin. (2007, December 24). "New Urbanism Examined by Time Magazine, Andres Duany," *Planetizen*, http://www.planetizen.com/node/29063.

DREW, Rachel Bogardus and HERBERT, Christopher. (2012, August). "Post-Recession Drivers or Preferences for Homeownership," *Joint Center for Housing Studies*, Harvard University, http://www.jchs.harvard.edu/sites/jchs.harvard.edu/files/w12-4_drew_herbert.pdf.

DUANY, Andres, PLATER- ZYBERK, Elizabeth, and SPECK, Jeff. (2000). *Suburban Nation: The Rise of Sprawl and the Decline of the American Dream*, New York: North Point Press.

DUCKER, Adam and GARDNER, Bob. (2011, August). "Anticipating the Upscale Empty-Nester Condo Market Recovery," *RCLCO*, http://www.rclco.com/generalpdf/general_Aug232011855_RCLCO_Advisory_August_2011.pdf.

DUELL, Mark. (2011, June 30). "Census reveals African-American children are leaving large U.S. cities as their young parents head for better life in suburbs," *Daily Mail*, http://www.dailymail.co.uk/news/article-2009903/African-American-children-leaving-biggest-U-S-cities-young-parents-head-suburbs.html.

DUNN, Ross E. (1987). *The Adventures of Ibn Battuta: A Muslim Traveler of the 14th Century*, Berkeley: University of California Press.

DURKIN, Martin. (2012, January 13). "Three Cheers for Urban Sprawl," *New Geography*, http://www.newgeography.com/content/002622-three-cheers-urban-sprawl.

DYOS, H.J. et al. (1968). "Agenda for Urban Historians," *The Study of Urban History*, New York: St. Martin's Press.

EARNSHAW, Martin. (2008). "Communities on the Couch," *The Future of Community*, London: Pluto Press.

EASTERBROOK, Gregg. (1999, March 15). "Suburban Myths," *The New Republic*.

EBERSTADT, Nicholas. (2005, November 15). "Old Age Tsunami," *American Enterprise Institute*, https://www.aei.org/publication/old-age-tsunami/.

——— (2010, November/December). "The Demographic Future," *Foreign Affairs*, http://www.foreignaffairs.com/articles/66805/nicholas-eberstadt/the-demographic-future.

——— (2015, February 21). "The Global Flight From the Family," *Wall Street Journal*, http://www.wsj.com/articles/nicholas-eberstadt-the-global-flight-from-the-family-1424476179.

EDSALL, Thomas B. (2013, October 22). "Bill de Blasio and the New Urban Populism," *New York Times*, http://www.nytimes.com/2013/10/23/opinion/edsall-bill-de-blasio-and-the-new-urban-populism.html.

EFRATI, Amir. (2006, June 2). "The Suburbs Under Siege," *Wall Street Journal*, http://www.wsj.com/articles/SB114921327859169468.

EHRLICH, Paul. (1968). *The Population Bomb*, New York: Ballantine Books.

EISCHEN, Kyle. (2000, March 19). "India's high-tech marvel makes abstract real," *San Jose Mercury*.

ELDRIDGE, H. Wentworth. (1975). "Urbanization: A Never Ending Process," *World Capitals: Toward Guided Urbanization*, Garden City: Anchor Press.

ELLIOT, Ross. (2013, October 18)."Bubble, bubble, toil and trouble," *The National Forum*, http://www.onlineopinion.com.au/view.asp?article=15588.

El NASSER, Haya. (2008, April 18). "Modern suburbia not just in America anymore," *USA Today*, http://usatoday30.usatoday.com/news/world/2008-04-15-suburbia_N.htm.

ELSEA, Daniel. (2005, April 24). "China's chichi suburbs/American-style sprawl all the rage in Beijing," *SFGate*, http://www.sfgate.com/opinion/article/China-s-chichi -suburbs-American-style-sprawl-2686119.php.

EMRATH, Paul and SINIAVSKAIA, Natalia. (2009). "Household Type, Housing Choice, and Commuting Behavior," National Association of Home Builders, https://www .nahb.org/en/research/housing-economics/special-studies/household-type-housing -choice-and-commuting-behavior-2009.aspx.

ENGELHART, Gary V. (2006, December 1). "Study on Housing Trends Among Baby Boomers," *Research Institute for Housing America*, http://www.housingamerica.org /Publications/StudyonHousingTrendsAmongBabyBoomers.htm.

ENGELKE, Peter and NORDENMAN, Magnus. (2014, January 30). "Megacity Slums and Urban Insecurity," *Atlantic Council*, http://www.atlanticcouncil.org/blogs /futuresource/megacity-slums-and-urban-insecurity.

ENGELS, Frederick. (2009). *The Condition of the Working Class in England*, Oxford: Oxford University Press.

ENGLEN, Theo. (2003). "Demographic Aspects of the European Family," *Family Life in the 20th Century, The History of the European Family*, New Haven: Yale University Press.

ENGLISH.NEWS.CN. (2014, January 30). "Singapore's total fertility rate slips again in 2013," http://news.xinhuanet.com/english/health/2014-01/30/c_133085388.htm.

ERDBRINK, Thomas. (2012, June 12). "Single Women Slowly Gain Acceptance in Iran," *New York Times*, http://www.nytimes.com/2012/06/13/world/middleeast/single -women-gaining-limited-acceptance-in-iran.html.

ESKENAZI, Joe. (2012, March 9). "Newsflash: San Francisco Expensive, Minorities and Families Leaving," *SF Weekly*, http://www.sfweekly.com/thesnitch/2012/03/09 /newsflash-san-francisco-expensive-minorities-and-families-leaving.

ESPINOSA, Julio Serrano and CASANOVA, Rosa. (2008, October 12). *Nos Movemos? La Movilidad Social en Mexico*, Fundacion ESRU.

EURACTIV.COM. (2011, August 23). "Europeans overwhelmingly against immigration: Poll," http://www.euractiv.com/future-eu/europeans-overwhelmingly-immigration -poll-news-507074.

EUROPEAN CHAMBER AND ROLAND BERGER STRATEGY CONSULTANTS. (2011, April 11). "Europe Business in China: Asia-Pacific Headquarters Study," http://www.rolandberger.com/media/publications/2011-04-11-rbsc-pub-Asia_Pacific _Headquarters_study.html

EUROPEAN ENVIRONMENT AGENCY REPORT. (2006, October). "Urban sprawl in Europe," http://www.eea.europa.eu/publications/eea_report_2006_10. FACKLER, Martin. (2008, March 27). "The Builder Who Pushes Tokyo Into the Clouds," *New York Times*, http://www.nytimes.com/2008/03/27/business/worldbusiness/27mori .html.

———— (2010, October 16). "Japan Goes From Dynamic to Disheartened," *New York Times*, (http://www.nytimes.com/2010/10/17/world/asia/17japan.html.

FAHMY, Dalia. (2014, May 27). "25 Years After Communism, Eyesores Spur Landmark Debate," *Bloomberg Business,* http://www.bloomberg.com/news/articles/2014-05-26 /25-years-after-communism-eyesores-spur-landmark-debate.

FAINSTEIN, Susan. (1994). *The City Builders: Property, Politics and Planning in London and New York,* London: Blackwell Publishers.

FARAGE, Nigel. (2014, December 18). "Surprise, surprise: tens of thousands of illegal immigrants have dropped off the Home Office's radar," *The Independent,* http://www .independent.co.uk/voices/comment/surprise-surprise-tens-of-thousands-of-illegal -immigrants-have-dropped-off-the-home-offices-radar-9934496.html

FARRAR, Lara. (2008, June 21). "Is America's suburban dream collapsing into a nightmare?," *CNN,* http://www.cnn.com/2008/TECH/06/16/suburb.city/index.html.

FASHIONUNITED. (2013). "Facts and Figures about the Fashion Industry," http://www .fashionunited.co.uk/facts-and-figures-in-the-uk-fashion-industry.

FEARN, Jonathan, PINKSTON, Denise, and ARENSON, Nicolas. (n. d.). "The Bay Area Housing Crisis: A Developer's Perspective," *Submittal to Plan Bay Area.*

FEDERAL BUREAU OF INVESTIGATION. (2011). "Violent Crime," http://www.fbi.gov /about-us/cjis/ucr/crime-in-the-u.s/2011/crime-in-the-u.s.-2011/violent-crime /violent-crime.

FEDERAL HIGHWAY ADMINISTRATION. (2012, December). "Traffic Volume Trends," http://www.fhwa.dot.gov/policyinformation/travel_monitoring/12dectvt/12dectvt.pdf.

FEHRENBACHER, Katie. (2013, June 21). "London's tech startup scene is hot—just don't compare it to Silicon Valley," *Gigaom,* http://gigaom.com/2013/06/21/londons-tech -startup-scene-is-hot-just-dont-compare-it-to-silicon-valley/.

FERGUSON, Rick and PEAKE, Richard. (2013). "Born This Way: The Australian Millennial Loyalty Survey," *Aimia.*

FESUS, Gabriella, et al. (2008, November). "Regions 2020: Demographic Challenges for European Regions," *Commission of the European Communities,* http://ec.europa .eu/regional_policy/sources/docoffic/working/regions2020/pdf/regions2020 _demographic.pdf.

FIGES, Orlando. (1996). *A People's Tragedy: The Russian Revolution 1891–1924,* New York: Penguin Press.

FISCHEL, William. (1995). *Regulatory Takings, Law, Economics and Politics,* Cambridge: Harvard University Press.

FISCHLER, Marcelle S. (2011, December 1). "Long Island/In the Region—'Walkable' Steps Into the Sunlight," *New York Times,* http://www.nytimes.com/2011/12/04 /realestate/long-island-in-the-region-walkable-steps-into-the-spotlight.html.

FISHER, Bruce. (2012, July 5). "Abundant Oil Again?," *Artvoice,* http://artvoice.com /issues/v11n27/news_analysis.

FISHMAN, Robert. (1997, Winter/Spring). "Cities After the End of Cities: towards an urban pluralism," *Harvard Design Magazine.*

FISHMAN, William. (1979). *The Streets of East London,* London: Duckworth.

FLEMING, Amy and ARNETT, George. (2014, February 24). "Interactive map: do city residents live longer?," *The Guardian,* http://www.theguardian.com/cities/datablog /ng-interactive/2014/feb/24/interactive-map-do-people-living-in-cities-live-longer.

FLEW, Terry. (2011). "Right to the City, Desire for the Suburb?," *M/C Journal,* vol. 14, no. 4, http://journal.media-culture.org.au/index.php/mcjournal/article/viewArticle/368.

FLORCRUZ, Michelle. (2015, February 7). "China's Housing Market Bubble: Home Ownership Elusive for Young Buyers and Renters," *International Business Times,* http://www.ibtimes.com/chinas-housing-market-bubble-home-ownership-elusive -young-buyers-renters-1808472.

FLORIDA, Richard. (2009, March). "How the Crash Will Reshape America," *The Atlantic,* http://www.theatlantic.com/magazine/archive/2009/03/how-the-crash-will -reshape-america/307293/.

———— (2012, July 31)."Want To Make a Creative City? Build Out, Not Up," *NPR,* http:// www.npr.org/2012/07/31/157664837/want-to-make-a-creative-city-build-out-not-up.

———— (2013, January 31). "The Fading Differentiation between City and Suburb," *Urban Land,* http://urbanland.uli.org/economy-markets-trends/the-fading-differentiation -between-city-and-suburb/.

———— (2013, April 4). "America's Most (and Least) Religious Metro Areas," *CityLab,* http://www.theatlanticcities.com/neighborhoods/2013/04/americas-most-and-least -religious-metro-areas/5180/.

———— (2013, October 24). "America's Top 25 High-Tech Spots," *The Atlantic CityLab,* http://www.theatlanticcities.com/jobs-and-economy/2013/10/americas-top-25-high -tech-hotspots/7335/.

———— (2014, May 8). "What is the World's Most Economically Powerful City?," *The Atlantic,* http://www.theatlantic.com/business/archive/2012/05/what-is-the-worlds -most-economically-powerful-city/256841/.

FLORIDA, Richard and JOHNSON, Sara. (2012, September 7). "The World's Leading Cities for Fashion," *CityLab,* http://www.citylab.com/work/2012/09/worlds-leading -cities-fashion/3182/.

FOGELSON, Robert. (2001). *Downtown: Its Rise and Fall 1880–1950,* New Haven: Yale University Press.

FOLEY, John. (2009, December 30). "Three Hurdles for China in the Year of the Tiger," *New York Times,* http://www.nytimes.com/2009/12/30/business/30views.html.

FORD, Ford Madox. (1995). *The Soul of London,* London: Orion Publishing.

FORREST, Ray and YIP, Ngai ming. (2013). *Young People and Housing,* Abingdon: Routledge.

FORSYTH, Ann. (2005, May). "Grading the Irvine Ranch," *American Planning Association,* http://marketing.irvinecompany.com/public_affairs/bren/planning/planning _grading_p1.html.

FOX, Andie. (2014, January 14). "Why Suburbia Snobs are Wrong," *The Guardian,* http://www.theguardian.com/commentisfree/2014/jan/15/why-suburbia-snobs-are -wrong.

FOXMAN, Simone and FERDMAN, Roberto A. (2013, June 3). "At the heart of Istanbul's political upheaval is a whirlwind of authoritarian building," *Quartz,* http://qz.com /90304/at-the-heart-of-turkeys-political-upheaval-is-a-whirlwind-of-authoritarian- building/.

FRANCOIS, Etienne. (1990). "The German Urban Network between the Sixteenth and Eighteenth Centuries," *Urbanization in History: A Process of Dynamic Interactions,* London: Clarendon Press.

FREEMAN, Mike. (2008, December 7). "Condo calamity," *UT San Diego,* http://www .utsandiego.com/uniontrib/20081207/news_mz1b7condo.html.

FREIDMAN, Benjamin M. (2005). *The Moral Consequences of Economic Growth*, New York: Knopf.

FREIDMAN, David and HERNANDEZ, Jennifer. (2015). "California Environmental Quality Act, Greenhouse Gas Regulation and Climate Change," Chapman University Press, http://www.chapman.edu/wilkinson/_files/GHGfn.pdf.

FREJKA, Tomas, JONES, Gavin W., and SARDON, Jean-Paul. (2010, September). "East Asian Childbearing Patterns and Policy Developments," *Population and Development Review*, vol. 36, http://www.ncbi.nlm.nih.gov/pubmed/20882707.

FREY, William H. (2011, May). "Melting Pot Cities and Suburbs: Racial and Ethnic Change in Metro America in the 2000s," *State of Metropolitan America*, http://www .brookings.edu/~/media/research/files/papers/2011/5/04%20census%20ethnicity %20frey/0504_census_ethnicity_frey.pdf.

———— (2015, April 8). "Migration to the suburbs and Sun Belt picks up," *Brookings*, http://www.brookings.edu/research/opinions/2015/04/08-migration-suburbs-sun -belt-frey.

FRIES, John. (2012). "2012 Member Opinion Survey," *AARP Research & Strategic Analysis*, http://www.aarp.org/content/dam/aarp/research/surveys_statistics/general/2013 /2012-Member-Opinion-Survey-Issue-Spotlight-Home-and-Family-AARP.pdf.

FUHR, Joseph, Jr. and POCIASK, Stephen. (2007, October 31). "Broadband Services: Economic and Social Benefits," *American Consumer Institute*.

FURRY BROWN DOG BLOG. (2010, August 6). "Putting Singapore's GDP in perspective," http://furrybrowndog.wordpress.com/2010/08/06/putting-singapores -gdp-in-perspective/.

FUSTGEL de COULANGES, Numa Denis. (1980). *The Ancient City: A Study of Religion, Laws and Institutions of Greece and Rome*, Baltimore: Johns Hopkins University Press.

GAFFNEY, Declan, et al. (2002). "London Divided: Income inequality and poverty in the capital: summary," *Greater London Authority*.

GALE CENGAGE LEARNING. (2014, January 14). "City Parks Boost Mood, Study Suggests; Moving to greener urban areas was associated with mental-health improvements," http://go.galegroup.com/ps/i.do?id=GALE%7CA355622748&v=2.1 &u=chap_main&it=r&p=ITOF&sw=w&asid=b24cccb4b028d6c2711cf2ab60ed4fa0.

GALLAGHER, Leigh. (2013). *The End of Suburbs*, New York: Penguin.

GALYEAN, Crystal. (2015, April 10). "Levittown: The Imperfect Rise of the American Suburbs," *US History Scene*, http://www.ushistoryscene.com/uncategorized /levittown/.

GANESH, Janen. (2014, June 28). "Being childless," *Financial Times*, http://www.ft.com /intl/cms/s/2/675071ac-fcc0-11e3-81f5-00144feab7de.html.

GARDINER, Juliet. (2010, January 29). "How Britain built Arcadia: The growth of the suburbs in the Thirties brought a better life to millions," *Daily Mail*, http://www .dailymail.co.uk/femail/article-1247156/How-Britain-built-Arcadia-The-growth -suburbs-Thirties-brought-better-life-millions.html.

GARNETT, Nicole Stelle. (2007). "Suburbs as Exit, Suburbs as Entrance," *Scholarly Works*, Paper 105, http://scholarship.law.nd.edu/law_faculty_scholarship/105.

GARREAU, Joel. (2012, April 23). "Review: The Great Inversion and the Future of the American City," *New Geography*, http://www.newgeography.com/content/002787 -review-the-great-inversion-and-future-american-city.

GEE, Marcus. (2013, November 4). "Markham's rapid change into Canada's most diverse city," *The Globe and Mail*, http://www.theglobeandmail.com/news/toronto /markhams-rapid-change-into-canadas-most-diverse-city/article15087829/.

GEHRT, Stanley. (2014, October 20). "Coyotes in the Loop: A Close-Up of Survival in the Urban Core." Paper presented at the New Horizons in Science Conference, Columbus, Ohio.

GEIGER, Friedrich. (2014, December 22). "Germany's Big Firms Pay Price for Small-Town Ties," *Wall Street Journal*, http://www.wsj.com/articles/germanys-big-firms-pay -price-for-small-town-ties-1419305459.

GERMAN, Erik and PYNE, Solana. (2010). "Dhaka: fastest growing megacity in the world," *GlobalPost*, http://www.globalpost.com/dispatch/asia/100831/bangladesh -megacities-part-one.

———— (2010, September 10). "Disasters drive mass migration to Dhaka," *GlobalPost*, http://www.globalpost.com/dispatch/asia/100831/bangladesh-megacities-part-three -migrant.

GILBERT, Alan and GUGLER, Josef. (1991). *Cities, Poverty and Development: Urbanization in the Third World*, Oxford: Oxford University Press.

GIROUARD, Mark. (1985). *Cities and People: A Social and Architectural History*, New Haven: Yale University Press.

GITTELSOM, John. (2011, July 20). "U.S. Moves Toward Home 'Rentership Society,' Morgan Stanley Says," *Bloomberg Business*, http://www.bloomberg.com/news/2011 -07-20/u-s-moves-to-rentership-society-as-owning-tumbles-morgan-stanley-says.html.

GLAESER, Edward. (2009). "Why Has Globalization Led to Bigger Cities?," *New York Times*, http://economix.blogs.nytimes.com/2009/05/19/why-has-globalization-led-to -bigger-cities.

———— (2011, April 12). "The Value of Urban Clustering," *New York Times*, http://economix .blogs.nytimes.com/2011/04/12/the-value-of-urban-clustering/.

———— (2015). *Triumph of the City: How Our Greatest Invention Makes Us Richer, Greener, Healthier and Happier*, New York: Penguin.

GLAESER, Edward L. and KHAN, Matthew E. (2003, May 13). "Sprawl and Urban Growth," *Handbook of Urban Regional Economics*, http://www.brown.edu/Departments /Economics/Faculty/henderson/sprawl.pdf.

GLAESER, Edward L. and SHAPIRO, Jesse. (2001, June). "Is There a New Urbanism? Growth of US Cities in the 1990s," *Discussion paper 1925*, Harvard Institute of Economic Research.

GLOBAL WORKPLACE ANALYTICS. "Pros and Cons," http://globalworkplaceanalytics .com/pros-cons.

GLOBALIZATION AND WORLD CITIES RESEARCH NETWORK. (2014, January 13). "The World According to GaWC 2012," http://www.lboro.ac.uk/gawc/world2012t.html.

GONZALEZ-RIVERA, Christian. (2013, April). "Low-Wage Jobs, 2012," *Center for an Urban Future*, http://nycfuture.org/data/info/low-wage-jobs-2012.

GOODMAN, Leslee. (2009, October). "The Decline and Fall of the Suburban Empire," *The Sun*, http://thesunmagazine.org/issues/406/the_decline_and_fall_of_the _suburban_empire.

GOOGLE CAREERS. "Google New York," http://www.google.com/about/jobs/locations /new-york/.

GORDON, David L.A. and SHIROKOFF, Isaac. (2014, July). "Suburban Nation? Population Growth in Canadian Suburbs, 2006–2011," Working Paper #1, Council for Canadian Urbanism, Toronto, Ontario, http://www.canadianurbanism.ca/canu _workingpaper1_suburban_nation/.

GORDON, Peter and RICHARDSON, Harry W. (2000, January 24). "Critiquing Sprawl's Critics," *Policy Analysis No. 365,* http://object.cato.org/sites/cato.org/files/pubs/pdf /pa365.pdf.

——— (2001). "Transportation and Land Use," *Smarter Growth: Market Strategies for Land Use Planning in the 21st Century,* Westport: Greenwood Press.

GORDON, Rachel. (2005, October 22). "Many with children planning to leave city /Survey finds them upset with safety, housing, schools," *SFGATE,* http://www.sfgate .com/bayarea/article/SAN-FRANCISCO-Many-with-children-planning-to-2600243. php.

GORNEY, Cynthia. (2011). "Brazil's Girl Power," *National Geographic,* http://ngm.nationalgeographic.com/2011/09/girl-power/gorney-text.

GOTTMANN, Jean. (1983). *The Coming of the Transactional City,* College Park: University of Maryland Institute for Urban Studies.

GOUGH, Neil. (2013, September 23). "Singapore to Give Citizens Priority for Job Openings," *New York Times,* http://www.nytimes.com/2013/09/24/business/global /singapore-seeks-to-put-locals-first-in-line-for-jobs.html.

GRAHAM, Suzanne E. and PROVOST, Lauren E. (2012, June 1). "Mathematics Achievement Gaps Between Suburban Students and Their Rural and Urban Peers Increase Over Time," The Carey Institute, University of New Hampshire, http://scholars.unh.edu/cgi/viewcontent.cgi?article=1171&context=carsey.

GRANT, Jonathan. (2005). "Population Implosion? Low Fertility Rates and Policy Responses in the European Union," *Rand Corporation,* http://www.rand.org/pubs /research_briefs/RB9126.html.

GRANT, Michael. (1969). *The Ancient Mediterranean,* New York: Scribner.

GRATZ, Roberta Brandes. (1995, November). "Americans Want What Czechs Have," *Association for Thrifty Transport,* http://doprava.ecn.cz/en/Amerika.php.

GREEN, Emma. (2015, March 27). "The Sexually Conservative Millennial," *The Atlantic,* http://www.theatlantic.com/politics/archive/2015/03/the-sexually-conservative -millennial/388832/.

GREENHOUSE, Steven. (2006, September 4). "Many Entry-Level Workers Feel Pinch of Rough Market," *New York Times.* http://www.nytimes.com/2006/09/04/us/04labor .html.

GRINDROD, John. (2003, September 19). "The answer to Britain's lack of homes is a new wave of new towns," *Financial Times,* http://www.ft.com/intl/cms/s/0/7301c738 -10dc-11e3-b291-00144feabdco.html.

GROENVELD, Simon. (1997). "For The Benefit of the Poor: Social Assistance in Amsterdam," *Rome*Amsterdam: Two Growing Cities in 17th Century Europe,* Amsterdam: Amsterdam University Press.

GROSS, Daniel. (2012, May 5). "Renting Prosperity," *Wall Street Journal,* http://www.wsj .com/articles/SB10001424052702304746604577382321021920372.

GROSS, Jane. (2008, November 18). "Boomerang Parents," *New York Times,* http://newoldage.blogs.nytimes.com/2008/11/18/boomerang-parents/.

GU, Baochang and YONG, Cai. (2009, December 2–4.). "Fertility Prospects in China." Paper presented at the Expert Group Meeting on Recent and Future Trends in Fertility at the United Nations Headquarters, New York City, New York. http://www.un.org /esa/population/publications/expertpapers/2011-14_Gu&Cai_Expert-paper.pdf.

GUELPHMERCURY.COM. (2010, August 18). "'50's era has an allure for Conservatives," http://www.guelphmercury.com/opinion-story/2680356--50s-era-has-an-allure-for -conservatives/.

GUNTHER, John. (1997). *Inside USA,* New York: The New Press.

GUTIERREZ, Patricio Solis. (2012). "Social Mobility in Mexico: Trends, Recent Findings, and Research Challenges," *Trace (México, DF),* vol. 62.

GUTNOV, Alexi, et al. (1971). *The Ideal Communist City,* New York, George Braziller.

HA, Eun-Hee, et al. (2001). "Is Air Pollution a Risk Factor for Low Birth Weight in Seoul?," *Epidemiology,* vol. 12, http://www.jstor.org/stable/3703182.

HADDEN, Jeffrey K. and BARTON, Joseph J. (1977). "Thoughts on the History of Anti-Urban Ideology," *New Towns and the Suburban Dream,* Port Washington: Kennikat Press.

HAINES, Michael. (2011). "Homeownership and Housing Demand in Late Nineteenth Century America: Evidence from State Labor Reports," Working Paper, Colgate University, http://isites.harvard.edu/fs/docs/icb.topic868135.files/Kansas91_all.pdf.

HAJELA, Deepti and PELTZ, Jennifer. (2015, April 18). "In NYC, debate over saving small shops amid chains' rise," *myway,* http://apnews.myway.com/article/20150418/us --nyc-saving_storefronts-ee226dc5df.html.

HALES, Mike et al. (2015, May 20). "Global Cities 2015," *ATKearney,* http://www .atkearney.com/research-studies/global-cities-index.

HALL, Peter. (1998). *Cities in Civilization,* New York: Random House.

———— (1995, August). "Globalization and the World Cities." Paper presented at the Pre-Habitate II Conference on World Cities and the Urban Future, Tokyo, Japan. http://archive.ias.unu.edu/resource_centre/UNU-IAS%20Working%20Paper %20No.12.pdf.

HALLEGATTE, Stephane, et al. (2013, August 18). "Future flood losses in major coastal cities," *Nature Climate Change,* no. 9, doi: 10.1038/nclimate1979.

HALTER, Nick. (2014, November 26). "Kraus-Anderson wants Southtown re-zoning delayed," *Minneapolis/St.Paul Business Journal,* http://www.bizjournals.com /twincities/news/2014/11/26/kraus-anderson-wants-southtown-re-zoning-delayed .html.

HAMEL, Pierre and KEIL, Roger. (2015, January 14). *Suburban Governance: A Global View,* Toronto: University of Toronto Press.

HAMER, David. (1990). *New Towns in the New World,* New York: Columbia University Press.

HANLEY, Sean. (1999, February 15). "Civil Society: An Idea Whose Time Has Gone?," *Central Europe Review,* vol. 0, no. 21, http://www.ce-review.org/authorarchives /hanley_archive/hanley21old.html.

HANNAH-JONES, Nikole. (2011, May 6). "In Portland's heart, 2010 Census shows diversity dwindling," *Oregonian,* http://www.oregonlive.com/pacific-northwest-news /index.ssf/2011/04/in_portlands_heart_diversity_dwindles.html.

HANNAN, Daniel. (2010, August 20). "The Internet is dragging Britain away from Europe and towards the Anglosphere," *Daily Telegraph*, http://blogs.telegraph.co.uk /news/danielhannan/100051187/the-internet-is-gradually-reorienting-britain-away -from-europe-and-toward-the-anglosphere/.

HAR.COM. (2014). "Cinco Ranch High School," http://www.har.com/school/101914007 /cinco-ranch-high-school.

HARDEN, Blaine. (2010, March 13). "Experts: Japanese women competing to be thin," *Statesman*, http://www.statesman.com/news/news/world/experts-japanese-women -competing-to-be-thin/nRrGd/.

HARDOY, Jorge E. (1975). "Two Thousand Years of Latin American Urbanization," *Urbanization in Latin America: Approaches and Issues*, Garden City: Anchor Books.

HARDY, Matthew. (2003, September). "The Renaissance of the Traditional City," *Axess Magazine*, http://www.academia.edu/2129665/The_Renaissance_of_the_Traditional _City_Axess_September_2003.

HARRIS, Elizabeth A. (2013, February 11). "Paying Top Dollar for Condos, and Leaving Them Empty," *New York Times*, http://www.nytimes.com/2013/02/12/nyregion /paying-top-dollar-for-condos-and-leaving-them-empty.html.

HAYDEN, Dolores. (2003). *Building Suburbia*, New York: Vintage Books.

HAYES, Patrick. (2011). "The Crowded City," *The Lure of the City: From Slums to Suburbs*, London: Pluto Press.

HEARTFIELD, James. (2006). *Let's Build: Why We Need Five Hundred Million New Homes in the Next Ten Years*, London: Audacity.

———— (2008). *Green Capitalism: Manufacturing Scarcity in an Age of Abundance*, Berlin: Mute Publishing.

HEATHCOTE, Edwin. (2006, May 10). "I love the vitality of this high rise city," *Financial Times*.

HEAVENS, Al. (2004, October 13). "Active-Adult Boomers Still Favor Suburbs," *Realty Times*, http://realtytimes.com/consumeradvice/newhomeadvice1/item/11550 -20041014_boomers.

HEDRICK-WONG, Yuwa. (2013). "Top 20 Destination Cities in 2013," *Mastercard*, http://insights.mastercard.com/position-papers/top-20-global-destination -cities-in-2013/.

HEERS, Jacques. (1976). *Family Life in the Middle Ages*, trans. Barry Herbert, Amsterdam: North-Holland Publishing Company.

HEGEWISCH, Ariane, LOWELL, Vicky, and HARTMANN, Heidi. (2007, May 23). "An economy that puts families first," *Economic Policy Institute*, http://www.epi.org /publication/bp190/.

HEILIG, Gerhard K. (2012). "World Urbanization Prospects, the 2011 Revision," *United Nations, Department of Economic and Social Affairs, Population Division, Population Estimates and Projections Section*, http://www.un.org/en/development/desa /population/publications/pdf/urbanization/WUP2011_Report.pdf.

HEINEMAN, Ben W. (2011, October). "In Russia, a Demographic Crisis and Worries for Nation's Future," http://www.theatlantic.com/international/archive/2011/10 /in-russia-a-demographic-crisis-and-worries-for-nations-future/246277/.

HERBIG, Paul A. and Pat BORSTORFF. (1995). "Japan's Shinjinrui: the new breed," *International Journal of Social Economics*, vol. 22. doi: 10.1108/03068299510104750.

HERSHATTER, Andrea. (2010, June). "Millennials and the World of Work: An Organization and Management Perspective," *Journal of Business and Psychology*, vol. 25. doi: 10.1007/s10869-010-9160-y.

HERTZ, Daniel Kay. (2014, March 31). "Watch Chicago's Middle Class Vanish Before Your Very Eyes," *City Notes*, http://danielkayhertz.com/2014/03/31/middle-class/.

HESS, Ken. (2014, June 2). "Death of the office and rise of the telecommuter," *ZDNet*, http://www.zdnet.com/article/death-of-the-office-and-rise-of-the-telecommuter/.

HICKMAN, Robin, HALL, Peter, and BANISTER, David (2013). "Planning more for sustainable mobility," *Journal of Transport Geography*, vol. 33, doi: 10.1016/j.jtrangeo .2013.07.004.

HILLS, John. (2007, February). "Ends and Means: The Future Role of Social Housing in England," ESRC Research Center for Analysis of Social Exclusion, CASEreport 34.

HIRAYAMA, Yosuke. (2013). "Housing and generational fractures in Japan," *Young People and Housing*, Abingdon: Routledge.

HIRSCH, Fred. (1976). *Social Limits to Growth*, Cambridge: Harvard University Press.

HISE, Greg and DEVERELL, William. (2000). *Eden By Design: The 1930s Olmsted-Bartholomew Plan for the Los Angeles Region*, Berkeley: University of California Press.

HISTORY STOCK EXCHANGE. (2014, May 25). "How wealthy was Singapore at its independence (1965)?," http://history.stackexchange.com/questions/12950/how -wealthy-was-singapore-at-its-independence-1965.

HOBSBAWM, E.J. (1962). *The Age of Revolution*, New York: Mentor.

HOBSON, Jeremy and GALLAGHER, Leigh. (2014, July 27). "Millennials Prefer City Life to Suburban Life," *Here & Now*, http://hereandnow.wbur.org/2014/06/27 /millennials-america-suburbs.

HOGE, Patrick. (2006, Feburary 28). "Your Commute is Shrinking/Bay Area workers drive less as more jobs move out of suburbs," *SFGate*, http://www.sfgate.com /bayarea/article/YOUR-COMMUTE-IS-SHRINKING-Bay-Area-workers-2540280.php.

HOLTHAUS, Eric. (2015, January 23). "Hundreds of Private Jets Delivered People to Davos. Also, It's Climate Change Day at Davos," *Slate*, http://www.slate.com/blogs /future_tense/2015/01/23/davos_climate_change_hundreds_of_private_jets_at_the _world_economic_forum.html.

HOOI, Joyce. (2012, October 9). "More than half of S'poreans would migrate if given a choice: Survey," *AsiaOne*, http://news.asiaone.com/News/Latest+News/Singapore /Story/A1Story20121007-376116.html.

HOPE, Katie. (2014, March 24). "Next Silicon Valleys: Why Cambridge is a start-up city," *BBC*, http://www.bbc.com/news/technology-26668034.

HORAN, Thomas. (2000). *Digital Places: Building Our City of Bits*, Washington, DC: Urban Land Institute.

HOROWITZ, Alana. (2015, January 29). "Marine Le Pen Leads French Presidential Poll," *The World Post*, http://www.huffingtonpost.com/2015/01/29/marine-le-pen-president -poll-_n_6573356.html.

HOURANI, Albert. (1991). *A History of the Arab Peoples*, New York: Warner Books.

HOWARD, Ebenezer. (1902). *Garden Cities of Tomorrow*, London: S. Sonnenschein & Co., Ltd.

HOWARD, Hilary. (2012, August 3). "Four Men, Sharing Rent, and Friendship, for 18 Years," *New York Times*, http://www.nytimes.com/2012/08/05/nyregion/four-men -sharing-rent-and-friendship-for-18-years.html.

HOWE, Anna L. (2003, November). "Housing an Older Australia: More of the Same or Something Different?," *Housing Futures in an Ageing Australia Conference, Melbourne*.

HOWE, Jeffery, (n. d.). "LeCorbusier—Villa Savoye," *Boston College Fine Arts Department*, http://www.bc.edu/bc_org/avp/cas/fnart/Corbu.html.

HOWE, Neil. (2014, March 24). "Don't Worry, America: Millennials Still Want to Marry," *Forbes*, http://www.forbes.com/sites/realspin/2014/03/25/dont-worry-america -millennials-still-want-to-marry/.

HUCKER, Charles. (1975). *China's Imperial Past*, Stanford: Stanford University Press.

HUDSON, Kris. (2012, October 5). "Checking In and Never Leaving," *Wall Street Journal*, http://www.wsj.com/articles/SB10000872396390444180004578018843635395034.

———— (2015, January 21). "Generation Y Prefers Suburban Home Over City Condo," *Wall Street Journal*, http://www.wsj.com/articles/millennials-prefer-single-family -homes-in-the-suburbs-1421896797.

HUFFINGTON POST. (2012, March 11). "Families Flee San Francisco: City Has Lowest Percentage Of Kids Of Any Major U.S. City," http://www.huffingtonpost.com/2012 /03/09/families-flee-san-francisco_n_1335639.html.

HUI, E.M. and S.M. HO. (2000). *Relationship between the Land-Use Planning System, Land Supply and Housing Prices in Hong Kong*, Hong Kong: Hong Kong Polytechnic University.

HURLEY, Amanda Kolson. (2014, Mary 12). "Skyscrapers in the Subdivision," *NextCity*, http://nextcity.org/features/view/suburbs-are-not-dead-the-future-of-retrofitted -suburbia.

HUXLEY, Aldous. (1969). *Brave New World*, New York: Harper Perennial.

HYMOWITZ, Kay S. (2006). *Marriage and Caste in America*, New York: Dee.

———— (2009, July 3). "Losing Confidence in Marriage," *Wall Street Journal*, http://www.wsj.com/articles/SB124658294270189935.

INGERSOLL, Richard. (2003). "A Post-Apocalyptic View of Ecology and Design," *Harvard Design Magazine*, no. 8, http://www.dyd.com.ar/biblioteca/selecciona79.html.

INSEE. (2011). "Parc des logements selon le type et le nombre de pièces au 1er janvier 2011," http://www.insee.fr/fr/themes/tableau.asp?reg_id=20&ref_id=soctc05201.

————, 2014, "Evolution de la population au 1er janvier 2014," http://www.insee.fr/fr /themes/tableau.asp?reg_id=20&ref_id=poptc02101 (webpage discontinued).

IP, Greg. (2008, July 17). "The Declining Value of Your College Degree," *Wall Street Journal*, http://www.wsj.com/articles/SB121623686919059307.

IRETON, Michael. (2005, August 16). "New Urbanism anything but authentic," *FFWD Weekly*.

ISRAEL, Jonathan I. (1995). *The Dutch Republic: Its Rise, Greatness and Fall*, Oxford: Oxford University Press.

ISSACS, Julia B. (2009, November). "Spending on Children and the Elderly," *Brookings*, http://www.brookings.edu/research/reports/2009/11/05-spending-children-isaacs.

ISTRATE, Emilia and NADEAU, Carey Anne. (2012, November 30). "Global Metro Monitor 2012: Slowdown, Recovery, and Interdependence," *The Brookings Institution*, http://www.brookings.edu/research/reports/2012/11/30-global-metro-monitor.

ITOK, Aki. (2011, March 28). "Kan Told To Decentralize Japan on Tokyo Annihilation Danger," *Bloomberg*, http://www.bloomberg.com/news/articles/2011-03-27/kan-told -to-decentralize-japan-as-aide-says-big-one-may-annihilate-tokyo.

ITV. (2015, April 14). "Liberal Democrats plan at least 10 new garden cities," http://www .itv.com/news/2015-04-14/liberal-democrats-plan-at-least-10-new-garden-cities/.

JACKSON, Gabrielle. (2015, January 8). "Is it really fair that young people can't buy a flat because their parents bought too many?," *The Guardian*, http://www.theguardian. com/commentisfree/2015/jan/09/gab-jackson-housing-piece.

JACKSON, Kenneth. (1985). *Crabgrass Frontier: The Suburbization of the United States,* New York: Oxford University Press.

JACOBS, Andrew and CENTURY, Adam. (2012, September 6). "As China Ages, Beijing Turns to Morality Tales to Spur Filial Devotion," *New York Times,* http://www.beijing -kids.com/forum/2012/09/06/NY-Times-As-China-Ages-Beijing-Turns-to-Morality -Tales-to-Spur-Filial-Devotion.

JACOBS, Jane. (2004). *Dark Ages Ahead,* New York: Penguin.

JACOBS, Karrie. (2003, April 19). "It's a Small World: The newest trend in urban development? Micro Units," *Metropolis Magazine.*

JACOBSEN, Linda A., MATHER, Mark and DUPUIS, Genevieve. (2012, September). "Household Change in the United States," *Population Reference Bureau,* http://www .prb.org/Publications/Reports/2012/us-household-change.aspx.

JACQUEMIN, Alain R.A. (1999). *Urban Development and New Towns in the Third World,* Aldershot: Ashgate.

JAKARTA GLOBE. (2011, December 14). "Singapore's Orchard Road Floods—Again," http://jakartaglobe.beritasatu.com/archive/singapores-orchard-road-floods-again/.

JANSSENS, Angelique. (2003). "Economic Transformation, Women's Work and Family Life in The History of the European Family," vol. 3: *Family Life in the 20th Century,* New Haven/London: Yale University Press

JAPAN TIMES. (2012, September 4). "Population of Tokyo to drop to half by 2100," http://populyst.net/2012/09/04/japan-times-population-of-tokyo-to-drop-by -half-by-2100/.

JAPANESE STATISTICS BUREAU. (2015). *2013 Land and Housing Survey,* http://www.e-stat.go.jp/SG1/estat/NewListE.do?tid=000001063455.

JIANYUE, Xue. (2014, January 22). "19,000 stranded by third train delay in a week," *Today,* http://www.todayonline.com/singapore/19000-stranded-third-train-delay-week.

JOHNSON, Ian. (2009, April 28)."China Faces a Grad Glut After Boom at Colleges," *Wall Street Journal,* http://www.wsj.com/articles/SB124087181303261033.

———— (2013, June 16). "China's Great Uprooting: Moving 250 Million into Cities," *New York Times,* http://www.nytimes.com/2013/06/16/world/asia/chinas-great-uprooting -moving-250-million-into-cities.html.

JONES, E. Michael. (2004). *The Slaughter of Cities: Urban Renewal as Ethnic Cleansing,* South Bend: St. Augustine Press.

JONES, Emrys. (1990). *Metropolis: The World's Great Cities,* Oxford: Oxford University Press.

JONES, Francis M. (1973). "The Aesthetic of the Nineteenth-Century Industrial Town," *The Victorian City: Images and Realities,* London: Routledge & Kegan Paul.

JONES, Gavin W. (2009, December 2–4). "Recent Fertility Trends, Policy Responses and Fertility Prospects in Low Fertility Countries of East and Southeast Asia." Paper presented at the United Nations Expert Group Meeting on Recent and Future Trends in Fertility, New York City, New York. http://www.un.org/esa/population/meetings /EGM-Fertility2009/Jones.pdf.

JONES, Gavin, TAY-STRAUGHAN, Paulin and CHAN, Angelique. (2008). *Ultra Low Fertility in Pacific Asia: Trends, Causes and Policy Issues*, London: Routledge.

JONES, Jeffrey M. (2014, February 13). "In US, 14% of Those Aged 24 to 34 Are Living With Parents," *Gallup*, http://www.gallup.com/poll/167426/aged-living-parents.aspx.

JORDAN, Miriam. (2015, March 3). "Federal Agents Raid Alleged 'Maternity Tourism' Businesses Catering to Chinese," *Wall Street Journal*, http://www.wsj.com/articles /us-agents-raid-alleged-maternity-tourism-anchor-baby-businesses-catering-to -chinese-1425404456.

JOSEY, Alex. (1971). *Lee Kuan Yew*, Singapore: Asia Pacific Press.

JOVIET, Muriel. (1997). *Japan: The Childless Society?: The Crisis of Motherhood*, London: Routledge.

JUNG-YOUN, Park. (2015, May 2). "Survey finds young Koreans without hope," *Korea Joongang Daily*, http://koreajoongangdaily.joins.com/news/article/Article.aspx ?aid=3003733.

KALISKI, John. (2008). "The Present City and the Practice of City Design," *Everyday Urbanism*, New York: The Monacelli Press.

—— *The Next American Suburb: Desire and the Middle Landscape*, Arcca, vol. 1. no. 2.

KANDELL, Jonathan. (1988). *La Capital: The Biography of Mexico City*, New York: Random House.

—— (1995). "Mexico's Megalopolis," *I Saw A City Invincible: Urban Portraits of Latin America*, Wilmington: SR Books.

KANTOR, Stu. (2012, February 2). "How Do the Top 100 Metro Areas Rank on Racial and Ethnic Equity?," *Urban Institute*, http://www.urban.org/publications/901478 .html (webpage discontinued).

KASARDA, Jack. (2008). "The Evolution of Airport Cities and the Aerotropolis," *Airport Cities: The Evolution*, London: Insight Media.

KATO, Mariko. (2010, January 5). "Experts say Japan must change how it is handling low birthrate," *Japan Times*, http://www.japantimes.co.jp/news/2010/01/05/national /experts-say-japan-must-change-how-it-is-handling-low-birthrate/.

KATTI, Madhu. (2014, January 29). "Biodiversity Can Flourish on an Urban Planet," *Sustainable Cities Collective*, http://sustainablecitiescollective.com/nature-cities /218411/biodiversity-can-flourish-urban-planet.

KATZ, Peter. (2000). "The New Urbanism in the New Millenium: A Postcard to the Future," *Cities in the 21st Century*, Washington, DC: Urban Land Institute.

KAUFMANN, Eric. (2010). *Shall the Religious Inherit the Earth: Demography and Politics in the 21st Century*, London: Profile Books.

KEESMAAT, Jennifer. (2014, May 16). "Here's How to Change Canada from a Suburban to an Urban Nation," *The Global and Mail*, http://www.theglobeandmail.com /globe-debate/heres-how-to-change-canada-from-a-suburban-to-an-urban-nation /article18606842/.

KELLY, Hugh F. and WARREN, Andrew. (2014). *Emerging Trends in Real Estate*, Washington, DC: PwC and Urban Land Institute.

KENDZIOR, Sarah. (2013, December 17)."Expensive cities are killing creativity," *Al Jazeera*, http://m.aljazeera.com/story/201312106585692246I.

KENNEDY, Alex. (2011, February 17). "Stagnant wages, immigration fuel Singapore squeeze," *Bloomberg Business*, http://www.businessweek.com/ap/financialnews /D9LEGSSG0.htm.

KENNY, Charles. (2012, August 13). "In Praise of Slums: Why millions of people choose to live in urban squalor," *Foreign Policy*, http://www.foreignpolicy.com/articles/2012 /08/13/in_praise_of_slums.

KENYON, Peter. (2012, February 1). "In Booming Istanbul, A Clash Between Old and New," *NPR*, http://www.npr.org/2012/02/01/146153016/in-booming-istanbul-a-clash -between-old-and-new.

KERSTEN, Katherine. (2014, May 19). "Turning the Twin Cities Into Sim City," *Wall Street Journal*, http://www.wsj.com/articles/SB10001424052702304536104579560042268686598.

KEYDERY, Çağlar. (2009, November). "Istanbul in a Global Context," *LSE Cities*, http://lsecities.net/media/objects/articles/istanbul-in-a-global-context/en-gb/.

KHAZAN, Olga. (2015, April 29). "The Childless Millennial," *The Atlantic*, http://www .theatlantic.com/health/archive/2015/04/millenials-not-having-babies/391721/.

KIM, Joolchul and CHOE, San-Chuel. (1970). *Seoul: The Making of a Metropolis*, New York: Wiley.

KIMMELMAN, Michael. (2015, February 12). "Paris Aims to Embrace Its Estranged Suburbs," *New York Times*, http://www.nytimes.com/2015/02/13/world/europe/paris -tries-to-embrace-suburbs-isolated-by-poverty-and-race.html.

——— (2013, July 24). "The Plan to Swallow Midtown," *New York Times*, http://www .nytimes.com/2013/07/25/arts/design/the-plan-to-swallow-midtown.html.

KIRBY, Andrew. (October 2004). "On 'Sprawl'," *Cities*, vol. 21, no. 5, pp. 369–468.

KIRKHAM, Chris. (2015, January 1). "California's high housing costs drive out poor, middle-income workers," *Los Angeles Times*, http://www.latimes.com/business/la-fi -california-migration-20150101-story.html.

KISCHENBLATT-GIMBLETT, Barbara. (2008). "Performing the City: Reflections on the Urban Vernacular," *Everyday Urbanism*, New York: The Monacelli Press.

KLEEMAN, Jenny. (2010, October 15). "Manila: A megacity where the living must share with the dead," *The Guardian*, http://www.theguardian.com/world/2010/oct/15 /philippines-overpopulation-crisis.

KLINENBERG, Eric. (2012). *Going Solo: The Extraordinary Rise and Surprising Appeal of Living Alone*, New York: Penguin Press.

KNIGHT, Heather. (2013, June 10). "Families' exodus leaves S.F. whiter, less diverse," *SF Gate*, http://www.sfgate.com/bayarea/article/Families-exodus-leaves-S-F-whiter-less -diverse-3393637.php.

KNOWLES, L.C.A. (1924). *The Industrial and Commercial Revolutions in Great Britain during the 19th Century*, London: Routledge.

KNOX, Paul. (1995). *World Cities in a World-System*, Cambridge: Cambridge University Press.

———— (2005). "Vulgaria: The Re-Enchantment of Suburbia," *Opolis: An International Journal of Suburban and Metropolitan Studies*, vol. 1, no. 2, http://escholarship.org/uc/item/5392f4vq.

KNOX, Paul and PINCH, Steven. (2013). *Urban Social Geography: An Introduction*, New York: Routledge.

KOCAK, Nazan. (2014). "Planning Sustainable Mobility in Polycentric Regions: Testing a Participatory Approach in Six Regions of Europe," *Transporation Research Procedia*, no. 4, doi:10.1016/j.trpro.2014.11.025.

KOCHAN, Ben. (2007, July). *Achieving a Suburban Renaissance—the Policy Challenge*, London: TCPA.

KOLKO, Jed. (2014, July 16). "The Recession's Lost Generation of Homeowners Isn't Millennials—It's the Middle-Aged," *Trulia*, http://www.trulia.com/trends/2014/07/recessions-lost-generation/.

———— (2015, January 22). "Urban Headwinds, Suburban Tailwinds," *Trulia*, http://www.trulia.com/trends/2015/01/cities-vs-suburbs-jan-2015/.

———— (2015, February 5). "No, Suburbs Aren't All the Same. The Suburbiest Ones Are Growing Fastest," *The Atlantic*, http://www.citylab.com/housing/2015/02/no-suburbs-arent-all-the-same-the-suburbiest-ones-are-growing-fastest/385183/.

———— (2015, May 21). "How Suburban Are Big American Cities?," *FiveThirtyEightEconomics*, http://fivethirtyeight.com/features/how-suburban-are-big-american-cities/.

KOLSON, Kenneth. (2001). *Big Plans: The Allure and Folly of Urban Design*, Baltimore: Johns Hopkins University Press.

KOOLHAUS, Rem and CASTELLS, Manuel. (1966). "The Generic City: Singapore or Bladerunner," *New Perspectives Quarterly*, vol. 13, no. 3, pp. 4–9.

KOSTELECKY, Tomas and VOBECKA, Jana. (2009). "Housing Affordability in Czech Regions and Demographic Behaviour—Does Housing Affordability Impact Fertility?," *Czech Sociological Review*, vol. 45, no. 6, pp. 1191–1213.

KOTKIN, Joel. (2012). "Let L.A. Be L.A.," *City Journal*, http://www.city-journal.org/2012/22_3_snd-los-angeles.html.

———— (2012, July 9). "The cities where a paycheck stretches the furthest," *New Geography*, http://www.newgeography.com/content/002950-the-cities-where-a-paycheck-stretches-the-furthest.

———— (2012, September 13). "The Changing Geography of Asian America: To the South and the Suburbs," *New Geography*, http://www.newgeography.com/content/003080-the-changing-geography-asian-america-to-the-south-and-the-suburbs.

———— (2012, December 14). "Aging America: The cities that are graying the fastest," *New Geography*, http://www.newgeography.com/content/003314-aging-america-the-cities-that-are-graying-the-fastest.

———— (2013, November 5). "American Cities May Have Hit 'Peak Office,' *New Geography*, http://www.newgeography.com/content/004033-american-cities-may-have-hit-peak-office.

———— (2013, December 9). "The Geography of Aging: Why Millennials Are Headed to the Suburbs," http://www.newgeography.com/content/004084-the-geography-of-aging-why-millennials-are-headed-to-the-suburbs.

———— (2013, December 19). "Where Working-Age Americans Are Moving," *New Geography*, http://www.newgeography.com/content/004100-where-working-age -americans-are-moving.

———— (2014). "Size Is Not the Answer: The Changing Face of the Global City," Singapore: Civil Service College, Singapore and Chapman University, https://www .cscollege.gov.sg/Knowledge/Documents/eBooks/The%20Changing%20Face%20 of%20the%20Global%20City.pdf.

———— (2014, March 21). "Where Inequality is Worst in the United States," *New Geography*, http://www.newgeography.com/content/004229-where-inequality-is -worst-in-the-united-states.

KOTKIN, Joel and COX, Wendell. (2015, March 9)."Asian Augmentation," *Orange County Register*, http://www.ocregister.com/articles/asian-653386-california-asians.html.

———— (2015, March 19). "The Evolving Geography of Asian America: Suburbs are High- Tech Chinatowns," *New Geography*, http://www.newgeography.com/content/004875 -the-evolving-geography-asian-america-suburbs-are-new-high-tech-chinatowns.

KOTKIN, Joel and SCHILL, Mark. (2015, April 15). "The Valley and the Upstarts: The Cities Creating the Most Tech Jobs," *New Geography*, http://www.newgeography.com /content/004899-the-valley-and-the-upstarts-the-cities-creating-the-most-tech-jobs.

KOTKIN, Joel and SHIRES, Michael. (2014, June 27)."The Cities Stealing Jobs from Wall Street," *New Geography*, http://www.newgeography.com/content/004390-the-cities -stealing-jobs-from-wall-street.

KOTKIN, Joel, SHROFF, Anuradha, MODARRES, Ali, and COX, Wendell. (2012). "The Rise of Post-familialism: Humanity's Future?" edited by Zina Klapper, Singapore: Civil Service College, Chapman University, https://www.chapman.edu/wilkinson /_files/The%20Rise%20of%20Post-Familialism.pdf.

KRUGMAN, Paul. (2008, January 23). "Home Not-So-Sweet-Home," *New York Times*, http://www.nytimes.com/2008/06/23/opinion/23krugman.html.

KULU, Hill, BOYLE, Paul J., and ANDERRSON, Gunnar. (2009, December). "High suburban fertility: Evidence from four Northern European countries," *Demographic Research*, vol. 21, no. 23, pp. 915–944, doi: 10.4054/DemRes.2009.21.31.

KUMO, Kazuhiro. (2010, June 2). "Explaining fertility trends in Russia," *VoxEU.org*, http://www.voxeu.org/article/explaining-fertility-trends-russia.

KUNSTLER, James Howard. (2004, February). "The ghastly tragedy of the suburbs," *TED*, http://www.ted.com/talks/james_howard_kunstler_dissects_suburbia.html.

———— (2005). *The Long Emergency: Surviving the Converging Catastrophes of the 21st Century*, New York: Atlantic Monthly Press.

KUNZIG, Robert. (2014, September 19). "A World with 11 Billion People? New Population Projections Shatter Earlier Estimates," *National Geographic*, http://news .nationalgeographic.com/news/2014/09/140918-population-global-united-nations -2100-boom-africa/.

KURTZ, Stanley. (2013, July 30). "Regionalism: Obama's Quiet Anti-Suburban Revolution," *National Review*, http://www.nationalreview.com/corner/354734 /regionalism-obamas-quiet-anti-suburban-revolution-stanley-kurtz.

KURTZLEBEN, Danielle. (2011, October 21). "Cities Where Women Are Having the Most Babies," *US News and World Report*, http://www.usnews.com/news/articles/2011/10 /21/cities-where-women-are-having-the-most-babies.

KUSHNER, James A. (2006). "Urban Planning and the American Family," *Stetson Law Review*, vol. 36, no. 67, http://www.stetson.edu/law/lawreview/media/urban-planning -and-the-american-family.pdf.

KWANG, Han Fook. (2013, June 18). "When wages fail to grow along with economy," *asiaone, http://www.askmelah.com/when-wages-fail-to-grow-along-with-economy/*.

LACHMAN, M. Leanne and BRETT, Deborah L. (2015). "Gen Y and Housing: What they want and where they want it," *Urban Land Institute*, http://uli.org/wp-content /uploads/ULI-Documents/Gen-Y-and-Housing.pdf.

LAM, Peng Er. (2009). "Declining Fertility Rates in Japan: An Ageing Crisis Ahead," *East Asia*, no. 26, doi: 10.1007/s12140-009-9087-y.

LAND, Michael. (2012). *Land of Promise*, New York: Harper.

LANG, Robert and LeFURGY, Jennifer. (2007, March). "Boomburg 'Buildout'," *Urban Affairs Review*, vol. 42, doi: 10.1177/1078087406295893.

LANZA, Mike. (2013, August 15). "Suburb-Hating is Anti-Child," *Playborhood*, http://playborhood.com/2013/08/suburb-hating-is-anti-child/.

LASCH, Christopher. (1991). *The True and Only Heaven*, New York: W.W. Norton.

LATEEF, Abdul Sahib A., et. al. (2010, March). "Geological constraints on urban sustainability, Kinshasa City, Democratic Republic of Congo," Environmental Geosciences, vol. 17, no. 1, pp. 17–35, doi: 10.1306/eg.04080908007.

LAU, Siu-Kai. (1981). "Utilitarianistic Familialism: The Basis of Political Stability," *Social Life and Development in Hong Kong*, Hong Kong: Chinese University Press.

LAUF, Jay. (2012, April 17). "'Focus: Sustainability' Launches on the Atlantic Coast," *The Atlantic*, http://www.theatlantic.com/personal/archive/2012/04/focus-sustainability -launches-on-the-atlantic-cities/255984/.

LAWLESS, Tim. (2012, May 25). "Population growth across the suburbs: Who's moving where and why," *CoreLogic*, http://blog.corelogic.com.au/2012/05/population-growth -across-the-suburbs-whos-moving-where-and-why/.

LE-CLAIRE, Jennifer. (2014, December 8). "Why Mixed-Use is Staple of New Construction," *GlobeSt.com*, http://www.globest.com/news/12_1002/miami /development/Why-Mixed-Use-is-Staple-of-New-Construction-353215.html.

LE CORBUSIER. (1987). *The City of Tomorrow and its Planning*, New York: Dover Publications.

———— (2002). "The Fairy Catastrophe," *Empire City*, New York: Columbia University Press.

LEE, John. (2009, October 6). "No More Excuses for Growing Rich-Poor Gap," *Spiegel*, http://www.spiegel.de/international/business/china-at-60-no-more-excuses-for -growing-rich-poor-gap-a-653438.html.

LEES, Andrew. (1985). *Cities Perceived: Urban Society in European and American Thought: 1820–1940*, New York: Columbia University Press.

LEHRER, Jonah. (2009, January 2). "How the city hurts your brain," *Boston.com*, http://www.boston.com/bostonglobe/ideas/articles/2009/01/04/how_the_city _hurts_your_brain/.

LEHRER, Sharon. (2007, March 4). "The Motherhood Experiment," *New York Times*, http://www.nytimes.com/2007/03/04/magazine/04wwlnidealab.t.html.

LEINBERGER, Christopher B. (2011, November 25). "The Death of the Fringe Suburb," *New York Times*, http://www.nytimes.com/2011/11/26/opinion/the-death-of-the -fringe-suburb.html.

LELAND, John. (2007, August 13). "Off to Resorts, and Carrying Their Careers," *New York Times*, http://www.nytimes.com/2007/08/13/us/13steamboat.html.

LERUP, Lars. (2011). *One Million Acres and No Zoning*, London: Architectural Association.

LEVIN, Dan. (2014, February 25). "Many in China Can Now Have a Second Child, but Say No," *New York Times*, http://www.nytimes.com/2014/02/26/world/asia/many -couples-in-china-will-pass-on-a-new-chance-for-a-second-child.html.

LEVIN, Tamar. (2008, February 29). "Families Help Care for Half of U.S. Preschoolers, Census Says," *New York Times*, http://www.nytimes.com/2008/02/29/us/29child .html.

LEWIS, Roger K. (2002, November 2). "Will Forces of Globalization Overwhelm Traditional Local Architecture?" *Global Policy Forum*, https://www.globalpolicy.org /component/content/article/162/27593.html.

LI, William D. H. (2013). "The Living Arrangements of Just-Married Young Adults in Taiwan," *Young People and Housing*, New York: Routledge.

LICHTNER, Cornelia. (2008, December 9). "More than one out of three Germans lives alone," *Gfk GeoMarketing*, http://archiv.gfk-geomarketing.de/press/20081209 _demographics_germany.pdf.

LIDA, David. (2008). *First Stop in the New World: Mexico City, The Capital of the 21st Century*, New York: Riverhead Books.

LIEBERG, Mats. (2013). "Youth Housing and Exclusion in Sweden," *Young People and Housing*, New York: Routledge.

LINCOLN, W. Bruce. (2002). *Sunlight at Midnight: St. Petersburg and the Rise of Modern Russia*, New York: Basic Books.

LIPIK, Vitaly. (n. d.). "The Big Achievement of a Small Country," *103 Meridian East*, http://meridian103.com/issue-7/made-in-singapore/global-ratings/.

LIPMAN, Barbara, LUBELL, Jeffrey, and SALOMON, Emily. (2012). "Housing an Aging Population: Are We Prepared?," *Center for Housing Policy*, http://www.nhc.org/media /files/AgingReport2012.pdf.

LLANA, Sara Miller. (2014, December 16)."In Germany, Anti-Islam voices grow louder, worrying leaders," *Christian Science Monitor*, http://www.csmonitor.com/World /Europe/2014/1216/In-Germany-anti-Islam-voices-grow-louder-worrying-leaders -video?cmpid=TW.

LOGAN, John R. and MOLOTCH, Harvey. (1987). *Urban Fortunes: The Political Economy of Place*, Berkeley: University of California Press.

LONGMAN, Phil. (2004). *The Empty Cradle: How Falling Birthrates Threaten World Prosperity and What to Do About It*, New York: Basic Books.

LONGWORTH, Richard C. (2013, November 8). "Perspective: Saving Chicago," *Chicago Tribune*, http://articles.chicagotribune.com/2013-11-08/news/ct-perspec-1108 -rebirth-20131108_1_saving-chicago-school-loans-new-plan.

LUCE, Edward. (2007). *In Spite of the Gods: The Strange Rise of Modern India*. New York: Doubleday.

LUCK, G.W. (2007). "A review of the relationships between human population density and biodiversity," *Biological Reviews of the Cambridge Philosophical Society*, vol. 82, no. 4, pp. 607–645.

LUHNOW, David. (2010, September 11). "Expats Flee Mexico's Business Capital," *Wall Street Journal*.

LUO, Rui. (2014). "Senior Co-Housing Design in China's Suburban Environment," (masters thesis, University of Texas at Austin), http://repositories.lib.utexas.edu /bitstream/handle/2152/25061/MDS2014-Luo.pdf?sequence=2.

LUTZ, Wolfgang, SKIRBEKK, Vegard, and TESTA, Maria Rita. (2006). "The Low Fertility Trap Hypothesis: Forces that may lead to further postponement and fewer births in Europe," *Vienna Yearbook of Population Research*, dio: 10.1553 /populationyearbook2006s167.

LUTZ, Wolfgang, TESTA, Maria Rita and PENN, Dustin J. (2007). "Population Density Is a Key Factor in Declining Human Fertility," *Population and Environment*, vol. 28.2.

LYNCH, Katherine. (2003). *Individuals, Families and Communities in Europe 1200–1800*, Cambridge: Cambridge University Press.

MA, Damien and ADAMS, William. (2013, November 7). "If You Think China's Air Is Bad . . .," *New York Times*, http://www.nytimes.com/2013/11/08/opinion/if-you-think -chinas-air-is-bad.html.

MA, Laurence C.J. (1971). *Commercial Development and Urban Change in Sung China*, Ann Arbor: University of Michigan, Department of Geography.

MACEWEN, Angella. (2012). "Working After Age 65," *Canadian Centre for Policy Alternatives*, http://www.policyalternatives.ca/sites/default/files/uploads /publications/National%20Office/2012/04/WorkingAfter65.pdf.

MAHTANI, Shibani. (2012, May 25). "Ferrari Crash Foments Antiforeigner Feelings in Singapore," *Wall Street Journal*, http://online.wsj.com/news/articles/SB10001424052 702304707604577423880540657976.

——— (2013, March 7). "Wealth Over the Edge: Singapore," *Wall Street Journal*, http:// online.wsj.com/news/articles/SB10001424127887324662404578334330162556670.

MAIDMENT, Paul. (2009, July 24). "China's Aging Population," *Forbes.com*, http://www.forbes.com/2009/07/24/china-shanghai-demography-population -opinions-columnists-one-child-policy.html.

MANDEL, Michael. (2007, September 4). "What The Income Report Tells Us About College Grads," *Businessweek*, http://www.businessweek.com/the_thread /economicsunbound/archives/2007/09/what_the_income.html.

MANGO, Cyril. (1980). *Byzantium: The Empire of New Rome*, New York: Scribner.

MANTURUK, K. (2010). "Friends and Neighbors: Homeownership and Social Capital Among Low-to Moderate-Income Families," *Journal of Urban Affairs*, vol. 32.

MARCHE, Stephen. (2012, May). "Is Facebook Making Us Lonely?," *The Atlantic*, http://www.theatlantic.com/magazine/archive/2012/05/is-facebook-making-us -lonely/308930/.

MARR, Andrew. (2013, December 14). "London is being hollowed out by global investors," *Spectator*, http://blogs.spectator.co.uk/coffeehouse/2013/12/london-is -being-hollowed-out-by-global-investors/.

MARTELLE, Scott. (2012). *Detroit: A Biography*, Chicago: Chicago Review Press.

MARTIN, Andrew and LEHREN, Andrew W. (2012, May 13). "A Generation Hobbled by the Soaring Cost of College," *New York Times*, http://www.nytimes.com/2012/05/13 /business/student-loans-weighing-down-a-generation-with-heavy-debt.html.

MARX, Karl. (1977). *Capital: Volume One*, trans. Ben Fowkes, New York: Vintage.

MASTER BLASTER. (2012, December 21). "Asia Found to be the Least Religious Place on Earth, China Tops List with Japan Coming in Second," *RocketNews24*, http://en. rocketnews24.com/2012/12/21/asia-found-to-be-the-least-religious-place-on-earth -china-tops-list-with-japan-coming-in-second/.

MATHIS, Sommer. (2014, January 30). "The Future of the Suburbs Is Unfolding in Arizona's East Valley," *CityLab*, http://www.citylab.com/work/2014/01/future -suburbs-unfolding-arizonas-east-valley/8251.

MAUGH, Thomas II. (2007, September 1). "Outskirts may have preceded early city," *Los Angeles Times*, http://articles.latimes.com/2007/sep/01/science/sci-city1.

McARDLE, Megan. (2015, April 17). "New Starter Homes Hit a Dead Stop," *Bloomberg View*, http://www.bloombergview.com/articles/2015-04-17/new-starter-homes-hit-a -dead-stop.

McBRIDE, Sarah. (2013, December 10). "Google bus blocked in San Francisco gentrification protest," *Reuters*, http://www.reuters.com/article/2013/12/10/us-google -protest-idUSBRE9B818J20131210.

McCLAIN, James L. and MERRIMAN, John M. (1997). "Edo and Paris: Cities and Power," *Edo and Paris: Urban Life in the Early Modern Era*, Ithaca: Cornell University Press.

McGEE, Henry W., Jr. (2007). "Gentrification, Integration or Displacement?: The Seattle Story," *BlackPast.org*, http://www.blackpast.org/perspectives/gentrification-integration -or-displacement-seattle-story.

McGEEHAN, Patrick. (2012, May 20) "More Earners at Extremes in New York Than in U.S.," *New York Times*, http://www.nytimes.com/2012/05/21/nyregion/middle-class -smaller-in-new-york-city-than-nationally-study-finds.html.

McKENNA, Phil. (2009, September 3). "Forget Curbing Suburban Sprawl," *MIT Technology Review*, http://www.technologyreview.com/news/415135/forget-curbing -suburban-sprawl/.

McKINSEY & COMPANY and *THE CONFERENCE BOARD*. (2007). *Reducing U.S. Greenhouse Gas Emissions: How Much at What Cost?*

McWHORTER, John. (2011, January 17). "Why Learn Mandarin? China Won't Make You Speak It," *Newsweek*, http://www.newsweek.com/why-learn-mandarin-china-wont -make-you-speak-it-66849.

MEHTA, Suketu. (2004). *Maximum City: Bombay Lost and Found*, New York: Vintage.

MELANSON, Trevor. (2013, October 3). "A Fascinating New Map of Toronto's Ethnic Distribution," *Canadian Business*, http://www.canadianbusiness.com/blogs-and -comment/a-fascinating-new-map-of-torontos-ethnic-distribution/.

MENCARINI, Letizia and TANTURRI, Maria Letizia. (2006, April). "High Fertility or Childlessness: Micro-Level Determinants of Reproductive Behaviour in Italy," *Population*, no. 61, doi: 10.3917/pope.604.0389.

MERRILL LYNCH. (2014, August). "Home in Retirement: More Freedom, New Choices," https://mlaem.fs.ml.com/content/dam/ML/Articles/pdf/AR6SX48F.pdf.

MICALLEF, Shawn. (2013, October 5). "The View From Toronto," *New York Times*, http://www.nytimes.com/2013/10/06/opinion/sunday/the-view-from-toronto.html.

MILLER, Carolyn, et al. (2012, September 26). "Main Report," *Pew Research Center,* http://www.pewinternet.org/2012/09/26/main-report-13/.

MILLER, Donald L. (2002). *Lewis Mumford: A Life,* New York: Grove Press.

MILLER, H. Max and SINGH, Ram N. (1994). "Urbanization during Postcolonial Days," *Urbanization in Africa: A Handbook,* Westport: Greenwood Press.

MILLS, Edwin S. (1984). *Urban Economics,* Glenview: Scott, Foresman & Co.

MINISTRY OF HEAVY INDUSTRIES & PUBLIC ENTERPRISES, GOVT. OF INDIA. (2006). "Automotive Mission Plan, 2006–2016: A Mission for Development of Indian Automotive Industry."

MINISTRY OF REGIONAL DEVELOPMENT CZ and INSTITUTE FOR SPATIAL DEVELOPMENT. (2014, July). "Selected Data on Housing 2013," http://www.mmr.cz /getmedia/1e967746-c803-44e9-90e1-e2008c337f1e/Selected-data-housing-2013.pdf.

MISHRA, Pankaj. (2006, July 6). "The Myth of the New India," *New York Times,* http://www.nytimes.com/2006/07/06/opinion/06mishra.html.

MODELL, John. (1980). "An Ecology of Family Decisions: Suburbanization, Schooling and Fertility in Philadelphia, 1880–1920," *Journal of Urban History,* no. 6.

MOGILEVICH, Mariana. (2003, October). "Big Bad Buildings: The Vanishing Legacy of Minoru Yamasaki," *The Next American City,* no. 3.

MOMMSEN, Theodore. (1958). *The History of Rome,* New York: Meridian Press.

MONAGHAN, Tony. (2013, January 30). "Perth—Australia's most diverse capital," *Committee for Perth,* http://www.committeeforperth.com.au/pdf/Advocacy /ReleaseCulturalDiversityJan2013.pdf.

MONTEFIORE, Simon Sebag. (2011). *Jerusalem: The Biography,* New York: Knopf.

MOORE, Rowan. (2015, March 14). "Britain's Housing crisis is a human disaster. Here are 10 ways to solve it," *The Guardian,* http://www.theguardian.com/society/2015 /mar/14/britain-housing-crisis-10-ways-solve-rowan-moore-general-election.

MORGAN, Edward. (2012, August 14). "Sex (Or Not) and the Japanese Single," *New Geography,* http://www.newgeography.com/content/003019-sex-or-not-and-japanese -single.

MOROZOV, Evgeny. (2011, January 8). "A Walled Wide Web for Nervous Autocrats," *Wall Street Journal,* http://online.wsj.com/news/articles/SB10001424052748704415104576065641376054226.

MORRILL, Dick. (2009, June 16). "The Geography of Class in Greater Seattle," *New Geography,* http://www.newgeography.com/content/00857-the-geography-class -greater-seattle.

———— (2011, April 29). "Seattle is shedding diversity; the state's minority populations grow," *Crosscut,* http://crosscut.com/2011/04/29/seattle/20804/Seattle-is-shedding -diversity-states-minority-popu/.

———— (2013, September 1). "Inequality of the Largest U.S. Metropolitan Areas," *New Geography,* http://www.newgeography.com/content/003921-inequality-largest-us -metropolitan-areas.

MORRIS, C. Zawadi. (2013, February 11). "New City Council Study Shows NYC's Middle Class Shrinking Fast," *Bed-Stuy Patch,* http://bed-stuy.patch.com/articles/new-city -council-study-shows-nyc-s-middle-class-shrinking-fast.

MORRONE, Francis. (2007, November 23). "When Buildings Stopped Making Sense," *Wall Street Journal,* http://www.wsj.com/articles/SB119578134568501693.

MOSES, Paul. (2005, April 19). "'Discovering' Williamsburg," *Village Voice,* http://www
.villagevoice.com/2005-04-19/news/discovering-williamsburg/full/.

MOZINGO, Louise A. (2014, February 14). *Pastoral Capitalism: A History of Suburban
Corporate Landscapes,* Cambridge: MIT Press.

MOZUR, Paul. (2011, May 11). "Taiwan's Demographic 'Time Bomb'," *Wall Street Journal,*
http://blogs.wsj.com/chinarealtime/2011/05/11/taiwans-demographic-time-bomb/.

MUIR, Hugh. (2013, January 14). "The ethnic mix of the suburbs is changing," *The
Guardian,* http://www.theguardian.com/uk/2013/jan/14/ethnic-mix-suburbs
-changing.

MUMFORD, Lewis. (1961). *The City in History,* New York: Harcourt.

———— (1956) *The Urban Prospect,* New York: HarcourtBrace.

MURPHY, Rhoades. (1974). "The City as a Center of Change: Western Europe and
China," *The City in the Third World,* New York: Macmillan.

MURRAY, Charles. (2010). *Coming Apart: The State of White America, 1960–2010,* New
York: Crown Forum.

———— (2012, January 21). "The New American Divide," *Wall Street Journal,* http://www
.wsj.com/articles/SB10001424052970204301404577170733817181646.

MUSTAFI, H., et al. (2012). "Main Air Pollutants and Myocardial Infarction," *Journal of
American Medical Association,* no. 307, doi: 10.1001/jama.2012.126.

MYERS, J.C. (2008, March 20). "Traces of Utopia: Socialist Values and Soviet Urban
Planning." Paper presented at the annual meeting of the Western Political Science
Association, San Diego, California.

MYRSKLA, Mikko, GOLDSTEIN, Joshua R., and CHENG, Yen-Hsin Alice. (2013, April).
"New Cohort Fertility Forecasts for the Developed World," MPIDR Working Paper
WP 2012–2014, Max Planck Institute for Demographic Research, Rostock, Germany,
http://www.demogr.mpg.de/papers/working/wp-2012-014.pdf.

NANGRIA, Vinita Dawra. (2014). "Is commute time taking over your life," *Times of India,*
http://timesofindia.indiatimes.com/life-style/Is-commute-time-taking-over-your-life
/articleshow/3508745.cms.

NATHAN, Max and URWIN, Chris. (2006, January 11). "City People: City Centre Living
in the UK," *Centre for Cities,* http://www.centreforcities.org/publication/city-people
-city-centre-living-in-the-uk/.

NATIONAL ASSOCIATION OF HOME BUILDERS. (2006, December 11). "Second and
Urban Homes Not a Big Lure for Baby Boomers," http://www.nbnnews.com/NBN
/issues/2006-12-11/Front+Page/3.html (webpage discontinued).

NATIONAL ASSOCIATION OF REALTORS. (2011, March). "2011 Community
Preference Survey," http://www.stablecommunities.org/sites/all/files/library/1608
/smartgrowthcommsurveyresults2011.pdf.

———— (2012, April). "Social Benefits of Homeownership and Stable Housing,"
http://www.realtor.org/sites/default/files/social-benefits-of-stable-housing-2012-04.pdf.

———— (2015, March 11). "Home Buyer and Seller Generational Trends," http://www
.realtor.org/reports/home-buyer-and-seller-generational-trends.

NATIONAL CENTER FOR EDUCATION STATISTICS. (2013, May). "The Status of Rural
Education," http://nces.ed.gov/programs/coe/indicator_tla.asp.

———— (1996, June 1). "Urban Schools: The Challenge of Location and Poverty,"
http://nces.ed.gov/pubs/web/96184ex.asp.

NATIONAL YOUTH COUNCIL OF SINGAPORE. (2011, January 21). "Youths today spend more time with family, have pragmatic life goals and are proud to be Singaporeans," https://nyc.gov.sg/component/k2/item/39-news-release-youths-today-spend-more-time-with-family-have-pragmatic-life-goals-and-proud-to-be-singaporeans.

NAVI MUMBAI MUNICIPAL CORPORATION. (n. d.). "Land Usage," http://www.nmmconline.com/web/guest/land-usage.

NEPRAM, Binalakshmi. (2013). "Ending violence against women from Northeast India," *Tehelka.com*, http://blog.tehelka.com/ending-violence-against-women-from-northeast-india/.

NEUHAUSER, Alan. (2013, July 2). "Majority of Manhattan Community Boards Oppose East Midtown Rezoning," *DNAinfo*, http://www.dnainfo.com/new-york/20130702/midtown/majority-of-manhattan-community-boards-oppose-east-midtown-rezoning.

NEW GEOGRAPHY. (2015, April 18). "Dispersion in Europe's Cities," http://www.newgeography.com/content/004901-dispersion-europes-cities.

NEW URBANISM. (n. d.)."Principles of Urbanism," http://www.newurbanism.org/newurbanism/principles.html.

NEW WORLD ENCYCLOPEDIA. (2013, June 17). "Constantinople," http://www.newworldencyclopedia.org/p/index.php?title=Constantinople&oldid=970032.

NEW YORK TIMES. (1955, October 27). "City Seen Choked By Fluid Suburbs."

NEWMAN, Andy. (2006, May 29). "Unto the City the Wildlife Did Journey," *New York Times*, http://www.nytimes.com/2006/05/29/nyregion/29animals.html.

NEWMAN, Peter and THORNLEY, Andy. (2005). *Planning World Cities*, New York: Palmgrave Macmillan.

NG, Samantha. (2013, June 21). "Singapore's Infrastructure Ranked Best in the World," *The Link*, http://blog.ctsi-global.com/post/2013/06/21/singapores-infrastructure-ranked-best-in-the-world.aspx.

NG, Yi Shu. (2014, August 10). "Mothership Q&A: Time Travellr app creators Calvin Soh and Saleem Jumabhoy," *mothership.sg*, http://mothership.sg/2014/08/mothership-qa-time-travellr-app-creators-calvin-soh-and-saleem-jumabhoy/.

NICOLAIDES, Becky. (2006). "How Hell Moved From the Cities to the Suburbs," *The New Suburban History*, Chicago: University of Chicago Press.

NIJMAN, Jan. (2006). "Mumbai's Mysterious Middle Class," *International Journal of Urban and Regional Research*, vol. 30, no. 4.

NIJMAN, Jan and SHIN, Michael. (2014). "The Megacity," *Atlas of Cities*, Princeton: Princeton University Press.

NIR, Sarah Maslin. (2013, November 22). "The End of Willets Point," *New York Times*, http://www.nytimes.com/2013/11/24/nyregion/the-end-of-willets-point.html.

NISBET, Robert. (1952). *The Quest for Community*, London: Oxford University Press.

NIVOLA, Peter. (1999). *Laws of the Landscape: How Policies Change Cities in Europe and America*, Washington, DC: Brookings Institution.

NOBEL, Justin. (2010, April 6). "Japan: 'Lonely Deaths' Rise Among Unemployed, Elderly," *Time*, http://content.time.com/time/world/article/0,8599,1976952,00.html.

NORQUIST, John O. (1998). *The Wealth of Cities: Revitalizing the Centers of American Life*, Reading: Perseus Books.

NUSTELING, Herbert. (1997). "Population of Amsterdam and the Golden Age," *Rome*Amsterdam: Two Growing Cities in 17th Century Europe,* Amsterdam: Amsterdam University Press, 71-84.

OBSTFELD, Maurice. (2009, March). "Time of Troubles: The Yen and Japan's Economy, 1985–2008," NEBER Working Paper, *The National Bureau of Economic Research,* http://www.nber.org/papers/w14816.

OBUDHO, Robert and Rose. (1994). "The Growth of Urban Population," *Urbanization in Africa,* Westport: Greenwood Press.

O'CONNOR, Kevin. (2010). "Global city regions and the location of logistics activity," *Journal of Transport Geography,* no. 18, doi: 10.1016/j.jtrangeo.2009.06.015.

O'CONNOR, Kevin and Ernest HEALY. (2004, January). "Rethinking Suburban Development in Australia: A Melbourne Case Study," *European Planning Studies,* no. 12. doi: 10.1080/0965431031000163569 8.

O'KELLY, Sebastian. (2010, March 1). "It's set to be Europe's biggest city . . . so should you buy in Istanbul?," *Daily Mail,* http://www.dailymail.co.uk/property/article -1254627/Its-set-Europes-biggest-city--buy-Istanbul.html.

OLIVER, Paul, DAVIS, Ian and BENTLEY, Ian. (1994). *Dunroamin: The Suburban Semi and its Enemies,* London: Random House UK.

OLMSTEAD, Frederick Law. (2005). "Selected Writings on Central Park," *Empire City: New York Through the Ages,* New York: Columbia University Press.

OLMSTEAD, Jennifer C. (2011). "Norms, Economic Conditions and Household Formation: A Case Study of the Arab World," *History of the Family,* no. 16.

O'NEILL, Brenden. (2009, November 19). "Too Many People? No, Too Many Malthusians," *spiked,* http://www.spiked-online.com/newsite/article/7723#.VVTK -pMYG48.

ONISHI, Norimitsu. (2012, May 14). "In San Francisco, Coyotes in Parks Are a Concern," *New York Times,* http://www.nytimes.com/2012/05/15/us/in-san-francisco-coyotes-in -parks-are-a-concern.html.

ORANGE COUNTY GREAT PARK ORGANIZATION. (2015). "Orange County Great Park," http://www.ocgp.org/.

ORILLION SOURCE. (2000, August). "Orillion India Thriving in Hyderabad."

OSBORN, Andrew. (2011, April 21). "Vladimir Putin promises to boost Russia's birth rate in possible campaign pitch," *Telegraph,* http://www.telegraph.co.uk/news/worldnews /europe/russia/8463908/Vladimir-Putin-promises-to-boost-Russias-birth-rate-in -possible-campaign-pitch.html.

OZMET, Steven. (1983). *When Fathers Ruled,* Cambridge: Harvard University Press.

——— (2001). *Ancestors: The Loving Family in Old Europe,* Cambridge: Harvard University Press.

PACE, Eric. (1994, January 29). "William J. Levitt, 86, Pioneer of Suburbs, Dies," *New York Times,* http://www.nytimes.com/1994/01/29/obituaries/william-j-levitt-86 -pioneer-of-suburbs-dies.html.

PADDOCK, Catherine. (2013, April 23). "Green Spaces Boost Wellbeing in Cities," *MNT,* http://www.medicalnewstoday.com/articles/259495.php.

PAGE, Jeremy, DAVIS, Bob, and AREDDY, James T. (2012, January 18). "China Turns Predominantly Urban," *Wall Street Journal,* http://www.wsj.com/articles/SB1000142 405297020373530457716665200236651 4.

PAGES, Erik. (2011, July 2). "Living and Working in the 1099 Economy," *New Geography*, http://www.newgeography.com/content/002314-living-and-working-1099-economy.

PARFREY, Eric. (n.d.). "What is Smart Growth?," Sierra Club, http://vault.sierraclub.org /sprawl/community/smartgrowth.asp.

PARK, Madison. (2014, May 8). "Top 20 most polluted cities in the world," *CNN*, http://www.cnn.com/2014/05/08/world/asia/india-pollution-who/.

PATRICK. (2011, December 10). "The Citigroup Plutonomy Memos: Two bombshell documents that Citigroup's lawyers try to suppress, describing in detail the rule of the first 1%," *Politicalgates*, http://politicalgates.blogspot.com/2011/12/citigroup -plutonomy-memos-two-bombshell.html.

PATTY, Anna. (2014, March 25). "ACTU to seek rise in minimum wages as home ownership becomes a pipedream," *Brisbane Times*, http://m.brisbanetimes.com.au /business/the-economy/actu-to-seek-rise-in-minimum-wages-as-home-ownership -becomes-a-pipedream-20140324-35eb1.html.

PEARCE, Fred. (2010). *The Coming Population Crash and Our Planet's Surprising Future*, Boston: Beacon.

PEARCE, Nick. (2012, December 8). "When young people buy their own homes, they feel like citizens with a stake in society," *The Guardian*, http://www.theguardian.com /commentisfree/2012/dec/09/home-ownership-young-people-falling.

PELTON, Joseph N. (2015, January/February). "The Rise of the Telecities," *The Futurist*.

PETERSON, Peter. (1999). *Gray Dawn: How the Coming Age Wave Will Transform America—and the World*, New York: Times Books.

PETERSON, William. (1977). "The Ideological Origins of Britain's New Towns," *New Towns and the Suburban Dream*, Port Washington: University Publications.

PEW RESEARCH CENTER. (2014, March 7). "Millennials in Adulthood," http://www .pewsocialtrends.org/2014/03/07/millennials-in-adulthood/.

——— (2015, March 12). "Wealthier Nations Less Religious; U.S. an Exception," http://www.pewresearch.org/fact-tank/2015/03/12/how-do-americans-stand-out -from-the-rest-of-the-world/ft_15-03-10_religiousgdpscatter/.

PFEIFFER, Deirdre. (2014, December 19). "Racial equity in the post-civil rights suburbs? Evidence from US regions 2000–2012," *Urban Studies*, doi: 10.1177/0042098014563652.

PIIPARIEN, Richney and RUSSELL, Jim. (2014, May 1). "Globalizing Cleveland: A Path Forward," *Maxine Goodman Levin College of Urban Affairs*, http://engagedscholarship .csuohio.edu/urban_facpub/1164.

PIKETTY, Thomas. (2014). *Capital in the 21st Century*, trans. by Arthur Goldhammer, Cambridge: Harvard University Press.

PILOT, Frederick L. (2015). *Last Rush Hour: The Decentralization of Knowledge Work in the Twenty-First Century*, Portland: Bookbaby.

PLATKIN, Dick. (2012, February 7). "Hollywood Needs More than Window Dressing and Bogus Claims to Boom Again," *City Watch*, http://www.citywatchla.com/archive/2787 -hollywood-needs-more-than-window-dressing-and-bogus-claims-to-boom-again.

PLOTNICK, Robert D. (2009). "Childlessness and the Economic Well-Being of Older Americans," *The Journals of Gerontology Series B: Psychological Sciences and Social Sciences* 6, doi: 10.1093/geronb/gbp023.

PLUMRIDGE, Hester. (2012, June 7). "Europe's Pension Crisis Yet to Come of Age," *Wall Street Journal*, http://www.wsj.com/articles/SB100014240527023032966045774504 83946387736.

POLLET, Thomas V., KUPPENS, Toon, and DUNBAR, Robin I.M. (2006). "When Nieces and Nephews become Important: Differences between Childless Women and Mothers in Relationships with Nieces and Nephews," *Journal of Cultural and Evolutionary Psychology*, no. 4, doi: 10.1556/JCEP.4.2006.2.1.

PONNURU, Ramesh. (2012, May 29). "The Empty Playground and the Welfare State," *National Review*, http://www.nationalreview.com/article/301108/empty-playground -and-welfare-state-ramesh-ponnuru.

PORTER, Douglas R. (2002). *Making Smart Growth Work*, Washington, DC: Urban Land Institute.

PRADHAN, Kanhu Charan. (2013). "Unacknowledged Urbanisation: New Census Towns of India," *Economic & Political Weekly*, vol. XLVIII, no. 36, http://www.cprindia.org /sites/default/files/articles/Unacknowledged_Urbanisation.pdf.

PRAENDL-ZIKA, Veronika. (2007)."Urban Sprawl in China—Land Use Change at the Transition from Village to Town," *Oikodrom-the Vienna Institute for Urban Sustainability*, http://download.holcimfoundation.org/1/docs/F07/WK-Grn/F07-WK -Grn-praendl02.pdf.

PREVILLE, Philip. (2011, September 14). "Exodus to the burbs: why diehard downtowners are giving up on the city," *Toronto Life*, http://www.torontolife.com /informer/features/2011/09/14/exodus-to-the-burbs-why-diehard-downtowners-are -giving-up-on-the-city/2/.

PRICE, David. (2014, April 14). "Home Matters!—Seven Policies That Could Prevent Roxbury's Gentrification," *Nuestra Communidad Development Corporation*, http://nuestracdc.org/seven-policies-that-could-prevent-roxburys-gentrification/.

PUROKAYASTHA, Devaprasad. (1998, May/June). "The New Technopolis," *Silicon India*.

PUTNAM, Robert. (2000). *Bowling Alone*, New York: Simon and Shuster.

QUI, Jane. (2012, October 12). "Megacities pose serious health challenge," *Nature*, http://www.nature.com/news/megacities-pose-serious-health-challenge-1.11495.

QUINT, Rose. (2015, January 28). "Most Millennial Buyers Want Single-Family Home in the Suburbs," *National Association of Home Builders*, http://eyeonhousing .org/2015/01/most-millennial-buyers-want-single-family-home-in-the-suburbs/.

RABINOVITCH, Simon. (2013, October 23). "Property prices in urban areas raise fears of overheating," *Financial Times*.

RAMESH, Randeep. (2011, December 5). "Income inequality growing faster in UK than any other rich country, says OECD," *The Guardian*, http://www.theguardian.com /society/2011/dec/05/income-inequality-growing-faster-uk.

RANDALL, Gregory C. (2010). *America's Original GI Town: Park Forest, Illinois*, Walnut Creek: Windsor Hill Publishing.

RAO, Krishna. (2014, April 15). "The Rent is Too Damn High," *Zillow*, http://www.zillow .com/research/rent-affordability-201394-6681/.

RAPAPORT, Richard. (1996, June 23). "Bangalore," *Wired*.

RAVI, Shamika, KAPOOR, Mudit, and AHLUWALIA, Rahul. (2012, August 9). "The Impact of NREGS on Urbanization in India," *Dartmouth.edu*, https://www.dartmouth .edu/~neudc2012/docs/paper_299.pdf.

RAYMOND, Andre. (2000). *Cairo*, trans. Willard Wood, Cambridge: Harvard University Press.

REEDER, D.A. (1968). "A Theater of Suburbs: Some Patterns of Development in West London, 1801-1911," *The Study of Urban History*, New York: St. Martin's Press.

RENN, Aaron M. (2009, October 18). "The White City," *New Geography*, http://www .newgeography.com/content/001110-the-white-city.

———— (2013, June 7). "Suburbs and Sacred Space," *New Geography*, http://www .newgeography.com/content/003762-suburbs-and-sacred-space.

———— (2014, April 15). "The Rise of the Executive Headquarters," *New Geography*, http://www.newgeography.com/content/004265-the-rise-executive-headquarters.

RES, Nar. (2012, November 10). "2012 Profile of Home Buyers and Sellers: Press Highlights," *National Association of Realtors*, http://www.slideshare.net/NarRes/2012 -profile-of-home-buyers-and-sellers-press-highlights.

REUTERS. (2014). "WHO most polluted cities list sees New Delhi smog trump Beijing," *Sydney Morning Herald*, http://www.smh.com.au/environment/who-most-polluted -cities-list-sees-new-delhi-smog-trump-beijing-20140508-zr6k4.html.

REYNOLDS, James. (2013, June 6). "Istanbul Gezi Park plan to proceed—Turkish PM Erdogan," *BBC*, http://www.bbc.com/news/world-europe-22801548.

RHODES, Elizabeth and MAYO, Justin. (2006, July 16). "Only Nine Areas in King County Left for Middle-Income Buyers," *Seattle Times*, http://community.seattletimes .nwsource.com/archive/?date=20060716&slug=homeappreciation16o.

RICHARDSON, Harry W. and GORDON, Peter. (1999, November). "Is Sprawl Inevitable? Lessons from Abroad." Paper presented at the ACSP Conference, Chicago, Illinois.

RICHARDSON, Michael. (2012, June 13). "China's demographic crunch," *Japan Times*, http://www.japantimes.co.jp/opinion/2012/06/13/commentary/chinas-demographic -crunch/.

RICHIE, Alexandra. (1998). *Faust's Metropolis: A History of Berlin*, New York: Carroll and Graf.

RICKETT, Jeff and Val. (n. d.)."Columbia, MD: It's All Here, Now," *NewTown Church*, http://pcamna.org/churchplanting/PDFs/ChurchPlanterProjectProfiles /ColumbiaMDRickettProject.pdf.

RIDLEY, Matt. (2014, April 25). "The World's Resources Aren't Running Out," *Wall Street Journal*, http://www.wsj.com/articles/SB10001424052702304279904579517862612 287156.

ROARK, James et. al. (2011). *Understanding the American Promise, Volume 2: From 1865: A Brief History of the United States*, Boston: Bedford/St. Martin's.

ROBERTS, Sam. (2012, September 20). "Rich Got Richer and Poor Poorer in N.Y.C., 2011 Data Shows," *New York Times*, http://www.nytimes.com/2012/09/20/nyregion/rich -got-richer-and-poor-poorer-in-nyc-2011-data-shows.html.

ROBSON, Garry and BUTLER, Tim. (2001, March). "Coming to Terms with London: Middle-class communities in a Global City," *International Journal of Urban & Regional Research*, no. 25, doi: 10.1111/1468-2427.00298.

ROGERS, Teri Karush. (2006, January 8). "Goodbye, Suburbs," *New York Times*, January 8, http://www.nytimes.com/2006/01/08/realestate/08cov.html.

ROGNILE, Matthew. (2014). "A Note on Piketty and diminishing returns on capital," *Capital in the Twenty-First Century*, President and Fellows of Harvard College, http://www.mit.edu/~mrognlie/piketty_diminishing_returns.pdf.

ROME, Adam. (2001). *The Bulldozer in the Countryside*, Cambridge: Cambridge University Press.

ROOCHNIK, David. (2013, April 30). "Review of Aristotle's Politics: Living Well and Living Together," *Bryn Mawr Classical Review*, http://bmcr.brynmawr.edu/2013/2013 -04-30.html.

ROSENBERG, Nathan and BIRDZELL, L.E., Jr. (1986). *How The West Grew Rich*, New York: Basic Books.

ROSENTHAL, Elizabeth. (2006, September 22). "In Northern Italy, the Agony of Aging Not So Gracefully," *New York Times*, http://www.nytimes.com/2006/09/22/world /europe/22genoa.html.

ROSENTHAL, Jack. (1974). "The Outer City: An Overview Suburban Turmoil in the United States," *Suburbia in Transition*, New York: New Viewpoints.

ROSS, Benjamin. (2014, May 4). "Disaster in the age of McMansions: America's dangerous addiction to suburban sprawl," *Salon*, http://www.salon.com/2014/05/04 /disaster_in_the_age_of_mcmansions_americas_dangerous_addiction_to_suburban _sprawl/.

ROTHMAN, Hal. (2003). *Neon Metropolis: How Las Vegas Started the 21st Century*, New York: Routledge.

ROXO, Sergio and HERDY, Thiago. (2013, June 13). "PM de SP usa tropa de choque para conter protestos em escalada de violencia," *Globo*, http://oglobo.globo.com/brasil/pm -de-sp-usa-tropa-de-choque-para-conter-protestos-em-escalada-de-violencia-8680923.

RT. (2012, July 2). "Big, big Moscow: City expands, thousands of officials pack," http:// rt.com/news/moscow-grow-double-parliament-155/.

RUFFENACH, Glenn. (2009, September 19). "Making Suburbia More Livable," *Wall Street Journal*, http://www.wsj.com/articles/SB10001424052970203674704574330 8 01650897252.

RUSHTON, Sharon. (2014, December 7). "Marin Voice: Flawed housing plan promotes higher densities," *marinij.com*, http://www.marinij.com/general-news/20141207 /marin-voice-flawed-housing-plan-promotes-higher-densities.

RYBCZYNSKI, Witold. (1995). *City Life: Urban Expectations in the New World*, New York: Scribner.

——— (2010). *Makeshift Metropolis; Ideas About Cities*, New York: Scribner.

——— (2013, December 3). "Behind the Façade of Prince Charles's Poundbury," *Architect*, http://www.architectmagazine.com/international-projects/behind-the -facade-of-prince-charless-poundbury.aspx.

SABATINI, Joshua. (2011, March 23). "San Francisco becoming a child-free zone as youth population declines," *The Examiner*, http://www.sfexaminer.com/sanfrancisco /san-francisco-becoming-a-child-free-zone-as-youth-population-declines /Content?oid=2171813.

SAGGS, H.W.F. (1962). *The Greatness That Was Babylon*, New York: Hawthorn.

SAINT, P. Michael and FARRELL, Robert J. (2009). *Nimby Wars: The Politics of Land Use*, Hingham: Saint University Press.

SANG-HUN, Choe. (2012, September 8). "A Writer Evokes Loss on South Korea's Path to Success," *New York Times*, http://www.nytimes.com/2012/09/08/world/asia/shin-kyung-sook-mines-south-koreas-sense-of-loss.html.

SAPORITO, Emanuela. (2011). "Mexico City. The marginal communities: social and ethnic segregation of the native population," *Territorio*, doi: 10.3280 / TR2011-057004.

SASSEN, Saskia. (2001). *The Global City: New York, London, Tokyo*, Princeton: Princeton University Press.

SAUL, Michael Howard. (2013, March 4). "New York City Leads Jump in Homeless," *Wall Street Journal*, http://online.wsj.com/article/SB10001424127887324539404578340731809639210.html.

SAUNDERS, Pete. (2014, December 12). "Two Chicagos, Defined," *New Geography*, http://www.newgeography.com/content/004795-two-chicagos-defined.

SAVAGE, Michael. (2009, January 3). "Poorer whites feel betrayed, says report," *Independent*, http://www.independent.co.uk/news/uk/home-news/poorer-whites-feel-betrayed-says-report-1222859.html.

SCHAMA, Simon. (1987). *The Embarrassment of Riches: The Interpretation of Dutch Culture in the Golden Age*, New York: Vintage.

SCHIAVENZA, Matt. (2013, September 13). "Mapping China's Economic Inequality," *The Atlantic*, http://www.theatlantic.com/china/archive/2013/09/mapping-chinas-income-inequality/279637/.

SCHIENBAUM, Diana. (2010). "Divided City: An Historical Perspective on Gated Communities in Mexico City," http://www.staff.uni-mainz.de/glasze/Abstracts_Papers_Paris_2007/Sheinbaum.pdf.

SCHIMEL, Elliot and MARCHETTI, Jennifer. (2012, October 22). "Next Generation of Homebuyers are Knowledgeable, Responsible and Savvy According to New Better Homes and Gardens Real Estate Survey," *Market Wired*, http://www.marketwired.com/press-release/next-generation-homebuyers-are-knowledgeable-responsible-savvy-according-new-better-nyse-rlgy-1716114.htm.

SCHNEIDER, William. (1992, July). "The Suburban Century Begins," *The Atlantic*, http://www.theatlantic.com/past/politics/ecbig/schnsub.htm.

SCHORSKE, Carl E. (1963). "The Idea of the City in European Thought," *The Historian and the City*, Cambridge: MIT Press.

SCHULZ, Matthew and CLARK, Blanche. (2014, March 6). "In defence of Sunshine: Surprising facts you may not know about Melbourne's sunny suburb," *Herald Sun*, http://www.heraldsun.com.au/news/victoria/in-defence-of-sunshine-surprising-facts-you-may-not-know-about-melbournes-sunny-suburb/story-fnkd6ppg-1226846852642.

SCHULZ, Nick. (2012, May 11). "The Life and Death of Great American Cities," *American Enterprise Institute*, http://www.aei.org/publication/the-life-and-death-of-great-american-cities/.

SCHWAB, Klaus. (2013). "The Global Competitiveness Report: 2013-2014," *World Economic Forum*, http://www3.weforum.org/docs/WEF_GlobalCompetitivenessReport_2013-14.pdf.

SCHWEIZER, Peter. (2015, January 20). "1,700 Private Jets Fly to Davos to Discuss Global Warming," http://www.breitbart.com/national-security/2015/01/20/1700-private-jets-fly-to-davos-to-discuss-global-warming/.

SCOMMENGA, Paola. (2014, September). "U.S. Baby Boomers Likely to Delay Retirement," *Population Reference Bureau,* http://www.prb.org/Publications /Articles/2014/us-babyboomers-retirement.aspx.

SCOTT, Mark. (2013, October 23). "Technology on the Thames," *New York Times,* http://www.nytimes.com/2013/10/24/technology/in-london-a-rising-silicon-upon -thames.html.

SCRUTTON, Alistair and AHLANDER, Johan. (2014, May 14). "Nordic tolerance under strain as anti-immigration parties grow," *Reuters,* http://uk.reuters.com/article/2014 /05/14/uk-europe-immigration-nordics-idUKKBN0DU0EE20140514.

SEARCEY, Dionne. (2014, August 21). "Marketers Are Sizing Up the Millennials," *New York Times,* http://www.nytimes.com/2014/08/22/business/marketers-are-sizing-up -the-millennials-as-the-new-consumer-model.html.

SELF, Will. (2013, January 18). "A Point of View: Staring at the Shard," *BBC,* http://www.bbc.com/news/magazine-21065706.

SELLERS, Christopher. (2012). *Crabgrass Crucible: Suburban Nature and the Rise of Environmentalism in Twentieth Century America,* Chapel Hill: University of North Carolina Press.

SENG, Loh Kah. (2011). "The British Military Withdrawal from Singapore and the Anatomy of a Catalyst," *Singapore in Global History,* Amsterdam: Amsterdam University Press.

SENIOR, Clarence. (1958). *Land Reform and Democracy,* Gainesville: University of Florida Press.

SETHI, Amit. (2014, July 12). "Are Mumbai's property-end users swifly moving towards the suburbs?," *Times of India,* http://epaperbeta.timesofindia.com/Article.aspx ?eid=31804&articlexml=Are-Mumbais-property-end-users-swiftly-moving-towards -1207201430IOI5.

SEVERINO, Ryan. (2015, April 1). "Why Older Millennials Are Leaving the Urban Core and Younger Millennials Aren't Far Behind," *Multifamily Executive,* http://www .multifamilyexecutive.com/news/why-older-millennials-are-leaving-the-urban-core -and-younger-millennials-arent-far-behind_0.

SHARMA, Kalpana, KHAN, Sameera, and WARWICK, Kitty. (2000). "Governing Our Cities," *Panos Institute.*

SHARMA, R.N. and SHABAN, Abdul. (2006). "Metropolitanization of Indian Economy: Lessons in Urban Development," *The ICFAI Journal of Governance and Public Policy,* vol. 1, no. 2.

SHARRO, Karl. (2008). "Density or Sprawl," *The Future of Community (Reports of a Death Greatly Exagerrated),* London: Pluto Press.

SHAVER, Les. (2015, April 14). "The Demise of the Starter Home," *Architect,* http://www .architectmagazine.com/practice/market-intel/the-demise-of-the-starter-home_s.

SHAW, Annapurna and SHARMA, R.N. (2006). "The Housing Market in Mumbai Metropolis and its Irrelevance to the Average Citizen," *Indian Cities in Transition,* Chennai: Orient Longman.

SHAW, Jane S. (2004, May 1). "Suburban Development Benefits Wildlife," *Heartland,* http://news.heartland.org/newspaper-article/2004/05/01/suburban-development -benefits-wildlife.

SHAW, Jane and UTT, Ronald. (2000). *A Guide to Smart Growth: Shattering Myths, Providing Solutions,* Washington, DC: Heritage Foundation.

SHEINBAUM, Diana. (2007). "Divided City: An Historical Perspective on Gated Communities in Mexico City," http://www.staff.uni-mainz.de/glasze/Abstracts _Papers_Paris_2007/Sheinbaum.pdf.

SHELLENBERGER, Michael and NORDHAUS, Ted. (2012). "Why Emissions Are Declining in the U.S. But Not in Europe," *New Geography,* April 21, http://www .newgeography.com/content/002786-why-emissions-are-declining-us-but-not-europe.

SHENZHEN MUNICIPAL E-GOVERNMENT RESOURCES CENTER. (n. d.). "Overview," *ShenZen Government Online,* http://english.sz.gov.cn/gi/.

SHIN, Kyoung-ho- and TIMBERLAKE, Michael. (2006). "Korea's Global City Structural and Political Implications of Seoul's Ascendance in the Global Urban Hierarchy," *International Journal of Comparative Sociology,* no. 47, pp. 145–173.

SHUQING, Zhao, et al. (2006). "Land use change in Asia and the ecological consequences," *Ecological Research,* no. 21. doi: 10.1007/s11284-006-0048-2.

SIEGEL, Fred. (1997). *The Future Once Happened Here: New York, D.C., L,A, and the Fate of America's Big Cities, Uncorrected Proof,* New York: Free Press.

SIEGEL, Harry. (2011, July 20). "Citizen Bloomberg," *Village Voice,* http://www .villagevoice.com/2011-07-20/news/michael-bloomberg-harry-siegel-citizen -bloomberg/.

SIMONITCH, Steven. (2012, August 12). "Young Japanese women becoming less interested in sex, survey says," *Japan Today,* http://www.japantoday.com/category /national/view/young-japanese-women-becoming-less-interested-in-sex-survey-says.

SIRABIAN, Robert. (2015, July). "Enclosure Acts," *University of Wisconsin Stevens Point,* http://www4.uwsp.edu/english/rsirabia/notes/212/enclosureActs.pdf.

SIT, Victor F.S. (1995) *Beijing: The Nature and Planning of a Chinese Capital City,* New York: John Wiley.

SMIL, Vaclav. (2007, April 19). "The Unprecedented Shift in Japan's Population: Numbers, Age, and Prospects," *The Asia-Pacific Journal: Japan Focus,* http://www .japanfocus.org/-Vaclav-Smil/2411.

SMITH, Michael Peter. (2001). *Transnational Urbanism: Locating Globalization,* Malden: Blackwell.

SNYDER, Mike. (2005, June 13). "As Houston adds sprawl, consequences multiply," *Chron,* http://www.chron.com/news/houston-texas/article/As-Houston-adds-sprawl -consequences-multiply-1549148.php.

SOBLE, Jonathan. (2015, March 19). "Japan's Recovery Is Complicated by a Decline in Household Savings," *New York Times,* http://www.nytimes.com/2015/03/20 /business/international/japans-recovery-is-complicated-by-a-decline-in-household -savings.html.

SOON, Debbie. (2010). "Choice: The 6th C," *Institute for Policy Studies,* http://lkyspp.nus .edu.sg/ips/wp-content/uploads/sites/2/2013/04/Debbie_Choice-The-Sixth-C _011210.pdf.

SORENSEN, Andre. (2001). "Subcentres and Satellite Cities: Tokyo's 20th Century Experience of Planned Polycentrism," *International Planning Studies,* vol. 6, doi:10.1080/13563470120026505.

SOUTH CHINA MORNING POST. (2013, September 27). "Hong Kong's Quality of Life Index dips as home prices soar," http://www.scmp.com/news/hong-kong/article /1318491/hong-kongs-quality-life-index-dips-home-prices-soar.

SOWELL, Thomas. (2013). "Liberalism Versus Blacks," *creators.com*, http://www.creators .com/conservative/thomas-sowell/liberalism-versus-blacks.html.

SPAN, Paula. (2011, March 25). "New Old Age," *New York Times*, http://newoldage.blogs .nytimes.com/2011/03/25/aging-without-children.

SPECK, Jeff. (2000, September 3). "Sprawl and the Future of the Old Neighborhood," *Asheville Citizen Times*.

SPEZZAFERRO, Luigi. (1997). "Baroque Rome: 'A Modern City'," *Rome*Amsterdam: Two Growing Cities in 17th Century Europe*, Amsterdam: Amsterdam University Press.

SQUADRON, Daniel L. (2013, May 24). "Can a Tree Grow in the Bronx?," *New York Times*, http://www.nytimes.com/2013/05/25/opinion/can-a-tree-grow-in-brooklyn.html.

STANLEY, B. (2003). "Going Global and Wannabe World Cities: (Re) Conceptualizing Regionalism in the Middle East," *Emerging Issues in the 21st Century World System*, vol. 1, Westport: Praeger.

*STATISTICS CANADA. (*2013, April 16). "2011 Census: Population and dwelling counts," http://www.statcan.gc.ca/daily-quotidien/120208/dq120208a-eng.htm.

———— (2014, December 19). "NHS Profile, Canada, 2011," https://www12.statcan.gc.ca /nhs-enm/2011/dp-pd/prof/details/page.cfm?Lang=E&Geo1=PR&Code1=01&Data =Count&SearchText=canada&SearchType=Begins&SearchPR=01&A1=All&B1=All.

STERN, Robert A. M. (2013, April 21). "A Modern City in East Midtown?," *New York Times*, http://www.nytimes.com/2013/04/22/opinion/a-smart-way-to-revive-east -midtown.html.

STEVENSON, Mark. (2011, March 3). "Mexican Census: Fewer migrating, many returning," *Washington Post*, http://www.washingtonpost.com/wp-dyn/content /article/2011/03/03/AR2011030303965.html.

STONE, Brian. (2009). "Land Use as Climate Change Mitigation," *Environmental Science and Technology*, vol. 43.

SULLIVAN, Melissa. (2015, April 20). "Survey also reveals Millennials are 'boomeranging'," *Mayflower*, http://www.mayflower.com/about-us/news/boomerang -press-release.

SUMO, Vanessa and LAMBERT, Emily. (2014, February 26). "What is the key to gentrification?," *Capital Ideas*, http://www.chicagobooth.edu/capideas/magazine /spring-2014/what-is-the-key-to-gentrification.

SWIDY, Neil. (2006, May 28) "Full house," *Boston Globe*, http://www.bostonglobe.com /magazine/2006/05/28/their-house-three-homes-managed-budgets-schedules -teeming-towns-especially-affluent-ones-four-more-work-doing-three-educated-moms -same/doZDGFfHzVO92ye6jrIhQP/story.html.

SYED, Saira. (2012, October 12). "Singapore: Economic slowdown opens foreign labour debate," *BBC News*, http://www.bbc.co.uk/news/business-19906139.

SZIKLA, Alexandra J. (2014, April 4). "Reflections from South Korea," *The World Post*, http://www.huffingtonpost.com/alexander-j-szikla/south-korea-real-estate_b_5121329 .html/.

SZIRMAI, Viktoria. (2011). *Urban Sprawl in Europe*, Budapest: Aula Kiado.

SZUCHMAN, Mark D. (1995). "The City as Vision—the Development of Urban Culture in Latin America" *I Saw A City Invincible: Urban Portraits of Latin America*, Oxford: SR Books.

TABUCHI, Hiroko. (2012, April 26). "An Aging Japanese Town Bets on Young Mayor for Its Revival," *New York Times*, http://www.nytimes.com/2012/04/27/business/global /aging-japanese-town-bets-on-a-young-mayor.html.

———— (2010, January 2). "For Some in Japan, Home is a Plastic Bunk," *New York Times*, http://www.nytimes.com/2010/01/02/business/global/02capsule.html.

TAIT, Malcolm. (2003). "Urban Villages as self-sufficient, integrated communities: a case study of London's Docklands," *Urban Design International*, no. 8.

TAM, Winsome. (2010, May 4). "The History of a 'City Without History'," *Asia Society*, http://asiasociety.org/business/development/history-city-without-history.

TARR, Joel A. and ZIMRING, Carl. (1997). "The Struggle for Smoke Control in St. Louis: Achievement and Emulation," *Common Fields: An Environmental History of St. Louis*, St. Louis: Missouri Historical Society Press.

TARWATER, Patrick Maybery. (1999, January 1). "The Effects of Population Density on the Spread of Disease," Texas Medical Center Dissertations (via ProQuest). Paper AAI9929469. http://digitalcommons.library.tmc.edu/dissertations/AAI9929469.

TATSUO, Hatta. (2008, October 31). "Learning the basics: Tokyo and nine regional cities," *Nikkei Real Estate*, http://realestate.nikkeibp.co.jp/re/members/news /20081031/527561/.

TAVARES, António F. and CARR, Jered B. (2013). "So Close, Yet So Far Away? The Effects of City Size, Density and Growth on Local Civic Participation," *Journal of Urban Affairs*, no. 35.3, Wiley Online Library, http://onlinelibrary.wiley.com/doi /10.1111/j.1467-9906.2012.00638.x/abstract.

TAVES, Max. (2015, March 31). "City Comes to the Suburbs in New Developments," *Wall Street Journal*, http://www.wsj.com/articles/city-comes-to-the-suburbs-in-new -developments-1427837530.

TAYLOR, P.J. (2013, February 21). "The Remarkable Legacy of Peter Hall's (1966) *The World Cities*," Globalization and World Cities Research Network, http://www.lboro .ac.uk/gawc/rb/rb423.html.

TAYLOR, Paul, et al. (2010, March 18). "The Return of the Multi-Generational Family Household," Pew Research Center, http://www.pewsocialtrends.org/2010/03/18/the -return-of-the-multi-generational-family-household/.

TEAFORD, Jon C. (2008). *The American Suburb: The Basics*, New York: Routledge.

———— (1993). *Cities of the Heartland: The Rise and Fall of the Industrial Midwest*, Bloomington: Indiana University Press.

———— (1997). *Post-Suburbia: Government and Politics in Edge Cities*, Baltimore: Johns Hopkins Press.

TEIXEIRA, Ana Claudia and BAIOCCHI, Gianpaolo. (2013, August 1). "Who Speaks for Brazil's Streets?," *Real Clear World*, http://www.realclearworld.com/articles/2013/08 /01/who_speaks_for_brazils_streets_105361-2.html.

TEMBHEKAR, Chittaranjan. (2009). "Mumbaikars die younger than other Indians: Study," *The Times of India*, http://timesofindia.indiatimes.com/india/Mumbaikars -die-younger-than-other-Indians-Study/articleshow/5190726.cms.

TEO, Nicholas. (2013, July 22). "Singaporeans among world's top 10 pessimists: survey," *Yahoo! News*, https://sg.news.yahoo.com/singaporeans-among-world%E2%80%99s -top-10-pessimists--survey-085155360.html.

TERJUNB, Werner H. and LAURIE, Stella S-F. (1973). "Solar Radiation and Urban Heat Islands," *Annals of the Association of American Geographers*, vol. 63, no. 2, pp. 181–207.

TERTIUS, Chandler. (1987). *Four Thousand Years of Urban Growth: An Historical Census,* Lewiston: St. David's University Press.

TERTIUS, Chandler and FOX, Gerald. (1974). *Three Thousand Years of Urban Growth,* New York: Academic Press.

THAKUR, Pooja. (2012, April 24). "Singapore "Shoebox' Condo Sales May Prompt Extra Taxes," *Bloomberg,* http://www.bloomberg.com/news/articles/2012-04-24/singapore -shoebox-condo-sales-may-prompt-extra-taxes.

THE CONFERENCE BOARD. (2014, September 16). "Millennials Will Play a Large Role in Shaping Housing Demand, Reports the Demand Institute," https://www.conference -board.org/press/pressdetail.cfm.

THE CUSTOMER BOARD. (2007, November). "Reducing US Greenhouse Gas Emissions: How Much at What Cost?," http://www.conference-board.org/publications /publicationdetail.cfm.

THE ECONOMIC TIMES. (2014, October 14). "Jobs across sectors moving to smaller cities," http://articles.economictimes.indiatimes.com/2014-10-14/news/55014467_1 _smaller-cities-recruitex-sectors.

THE ECONOMIST. (1998, June 22). "Belt loosening," http://www.economist.com /node/603171.

———— (2014, September 24). "Don't Panic," http://www.economist.com/news /international/21619986-un-study-sparks-fears-population-explosion-alarm -misplaced-dont-panic.

———— (2013, February 21). "Forgotten in the banlieues," http://www.economist.com /news/europe/21572248-young-diverse-and-unemployed-forgotten-banlieues.

———— (2014, March 25). "The incredible shrinking country," http://www.economist .com/blogs/banyan/2014/03/japans-demography.

———— (2006, October 26). "The forgotten underclass," http://www.economist.com /node/8089315.

———— (2014, February 6). "Into the melting pot," http://www.economist.com/news /britain/21595908-rapid-rise-mixed-race-britain-changing-neighbourhoodsand -perplexing.

———— (2005. June 2). "Wisteria Lane: How John Prescott and Prince Charles are reshaping the suburbs," http://www.economist.com/node/4033449.

THE HACKNEY CITIZEN. (2011, June 7). "Residents Oppose Hackney high-rise at London Fields," *Hackney Citizen,* http://hackneycitizen.co.uk/2011/06/07/residents -oppose-hackney-high-rise-at-london-fields/.

THE INDEPENDENT. (2014, May 11). "Britain: The global capital for billionaires," http://www.independent.co.uk/voices/editorials/britain-the-global-capital-for -billionaires-9351290.html.

THE NATION. (2013, August 1). "Asian investors may boost global property portfolio by more than $150 billion in next five years: CBRE," http://www.nationmultimedia.com /business/Asian-investors-may-boost-global-property-portfoli-30211596.html.

———— (2014, September 16). "Kingdom of Slaves in the Persian Gulf," http://www .thenation.com/blog/181626/kingdom-slaves-persian-gulf.

THE STRANGER. (2004, November 11). "The Urban Archipelago," http://www .thestranger.com/seattle/the-urban-archipelago/Content?oid=19813.

THE UNIVERSITY OF SUNDERLAND, GB. (1999, February 13). "Les Annees banlieues," http://eserve.org.uk/tmc/contemp1/banlieue.htm.

THE VANCOUVER SUN. (2008, November 12). "Depreciation of city condos expected to exceed that of suburban houses," *Canada.com*, http://www.canada.com/vancouversun /news/business/story.html?id=9a304820-0166-4a0b-97ef-02012052acca.

THE WASHINGTON POST. (2004, March 25). "At Home With His Creation; Founder of Reston Living Out Dream," *HighBeam Research*, http://www.highbeam.com/doc /1P2-164114.html.

THOMAS, Landon Jr. (2013, August 20). "Istanbul Skyline Reflects Cheap Dollars Now Growing Scarce," *New York Times*, http://www.nytimes.com/2013/08/21/business /global/turkish-skyline-foreshadows-emerging-market-slowdown.html.

———— (2014, January 28). "'Fragile Five' Is the Latest Club of Emerging Nations in Turmoil," *New York Times*, http://www.nytimes.com/2014/01/29/business /international/fragile-five-is-the-latest-club-of-emerging-nations-in-turmoil.html.

———— (2014, May 21). "Alarm Over Istanbul's Building Boom," *New York Times*, http://www.nytimes.com/2014/05/21/realestate/commercial/after-istanbuls-building -boom-come-worries-of-a-bust.html.

THOMAS, Melanie. (2008). "Totally Devo: Generation Y and Housing," *Carpe Diem, The Australian Journal of Business and Informatics*, no. 4.

THOMPSON, Jenny. (2014, September 4). "Bright Lights, Big City: Early 1980s New York," *the American past: NYC in focus*, http://americanpast.blogspot.com/2014/09 /bright-lights-big-city-early-1980s-new.html.

THURLOW, Rebecca. (2015, February 10). "Australia's Property Boom Spurs Interest in 'Granny Flat'," *Wall Street Journal*, http://www.wsj.com/articles/australias-property -boom-spurs-interest-in-granny-flats-1423593357.

TIEFENSEE, Wolfgang and PFISTER, Ernst. (2006, June 30). "Concepts and Strategies for Spatial Development in Germany," *Federal Ministry of Transport, Building and Urban Affairs*, http://www.bbsr.bund.de/BBSR/EN/Publications/BMVBS /SpecialPublication/2007_2009/DL_ConceptsStrategies.pdf.

TIMIRAOS, Nick. (2009, March 13). "Revival of Downtown Los Angeles Stalls," *Wall Street Journal*, http://www.wsj.com/articles/SB123690304370913677.

TOBIN, Lucy. (2013, September 27). "London has a soul that the Chinese can never buy," *London Evening Standard*, http://www.standard.co.uk/comment/lucy-tobin-london -has-a-soul-that-the-chinese-can-never-buy-8844198.html.

TOFFLER, Alvin. (1980). *The Third Wave*, New York: Bantam Books.

TORTAJADA, Cecilia. (2008). "Challenges and Realities of Water Management of Megacities." *Journal of International Affairs*, vol. 61, no. 2, http://www .thirdworldcentre.org/wp-content/uploads/2015/04/challengesmexicocity.pdf.

TOULMIN, Steven. (1990). *Cosmopolis: The Hidden Agenda of Modernity*, Chicago: University of Chicago Press.

TRANSPORT CANADA. (2006, April). *The Cost of Urban Congestion in Canada*, http://www.adec-inc.ca/pdf/02-rapport/cong-canada-ang.pdf.

TRANSPORTATION RESEARCH BOARD and COX, W. (2011). "Reducing Greenhouse Gases from Personal Mobility: Opportunities and Possibilities," *Reason Foundation*.

TRAUD, Amy. (2015, March 10). "The Racial Wealth Gap: Why Policy Matters," *Demos*, http://www.demos.org/publication/racial-wealth-gap-why-policy-matters.

TREANOR, Paul. (2007, June). "All 10 Million Europeans," http://web.inter.nl.net/users/Paul.Treanor/nohumans.html.

TRINITY RIVER CORRIDOR PROJECT. (2011). http://www.trinityrivercorridor.com/.

TURNBULL, C.M. (2009). *A History of Modern Singapore 1819–2005*, Singapore: NUS Press.

ULRICH, Roger S. (1984). "View though a window may influence recovery from surgery," *Science*, doi: 10.1126/science.6143402.

UNITED NATIONS. (2014). "United Nations World Urbanization Prospects: The 2014 Edition," http://esa.un.org/unpd/wup/.

UNIVERSITY OF MICHIGAN. (2015, July 31). "Monitoring the Future," http://monitoringthefuture.org/.

US CENSUS BUREAU. (2011, October 6). "2011 Census Shows Second Highest Homeownership Rate on Record Despite Largest Decrease since 1940," http://www.census.gov/2010census/news/releases/operations/cb11-cn188.html.

USEPA. (2004). "Air Quality Criteria for Particulate Matter," Final Report, Washington, DC, EPA 600/P-99/002aF-bF, http://cfpub.epa.gov/ncea/risk/recordisplay.cfm?deid=87903.

———— (2014, August 15). "Nitrogen Dioxide: Health," http://www.epa.gov/oaqps001/nitrogenoxides/health.html.

UTT, Ronald D. (2009, November 10). "The Oberstar Transportation Plan: A Costly Exercise in Lifestyle Modification," *Heritage Foundation Web Memo.* http://www.heritage.org/research/reports/2009/11/the-oberstar-transportation-plan-a-costly-exercise-in-lifestyle-modification.

van KESSEL, Peter and SCHULTE, Elisja. (1997). *Rome*Amsterdam: Two Growing Cities in 17th Century Europe*, Amsterdam: Amsterdam University Press.

van ONSELEN, Leith. (2014, September 10). "Choked housing supply is very real," *Macro Business*, http://www.macrobusiness.com.au/2014/09/choked-housing-supply-is-very-real/.

———— (2013). "HIA: Construction recovery weak, reform needed," *Macro Business*, http://www.macrobusiness.com.au/2013/07/hia-construction-recovery-weak-reform-needed/.

VELA, Justin. (2012). "Cities of Dreams," *Wall Street Journal*, http://online.wsj.com/news/articles/SB10001424052702303425504577353460769167448.

VELSEY, Kim. (2013, February 19). "Same As It Ever Was: Hipsters Move to the Suburbs, Fancy Themselves Pioneers," *Observer*, http://observer.com/2013/02/same-as-it-ever-was-hipsters-move-to-the-suburbs-fancy-themselves-pioneers/.

VOLCOVICI, Valerie and LEWIS, Matthew. (2014, April 15) "U.S. greenhouse gas emissions fall 10 pct since 2005: EPA," *Reuters*, http://www.reuters.com/article/2014/04/15/us-usa-climate-carbon-idUSBREA3EIXD20140415.

VOLKOGONOV, Dmitri. (1998). *Autopsy for an Empire: The Seven Leaders Who Built the Soviet Union*, Harold Shukman trans., New York: Free Press.

———— (1991). *Stalin: Triumph and Tragedy*, Harold Shukman trans., New York: Grove Wiedenfield.

vom HOVE, Tann. (2008, November 27). "China's urban transition causes growing inequality," *UN Habitat*, http://www.citymayors.com/habitat/habitat08-china.html.

von HOFFMAN, Alexander and FELKNER, John. (2002, January). "The Historical Origins and Causes for Urban Decentralization in the United States," Working Paper, *Joint Center for Housing Studies*, Harvard University, http://www.jchs.harvard.edu/research/publications/historical-origins-and-causes-urban-decentralization-united-states.

WADE, Geoff. (2009). "An Early Age of Commerce in Southeast Asia, 900–1300 CE," *Journal of Southeast Asian Studies*, no. 40, doi:10.1017/S0022463409000149.

WADE, Lisa. (2010, January 2). "Changes in Ideal Family Size," *Pew Research*, http://thesocietypages.org/socimages/2010/06/02/change-in-the-ideal-family-size/.

WAGENAAR, Michael. (1992, November). "Conquest of the Center or Flight to the Suburbs?: Divergent Metropolitan Strategies in Europe, 1850–1914," *Journal of Urban History*, no. 19.

WALDIE, D.J. (2000, March 3). "Do the Voters Really Hate Sprawl?," *New York Times*.

——— (2013, June 8). "Falling in Love Where You Are," *New Geography*, http://www.newgeography.com/content/003763-falling-in-love-with-where-you-are.

WALKER, Marcus. (2006, October 20). "In Estonia, paying women to have babies pays off," *Pittsburgh Post-Gazette*, http://www.post-gazette.com/life/lifestyle/2006/10/20/In-Estonia-paying-women-to-have-babies-pays-off/stories/200610200166.

WALKER, Peter and HURLEY, Patrick. (2011). *Planning in Paradise: Politics and Visioning of Land Use in Oregon*, Tucson: University of Arizona Press.

WALTERS, Stephen J.K. (2014). *Boom Towns: Restoring the Urban American Dream*, Stanford: Stanford University Press.

WANG, Feng. (2013, October 18). "Beijing as a Globally Fluent City," *Brookings*, http://www.brookings.edu/research/papers/2013/10/19-beijing-global-city.

WANG, Shirley S. (2015, January 26). "The Fight to Save Japan's Young Shut-Ins," *Wall Street Journal*, http://www.wsj.com/articles/the-fight-to-save-japans-young-shut-ins-1422292138.

WANG, Wendy and Paul TAYLOR. (2011, March 9). "For Millennials, Parenthood Trumps Marriage," *Pew Research Center*, http://www.pewsocialtrends.org/2011/03/09/for-millennials-parenthood-trumps-marriage/.

WARNER, Jeremy. (2013, October 22). "The housing bubble goes global—again," *Telegraph*, http://blogs.telegraph.co.uk/finance/jeremywarner/100025864/the-housing-bubble-goes-global-again/.

WARREN, Richard. (2013, August 9). "Dizzy heights," *Luxehomes*, http://www.luxehomes.com.hk/articles/dizzy-heights.

WATERFIELD, Bruno. (2012, April 4). "Germany to impose tax on the young to help the old," *Telegraph*, http://www.telegraph.co.uk/news/worldnews/europe/germany/9186111/Germany-to-impose-tax-on-the-young-to-help-the-old.html.

WEBB, R.K. (1971). *Modern England: From the Eighteenth Century to the Present*, New York: Dodd, Mead, and Company.

WEBER, Max. (1978). *Economy and Society*, vol. 2, Berkeley: University of California Press.

WEIDENBAUM, Murray and HUGHES, Samuel. (1996). *The Bamboo Network: How Expatriate Chinese Are Creating A New Economic Superpower in Asia*, New York: Free Press.

WEISE, Karen. (2014, October 15,)."Why Are Chinese Millionaires Buying Mansions in an L.A. Suburb?," *Bloomberg Business*, (http://www.businessweek.com/articles/2014 -10-15/chinese-home-buying-binge-transforms-california-suburb-arcadia.

WEITZ, Eric D. (2007). *Weimar Germany: Promise and Tragedy*, Princeton: Princeton University Press.

WELLS, Amy Stuart. (2014, October 3). "The Diverse Suburbs Movement Has Never Been More Relevant," *The Atlantic*, http://www.citylab.com/politics/2014/10/the -diverse-suburbs-movement-has-never-been-more-relevant/381061/.

WELLS, H.G. (1999). *Anticipations of the Reaction of Mechanical and Scientific Progress Upon Human Life and Thought*, Mineola: Dover.

WERDIGIER, Julia. (2011, June 23). "For Many in Britain, Being a Homeowner is a Fading Dream," *New York Times*, http://www.nytimes.com/2011/06/24/business /global/24rent.html.

WERTHEIMER, Jack. (2005, October). "Jews and the Jewish Birthrate," *aish.com*, http://www.aish.com/jw/s/48899452.html.

WHYTE, William H. (1965). "The Anti-City," *Metropolis: Values in Conflict*, Belmont: Wadsworth.

WILFORD, John Noble. (2000, December 19). "In Maya Ruins, Scholars See Evidence of Urban Sprawl," *New York Times*, http://www.nytimes.com/2000/12/19/science/in -maya-ruins-scholars-see-evidence-of-urban-sprawl.html.

WILKINSON, Francis. (2014, April 9). "Why are Liberal Cities Bad for Blacks?" *Bloomberg View*, http://www.bloombergview.com/articles/2014-04-09/why-are-liberal -cities-bad-for-blacks.

WILKINSON, Thomas O. (1965). *The Urbanization of Japanese Labor: 1868–1955*, Amherst: The University of Massachussetts Press.

WILLIAMS, Alex. (2013, February 15). "Creating Hipsturbia in the Suburbs of New York," *New York Times*, http://www.nytimes.com/2013/02/17/fashion/creating-hipsturbia-in -the-suburbs-of-new-york.html.

WILLIAMS, Austin. (2008). *The Enemies of Progress: The Dangers of Sustainability*, London: Societas.

WILLIAMS, Richard. (2008). "Public Space: Designing in Community," *The Future of Community*, Pluto Press.

WILLIAMS, Thomas Chatterton. (2013, November 8). "How Hispters Ruined Paris," *New York Times*, http://www.nytimes.com/2013/11/10/opinion/sunday/how-hipsters -ruined-paris.html.

WILSON, A.N. (2004). *London: A History*, New York: Modern Library.

WILSON, Jill H. and SVALJENKA, Nicole Prchal. (2014, October 29). "Immigrants Continue to Disperse, with Fastest Growth in the Suburbs," *Brookings*, http://www .brookings.edu/research/papers/2014/10/29-immigrants-disperse-suburbs-wilson -svajlenka.

WILSON, Lindsay. (2013, March). "America's Carbon Cliff: Dissecting the decline in US carbon emissions," *Shink That Footprint*, http://shrinkthatfootprint.com/wp-content /uploads/2013/03/Americas-Carbon-Cliff.pdf.

WINOGRAD, Morley and Michael D. HAIS. (2010, April 19). "The Millennial Metropolis," *New Geography*, http://www.newgeography.com/content/001511-the -millennial-metropolis.

WOLFF, Edward N. (2012, November). "The Asset Price Meltdown and the Wealth of the Middle Class," Working Paper 18559, The National Bureau of Economic Research, http://www.nber.org/papers/w18559.pdf.

WONG, Chun Han. (2013, September 23). "Singapore Tightens Hiring Rules for Foreign Skilled Labor," *Wall Street Journal,* http://online.wsj.com/articles/SB1000142405270 2303759604579092863888803466.

WONG, Edward. (2009, January 25). "College Educated Chinese Feel Job Pinch," *New York Times,* http://www.nytimes.com/2009/01/25/world/asia/25china.html.

——— (2013, November 23). "Urbanites Flee China's Smog for Blue Skies," *New York Times,* http://www.nytimes.com/2013/11/23/world/asia/urbanites-flee-chinas-smog -for-blue-skies.html.

WOODS, Ginny Parker. (2004, December 29). "In Aging Japan, Young Slackers Stir up Concerns," *Wall Street Journal,* http://www.wsj.com/articles/SB113581461811933422.

WORLD BANK. (2009). "World Development Report: Reshaping Economic Geography," https://openknowledge.worldbank.org/handle/10986/5991.

WORLD FEDERATION OF EXCHANGES. "Domestic Market Capitalization," http://www.world-exchanges.org/statistics/domestic-market-capitalization (webpage discontinued).

WORLD HEALTH ORGANIZATION. (2014). "Ambient (outdoor) air pollution in cities database 2014," http://www.who.int/phe/health_topics/outdoorair/databases/cities /en/.

WORLD SHIPPING COUNCIL. (n. d.). "Top 50 World Container Ports," http://www .worldshipping.org/about-the-industry/global-trade/top-50-world-container-ports.

WORONOFF, Jan. (1984). *Japan: The Coming Social Crisis,* Tokyo: Lotus Press.

WOUDHUYSEN, James. (2007, March 8). "In praise of big cities," *spiked,* http://www .spiked-online.com/newsite/article/2942.

WRIGHT, Frank Lloyd. (1958). *The Living City,* New York: New American Library.

WRIGHT, Tom and GUPTA, Harsh. (2011, April 29). "India's Boom Bypasses Rural Poor," *Wall Street Journal,* http://www.wsj.com/articles/SB1000142405274870408160 4576143671902043578.

WRIGLEY, E.A. (1990). "Brake or Accelerator? Urban Growth and Population Growth before the Industrial Revolution," *Urbanization in History: A Process of Dynamic Interactions,* London: Clarendon Press.

WU, Lemin. (2012, October 9). "Does Malthus Really Explain the Constancy of Living Standards?," *University of California, Berkeley,* http://eml.berkeley.edu/~webfac /obstfeld/wu.pdf.

WULFF, Maryann, HEALY, Ernest and REYNOLDS, Margaret. (2004). "Why Don't Small Households Live in Small Dwellings?—Disentangling a Planning Dilemma," *People and Place,* vol. 12, no. 1.

YANG, Calvin. (2013, September 25). "Singapore Looks Below for More Room," *New York Times,* http://www.nytimes.com/2013/09/26/business/international/crowded -singapore-looks-below-for-room-to-grow.html.

YAP, Mui Teng. (2003). "Fertility and Population Policy: The Singapore Experience," *Journal of Population and Social Security (Population),* no. 1, http://www.ipss.go.jp /webj-ad/webjournal.files/population/2003_6/24.yap.pdf.

YEANDLE, Mark. (2015, March). "The Global Financial Centres Index 17," *Qatar Financial Centre*, http://www.longfinance.net/images/GFCI17_23March2015.pdf.

YEW, Lee Kwan. (2000). *From Third World to First: The Singapore Story: 1965-2000*, New York: Harper Collins.

YGLESIAS, Matthew. (2014, November 12). "The best cure for wage stagnation nobody in Washington is talking about," *Vox Media*, http://www.vox.com/2014/11/12/7193609/zoning-wage-stagnation.

YI, Daniel. (2003, November 22). "My Other Door Is For My Customers," *Los Angeles Times*, http://articles.latimes.com/2003/nov/22/local/me-homebiz22.

YIM, Steve H.L. and BARRETT, Steven R.H. (2012). "Public Health Impacts of Combustion Emissions in the United Kingdom," *Environmental Science & Technology* no. 46. doi: 10.1021/es2040416.

YODER, Steve. (2013, June 6). "Millions of Seniors Are Moving Back to Big Cities," *Business Insider*, http://www.businessinsider.com/millions-of-seniors-are-moving-to-cities-2013-6.

Z/YEN GROUP. (2014, September). "GFCI—Global Financial Centres Index," http://www.zyen.com/research/gfci.html.

ZAHNISER, David. (2007, May 30). "Do As We Say, Not As We Do," *LA Weekly*, http://www.laweekly.com/2007-05-31/news/do-as-we-say-not-as-we-do/.

ZELNICK, Reginald E. (1971). *Labor and Society in Tsarist Russia*, Stanford: Stanford University Press.

ZHANG, Ping, et al. (2010). "Potential Drivers of Urban Heat Islands in the Northeast USA," *NASA*, http://www.nasa.gov/pdf/505254main_zhang.pdf.

ZHAO, Dayong, et al. (2011). "Reproductive toxicity in male mice exposed to Nanjing City tap water," *Exotoxicology*, no. 20, doi: 10.1007/s10646-011-0644-y.

ZHONG, Raymond and DUTTA, Saptarishi. (2014, April 13). "As Growth Slows in India, Rural Workers Have Fewer Incentives to Move to Cities," *Wall Street Journal*, http://online.wsj.com/news/articles/SB10001424052702304732804579423221004363850.

ZHU, Yapeng. (2013). "Youth Housing Problems in China," *Young People and Housing*, New York: Routledge.

ZIJDERVELD, Anton C. (1998). *A Theory of Urbanity: The Economic and Civic Culture of Cities*, New Brunswick: Transaction Publishers.

ZILLOW. "Zillow Real Estate Research," http://www.zillow.com/research/data/.

ZUCKERMAN, Phil. (2009). "Atheism, Secularism and Well-Being," http://pitweb.pitzer.edu/academics/wp-content/uploads/sites/38/2014/12/FAC-Zuckerman-Sociology-Compass.pdf.

ZUKIN, Sharon. (2009). *"Destination Culture: How Globalization Makes All Cities Look the Same,"* Inaugural Working Paper Series, vol. 1, no 1, Center for Urban and Global Studies, Trinity College, http://www.trincoll.edu/UrbanGlobal/CUGS/Faculty/Rethinking/Documents/Destination%20Culture.pdf.

ENDNOTES

INTRODUCTION

1   Braudel, 1979, p. 30.

2   http://www.newgeography.com/files/Kotkin-What-is-a-City-For-LKYCIC.pdf.

3   Easterbrook, 1999, p. 20.

CHAPTER 1

1   Roochnik, 2013.

2   http://esa.un.org/unpd/wup/. See United Nations,2014.

3   Cox, "Half-Urban World."

4   http://www.thestranger.com/seattle/the-urban-archipelago/Content?oid=19813. See *The Stranger*, 2004.

5   Another definition of the city is the "metropolitan area." This includes the urban area and those areas beyond the urban area from which people commute in sufficient numbers to employment in the urban area.

6   Wright, 1958, p. 87.

7   Chang, 2014.

8   Le Corbusier, 1987, p. xvii.

9   Le Corbusier in *Empire City*, 2002, p. 610–18.

10   Mumford, 1961, p. 197.

11   See Le Corbusier, 1987, p. xxi, xxiv–v, 15, 93, 301.

12   Fogelson, 2001, p. 240–8.

13   Colin Buchanan and Partners, 2008.

14   http://www.newgeography.com/content/002987-density-not-issue-the-urban-scaling-research

15   Author's analysis of EMSI 2015.2 employment data.

16   http://www.slate.com/articles/business/metropolis/2015/06/san_francisco_rent_crisis_the_solution_isn_t_in_the_city_it_s_in_the_suburbs.html

17   Cox, "2010 Major Metropolitan Area."

18   Kotkin and Schill, 2015.

19   http://www.theatlantic.com/business/archive/2010/09/the-power-of-density/62569/

20   See John G. Clark, et al., 1982, p. 499.

21   http://www.newgeography.com/content/004921-dispersion-and-concentration-metropolitan-employment

22   http://www.brookings.edu/%7E/media/Research/Files/Reports/2009/4/06 job sprawl kneebone/20090406_jobsprawl_kneebone.PDF

23   http://www.newgeography.com/content/004921-dispersion-and-concentration-metropolitan-employment

24   Brand, 2005.

25   Dreiling, 2007; Stone, 2009, pp. 9052–9056; and Utt, 2009.

26   Cohen, 2014.

27   Donald, 2008, p. 35.

28   http://davidowen.typepad.com/david_owen/biography.html; and Klinenberg, 2012, p. 207.

29   Cox, "Greenhouse Gas Emissions."

30   http://www.pnas.org/content/112/19/5985.abstract

31   http://www.propertyoz.com.au/library/RDC_ACF_Greenhouse-Report.pdf

32   CBC News, 2013.

33   Parfrey, "What is Smart Growth?"

34   Shaw and Utt, 2000, p. 18; and O'Neill, 2009.

35   http://sfpublicpress.org/news/2014-10/housing-solution-increase-density-in-western-neighborhoods-and-fix-transit and http://www.realclearpolicy.com/2014/08/29/the_biggest_thing_blue_states_are_screwing_up_21791.html

36   http://www.pdx.edu/realestate/sites/www.pdx.edu.realestate/files/Mildner_UGR_article_3.pdf

37   Fearn, Pinkston, and Arenson, "Bay Area Housing Crisis."

38   http://www.nytimes.com/2015/01/30/nyregion/long-lines-and-low-odds-for-new-yorks-subsidized-housing-lotteries.html

39   See, for example, Le-Claire, 2014; and Boucher, 2014.

40   See, for example, Belvedere, 2013; and also Yglesias, 2014; Nivola, 1999, p. 1; Duany, Plater-Zyberk, and Spec, 2000, pp. 44–46; Karrie Jacobs, 2003; and Constantineau, 2014.

41   http://qz.com/90304/at-the-heart-of-turkeys-political-upheaval-is-a-whirlwind-of-authoritarian-building/

42   http://taksimdayanisma.org/; see also, for example, Kenyon, 2012; Foxman and Ferdman, 2013; and Reynolds, 2013.

43   http://oglobo.globo.com/pais/pm-de-sp-usa-tropa-de-choque-para-conter-protestos-em-escalada-de-violencia-8680923. See Roxo and Herdy, 2013

44   http://www.realclearworld.com/articles/2013/08/01/who_speaks_for_brazils_streets_105361-2.html. See Teixeira and Baiocchi, 2013.

45   http://www.dnainfo.com/new-york/20130702/midtown/majority-of-manhattan
-community-boards-oppose-east-midtown-rezoning. See Neuhauser, 2013.

46   http://www.nytimes.com/2013/07/25/arts/design/the-plan-to-swallow-midtown.html.
See Kimmelman, 2013.

47   http://www.nytimes.com/2013/04/22/opinion/a-smart-way-to-revive-east-midtown
.html. See Stern, 2013.

48   See, for example, Kurtz, 2013; and also Florida, 2012.

49   Kotkin, 2012.

50   *Ibid.;* see also Platkin, 2012; Bennett, 2012; *The Hackney Citizen,* 2011; Self, 2013;
and Bennett, 2015.

51   Confessore, 2006 and Morrone, 2007.

52   Cox, "Growing and Becoming Less Dense."

53   Cox, "Dispersion in Urban Areas."

54   Angel, 2012, p. 7.

55   Calculated from Census Bureau data.

56   This actually understates the suburban growth, since many core cities have annexed
areas that were formerly suburban.

57   Cox, "Urban Cores."

58   http://longevity3.stanford.edu/wp-content/uploads/2012/10/PPAR- Graying_of
_the_Global_Population_Jan_20081.pdf

59   As quoted in Kushner, 2006.

60   Appleseed, 2011.

61   Calculated from American Community Survey, 2012.

62   Clark, et al., 2004, pp. 291–318; and also Clark and Inglehart, 1998, pp. 58–59.

63   http://www.un.org/esa/population/meetings/EGM-Fertility2009/P05_Jones.pdf.
See Gavin Jones, 2009.

64   http://blogs.wsj.com/chinarealtime/2013/08/12/hong-kongs-high-cost-of-living
-deters-would-be-parents/. See Chen, 2013.

65   http://news.asiaone.com/News/Latest+News/Singapore/Story/A1Story20121007
-376116.html. See Hooi, 2012.

66   See Brinkley, 2013; and also Chen and Young, 2013.

67   See, for example, Jordan, 2015; and also Kotkin and Cox, 2015.

68   Cox, "Exodus of School Children"; and Kotkin, 2013.

69   Bissinger, 1997, pp. 206–208.

70   http://playborhood.com/2013/08/suburb-hating-is-anti-child/. See Lanza, 2013.

71   See Cox, "Urban Core Millenials?" and "Plan Bay Area"; and Lanza, 2013.

72   Kotkin, "Working-Age Americans are Moving."

CHAPTER 2

1   Braudel, 1992, p. 29.

2   *Ibid.,* p. 481.

3   Kischenblatt-Gimblett, 2008, p. 19.

4   See, for example, CEOs for Cities and Lauf, 2012.

5   Dyos et al., 1968, p. 1.

6   Mumford, 1961, p. 49.

7   Dunn, 1987, p. 65.

8   Montefiore, 2011, pp. 26–27, 39, 144.

9   Bell and de-Shalit, 2011, p. 45.

10   Celorio, 2004, p. 33–34.

11   Saggs, 1962, pp. 36, 162.

12   Florida, "America's Most (and Least) Religious."

13   Renn, 2013.

14   As quoted in Brook, 2013, p. 31.

15   Toulmin, 1990, p. 66.

16   As quoted in Grant, 1969, pp. 192, 204–205 and de Coulanges, 1980, pp. 309–311.

17   Marx, 1977, p. 265.

18   See Balsdon, 1969, p. 109; and also Carcopino, 1940, pp. 10–12, 44; and Marx, 1977, pp. 233.

19   Weber, 1978, p. 1215.

20   See *New World Encyclopedia*, "Constantinople," 2013; and Mango, 1980, pp. 48–49, 75–76.

21   Richie, 1998, pp. 214–215.

22   Jones, 1990, p. 68.

23   Abbott, 1999, p. 180–184.

24   Dunn, 1987, pp. 58–60; and Sit, 1995, p. 351; Francois, 1990, pp. 78–79, 89.

25   See Braudel, 1992, p. 51; and also Weber 1978, pp. 1214–1216; Rosenberg and Birdzell, 1986, p. 60; and Mumford, 1961, p. 323.

26   Schama, 1987, pp. 174–175, 261, 301–304; and Groenveld, 1997, pp. 102–209.

27   Israel, 1995, pp. 113, 148–149, 547, 787; Braudel, 1979, p. 178; Rosenberg and Birdzell, 1986, pp. 131–134; and Butler, 2007.

28   Braudel, 1992, p. 495; Israel, 1995, pp. 330–331; and Hall, 1998, p. 117.

29   Toffler, 1980, pp. 53, 262–263.

30   Wrigley, 1990, p. 107.

31   See Toffler, 1980, p. 54; and Sirabian, 2015.

32   Marx, 1977, pp. 233, 365, 889.

33   Girouard, 1985, pp. 268–269; 282–283.

34   Braudel, 1979, p. 81; Hadden and Barton, 1977, p.36.

35   Marx, 1977, p. 813.

36   De Vries, 1984, p. 193.

37   http://laphamsquarterly.org/city/examining-costs-production

38   Haines, 2011.

39   See Fogelson, 2001, p. 321; and Teaford, 1993, pp. 7, 19.

40   Toffler, 1980, pp. 119–120; Boon and Modarres, 2006, p. 35; and Mumford, 1961, p. 475.

41   Wells, 1999, pp. 20–37; Bruegmann, 2005, p. 25; and Francis M. Jones, 1973, p. 259, 2716.

42   Cox, "Southeast England Population." Calculated from census data.

43   Cox, "World Megacities." Calculated from census data.

44   Peterson, 1977, pp. 62–65.

45   See Clapson, 2000, pp. 151–174.

46   Howard, 1902, p. 38.

47   See Peterson, 1977, pp. 62–65; and Schorske, 1963, p. 108.

48   Randall, 2010, pp. 18–19.

49   Hamer, 1990, pp. 42–47.

50   Jackson, 1985, p. 176.

51   Siegel, 1997, p. x.

52   Teaford, 1997, p. 10.

53   Miller, 2002, p. 204.

54   www.radburn.org

55   Donaldson, 1977, pp. 82–103.

56   Calculated from census data. See Cox, "Major Metropolitan Area: 1950 & 2010"; also Bissinger, 1997, p. xiii; Martelle, 2012, pp. 206–208; Waldie, 2000; Abrahamson, 2013, pp. 5–11; Land, 2012, pp. 341–2; and Cox, "How the Suburbs Made Us Rich."

57   Gottmannn, 1983, pp. 13, 28, 34, 37.

58   E. Michael Jones, 2004, pp. 423, 528; and Teaford, 1993, pp. 228–229.

59   Bissinger, 1997, p. xiii; and Martelle, 2012, pp. vii–xiii, 161.

60   Lasch, 1991, pp. 139–142; and Wells, 1999, pp. 154–158.

61   Applebaum, 2012, p. 364.

62   Figes, 1996, pp. 682–3.

63   As quoted in Lincoln, 2002, pp. 1–3.

64   Volkogonov, 1991, p. 234, and Volkogonov, 1998, pp. 184–185.

65   Appelbaum, 2012, pp. 364–365.

66   *Ibid.*, p. 380.

67   Gutnov, et al., 1971, p. 367.

68   *Ibid.*, 1971, p. 68.

69   *Ibid.*, pp. 2, 9.

70   *Ibid.*, p. 16.

71   *Ibid.*, p. 8.

72   Applebaum, 2012, pp. 236–364.

73   *Ibid.*, p. 383.

74   Hanley, 1999; and Borufka, 2010.

75   Richie, 1998, pp. 240–241, 383–385, 470–474.

76   Weitz, 2007, pp. 70–71.

77   Applebaum, 2012, pp. 365–367.

78   Richie, 1998, pp. 762–768; and Fahmy, 2014.

79   http://www.voxeurop.eu/en/content/article/40081-leipzig-mix

80   Castells, 1989, 149–50.

81   See, for example, https://www.pinterest.com/griggsy68/church-conversion; http://www.boston.com/realestate/gallery/0727churches/; and Bendavid, 2015.

82   Wilson, 2004, pp. 163–164; and Fainstein, 1994, p. 35.

83   Ford, 1995, p. 69.

84   Braudel, 1979, p. 629.

85   Rothman, 2003, p. 263.

86   Terry Nichols Clark, "Urban Amenities," p. 104.

87   Kotkin, "American Cities."

88   Logan and Molotch, 1987, p. 260.

89   http://blogs.wsj.com/metropolis/2013/09/20/mayor-bloomberg-wants-every -billionaire-on-earth-to-live-in-new-york-city/; and http://www.nytimes.com /2003/01/08/nyregion/mayor-says-new-york-is-worth-the-cost.html

90   Patrick, 2011.

91   http://www.nytimes.com/2012/05/21/nyregion/middle-class-smaller-in-new-york -city-than-nationally-study-finds.html. See McGeehan, 2012.

92   See Patrick, 2011.

93   Kolson, 2001, p. 123.

94   Walters, 2014, pp. 144–145.

95   https://www.bostonglobe.com/business/2014/11/23/shadow-future /s1KhT91Jlhyq SObVOb6GqL/story.html

96   Rybczynski, 2010, p. xiii.

97   Garreau, 2012; Saunders, 2014; and Hertz, 2014.

98   Jane Jacobs, 2004, p. 37.

99   http://www.creators.com/conservative/thomas-sowell/liberalism-versus-blacks.html. See Sowell, 2013.

100 http://www.oregonlive.com/pacific-northwest-news/index.ssf/2011/04/in_portlands _heart_diversity_dwindles.html. See Hannah-Jones, 2011.

101 http:/www.blackpast.org/perspectives/gentrification-integration-or-displacement -seattle-story. See McGee, 2007.

102 http://nuestracdc.org/seven-policies-that-could-prevent-roxburys-gentrification/. See Price, 2014.

103 Sumo and Lambert, 2014; and Renn, 2009.

104 Cortright and Mahmoudi, 2014.

105 https://culturalpolicy.uchicago.edu/sites/culturalpolicy.uchicago.edu/files/clark -amenities.pdf

106 Kolson, 2001, pp. 122–123.

107 Cox, "The Costs of Smart Growth."

108 Kolson, 2001, p. 123.

109 Williams, 2008, pp. 4–8, 13.

110 Bailey, 2014.

111 Glaeser, 2015, p. 205; and Zahniser, 2007.

112 Holthaus, 2015; and Schweizer, 2015.

113 Christie, 2015.

114 Wright, 1958, pp. 33, 57, 61, 83,85, 99–100.

115 Squadron, 2013.

116 Olmsted, 2005, pp. 278–279.

117 Orange County Great Park Organization, 2015.

118 http://www.wral.com/raleigh-formally-dedicates-28-mile-neuse-river-trail/12382796/

119 Buffalo Bayou Partnership, 2015; and Trinity River Corridor Project, 2011.

120 http://www.newgeography.com/content/003763-falling-in-love-with-where-you-are

CHAPTER 3

1 Bhagat, 2010.

2 Wright and Gupta, 2011.

3 http://www.newgeography.com/content/005029-poorer-nations-set-99-population-growth

4 http://www.un.org/en/development/desa/population/publications/pdf/urbanization/WUP2011_Report.pdf

5 "Urban areas" are the city in its physical form, and include only developed areas. This is in contrast to the city in its economic or functional form, which is called the "metropolitan area" (labor market areas). There are no international standards with respect to delineating metropolitan areas. Urban areas are called "built up urban areas" in the United Kingdom, "population centres" in Canada, and *unité urbaines* in France.

6 http://teacherweb.ftl.pinecrest.edu/snyderd/MWH/readings/Urban/City%20Pop%20-%20History.pdf

7 Cox, "Demographia World Urban Areas"; and Wilkinson, 1965, p. 67.

8 World Bank, 2009, p. 12.

9 Gilbert and Gugler, 1991, p. 13.

10 Wilkinson, 1965, pp. 21, 79.

11 O'Kelly, 2010.

12 Keyder, 2009.

13 Istrate and Nadeau, 2012.

14 Cox, "Evolving Urban Form: Tokyo."

15 Jacquemin, 1999.

16 World Bank, 2009, pp. 8, 12.

17 See Cox, "Pakistan."

18   See Hardoy, 1975, p. 51; Gerhard K. Heilig, 2012; and Szuchman, 1995, pp. 20–21. *One caveat*: Estimating population for comparably defined urban areas, particularly in the developing world, can be difficult. For example, there is considerable disagreement about the population of Lagos, where local officials claimed there were twice as many people in 2005 as were counted in the 2006 Nigerian census. Add the "missing" 8 million or more people, and the population would be 22 million this year. The higher local count, however, has not been broadly accepted. The population of Karachi is also disputed, with some claiming a somewhat lower population than reported. Part of the problem is that the latest completely reported census in Pakistan was in 1998, with only spotty data released from the most recent count.

19   Shenzhen Municipal E-Government Resources Center, "Overview."

20   Tam, 2010.

21   Based on UN estimates, analysis by Wendell Cox.

22   From the United Nations, national census authorities, and other sources.

23   Projection rates derived from the United Nations, national statistical agencies, and United States Conference of Mayors data.

24   Hall, 1998, p. 23; World Bank, 2009.

25   Ades and Glaeser, 1995, pp. 195–227; Charrier, 1988, p. 20–21.

26   Hales et al., 2015.

27   World Bank, 2009; Ahmed, 2010; and Schwab, 2013.

28   Kandell, 1988, p. 552.

29   Kandell, 1995, p. 187.

30   Lateef, 2010.

31   Vela, 2012; Thomas, "Alarm Over Istanbul's Building Boom"; and Thomas, "Fragile Five."

32   Lida, 2008, p. 10.

33   Barrionueva, 2010; Bevins, 2010; and Hardoy, 1975, p. 53.

34   Mehta, 2004, p. 491.

35   Mumford, 1961, pp. 237–240; and Hall, 1998, p. 35.

36   Boone and Modarres, 2006, pp. 11–17; and Carcopino, 1940, p. 20.

37   Mumford, 1961, pp. 205–221; and Carcopino, 1940, pp. 23, 47.

38   Boone and Modarres, 2006, pp. 136–7.

39   Bruegmann, 2005, p. 23.

40   Mango, 1980, pp. 62–68.

41   Braudel, 1992, pp. 493–495, 544–547; Murphy, 1974, pp. 54.

42   http://teacherweb.ftl.pinecrest.edu/snyderd/MWH/readings/Urban/City%20Pop%20-%20History.pdf

43   Dunn, 1987, pp. 45, 272, 266.

44   Fishman, 1979, p. 28.

45   Engels, 2009, p. 34.

46   Boone and Modarres, 2006, pp. 136–7.

47   Braudel, 1992, pp. 90–91, 281.

48   Richie, 1998, p. 164; and Mumford, 1961, p. 359.

49   Hall, 1998, p. 282; Bruegmann, 2005, p. 32.

50   Hall, 1998, pp. 176–177.

51   Lincoln, 2000, pp. 152, 242, 231–3; and Zelnick, 1971, p. 241.

52   Carmona, 2002, pp. 391–402.

53   Mumford, 1961, pp. 478–9.

54   Mills, 1984.

55   See, for example, Wu, 2012; and Gregory Clark, 2007.

56   Saporito, 2011; Miller and Singh, 1994, pp. 68–69; and Scheinbaum, 2010.

57   Wilkinson, 1965, p. 43.

58   Raymond, 2000, pp. 309–310, 337.

59   Zhong and Dutta, 2014; and Brook, 2013, pp. 202–203.

60   Christopher and Tarver, 1994, p. 46–7.

61   German and Pyne, "Dhaka."

62   Interview with author and Mira Advani.

63   See, for example, Johnson, 2013; Branigan, 2011; Davis and Page, 2011; and Schiavenza, 2013.

64   Anderlini, 2015.

65   Gutierrez, 2012, pp. 7–20.

66   Espinosa and Casanova, 2008, p. 91.

67   Azevedo and Bouillon, 2009.

68   Interview with author.

69   Shaw and Sharma, 2006, pp. 284–5; and Das, 2009.

70   http://www.satp.org/satporgtp/sair/Archives/sair12/12_7.htm

71   Berube, 2014.

72   Sharma and Shaban, 2006.

73   Engelke and Nordenman, 2014.

74   Nijman, 2006, pp. 758–777.

75   Abkowitz, 2015.

76   Boone and Modarres, 2006, p. 47.

77   Tembhekar, 2009.

78   See Fleming and Arnett, 2014.

79   Desai, 2009; and Scheinbaum, 2010.

80   German and Pyne, "Disasters drive mass migration"; and Mishra, 2006.

81   Critser, 2010.

82   Boone and Modarres, 2006, p. 57.

83   Shuqing, et al., 2006, pp. 890–896.

84   Kleeman, 2010.

85   Agence France Presse, 2013.

86   Tarwater, 1999.

87   Sarah Boseley, 2014.

88   Engelke and Nordenman, 2014.

89   Park, 2014; World Health Organization, 2014.

90   See Reuters, 2014; and Qui, 2012.

91   http://www.sos.org.au/ref3/ref15.html

92   Cox, "Smart growth"; and USEPA, 2014.

93   http://www.sos.org.au/ref3/ref17.html

94   Ha, et al., 2001.

95   http://www.sos.org.au/ref3/ref18.html

96   http://www.sos.org.au/ref3/ref20.html

97   USEPA, 2004; Mustafić, et al., 2012, pp. 713–721; and Yim and Barrett, 2012, pp. 4291–4296.

98   Dong, 2012.

99   Braudel, 1979, pp. 321, 582–3.

100 Richard Dobbs, et al., 2012.

101 http://www.ncbi.nlm.nih.gov/pubmed/17453349. See Campbell and Campbell, 2007.

102 Nepram, 2013.

103 Barta and Pokharek, 2009.

104 Nangia, 2008.

105 Mehta, 2004, pp. 16, 28, 122.

106 Calculated from American Community Survey data, 2009–2013.

107 Nijman and Shin, 2014, p. 153.

108 Sharma, Khan, and Warwick, 2000, p. 3.

109 Akhter and Ara, 2014.

110 Desouza, 2014.

111 Becerril and Jimenez, 2007.

112 Tortajada, 2008.

113 http://timesofindia.indiatimes.com/home/environment/global-warming/As-sea-level-rises-Chennai-areas-face-submersion-threat/articleshow/6966837.cms

114 Hallegatte, et al., "Future flood losses in major coastal cities."

115 http://www.narendramodi.in/rurbanization-my-idea-is-to-create-a-rural-urban-connect-where-the-soul-is-of-the-rural-bent-but-with-an-urban-touch-4707

116 Dong, 2012; and Wong, 2013; Brinkley, 2013; Ma and Adams, 2013; and Zhao, et al., 2011.

117 Sharma, Khan, and Warwick, 2000, p. 3.

118 Nijman and Shin, 2014, p. 151; and Wendell Cox, "Evolving Urban Form: Dhaka."

119 Interview with author and Mira Advani.

120 Interview with author.

121 Bosker, 2014. For a response see Cox, "Paving over Hunan?" 2014; and Praendl-Zika, 2007.

122 Glaeser, 2009.

123 Basulto, 2014.

124 Fackler, 2008.

125 See, for example, http://www.siemens.com/industryjournal/pool/3478_IJ_HMI
_201_Komplett_E.pdf; http://www.economist.com/news/business/21565244
-chinese-firms-are-new-challengers-global-construction-business-great-wall
-builders; and http://www.triplepundit.com/2011/05/megacities-economic-growth
-ecological-crisis/.

126 http://www.foreignpolicy.com/articles/2012/08/13/in_praise_of_slums. See Kenny,
2014.

127 Sharma, Khan, and Warwick., 2000, p. 3.

128 Draper, 2013.

129 Tortajada, 2008.

130 Brand, "Urban squatters save the world."

131 Engelke and Nordenman, 2014.

132 Lida, 2008, p. 326.

133 http://www.mckinsey.com/mgi/publications/urban_world/index.asp

134 Dobbs et al., 2011.

135 Eldridge, 1975, p. 19.

136 "Reshaping Economic Geography," p. 94; and Luhnow, 2010.

137 Cox, "Dispersion."

138 Calculated from data in the "World Urbanization Prospects, the 2011 Revision."
See Heilig, 2012.

139 Calculations based on UN data, analyzed by Wendell Cox.

140 Based on the end of 2013 municipal population estimates. Shanghai grew 3.5
percent annually from 2000 to 2010, but it only grew 1.9 percent from 2010 to
2014. Beijing's growth rates were 4 percent and 2.6 percent, respectively.

141 Anderlini, 2015.

142 http://www.newgeography.com/content/005074-rural-industrialization-asia-s-21st
-century-growth-frontier

143 See Mehta, 2004; Luce, 2007; Zhong and Dutta, 2014.

144 Ministry of Heavy Industries, 2006.

145 See Dobbs, et al., 2012; and Bellman, 2010.

146 See Bradsher, 2002; Orillion Source, 2000; Eischen, 2000; Rapaport, 1996;
Purokayastha, 1998; http://timesofindia.indiatimes.com/tech/jobs/5-Indian-cities
-score-high-in-global-IT-talent-survey/articleshow/37190952.cms; http://news.bbc
.co.uk/2/hi/business/6583203.stm; and http://www.nytimes.com/2010/10/24
/world/asia/24india.html.

147 Data from Cox, "Demographia World Urban Areas." Below 500,000 urban
population estimated (scaled) from 2000 data in Angel, 2012.

148 Interview with author.

149 Sharma and Shaban, 2006.

150 World Bank, 2009, p. 68.

151 Bajpai, 2012; Wilkinson, 1965, p. 66.

152 The National Rural Employment Guarantee Scheme is reputed to have reduced rural-to-urban migration by 28 percent (between 1999 and 2008). See Sharma and Shaban, 2006; Ravi, Kapoor, and Ahluwalia, 2012.

153 Pradhan, 2013; Bhaumik, Gangopadhyay, and Krishnan, 2009; and Bhagat, 2011.

154 Interview with author.

155 http://www.dailymail.co.uk/indiahome/indianews/article-2789398/modi -rolls-model-village-programme-transform-indian-infrastructure.html; and http://defence.pk/threads/welcome-to-the-billion-man-slum.330688/

156 Obudho, 1994, p. 62.

157 World Bank, 2009, pp. 9, 62.

158 *Ibid.*, p. 74.

159 *Ibid.*, pp. 81, 85.

160 Branigan, 2011.

161 Interview with author.

CHAPTER 4

1 Ng, 2014.

2 Bureau of Labor Statistics, 2012.

3 Mahtani, 2013.

4 http://www.askmelah.com/when-wages-fail-to-grow-along-with-economy/. See Kwang, 2013.

5 *Ibid.*; and Kennedy, 2011.

6 Teo, 2013.

7 Hooi, 2012.

8 The term "global cities" refers to entire metropolitan areas (labor market areas), which represent the functional economic definition of cities. Thus, New York refers not only to the well-known core of Manhattan, but also economically connected areas, such as nearby Westchester County or more distant Pike County, Pennsylvania. London includes not only the city, but also outside-the-greenbelt exurban communities such as Milton Keynes and Crawley. Hong Kong extends well beyond central areas to include new towns like Sha Tin, Yuen Long, and Sheung Shui. Metropolitan areas cross international or administrative boundaries (such as Hong Kong–Shenzhen) only where border controls permit free movement of labor, such as within the European Union.

9 Hall, 1995.

10 Taylor, 2013; and Wilson, 2004, p. 81.

11 Tertius and Fox, 1974, pp. 320, 482; and Curtin, 1984, pp. 128–129.

12 Wade, 2009, p. 221; Dunn, 1987, 258.

13 Charrier, 1988, pp. 20–21.

14 Los Angeles and Orange Counties.

15 Tokyo refers to the metropolitan area that stretches across the four prefectures of Tokyo, Kanagawa, Saitama, and Chiba (not to be confused with the Tokyo "metropolis," which refers to only the prefecture of Tokyo).

16   The San Francisco Bay Area (combined statistical area) includes the adjacent metropolitan areas of San Francisco and San Jose as well as adjacent smaller metropolitan areas (Santa Rosa, Napa, Vallejo, Santa Cruz, and Stockton).

17   Beaverstock, Taylor, and Smith, 1999; and O'Connor, 2010.

18   Sassen, 2001; and Globalization and World Cities Research Network, 2012.

19   Sassen, 2001.

20   Pages, 2011.

21   Emry, 1990, p. 11.

22   The term "region" is used as a synonym for "metropolitan area" (the functional definition of a city).

23   Knox, 1995, p. 6.

24   Schwab, 2013.

25   Hannan, 2010; and Morozov, 2011.

26   Florida, "America's Top 25 High-Tech Spots."

27   Cox, "Demographia World Urban Areas."

28   Knox, 1995, pp. 20–21, 24–32; and Ma, 1971, pp. 15, 29.

29   *Ibid.*

30   Braudel, 1979, p. 583.

31   World Shipping Council, "Top 50 World Container Ports."

32   Ng, 2013.

33   Kasarda, 2008, p. 4.

34   Stanley, 2003.

35   Curtin, 1984, pp. 11–12, 105; and Ma, 1971, p. 39.

36   van Kessel and Schulte, 1997, p. 81.

37   Braudel, 1979, p. 30.

38   Cooper, 2002, pp. 146–147.

39   Wilson, 2004, pp. 129, 177; http://www.pewforum.org/2011/01/27/future-of-the -global-muslim-population-regional-europe/; and http://www.dailymail.co.uk /debate/article-3223828/PETER-HITCHENS-won-t-save-refugees-destroying -country.html.

40   Statistics from Wendell Cox, the *Demographia* website, Sam Badger, Giorgio Cafiero, and Foreign Policy in Focus. Also see *The Nation*, 2014.

41   Batalova, 2015.

42   Braudel, 1992, p. 561.

43   Abbey, 2005.

44   McClain and Merriman, 1997, p. 12.

45   Hales, et al., 2015; and Kotkin, 2014; Florida, "World's Most Economically Powerful City"; and http://www.globalsherpa.org/cities-world-city.

46   Lees, 1985, p. 103.

47   Gottmann, 1983, pp. 23, 41.

48   Knowles, 1924, pp. 328–329.

49   McWhorter, 2011.

50   Z/Yen Group, 2014, "GFCI."

51   Yeandle, 2015.

52   Florida and Johnson, 2012; FashionUnited, 2013.

53   Scott, 2013.

54   Fehrenbacher, 2013.

55   Google Careers.

56   World Federation of Exchanges, "Domestic Market Capitalization."

57   Hedrick-Wong, 2013.

58   Kotkin, "Size is not the Answer."

59   See *Furry Brown Dog Blog*, 2010; and History Stock Exchange, 2014.

60   Seng, 2011.

61   Turnbull, 2009, p. 375.

62   Josey, 1971, p. 48.

63   See Lipik, "The Big Achievement of a Small Country"; and http://www.ncee.org /programs-affiliates/center-on-international-education-benchmarking/.

64   Yew, 2000, p. 603.

65   GDP-PPP, calculated from World Bank Data.

66   See European Chamber, 2011.

67   Wang, 2013.

68   Schama, 1987, pp. 15, 253, 294, 311; and Zijderveld, 1998, p. 34.

69   Hobsbawm, 1962, p. 207; and Israel, 1995, pp. 113, 330, 999, 1012–1013.

70   Beckert, 2001, p. 7.

71   Hall, 1998, p. 7.

72   Gunther, 1997, p. 549.

73   Castells, 1999, pp. 30–31; Ip, 2008; Mandel, 2007; Greenhouse, 2006; and Blanchflower, 2010.

74   Bell, 1973, p. 344.

75   Nir, 2013.

76   Hall, 1998, p. 961.

77   Heartfield, 2006, p. 182.

78   See Child Poverty Action Group, "Child poverty in London."

79   Hills, 2007, p. 6; Gaffney, et al., 2002, pp. 1–9; BBC News, 2013; *The Independent*, 2014; and Ramesh, 2011.

80   Barber, 2007.

81   Rhodes and Mayo, 2006; and Associated Press, 2006.

82   *The Economist*, "The incredible shrinking country."

83   Woronoff, 1984, p. 312.

84   *Ibid.*; see also Tabuchi, 2010; and Obstfeld, 2009.

85   Longworth, 2013; Braudel, 1979, p. 629; and Smith, 2001, pp. 82–84.

86   Moses, 2005.

87   De Lacey, 2012.

88   Gonzalez-Rivera, 2013; and McGeehan, 2012.

89   Piketty, 2014, p. 26.

90   Alter, 2014; McGeehan, 2012; and Hudson, 2012.

91   McGeehan, 2012; Roberts, 2012; and Morris, 2013.

92   http://www.nytimes.com/2015/11/20/nyregion/new-yorks-rise-in-homelessness
      -went-against-national-trend-us-report-finds.html

93   Barta and Hannon, 2009.

94   This is a higher figure than often quoted. It includes not only foreign non-residents,
      but also foreign-born citizens.

95   Ford, 1995, p. 12.

96   Llana, 2014.

97   Euractiv.com, 2011.

98   Horowitz, 2015.

99   Farage, 2014; and Savage, 2009.

100   Scrutton and Ahlander, 2014; and Darroch, 2014.

101   http://blogs.wsj.com/indonesiarealtime/2013/01/29/singapore-likes-a-crowd/;
      http://www.dailymail.co.uk/news/article-2562866/Romanians-Bulgarians-working
      -Britain-soars-40-year-BEFORE-work-curbs-lifted.html

102   Chia, 2013.

103   Wong, 2013.

104   Gough, 2013.

105   http://www.economist.com/blogs/banyan/2013/12/riot-singapore

106   *Jakarta Globe*, 2011; Jianyue, 2014; and Yang, 2013.

107   See *The Nation*, 2013; Mahtani, 2012; and Rabinovitch, 2013.

108   *The Nation*, 2013.

109   Brown, 2013.

110   Harris, 2013; and Campo-Flores and Dougherty, 2013.

111   See Batt, 2013; and Warren, 2013.

112   Except as described below, all data is from the 10th Annual Demographia
      International Housing Affordability Survey (http://www.demographia.com/dhi.pdf).
      Beijing and Shanghai data is broadly estimated from new house price-to-income
      data published by E-House China (http://src.fangchan.com/zhongfangwang
      /zhongfangwang/data/2013/09/yiju10.pdf). Since new houses tend to be more
      costly than existing houses, the median multiples for Beijing and Shanghai could
      be lower (Beijing and Shanghai could be more affordable than shown). Seoul data is
      from KB Kookmin Bank.

113   Reported housing price-to-income multiple is converted from disposable to gross
      income for Shanghai and Beijing by Wendell Cox, the *Demographia* website, and
      Candy Chan. Also see *South China Morning Post*, 2013.

114   Warner, 2013; and Brown, 2013.

115   Werdigier, 2011.

116   McBride, 2013.

117   See ABC7 News, 2013

118   Edsall, 2013.

119   See Wong, 2009; vom Hove, 2008; Dean, 2006; and Johnson, 2009.

120   Foley, 2009.

121   See Lee, 2009; Maidment, 2009; and Dean, 2006.

122   Weise, 2014; and Brook, 2013, p. 313.

123   Newman and Thornley, 2005, p. 13.

124   Dougherty, 1986, p. 105.

125   Howe, "LeCorbusier—Villa Savoye."

126   Chesterton, 2013.

127   Bell and de-Shalit, 2011, p. 5

128   *Ibid.*, p. 88.

129   Newman and Thornley, 2005, p. 1.

130   Koolhaus and Castells, 1966, p. 4.

131   Lewis, 2002.

132   *Ibid.*

133   See Williams, 2013; Chen, "Retail Rents Lose Their Shine"; and Hajela and Peltz, 2015.

134   Cha, 2008.

135   Zukin,2009, p. 3–4

136   Zukin, 2009, p. 4.

137   Zukin, 2009, p. 7.

138   Campanella, 2013.

139   Zukin, 2009; and Cho, 2010.

140   Kendzior, 2013.

141   Micallef, 2013; and Badger, 2015.

142   Alter, 2014.

143   Thakur, 2012; Marr, 2013; Alter, 2014; Kenyon, 2012; Foxman and Ferdman, 2013; Thomas, 2013; and http://www.treehugger.com/author/lloyd-alter/.

144   Tobin, 2013.

145   See Syed, 2012; http://www.thethinkingatheist.com/forum/Thread-Singapore-s -Little-India-Riot-A-Shock-But-Not-A-Total-Surprise; and Mahtani, 2012.

146   Dougherty, 1986, p. 105.

147   Lau, 1981.

CHAPTER 5

1   Based on American Community Survey, 2013, one year data.

2   See National Association of Realtors, 2011; and Brown, 2012.

3   Lynch, 2003, pp. 42–43.

4   Fustgel de Coulanges, 1980, pp. 77–85.

5   See Cohen, 1975, pp. 170–1; and Baucham, 2012. "Intentional childlessness was denounced as a serious sin," noted Cohen. "Children," he added, "were thought of as a precious loan from God to be guarded with loving and fateful care."

6   Hourani, 1991, p. 105.

7   http://www.familybuddhism.com/buddha_on_family.php. Noted the 13th-century Zen master Dogen, "Those who see worldly life as an obstacle to Dharma see no Dharma in everyday actions; they have not yet discovered that there are no everyday actions outside of Dharma."

8   Analysis by Anuhardra Schroft.

9   Barbier, 2011, p. 118.

10 See Aries, 1962, p. 128; Ozment, 2001, p. 54; and Lynch, 2003, pp. 44–47, 69.

11 Schama, 1987, pp. 481–561.

12 Lynch, 2003, pp. 46–47, 138–139; and Schama, 1987, pp. 260, 404–407.

13 Heers, 1976, pp. 217–222.

14 Ozment, 1983, pp. 1–2, 49.

15 Aries, 1962, p. 133; Ozment, 2001, pp. 54–55.

16 de Bary, et al., 1960, pp. 4–5, 28.

17 Hucker, 1975, pp. 10, 33, 57, 84.

18 Lau, 1981, p. 206.

19 Weidenbaum and Hughes, 1996, p. 30; and Gu and Yong, 2009.

20 Lynch, 2003, pp. 42–43.

21 De Vries, 1984, p. 193.

22 Braudel, 1992, p. 71.

23 Bock, 1955, pp. 17–21, 159; Burke, 1994, p. 129; Mommsen, 1958, p. 549; Mango, 1980, pp. 226–227; Spezzaferro, 1997, p. 52; and Nusteling, 1997, p. 73.

24 Barbier, 2011, pp. 84–85.

25 Braudel, 1992, pp. 71–73, 90, 194–195; Barbier, 2011, pp. 190–191; and Braudel, 1979, pp. 564–565.

26 Mumford, 1961, p. 475; and Carmona, 2002, p. 391.

27 Teaford, 1993, pp. 137–141.

28 Based upon an analysis of 2010 American Community Survey data for 422 counties comprising the largest metropolitan areas in the United States (over 1,000,000 population).

29 Calculated from 2012 American Community Survey.

30 Cox, "California declares war."

31 Calculated from American Community Survey, 2013, one year data.

32 San Francisco is the core municipality of the San Francisco Bay Area and is home to slightly more than 10 percent of its population, with 800,000 residents.

33 Onishi, 2012.

34 Calculated from American Community Survey, 2013, one year data.

35 City-Data.com, "San Francisco, California"; Sabatini, 2011; and Gordon, 2005; Huffington Post, 2012; Eskenazi, 2012; and Kotkin, "Aging America

36   Clark, 2012.

37   Analysis of Statistics Canada data. Urban cores include the Toronto Central Health Region, ville de Montreal, and city of Vancouver.

38   Klinenberg, 2012, p. 5; analysis of census data by Ali Modarres.

39   Myrskyla, et al., 2013.

40   Eberstadt, 2015.

41   Kulu, et al., 2009.

42   Bidoux, et al., 2010.

43   Lichtner, 2008.

44   Pearce, 2010, p. 100.

45   Mencarini and Tanturri, 2006; and Chamie and Mirkin, 2012.

46   Joviet, 1997.

47   Interview with author and Mika Toyota.

48   English.News.CN, 2014; Kotkin, et al, 2012.

49   Jones, 2009; and the China Statistical Yearbook 2014, http://www.stats.gov.cn/tjsj /ndsj/2014/indexeh.htm.

50   Levin, 2014.

51   Cox, "Demographia World Urban Areas."

52   http://www.smithsonianmag.com/travel/Seoul-of-a-New-Machine-174966501.html. See Downey, 2012.

53   http://www.worlddesigncapital.com/world-design-capitals/past-capital-seoul/. See "Past Capital: Seoul."

54   Calculated from United Nations and Korea census data.

55   Calculated from census data. Also see Cox, "Evolving Urban Form: Seoul"; and Kim and Choe, 1970, pp. 191, 199.

56   Jones, 2009; and Bowring, 2012.

57   Smil, 2007.

58   The United Nations's Population Prospects defines the "more developed world" as Europe (including Russia and Eastern Europe, Canada, the United States, Australia, New Zealand, and Japan). All other parts of the world are classified as the "less developed world." This inexplicable definition leaves out Singapore, which had the fourth highest GDP per capita in the world in 2010, according to the International Monetary Fund. It also excludes Hong Kong, South Korea, and a number of other regions. This report has reclassified the UN data into "higher income" and "medium and lower income" regions, with those above a 2010 GDP per capita $20,000 being "higher income."

59   Cox, "Evolving Urban Form: Seoul"; Tatsuo, 2008; and Shin and Timberlake, 2006.

60   Japan Times, 2012.

61   Calculated from Taiwan census data.

62   UN Population Prospects, 2010.

63   Pearce, 2010, p. xvi.

64   Mozur, 2011.

65   UN Population Prospects, 2010.

66 *Ibid.*

67 Pearce, 2010, pp. 228–230.

68 See Woods, 2004; Tabuchi, 2012; and Nobel, 2010.

69 Sang-Hun, 2012.

70 Lam, 2009.

71 UN Population Prospects, 2010.

72 Richardson, 2012.

73 Calculated from data in UN *World Population Prospects, 2012,* http://esa.un.org
    /wpp/unpp/p2kodata.asp.

74 Eberstadt, 2005.

75 Waterfield, 2012; and Eberstadt, 2010.

76 Basu, 2012; Soble, 2015; and Auslin, 2015.

77 Gorney, 2011; and Kotkin, et. al, 2012.

78 Carlson, 2006.

79 Zuckerman, 2009; and Kaufmann, 2010, p. 260.

80 Nisbet, 1952, p. 203.

81 Pew Research Center, 2015.

82 Master Blaster, 2012.

83 Kaufmann, 2010, pp. 9–10.

84 Murray, 2010, p. 154.

85 Wertheimer, 2005; and Kurtzleben, 2011.

86 Kaufmann, 2010, p. 65–67.

87 Olmstead, 2011; and Erdbrink, 2012.

88 De Paulo, 2006, p. 259.

89 Terry Nichols Clark, et al., "Amenities Drive Urban Growth."

90 See Klinenberg, 2012, pp.18–19; and Marche, 2012.

91 DePaulo, 2011, p. 259.

92 Plotnick, 2009: pp. 767–776.

93 Howard, 2012.

94 Klinenberg, 2012.

95 *Ibid.*

96 Janssens, 2003, p. 93.

97 Klineberg, 2012, p.14.

98 Bolick, 2011.

99 See Fackler, 2010; Simonitch, 2012; Morgan, 2012; and Harden, 2010.

100 Wang, 2015.

101 Cherlin, 2013.

102 Englen, 2003, p. 304.

103 Eberstadt, 2015.

104 Analysis by Mika Toyota, National University of Singapore, based on Japanese government statistics.

105 Frejka, et al., 2010.

106 Lutz, Skirbekk, and Testa, 2006.

107 Based on analysis by Eurostat (London) and Japanese statistics bureau (Tokyo) data.

108 Klineberg, 2012, pp. 37–38.

109 Murray, 2012; Hymowitz, 2009.

110 Ganesh, 2014.

111 Clark and Inglehart, 1998, pp. 9–65.

112 Interview with author.

113 Herbig and Borstorff, 1995, pp. 49–65.

114 Interview with author and Anuradha Shroff.

115 Klineberg, 2012, p. 207.

116 Jacobs, 2013.

117 Itoh, 2011; and Cox, "Evolving Urban Form: Tokyo."

118 Jones, Tay-Straughan, and Chan, 2008.

119 See Englen, 2003, op. cit., pp.286–290.

120 Kostelecky and Vobecka, 2009.

121 Cox and Pavletich, 2014.

122 *Ibid.*

123 *Ibid.*

124 Hui and Ho, 2000.

125 Interview with author.

126 Toffler, 1980, pp. 117, 437.

127 *Ibid.*, p. 210.

128 Coontz, 1992, pp. 155–165.

129 Frejka, Jones and Sardon, 2010, pp. 579–606.

130 Putnam, 2000, p. 189.

131 Lasch, 1991, p. 138.

132 Interview with author.

133 Hymowitz, 2006, p. 145.

134 Grant, 2005.

135 Soon, 2010.

136 Pearce, 2010, p. 134.

137 Lutz, Skirbekk and Testa, 2006.

138 *Ibid.*

139 Statistics Canada, 2013.

140 http://www.un.org/en/development/desa/population/publications/pdf/migration/migrationreport2013/Full_Document_final.pdf

141 Cox, "Evolving Urban Form: Milan"; and Rosenthal, 2006.

142 Longman, 2004, p. 67.

143   http://www.make-it-in-germany.com/en/making-it/aktuelles/press-release/

144   http://www.alternet.org/world/labor-shortage-germany-needs-more-immigrants

145   http://www.pewforum.org/2011/01/27/future-of-the-global-muslim-population
      -regional-europe/

146   http://www.dailymail.co.uk/debate/article-3223828/PETER-HITCHENS-won-t-save
      -refugees-destroying-country.html

147   http://www.theguardian.com/world/2010/oct/17/angela-merkel-german
      -multiculturalism-failed

148   Fesus, et al., 2008.

149   http://www.nytimes.com/2015/10/02/world/europe/despite-shrinking-populations-
      eastern-europe-resists-accepting-migrants.html

150   Walker, 2006.

151   Treanor, 2007; Heineman, 2011; Chelala, 2012; and Kumo, 2010.

152   Kotkin, et al., 2012.

153   Stevenson, 2011.

154   Lida, 2008, p. 133.

155   Huxley, 1969, p. 41.

156   *Ibid.*, pp. 5, 23–24.

157   Earnshaw, 2008, p. 149.

158   Pollet, Kuppens, and Dunbar, 2006, pp. 83–93.

159   Research has shown that the child-unfriendly policies that would force higher
      densities produce little or no reduction in greenhouse gas emissions and that less
      expensive (and less intrusive) alternatives are generally available. See, for example,
      McKinsey & Company and The Conference Board (2007), *Reducing U.S. Greenhouse
      Gas Emissions: How Much at What Cost?*, Board on Energy and Environmental
      Systems (2009), *Driving and the Built Environment: The Effects of Compact Develop-
      ment on Motorized Travel, Energy Use, and CO2 Emissions,* Transportation Research
      Board and Cox, W. (2011), "Reducing Greenhouse Gases from Personal Mobility:
      Opportunities and Possibilities," *Reason Foundation.*

160   Guelphmercury.com, 2010.

CHAPTER 6

1   See Cinco Ranch Life.

2   City-Data.com, "Cinco Ranch, Texas."

3   Snyder, 2005.

4   Crossley, 2009.

5   Lerup, 2011, p. 263.

6   http://www.cincoranch.com/

7   Binkovitz, 2015.

8   City-Data.com, "Cinco Ranch, Texas."

9   Har.com, 2014.

10   Calculated for urban areas within the 15 largest metropolitan areas, using University
     of Missouri radius data for the 2000 and 2010 censuses. The land area of each

urban area is idealized into a circle. The inner-third ring would be, for example, within a five-mile radius from city hall in an urban area with a total radius of 15 miles (an urban land area of approximately 707 square miles).

11   Braudel, 1992, p. 281.

12   Mumford, 1961, p. 511; and Braudel, 1992, p. 281.

13   Reeder, 1968, p. 253.

14   Wagenaar, 1992, pp. 60–83; and The University of Sunderland, 1999.

15   Calculated from INSEE 2014 and INSEE, 2011; see also Berger, 1996.

16   Wells, 1999, pp. 75–76.

17   City-Data.com, "Cinco Ranch, Texas."

18   City-Data.com, "New York, New York."

19   City-Data.com, "San Francisco, California"; Sabatini, "San Francisco becoming a child-free zone as youth population declines"; and Gordon, 2005.

20   Wells, 1999, p. 32.

21   Campanella, 2013.

22   Girouard, 1985, p. 254.

23   Bogart, 2006, p. 108.

24   Durkin, 2012.

25   *The Economist*, 2005.

26   Schulz, 2012.

27   *The Economist*, 2005.

28   Blake, 1979, p. 34.

29   Nicolaides, 2006, p. 87.

30   *Ibid.*, pp. 91–97.

31   Oliver, Davis, and Bentley, 1994, p. 40.

32   New York Times, 1955.

33   Fox, 2014.

34   Knox, 2005, pp. 33–46.

35   Dobriner, 1963, pp. 127–137; Brown, 2004; and Kirby, 2004, p. 369.

36   http://journal.media-culture.org.au/index.php/mcjournal/article/viewArticle/368

37   See Davies, 2012; and Flew, 2011.

38   http://blogs.crikey.com.au/theurbanist/author/davipoll/

39   Davies, 2012.

40   *The Economist*, 1998.

41   Sellers, 2012, pp. 288, 294–295.

42   Sharro, 2008, pp. 68–77; and Heathcote, 2006.

43   See Sharro, 2008, p. 67; Mark Clapson gathered surveys of people's living aspirations in *Suburban Century* (2003), pp. 55–7; Ben Kochan, in research for the *Town and Country Planning Association* and the *Joseph Rowntree Foundation*, collected more resent research on people's living aspirations and satisfaction, published in *Achieving a Suburban Renaissance—the Policy Challenge* (2007), pp. 4, 23.

44   Wilson, 2004, p. 119.

45   Gardiner, 2010.

46   Webb, 1971, pp. 576–577; and Freidman, 2005, pp. 20, 63.

47   Clapson, 1998, pp. 101–106.

48   Heartfield, 2006, p. 65; Sharro, 2008, p. 67.

49   Baltzell, 1950, pp. 196–209; and Modell, 1980, pp. 397–417.

50   Jackson, 1985, p. 176; and Clark, et al., 1977, p. 280.

51   Teaford, 1993, pp. 238–242.

52   Bruegmann, 2005, p. 65.

53   Galyean, 2015.

54   Coontz, 1991, p. 77; Abrahamson, 2013, p. 5; and Randall, 2010, p. 2.

55   Ross, 2014.

56   See, for example, National Association of Realtors, 2011; Abrahamson, 2013, p. 5; and Coontz, 1991, p. 77.

57   Calculated from Census Bureau data.

58   This actually understates the suburban growth, since many core cities have annexed areas that were formerly suburban.

59   Coontz, 1992, pp. 29, 61.

60   Senior, 1958, p. 11.

61   Glaeser and Shapiro, 2001.

62   Rogers, 2006; and Cox, "Flocking Elsewhere."

63   Abrahamson, 2013, p. 48.

64   Krugman, 2008.

65   Florida, "Crash Will Reshape America."

66   See, for example, Freeman, 2008; Timiraos, 2009; Bula, 2009; and *The Vancouver Sun*, 2008.

67   Bookman, 2009.

68   *Daily Mail Reporter*, 2012

69   Arieff, 2009.

70   Hardy, 2003.

71   See, for example, Dougherty, 2009; Leinberger, 2011; Kolko, "Suburbs Aren't All the Same"; and Badger, 2015.

72   Kolko, "How Suburban."

73   Calculated from US Census Bureau building permit data.

74   "Second Highest Homeownership"; and Cox, "Home Ownership."

75   Drew and Herbert, 2012.

76   Breen, "UConneticut/Hartford Courant Poll."

77   Analysis of Statistics Bureau of Japan data.

78   See Hirayama, 2013, p. 173; Sorensen, 2001, pp. 9–32; and Japanese Statistics Bureau, 2015.

79   See O'Connor and Healy, 2004, pp. 27–40; Wulff, Healy, and Reynolds, 2004, pp. 57–70; Tavares and Carr, 2013, pp. 283–302.

80   Cox, "Australia"; and Lawless, 2012.

81 http://www.ahuri.edu.au/publications/download/ahuri_10016; and Gordon and Shirokoff, 2014.

82 Statistics Canada, 2014.

83 Cox, "Special Report: Census 2011."

84 Keesmaat, 2014; and Gordon and Shirokoff, 2014.

85 *European Environment Agency Report,* 2006, p. 5.

86 Richardson and Gordon, 1999.

87 http://www.newgeography.com/content/003075-the-evolving-urban-form-z-rich

88 Derived from United Nations data and data from national statistics bureaus and Wendell Cox. See *New Geography,* 2015.

89 http://www.newgeography.com/content/002970-the-evolving-urban-form-london

90 *New Geography,* 2015.

91 Gordon and Richardson, 2001.

92 Cox, "Evolving Urban Form: Beijing."

93 *Ibid.*; Cox, "Evolving Urban Form: Shanghai." Based on end-of-2013 municipal population estimates. Shanghai grew 3.5 percent annually from 2000 to 2010, but only 1.9 percent from 2010 to 2014. Beijing's growth rates were 4.0 percent and 2.6 percent, respectively. Also see Cox, "China's Top Growth Cities."

94 See, for example, Angel, 2012, pp. 171–173; El Nasser, 2008; and Elsea, 2005.

95 Cox, "Densities Fall."

96 Angel, 2012, pp. 177–179.

97 Clark, et al., 1982, p. 469.

98 Galyean, 2015.

99 Jackson, 1985, p. 21. Also see Garnett, 2007.

100 Garnett, 2007.

101 Frey, 2011; and Duell, 2011.

102 Glaeser and Khan, 2003.

103 Frey, 2011.

104 Kotkin, 2012.

105 Kotkin and Cox, 2015; and Teaford, 2008, pp. 82–83.

106 Wilkinson, 2014.

107 Renn, 2009; Also see Kantor, 2012.

108 See, for example, Knight, 2013; Hannah-Jones, 2011; and Morrill, 2011.

109 Jackson, 1985, p. 70.

110 Rosenthal, 1974, p. 269.

111 Wilson and Svaljenka, 2014.

112 Calculated from the Census Bureau Current Population Survey for 2013 to 2014. The number is actually higher because this report uses the "principal cities" to identify non-suburban immigration. Principal cities include the core cities as well as municipalities that are suburban employment centers, which are overwhelmingly suburban in their built form. Also see Cox, "Urban Cores."

113 Binkovitz, 2015; and Pfeiffer, 2014.

114 Czekalinski, 2012.

115 http://www1.law.umn.edu/uploads/e0/65/e065d82a1c1daobfef7d86172ec5391e/Diverse_Suburbs_FINAL.pdf

116 Wells, 2014.

117 *The Economist*, 2006.

118 Muir, 2013.

119 *The Economist*, "Into the Melting Pot."

120 Boland and Simpson, 2010.

121 Clark, 2013; Melanson, 2013; and Gee, 2013.

122 Capuano, 2015.

123 See DPCD Spatial Analysis, 2009; City of Melbourne, "Multicultural communities; and Schulz and Clark, 2014.

124 Monaghan, 2013.

125 Whyte, 1965, p. 69.

126 See, for example, *The Economist*, 2013; Kimmelman, 2015; and Szirmai, 2011, p. 144.

127 Farrar, 2008; and Leinberger, 2011.

128 http://www.demographia.com/db-hcm.pdf

129 See, for example, Cox, 2013; DeParle, Gebeloff, and Tavernise, 2011.

130 Morrill, 2013.

131 The Gini index measures the extent to which the distribution of income (or, in some cases, consumption expenditure) among individuals or households within an economy deviates from a perfectly equal distribution. A Lorenz curve plots the cumulative percentages of total income received against the cumulative number of recipients, starting with the poorest individual or household. The Gini index measures the area between the Lorenz curve and a hypothetical line of absolute equality, expressed as a percentage of the maximum area under the line. Thus, a Gini index of 0 represents perfect equality, while an index of 100 implies perfect inequality. Also see http://data.worldbank.org/indicator/SI.POV.GINI.

132 Kotkin, "Where Inequality is Worst."

133 Hamel and Keil, 2015, p. 125.

134 Wolff, 2012.

135 See, for example, Gittelsom, 2011; Dewan, 2013; and Dougherty, 2009.

136 Traub, 2015.

137 Rognile, 2014.

138 Mumford, 1961, p. 512.

139 Norquist, 1998, p. 189.

140 Indeed, Phoenix is among the most dense US urban areas. Among the 51 metropolitan areas with more than 1,000,000 population in 2010, the principal urban area of Phoenix ranked 16th in density, and it was nearly as dense as Portland, Oregon, which is renowned for its densification policies.

141 See, for example, Duany, Plater-Zyberk, and Speck, 2000, pp. 5–9, 137; and Schneider, 1992.

142 Kunstler, 2004, p. 19.

143 Conn, 2004.

144 Ireton, 2005.

145 Williams, 2008, p. 57; and Gordon and Richardson, 2000, p. 5.

146 Kushner, 2006.

147 Gordon and Richardson, 2000.

148 Gratz, 1995; and Ministry of Regional Development, 2013.

149 Gordon and Shirokoff, 2014.

150 Brueckner and Largey, 2006.

151 Miller, et al., 2012.

152 Knox, 2005.

153 See Knox and Pinch, 2013 p.190.

154 Williams, 2008, p. 47–49.

155 See, for example, DiPasquale and Glaeser, 1998, pp. 354–384; and Manturuk, 2010, pp. 471–488.

156 National Association of Realtors, 2012.

157 CBC News, 2014.

158 Preville, 2011.

159 Bruegmann, 2005, p. 126.

160 Kushner, 2006.

161 New Urbanism, "Principles of Urbanism."

162 Porter, 2002, p. 68.

163 Nathan and Urwin, 2006.

164 Kotkin, "The Geography of Aging."

165 Siegel, 2011.

166 Shaw and Ronald Utt, 2000, p. 89.

167 Dillon, 2009.

168 Davidson, 2014.

169 Dillon, 2009.

170 Robson and Butler, 2001, p. 70–86.

171 Katz, 2000.

172 Shaw and Utt, 2000, p. 89.

173 National Center for Education Statistics, 2013; Dillon, 2009; Graham and Provost, 2012; Emrath and Siniavskaia, 2009; and National Center for Education Statistics, 1996.

174 Analysis of 2010 ACS data by Ali Modarres.

175 Anton, 2012.

176 Federal Bureau of Investigation, 2011.

177 Boland and Simpson, 2010.

178 Bruegmann, 2005, p. 111.

179 Maugh, 2007; Aristotle, 1984, p. 36–37; and Wilford, 2000.

180 Bruegmann, 2005, p. 126.

CHAPTER 7

1 Lutz, Testa, and Penn, 2007, pp. 69–81.

2 German and Pyne, 2010.

3 Mehta, 2004, p. 16.

4 Fishman, 1997, pp. 14–15.

5 Roark, et. al., 2011; and Pace, 1994.

6 Braudel, 1979, p. 503.

7 Navi Mumbai Municipal Corporation, "Land Usage"; and Jacquemin, 1999, pp. 272–273.

8 Ferguson and Peake, 2013, p. 2.

9 Searcey, 2014.

10 Demand Institute, 2013.

11 Hardy, 2003.

12 Katz, 2000; and Speck, 2000.

13 Barragan, 2014.

14 Hobson and Gallagher, 2014; and Gallagher, 2013, p. 19.

15 Zip codes (zip code tabulation areas) with population densities 7,500 per square mile and above and transit/walk/bicycle commute shares of 20 percent and above. See City Sector Model, at http://www.demographia.com/csmcriteria.png and http://www.newgeography.com/category/story-topics/city-sector-model.

16 Cox, "Dispersing."

17 Baker, 1981; and Thompson, 2014.

18 Cox, "Urban Core Millenials?" Analysis of rings by Wendell Cox.

19 Winograd and Hais, 2010.

20 Burbank and Keely, 2014.

21 Lachman and Brett, 2015.

22 Hudson, 2015; Quint, 2015.

23 Schimel and Marchetti, 2012.

24 The Conference Board, 2014.

25 Drew and Herbert, 2012.

26 Chevreau, 2015.

27 See, for example, Forrest and Yip, 2013, p. 42; Martin and Lehren, 2012; and Jones, 2014.

28 Pearce, 2012.

29 Thomas, 2008, pp. 111–119; Girouard, 1985, p. 362.

30 Thomas, 2008, pp. 111–119; Jackson, 2015.

31 Patty, 2014.

32 Li, 2013, p. 89.

33 Lieberg, 2013, p. 109.

34 Zhu, 2013, p. 156.

35 FlorCruz, 2015.

36   Jung-Youn, 2015; and Szikla, 2014.

37   Fischel, 1995.

38   Shaver, 2015; and McArdle, 2015.

39   Zillow, "Zillow Real Estate Research"; and Bivins, 2014.

40   Rao, 2014.

41   Kirkham, 2015.

42   Piiparinen and Russell, 2014.

43   Abley, 2009.

44   Moore, 2015.

45   Chu, 2014.

46   de Castella, 2011.

47   *Ibid.*

48   Woudhuysen, 2007.

49   van Onselen, 2014.

50   Elliot, 2013; and van Onselen, 2013.

51   Cox, "Australia's Housing Affordability 'Outrage'."

52   Dobbs, 2010; and http://www.economist.com/blogs/graphicdetail/2012/04/focus-4.

53   FlorCruz, 2015.

54   Winograd and Hais, 2010.

55   Clapson, 2000, pp. 151–174.

56   Hayden, 2003, pp. 45–67.

57   Hise and Deverell, 2000, pp. 12–15; and Bartlett, 1907, p. 17.

58   Hise and Deverell, 2000, pp. 1–11.

59   Hadden and Barton, 1977, p. 50.

60   Calculated from UN urban agglomeration data.

61   Donaldson, 1977, pp. 95–97.

62   See, for example, *The Washington Post*, 2004; Rickett and Rickett, "Columbia, MD"; and Forsyth, 2005.

63   Mathis, 2014.

64   Fischler, 2011; and Hurley, 2014.

65   Hershatter, 2010, pp. 211–223.

66   Williams, 2013.

67   Velsey, 2013.

68   See, for example, Florida, "Fading Differentiation"; Taves, 2015; and Jacobs, 2004, pp. 216–217.

69   Bruegmann, 2005, p. 61.

70   Efrati, 2006.

71   Lang and LeFurgy, 2007, pp. 533–552.

72   Teaford, 2008, p. 209; and Halter, 2014.

73   Rushton, 2014.

74   Donaldson, 1977, p. 16–17.

75 Garnett, 2007, p. 10.

76 See Hirsch, 1976, pp. 1–4, 33–38; Walker and Hurley, 2011, p. 180; Saint and Farrell, 2009, p. 13.

77 Breen, "Gayest Cities in America." Calculated from Williams Institute data.

78 See, for example, Khazan, 2015; Severino, 2015; and Astone, Martin, and Peters, 2015.

79 See Farrar, 2008; Morrill, 2009; interview with author; Leinberger, 2011.

80 Bruegmann, 2005, pp. 61, 81; and Coy, 2012.

81 Cox, "U.S. Sets New House Record."

82 Wulff, Healy, and Reynolds, 2004, pp. 57–70.

83 Green, 2015.

84 Pew Research Center, 2014.

85 Howe, 2014; Wang and Taylor, 2011; and University of Michigan, 2015.

86 Lutz, Testa, and Penn, 2006; and Lehrer, 2007.

87 National Youth Council of Singapore, "Youths today."

88 Swidy, 2006.

89 Wade, 2010.

90 Yoder, 2013.

91 Heavens, 2004; and Engelhart, 2006.

92 Res, 2012; and Merrill Lynch, 2014.

93 Ducker and Gardner, 2011; Engelhardt, "Study on Housing"; and National Association of Home Builders, 2006.

94 Howe, 2003.

95 Chevreau, 2015.

96 Scommenga, 2014.

97 Colebatch, 2012.

98 MacEwen, 2012.

99 Fries, 2012; and Lipman, Lubell, and Salomon, 2012. Also see http://www.housingwire.com/news/2008/11/26/3-4-boomers-arent-looking-move-report and https://mlaem.fs.ml.com/content/dam/ML/Articles/pdf/AR6SX48F.pdf.

100 Cannuscio, Block, and Kawachi, 2003, p. 395.

101 Ruffenach, 2009.

102 Span, 2011.

103 Jacobsen, Mather, and Dupuis, 2012.

104 Coontz, 1992, p. 183.

105 Sullivan, 2015.

106 Levin, 2008.

107 Gross, 2008.

108 Taylor, et al., 2010.

109 National Association of Realtors, 2015.

110 Alcantra, 2012.

111   Christie, 2012.

112   Thurlow, 2015.

113   Luo, 2014, p. 3; Lehrer, 2009.

114   Glaeser, 2011; and Cox, "Density is not the issue."

115   Cox, "10 most affluent cities."

116   See, for example, Kelly and Warren, 2014; Kotkin, "Where a paycheck stretches"; and Le-Claire, 2014.

117   Cox, "Dispersion and Concentration."

118   Cox, "Beyond polycentricity."

119   Donaldson, 1977, p. 101.

120   Calculated from American Community Survey, 2013, one year data.

121   Forsyth, 2005. Also see Dreier, Mollenkopf, and Swanstrom, 2002, p. 59.

122   Calculated from Census Bureau County Business Pattern data at the ZIP code (ZCTA) level.

123   Frey, 2015.

124   Tiefensee and Pfister, 2006.

125   Geiger, 2014.

126   David, et al., 2013, pp. 237–254.

127   See Hickman, Hall, and Banister, 2013, pp. 210–219; and Kocak, 2014, pp. 327–346.

128   World Bank, 2009.

129   Brown, 2015.

130   Basulto, 2014.

131   Cox, "2010 Major Metropolitan Area."

132   Kotkin and Schill, 2015.

133   Hope, 2014; Mozingo, 2014, p. 208–214.

134   Lida, 2008, pp. 49–53; Sheinbaum, 2007; and Angel, 2012, p. 174.

135   Sethi, 2014; and *The Economic Times*, 2014.

136   John G. Clark, et al., 1982, p. 499.

137   Bruegmann, 2005, p. 37.

138   *Ibid.*, p. 53.

139   Cox, "Dispersion and Concentration."

140   Basulto, 2014.

141   Renn, 2014.

142   Kotkin and Shires, 2014; and Fainstein, 1994, p. 25.

143   Cox, "New York, Legacy Cities."

144   Hoge, 2006; Barbour, 2006; and Gordon and Richardson, 2000.

145   Gordon and Richardson, 2001.

146   Federal Highway Administration, 2012; and Balaker and Staley, 2006, p. 45.

147   Bogart, 2006, p. 191.

148   Davies, 2015.

149   von Hoffman and Felkner, 2002.

150   Pelton, 2015.

151   Horan, 2000, p. 52.

152   http://www.newgeography.com/content/001798-decade-telecommute

153   Hess, 2014.

154   Yi, 2003.

155   Leland, 2007.

156   Pilot, 2015, pp. 4–15.

157   Global Workplace Analytics.

158   Fuhr and Pociask, 2007.

159   Toffler, 1980, pp. 42–45, 119–145, 195.

160   Ridley, 2014; Kunstler, 2005, p. 3; Kunstler, 2004; and Goodman, 2009.

161   Fisher, 2012.

162   See, for example, Dreiling, 2007; Stone, 2009, pp. 9052–9056; and Utt, 2009.

163   Calthorpe, 2011.

164   Wilson, 2013; Shellenberger and Nordhaus, 2012; and Volcovici and Lewis, 2014.

165   McKenna, 2009.

166   *Ibid.*; Rybczyniski, 2010, p. 186.

167   Cox, "California Declares War"; and The Customer Board, 2007.

168   Byrd, et al., 2013, pp. 944–952.

169   Boone and Modarres, 2006, p. 105.

170   Terjunb and Laurie, 1973, pp. 181–207.

171   Akbari, 2005; and Adachi, et al., 2014, p. 1886–1900.

172   Zhang, et al., 2010.

173   Transport Canada, 2006.

174   Alter, 2007; and Bernstein and Vara-Orta, 2007.

175   Friedman and Hernandez, 2015.

176   Donaldson, 1977, p. 57; Adam Rome, 2001, pp. 266–271; Teaford, 2008, p. 21.

177   See Sellers, 2012, pp. 16–17, 290–292; Donaldson, 1977, p. 57; and Rome, 2001, pp. 266–271.

178   Arendt, 1996, pp. 13, 121.

179   Luck, 2007, pp. 607–645; and Katti, 2014.

180   Gehrt, 2014; and Newman, 2006.

181   Shaw, 2004; and Heartfield, 2008, p. 11.

182   Dosick, 2012.

183   Ulrich, 1984; Gale Cengage Learning, 2014; and Paddock, 2013.

184   Ingersoll, 2003.

185   O'Neill, 2009.

186   Barbier, 2011, p. 89.

187   O'Neill, 2009; and Pearce, 2010, p. 6.

188   Bruegmann, 2005, p. 135.

189   Cox, "Declining Human Footprint." Based on data from the US Department of Agriculture.

190   Data from 2010 US census.

191   Cox, "Urban Policy"; and Cox, "Housing Affordability." Calculated from Statistics Canada data.

192   Australian Government Department of the Environment, 2011

193   Cox, "Declining Human Footprint" and Cox, "Melbourne."

194   Angel, 2012.

195   Barbier, 2011, p. 681.

196   Longman, 2004, pp. 7–13, 133; and Ehrlich, 1968, pp. 15–454, 66–7, 136–7.

197   Callenbach, 1975, pp. 61–67.

198   Collins, 2014; and Peterson, 1999, p. 13.

199   Kunzig, 2014; and *The Economist*, "Don't Panic."

200   Ponnuru, 2012.

201   See Kato, 2010; *Diversity Officer Magazine*, 2008; and Child Policy International, 2009. Also see Chen, 2012; and http://www.guardian.co.uk/world/2005/sep/22/france.jonhenley1

202   Chen, 2012.

203   Kotkin, et al., 2012.

204   Yap, 2003, pp. 643–58.

205   Hegewisch, Lowell, and Hartmann, 2007.

206   Cox and Pavletich, 2015.

207   Osborn, 2011.

208   RT, 2012.

209   Downs, 1994.

210   Jacobs and Century, 2012.

211   Mumford, 1961, p. 57.

212   Glaeser and Kahn, 2003.

213   Tarr and Zimring, 1997, pp. 199–220; and Mumford, 1961, p. 459.

214   Kersten, 2014.

215   Barkham, 2014; ITV, 2015; and Dominiczak, 2014.

216   Williams, 2008, p. 8.

217   Heartfield, 2006, pp. 21, 30–31.

218   Grindrod, 2003; and http://www.newgeography.com/content/003432-britains-housing-crisis-the-places-people-live.

219   http://www.newgeography.com/content/003432-britains-housing-crisis-the-places-people-live

220   Bajpai, 2012.

221   https://openknowledge.worldbank.org/bitstream/handle/10986/13105/757340PUB0EPI0001300pubdate02021013.pdf

222   Booth, 2009.

223   Rybczynski, 2013; Hayes, 2011; and Donald, 2011.

224 Daley and Wood, 2014.

225 Isaacs, 2009.

226 Plumridge, 2012.

227 Dr. Housing Bubble, 2012; and Kolko, 2014.

228 Gross, 2012.

229 Wright, 1958, pp. 83, 231.

230 Tait, 2003, pp. 37–52.

231 Kaliski, 2008.

232 Howe, "LeCorbusier—Villa Savoye."

233 Mogilevich, 2003.

234 Mumford, 1961, p. 544.

235 Mumford, 1956, p. 18.

236 Braudel, 1992, p. 562.

237 Lerup, 2011, p. 194.

INDEX